ENGLISH HERITAGE, ENGLISH CINEMA

English Heritage, English Cinema

Costume Drama since 1980

ANDREW HIGSON

OXFORD
UNIVERSITY PRESS

*This book has been printed digitally and produced in a standard specification
in order to ensure its continuing availability*

OXFORD
UNIVERSITY PRESS

Great Clarendon Street, Oxford OX2 6DP

Oxford University Press is a department of the University of Oxford.
It furthers the University's objective of excellence in research, scholarship,
and education by publishing worldwide in

Oxford New York

Auckland Cape Town Dar es Salaam Hong Kong Karachi
Kuala Lumpur Madrid Melbourne Mexico City Nairobi
New Delhi Shanghai Taipei Toronto
With offices in
Argentina Austria Brazil Chile Czech Republic France Greece
Guatemala Hungary Italy Japan South Korea Poland Portugal
Singapore Switzerland Thailand Turkey Ukraine Vietnam

Oxford is a registered trade mark of Oxford University Press
in the UK and in certain other countries

Published in the United States
by Oxford University Press Inc., New York

ISBN 978-0-19-925902-1

Printed and bound by CPI Antony Rowe, Eastbourne

For Val

Acknowledgements

THIS BOOK HAS been gestating for a shockingly long time, though I hope it's a better book for that! I'd like to thank OUP for persevering with me, and especially Andrew Lockett, who first commissioned the book, Matthew Hollis, who was very supportive during his time with the Press, Sophie Goldsworthy, who saw the book through its final stages, and crucially agreed to a longer publication than first planned, and Sophie's colleagues Sarah Hyland and Frances Whistler. My work on heritage films has benefited enormously from the work of others over the years. In particular, I'd like to acknowledge the intellectual stimulus provided by Patrick Wright's work on heritage culture, by Roger Sales's teaching and writing on Austen adaptations, by Pam Cook's writing on costume drama and national identity, by Claire Monk's publications on heritage cinema, and by Ann-Marie Cook's efforts to widen the definition of heritage cinema. The often trenchant criticisms of my work by Pam and Claire have been invaluable in enabling me to the reach the position I take in this book. Thomas Austin deserves mention too for helping me steer towards a reception studies approach, as do Richard Dyer and Ginette Vincendeau, whose work on European heritage cinema has also been influential.

I've been teaching courses about contemporary British cinema and about costume drama and heritage at the University of East Anglia (UEA) since the late 1980s and I owe an enormous debt to the many students, both undergraduate and postgraduate, who have helped me refine my views about heritage films. Particularly influential in this respect, though they may not have realized it at the time, were Matthew Brown, Ann-Marie Cook, Tim Bergfelder, and Michael Williams, the latter two both now lecturing at University of Southampton. Over the years, numerous postgraduate students have provided expert research assistance, including Ann-Marie Cook, Becky Innes, Rachel Moseley (now lecturing at University of Warwick), Miranda Bayer, Shoko Otsuyama, Michael Williams, and Lawrence Napper. Miranda Bayer as ever did a thoroughly professional job with the index. Peter Krämer, Sarah Street, and Thomas Austin all read and commented on early versions of some of the chapters. Peter's comments were particularly productive.

My colleagues in the School of English and American Studies at UEA—especially those in Film Studies—have supported my work on heritage cinema for many years, discussed ideas with me, provided intellectual stimulation, and created the space needed to complete the project. All in all, they have ensured that UEA has been the ideal environment in which to carry out such work. Research for the book was enabled by a research grant from the British Academy, a Research Leave Award from the Arts and Humanities Research Board, and two periods of Study Leave granted by UEA.

Some of the material in the book first appeared in 'Re-presenting the National Past: Nostalgia and Pastiche in the Heritage Film', in Lester Friedman (ed.), *Fires were Started: British Cinema and Thatcherism* (Minneapolis and London: University of Minnesota Press and UCL Press, 1993), in 'The Heritage Film and British Cinema', in *Dissolving Views: Key Writings on British Cinema* (London: Cassell, 1996), which I edited, and in 'Heritage Cinema and Television', in Dave Morley and Kevin Robins (eds.), *British Cultural Studies: Geography, Nationality and Identity* (Oxford: Oxford University Press, 2001). I would like to thank the editors and publishers of those books for allowing me to rework material from those publications.

Many of the arguments in the book were first explored in conference papers or invited talks. Conference papers were delivered at Birkbeck College ('Remembering the 1990s', 2000), University of Warwick ('The Spectacular: An International Conference', 2000; and 'The European Heritage Film', 1995), University of York/London Guildhall University ('The Idea of Heritage: Past, Present and Future', 1999), Birkbeck College/National Film Theatre ('Past Pleasures: The Costume Drama in Film', 1997), and University of Kingston ('The Revision of England', 1996). Invited lectures and research papers were given at University of Copenhagen (2001), University of Southampton (1998), Humboldt-Universitat, Berlin (1998), and University of Newcastle (1996). I would like to thank the organizers of these events for allowing me the opportunity to think through my ideas in a public setting.

Finally, I would like to thank my wife, Val, and my daughters, Billie and Luisa, for being there, even when I locked myself away in my study, for watching with me many of the films I discuss, and for constantly reminding me, in the best possible ways, that there's more to life than research and writing, and that there's no place like home. I dedicate the book to Val, with love and thanks.

Contents

List of Illustrations

BFI Collections provided the film stills and posters reproduced as illustrations 1, 2, 3, 4, 5, 10, 13, 14, 15, 16, 18, 27, and 30. The John Kobal Collection provided the film stills and posters reproduced as illustrations 19, 24, and 25. Merchant Ivory Productions Ltd. provided the stills, posters, and publicity materials reproduced as illustrations 7, 12, 20, 21, and 23. The photographs of original material for illustrations 6, 8, 9, 11, 17, 22, 26, 28, and 29 were taken by Maxine Adcock, © Maxine Adcock. Whilst every effort has been made to identify copyright holders, that has not been possible in a few cases. We apologize for any apparent negligence and any omissions brought to our attention will be remedied in any future editions.

Introduction

Cinema, one of the most important social and cultural forces of the twentieth century, seemed in the early 1980s in Britain to be on its last legs. The numbers of people watching films at the cinema were at their lowest ebb, while British film production had all but disappeared. Since the mid-1980s, with the rise of the multiplex and the blockbuster success of a few huge Hollywood films each year, audiences, remarkably, have risen once more, and quite dramatically. The development of the home video market, new terrestrial television channels, cable, and satellite have further ensured that film is once more a central part of British popular culture. In that same period, British film-making, while never exactly financially stable, maintained a vigorous critical presence, a new British art cinema emerged, and a select band of films achieved considerable box-office success both at home and internationally.

One of the most visible production trends in Britain in this period was the quality costume drama. From *Chariots of Fire* in 1981 to *The Golden Bowl* in 2000, via *A Room with a View* (1986), *The Madness of King George* (1995), *Sense and Sensibility* (1996), *Shakespeare in Love* (1998), and well over 100 comparable films (see the Filmography at the back of the book), the quality costume drama has proved both critically successful and of significant box-office interest in Britain, but also in other markets, especially the USA. In various ways, these films engage with subject-matter and discourses that have traditionally played a major part in determining how the heritage and identity of England and Englishness have been understood. These are films set in the past, telling stories of the manners and proprieties, but also the often transgressive romantic entanglements of the upper- and upper middle-class English, in carefully detailed and visually splendid period reconstructions. The luxurious country-house settings, the picturesque rolling green landscapes of southern England, the pleasures of period costume, and the canonical literary reference points are among the more frequently noted attractions of such films—although there are of course exceptions, costume dramas or period films that eschew such attractions.

In this same period, cultural commentators identified what they saw as the consolidation of a heritage industry: a potent marketing of the past as part of the new enterprise culture, a commodification of museum culture. The English costume dramas of the last two decades seem from one point of view a vital part of this industry. For this reason, I and others have labelled them heritage films, though this is not a term that their producers or indeed many of their audiences would be familiar with or even approve of. I shall certainly be examining the extent to which this label might be appropriate—but I shall also look at other ways of making sense of such films, and other ways of categorizing and naming them.

There is considerable debate about how such films should be interpreted, both in academic circles and in the mainstream press and more specialist film publications. The debate takes in questions of politics as well as aesthetics, and it raises important questions about the nature and practice of interpretation, how audiences use texts, and how meanings accrue to those texts. It is this debate, as much as the films themselves, that interests me. Given the cultural presence of these films in what we can only with some difficulty call British cinema, and given the way in which they engage with heritage discourses, my examination of these films will also allow me to raise important questions about national cinema and cultural identity in the 1980s and 1990s.

First, though, it will be necessary to establish the extent and limits of this production trend. What are the key characteristics of the films that make up this production trend, in terms of subject-matter, sources, production personnel, cast, and style? To what extent do they constitute a distinct genre? How appropriate is it to erect critical demarcations between one set of films and another? These are some of the questions I shall be seeking to explore in the first chapter. One of the surprises in researching this book was discovering quite how many films might be seen as belonging to this production trend. In the second chapter, I begin to explore how audiences have made sense of the films and put them to use in contemporary culture. I concentrate on the very specific audience of professional cultural commentators, film critics, and academics. In examining the critical debate about these recent costume dramas, I consider the extent to which the films relate to the heritage and tourism industries. I also consider the ways in which discussion about these films has posed questions about Englishness, national identity, and national cinema, and about class, gender, and taste.

In the third and fourth chapters, I explore another set of questions about the production, distribution, marketing, and exhibition of the films, and the audiences they have reached. Why have quality costume dramas with an English subject-matter or setting been so frequently produced in the 1980s and 1990s? What sources of funding have been available to producers, and what levels of budget have been deemed apropriate? Why have specialist distributors so often seemed keen to take on these films, especially for the American market? How have these films been pitched at particular audiences? Which aspects of the films are stressed in their promotion? To which audiences have these films appealed? In Chapter 3, I concentrate on the British production context and the types of exhibition the films were given. In Chapter 4, I examine the American commercial interest in English heritage films.

Finally, there are two case studies, which apply these questions to individual films that proved particularly successful instances of the production trend. First, I look at the Merchant Ivory adaptation of E. M. Forster's Edwardian novel *Howards End*, released in 1992. Secondly, I examine the 1998 Working Title production of *Elizabeth*, about the early years of England's sixteenth-century monarch. Both films, interestingly, were directed by foreigners—James Ivory, an American, and Shekhar Kapur, an Indian—and both films raise productive questions about England and Englishness. The critical reception of both films also yields important insights about the diversity of interpretations any film can generate, and the particular emphases one can discern in relation to these two films.

As the questions I pose above should make clear, one of my aims in this book is to produce a reasonably comprehensive map of English costume dramas of the 1980s and 1990s. Another is to test theories of genre and practices of textual analysis and cultural criticism in relation to both industrial concerns and the evidence of reception. A third is to engage with debates about British cinema as a national cinema by exploring a particular production trend. At times, the debate about heritage films has become unnecessarily polarized, and it is as much the polarities of the debate as the films themselves that I want to examine. I will of course be building on my previous work on heritage films here—and two publications in particular, which have in themselves provoked a fair bit of criticism.[1] Much of that criticism seems to me well-founded, so while I'll incorporate some of the arguments from my earlier publications (especially in Chapters 1 and 2), I'll also be revising those arguments in various ways. One of the developments I'll need to confront is the films of the late 1990s which were specifically designed to widen the appeal of the costume drama, and thereby to address more diverse audiences. Such films mean that the debate must take a new turn.

I've used a variety of methods in researching this field. That variety is in itself an important strategy, since it allows different types of questions to be addressed and for answers to be framed in ways that are appropriate to the subject-matter. Central to the project is the process of empirical investigation: of industry developments, of marketing and promotional discourses and practices, of box-office statistics, of critical reception and reviewing trends, and of ways in which the tourism and heritage industries have taken up the films in question. In examining the production context of the films and the markets in which they circulate, I will draw in part upon the discourse of political economy, while analysis of film style will be used to yield insights about how the films themselves work as texts. Although my research will at times draw on the formalist analysis of meaning construction, this will always be tested against the evidence of critical reception and/or internet discussion by fans, not least in order to underline the limitations of such formalist analysis.

In broad terms, the subject-matter of the book is 'British' costume dramas released between 1980 and 2000. Such films belong at the same time to wider and longer standing traditions, especially in Europe. The idea of Europe as old, a place of history and antiquity, and as the font of Western culture, plays a crucial part in the play of European identity. As Richard Dyer and Ginette Vincendeau point

---

[1] 'Re-presenting the National Past: Nostalgia and Pastiche in the Heritage Film', in Lester Friedman (ed.), *Fires were Started: British Cinema and Thatcherism* (Minneapolis and London: University of Minnesota Press and UCL Press, 1993), 109–29; and 'The Heritage Film and British Cinema', in Andrew Higson (ed.), *Dissolving Views: Key Writings on British Cinema* (London: Cassell, 1996), 232–48. See also 'Heritage Cinema and Television', in David Morley and Kevin Robins (eds.), *British Cultural Studies* (Oxford: Oxford University Press, 2001), 249–60.

out, the heritage film draws on this idea of European culture in a variety of ways, retelling old stories about its monarchs, for instance, and adapting its canonical literature.[2] Hollywood has also tapped into this tradition in all sorts of ways, but American films have also told stories about the American past, whether in the form of the Western genre, or in literary adaptations such as *The Last of the Mohicans* (1992), *The Age of Innocence* (1993), and *Little Women* (1994). While such films are strictly outside the boundaries of my study, they will occasionally merit a mention. But the boundaries are never clear cut—the English film-maker Terence Davies, for instance, made a film of Edith Wharton's classic American novel *The House of Mirth* (2000), with substantial British funding and mainly British locations—and the film was officially regarded as a co-production between the USA and the UK.

But I've had to draw boundaries somewhere to prevent the book from spiralling out of control. Consequently, I'm not going to be dealing centrally with the many British television costume dramas and literary adaptations of the 1980s and 1990s—although again I shall occasionally refer to such productions. Nor will I be focusing centrally on Welsh or Irish or Scottish heritages, although it will be important to find a place for such films as *Rob Roy* and *Braveheart* (both 1995)— and of course *Chariots of Fire* deals nearly as much with Scottishness as it does with Englishness. Another line I've drawn makes a chronological distinction. For reasons I'll explain in Chapter 1, I've decided not to include much discussion of films set mainly during or after the Second World War. Such films are still clearly costume dramas, they are still about the past—but they deal with the more recent past, and I needed to end my discussion somewhere. So for the purposes of this book, I won't very often venture beyond the Second World War.

I should also point out that, while the majority of films that I discuss are literary adaptations of one sort or another, I won't spend much time exploring the processes of adaptation. What interests me is the fact of adaptation—and the status that lends many of the films. In any case, there is a huge scholarly and critical industry dedicated to exploring the details of literary adaptation, so these sorts of issues are well covered elsewhere.

But even if I've had to draw some artificial boundaries around the films I discuss, that still leaves me with a fairly sizeable body of films to deal with— indeed, a much larger body of films than I had initially anticipated. Many of those films have an important place in English cinema history, not least for the role they played in securing a reputation for quality English film-making. Upmarket literary adaptations and 'tasteful' period dramas, along with the documentary-realist tradition, have held pride of place in the ongoing debates about what constitutes English national cinema. (The classic serial and other reverential adaptations of canonical literature on television have also of course been one of the cornerstones of the public service broadcasting schedule.) With the demise of popular,

[2] Richard Dyer and Ginette Vincendeau, 'Introduction', in Dyer and Vincendeau (eds.), *Popular European Cinema* (London: Routledge, 1992), 6.

indigenous genre cinema in the 1980s and 1990s, the rise of the British art-house film, and the dedicated exploitation of the crossover market, the place of the costume drama in the development of English national cinema became even more important.

Heritage films operate at very much the culturally respectable, quality end of the market, and are key players in the new British art cinema, which straddles the traditional art-house circuit and the mainstream commercial cinemas in Britain—'one of the better kinds of British film', as the *Daily Mail* remarked of *Howards End*.[3] These are the sort of films that are invited to festivals and that win prizes (Oscars awarded to English costume dramas are listed in the Filmography). They are discussed in terms of an authorship which, at least in the case of the literary adaptations, is doubly coded—in terms of both film director and author of the source novel. A significant section of their audiences is middle class, and significantly older than the mainstream film audience, and they appeal to a film culture which is closely allied to educational discourses, English literary culture, and the canons of good taste.

The aura of art and quality around the heritage film does not simply afford it a special place in the contemporary national culture. This is also the type of English film that is frequently sold in export markets. Many of the films discussed received an art-house release overseas, or were otherwise promoted to 'discerning' international audiences. Some even did well in mainstream cinemas. As such, these films operate as cultural ambassadors, promoting certain images of Englishness. But does it still make sense in the global cultural economy to describe a film as 'British' or 'English'? It is rare today to find a film that is not designed for both domestic and export markets, and which is not therefore funded from a variety of sources or created by a multinational team. Many of the costume dramas considered here were either funded by American companies, or made as co-productions. In this context, should we not accept that what may seem to be a national representation is in reality an international mythology—that is, a story and characters that are assumed to have meaning, significance, and poignancy for international audiences?

Perhaps this simply underlines rather more obviously the constructed nature of representations of the English national past, which, in an era of intense globalization, is perhaps inevitable. But should we not be defending national cinema against such identity-blurring developments? Some of the films do indeed seem to engage in this sort of activity, by addressing the issue of Americanization, for instance. Thus in *Chariots of Fire* Englishness is specifically set against the modernity of America, while in *The Remains of the Day* (1993), some of the traditions of the stately home at the heart of the narrative are eroded when it is bought by an American. English national cinema in such instances is thus defined as quite distinct from the culture of Hollywood, even as it depends on Hollywood funding and the access it affords to the huge American market. Such films, and some of

---

[3] Shaun Usher, 'Fine Probe into Past Prejudices', *Daily Mail* (1 May 1992), 34.

the claims made for them, often seem to insist on the purity and distinctiveness of a traditional Englishness and eschew the particular type of cross-cultural intertextuality that is such a strong feature of contemporary aesthetics. Such films seem to articulate a version of the national heritage that contributes to a core English identity. But it is also possible, as we shall see, to read these films differently—to see them as critiques of heritage Englishness, for instance. It is certainly not the case that all audiences read the films as articulating nostalgic, conservative versions of Englishness. On the other hand, it is clearly *possible* to read them in this way (and certainly many commentators have read them in this way).

This is something to which we will continually return: that such films have generated different interpretations. If we also take into account that identity is never fixed, natural, or essential, and that national identity is always to some extent a mythic construction, and very often contested, it is difficult to know exactly how or why or against what one might defend a national cinema. English cinema has never been a 'purely national' cinema, whatever that might mean, and recent developments hardly transform the situation that has prevailed since the First World War.[4] Yet there is much public debate over the Englishness of English cinema, or the Britishness of British cinema, and the status of those cinemas in the global cultural marketplace. The debate is at its most shrill when 'British' films are in the running for the world's most prestigious film awards, the Oscars. Even though these are American awards, the publicity generated around Oscar ceremonies has long been used to draw attention to the quality of 'British' cinema.

When *Chariots of Fire* won four Oscars in 1982, Colin Welland, the scriptwriter, proclaimed that 'the British are coming!' When Anthony Minghella accepted his Best Director Oscar for *The English Patient* (1996) in 1997, he declared 'it's a great day for the Isle of Wight' (the small island off the south coast of England where he was born). *Chariots* was funded by Twentieth Century Fox, one of the American majors, and Allied Stars, run by the Egyptian Dodi Fayed. *The English Patient* was funded by Miramax, then part of the Disney empire. Both have strong British connections, in setting, characters, cast, and crew, but *The English Patient's* American producer, Saul Zaentz, was probably being more honest when he described it as 'an international film' ('Hell, even the English patient was a Hungarian!')—hence Minghella's satirical coup in claiming the film for the Isle of Wight.[5]

Even so, in the British press, there was a great deal of ballyhoo around the Britishness of both films, and about other major Oscar winners with British connections, such as *Gandhi* (1982) and *Shakespeare in Love*. In part, this is a question of promotion, a means of forging a brand image, an assertion of difference from Hollywood—for all the dependence of the films on Hollywood money. In part, though, the ballyhoo expressed an anxiety about national identity and

[4] See my 'The Instability of the National', in Justine Ashby and Andrew Higson (eds.), *British Cinema, Past and Present* (London: Routledge, 2000), 35–47.

[5] All quotations from Rachel Halliburton and Peter Guttridge, 'Best of British', *Independent*, Film section (27 Mar. 1997), 8–9.

national status. As one journalist put it, the question of what counts as a British film is 'the single most vexed question in national cinematic self-promotion . . . [A] film's Britishness is a much-chewed over issue because so much national self-esteem is tied up in the success of these keystone movies'.[6] To proclaim a film 'British' is thus often to claim ownership of a film of which the British may be proud, and which can give the British film industry some kudos. As the same journalist had commented previously, 'international co-productions are so commonplace that seeking out the national identity of any given film is largely a matter of public relations'.[7]

There is also an economic dimension, however, since there are official definitions of a film's national identity in place to determine which films should receive subsidies or tax relief. (*The English Patient*, for instance, was not officially registered as a British film.) It is also the case that the financing of a 'British' film by an American company may leave its British film-makers with little control over the decision-making process, and may ensure that much of the revenue generated at the box office goes back to USA. Despite such problems, government policy in the 1990s, under both Conservative and Labour, was designed to encourage more production activity in the UK by American companies, since such activity was deemed good for the economy generally, regardless of the cultural issues at stake.

On the one hand, then, globalization is recognized as a fact of life, and strategies are devised to make the most of its incursions into the traditional nation-state. On the other hand, national identity and pride is constantly reasserted. When *Titanic* (1997) swept the board at the Oscars in 1998, one journalist urged his fellow Americans to 'forget those charming little dramas that pour out of the British Isles. This was a competition for the big boys.'[8] Should we also forget that those charming little dramas were actually funded by the big boys, or at least their younger brothers? In fact, the Oscar ceremony is crucial to the cultural and economic well being of heritage films and other such quality productions. Miramax in particular campaigned hard to get titles like *Mrs Brown* (1997), *The Wings of the Dove* (1997), and *Shakespeare in Love* nominated for Oscars. Release patterns for such films are frequently designed to make the most of the publicity and kudos an Oscar nomination secures—since it can have a significant impact on box-office success, boosting admissions and extending the shelf-life of a film. After the success of *Chariots* at the Oscars in 1982, for instance, it was predicted that $5–6 million would be added to the film's gross takings.[9]

Because of the complexity of these issues, there is inevitably a degree of vagueness when identifying films in this book. Most of the films discussed have an English setting or deal with the English abroad, or are otherwise culturally

---

[6] Andrew Pulver, 'Bard to Worse at the Multiplex', *Guardian* (5 Feb. 1999), 19.

[7] Andrew Pulver, 'Today the Government will Pledge More Millions for British Film', *Guardian*, G2 (24 July 1997), 4.

[8] Bob Thomas, quoted in Dan Glaister, 'Titanic Sinks British Oscar Hopes', *Guardian* (25 Mar. 1998), 5.

[9] Quentin Falk, 'Chariots Came, Saw and Conquered . . .', *Screen International* (3 Apr. 1982), 2.

English, and most were made in England. Most are officially recorded as British productions, but some are not, and many are either co-productions, or have received funding from overseas partners—but as I've just noted, even those that are not officially recorded as British are often claimed as British. Only too aware of these difficulties, but wanting to discuss these films as a group, I've often resorted to putting 'British' in inverted commas when referring to the national identity of the films in an economic sense. When I refer specifically to the cultural identity of the films, I tend to use the adjective English. It's not a perfect solution, but it is pragmatic!

By comparison with mainstream Hollywood star vehicles, heritage films are relatively low-budget productions, with the emphasis on authorship, craft, and artistic value. They are valued as much, perhaps more, for their cultural significance as for their box-office takings—though profitability clearly cannot be removed from the equation altogether. Distribution tends to be specialized, with films carefully geared to target audiences and enjoying exclusive runs in the right sorts of cinemas rather than saturation release, especially in the crucial North American market. These films thus operate as a middle-brow version of quality, pitched somewhere between modernism and the more high-brow elements of art cinema on the one hand, and low-brow popular culture on the other—whether it is the popular culture of Hollywood or indigenous popular culture. Of course, there are self-consciously (post)modernist period films (the work of Sally Potter, Derek Jarman, and Peter Greenaway comes to mind), and of course some of the films are adapted from modernist literary classics. In broad terms, however, it is the middle-brow that claims these films. This inevitably upsets commentators with little sympathy for middle-brow versions of quality: as we shall see, both those attached to popular culture and those with a greater investment in the high brow have difficulties with the films. The varying response to such films thus forms quite a large part of what follows. I begin this discussion with the question of naming: what labels have been applied to such films, and why?

1
The English Heritage Film in the 1980s and 1990s: Mapping the Field

It is one thing to gather together a group of films and give them a collective name. It is another thing to justify that process of grouping and naming. I've deliberately used a variety of terms for the films this book is about: heritage films, costume dramas, period films. We might add others, some facetious (white flannel films, frock flicks, Brit-Lit movies), some focused on particular cycles (post-heritage films, the Edwardian genre), some ideologically grounded (nostalgic screen fictions). Some of these films have also been discussed under the more general rubrics of the woman's picture, the art-house film, and the quality film. The proliferation of labels is an indication of the diversity and richness of the films they identify, the range of interpretations generated around them, and the hybridity and interconnectedness of genre categories. This shouldn't worry us unduly. They are just labels after all. On the other hand, academic film studies has invested much in the analysis of genre and of particular genres, establishing conventions and compiling taxonomies.

So is heritage cinema a genre? That depends what we mean by the term heritage cinema. Thus, are all period films and costume dramas by definition heritage films? If not, what is the relation of the heritage film to these other genres? Is it distinct from them, a cycle within them, or another name for them? If, like Ann-Marie Cook, we define a heritage film as any film set in the past,* we might reasonably ask why apply a new label when perfectly serviceable terms for such films already exist. If we define the heritage film more tightly—only films dealing with the English past, for instance, or only films made in or depicting a certain period, or of a particular style—we run into all the problems that arise once we start devising rules and regulations. Who devises the rules? Who decides which films are to be included and excluded, which films are central to the genre and which peripheral? On what grounds should such decisions be made? What if others disagree with the decisions? These are the problems of genre definition: where to draw the boundaries, how to limit the category of the heritage film, how to speak with any authority about why this film is in but not that one.

*In her forthcoming Ph.D. thesis 'Parallels to the Past: The Politics of Heritage Cinema in Britain in the 1990s', which has helpfully stimulated my thinking.

We will run into just as many problems if we do away with labels altogether. My task, after all, is to discuss some of the shared characteristics of a range of 'British' films produced in the 1980s and 1990s, and I need to be able to give these films a name. For the purposes of debate and analysis, in other words, I need to be able to categorize the films, to distinguish them from other films. There clearly is some benefit in discussing these films as a genre, some benefit in drawing on the established practices of genre study. But I want to avoid constructing an elaborate, rule-governed, and exclusive category—much better, it seems to me, to acknowledge the degree to which one group of films overlaps with other groups. In our case, for instance, many heritage films (I've had to use some label!) are also literary adaptations, but not all literary adaptations are set in the past, and not all costume dramas are literary adaptations. All genres and cycles are in fact best understood as loose, leaky, hybrid categories, drawing on a variety of influences, building on an eccentric range of sources, references, and representational practices, filmic and otherwise. Each film is the product of its particular historical conditions of existence, each cycle or genre emerges as it evolves, constructing its own terms of reference, its own intertexts.

Inevitably, I've had to make some decisions about what to include in this book, and what to exclude. The decisions have been made primarily on the basis of the date when the film was made and the period and place in which it is set. Those decisions aren't intended as the basis for a genre definition; on the contrary, they simply limit the scope of this study so that it becomes manageable and focused. As I've already explained, I'll be concentrating primarily on films made in the 1980s and 1990s that either depict some aspect of the English past before the Second World War or are adapted from a canonical English literary text. Most of the films I discuss have some British element in their production, and are classified as either British films, or British co-productions. But there are a number of films classified solely as American which have such a strong emphasis on English culture and history that I've felt it necessary to take those films on board too. The Filmography at the end of the book reflects this thinking and indicates the range of films I'll be dealing with (although often only in passing).

The parameters I've adopted will allow me to discuss a film like *The Wings of the Dove* (1997), set in Edwardian Britain, even though it was adapted from a novel by Henry James, an American, and the protagonists spend some of their time in Italy. Indeed, the antics of the English abroad feature in several of the films I'll be discussing. The limits I've set also allow me to discuss a film like *Elizabeth* (1998), set in sixteenth-century England, even though it was directed by an Indian, Shekhar Kapur. *Robin Hood: Prince of Thieves* (1991) is more difficult to justify because it was classified as an American production; even so, it was set in twelfth-century England, shot on English locations, and includes numerous British actors.[1] Shakespeare adaptations that don't have an English setting are included as

---

[1] There are in fact fourteen films in the Filmography that were classified solely as American productions; all are either set in England, or about the English; several are adaptations of English literary or dramatic properties; several others are about English or Scottish folk heroes.

well—so long as there's also a strong British element in the production circum-stances. But the American production of *Great Expectations* (1997), updated so that it takes place in present-day Florida, is stretching things too far for it to be in any way central to my discussions. Even so, neither it nor, say, *Clueless* (1995), an updating and Americanizing of Jane Austen's *Emma*, should be disregarded altogether. It would be equally rash to overlook Martin Scorsese's *The Age of Inno-cence* (1993), Jane Campion's *The Piano* (1993), or James Cameron's *Titanic* (1997), parallel texts, as it were, even though none is a British production, and the first has very few British connections at all. Thus, while they remain films that must be kept in the frame, they do not appear in the Filmography. *The House of Mirth* (2000), like *The Age of Innocence* (1993) adapted from an Edith Wharton novel and set in late nineteenth-century New York, is easier to reconcile, since it was very much a British production, shot on location in Glasgow and elsewhere, by the British director Terence Davies.

The heritage film label is of course a critical invention of recent years, emerg-ing in a particular cultural context to serve a specific purpose.[2] In an earlier pub-lication, 'Re-presenting the National Past', which appeared in 1993, I applied the label loosely to a relatively small group of 'British' costume dramas of the 1980s and early 1990s that detailed aspects of the English past and that shared various circumstantial, formal, and thematic characteristics, especially their emphasis on the upper and upper middle classes in the early decades of the twentieth century.[3] The term heritage cinema seemed appropriate since I and others identified these films as the products of a culture and an economy in which what had come to be called the heritage industry—the commodification of the past—had become highly visible. I was not alone in thinking that a number of English period films of the 1980s and 1990s displayed a marked generic intertextuality. Cairns Craig, for instance, was adamant that there was an identifiable genre with common themes, literary sources, and a repertory cast, and already in 1991 thought the genre was 'in danger of turning into a parody of itself'.[4] Craig's article was an important early attempt to define this category of film-making and to situate it in relation to the heritage industry, but his views were by no means unique, and even those who disagree with his critical disparagement of the genre accept the idea that something akin to a generic category has emerged.

The way I defined heritage cinema in 'Re-presenting the National Past' was much more tightly circumscribed than what I'm proposing here. Other writers such as Craig and Tana Wollen also focused on a fairly limited group of films.[5]

[2] See Claire Monk, 'The British Heritage-Film Debate Revisited', in Claire Monk and Amy Sargeant (eds.), *British Historical Cinema* (London: Routledge, 2002), 176–98.

[3] See Andrew Higson, 'Re-presenting the National Past: Nostalgia and Pastiche in the Heritage Film', in Lester Friedman (ed.), *Fires were Started: British Cinema and Thatcherism* (Minneapolis and London: University of Minnesota Press and UCL Press, 1993), 109–29.

[4] Cairns Craig, 'Rooms without a View', *Sight and Sound*, 1/2 (1991), 10; see also Tana Wollen, 'Over our Shoulders: Nostalgic Screen Fictions for the Eighties', in John Corner and Sylvia Harvey (eds.), *Enterprise and Heritage: Crosscurrents of National Culture* (London: Routledge, 1991), 178–93.

[5] Wollen, 'Over our Shoulders'.

What we were interested in was how certain English costume dramas of the period seemed to articulate a nostalgic and conservative celebration of the values and lifestyles of the privileged classes, and how in doing so an England that no longer existed seemed to have been reinvented as something fondly remembered and desirable. Such films seemed to represent a particular relationship to the past—hence the heritage label—and as such, seemed symptomatic of so much cultural activity of the period. I still think it's a good argument, and a reasonable interpretation of the films in question—but it is just an interpretation, and other interpretations are possible. To insist that the films be called heritage films, and are best understood in terms of the relationships they establish between past and present, is to limit access to other ways of understanding these films and the varied social functions they perform. But all labels run that risk, and the heritage cinema label has acquired a certain cachet through its repeated use in academic debate, so I'm going to continue to use it. Not exclusively, though, since I don't want to make too much of a fetish of it. I'll therefore sometimes call the same group of films by other names, primarily the costume drama and the period film.

In academic film studies, it has become conventional to make a distinction between the historical film and the costume drama. The historical film is often understood to comprise films that depict actual figures from history, in their historical context. The costume drama label, on the other hand, is sometimes reserved for films that present fictional characters in historical settings.[6] If the historical film is perceived as tending to dwell on public events in the public sphere, the costume drama dwells on events in the private sphere. The boundaries soon become blurred, however, with 'historical' films from *The Private Life of Henry 8th* (1933), *Victoria the Great* (1937), and *The Private Lives of Elizabeth and Essex* (1939) to *The Madness of King George* (1995), *Mrs Brown* (1997)—about Queen Victoria's relationship with one of her staff—and *Elizabeth* spending much of their time dealing with events in the private sphere. It's also the case that many so-called costume dramas seek to authenticate their fiction by constructing a 'historically accurate' setting. The distinction between historical films and costume dramas thus seems to me difficult to maintain—and I don't intend to maintain it here. For the most part, then, I shall avoid the term historical film, and assume that the costume drama label covers all period films, whether they depict actual historical figures or clearly fictional figures.

The problem with the conventional distinction between the historical film and the costume drama is precisely that it depends on a rather rigid and unwavering set of rules. Genre study needs to be flexible, and to recognize that boundaries are artificial, discursive constructs produced in pieces of writing like this. As Steve Neale writes, 'a genre's history is as much the history of the term as it is of the films to which the term has been applied; [it] is as much a history of the conse-

---

[6] See e.g. Marcia Landy, 'Looking Backward: History and Thatcherism in the Recent British Cinema', *Film Criticism*, 15/1 (1990), esp. 17–22; also several of the essays in Monk and Sargeant (eds.), *British Historical Cinema*.

quently shifting boundaries of a corpus of texts as it is of the texts themselves. The institutionalisation of any generic term is a key aspect of [its] social existence.[7] In the case of this book, I need to map the field of films on which I'm going to concentrate, but it's important to recognize that the map could be drawn differently. If we construct limits, we must be prepared to deconstruct them as well. There is no point in defining a term like heritage cinema too tightly—no point, for instance, in saying that the heritage film never deals with the great events of national history (that would exclude a film like *Elizabeth*), or that all heritage films are literary adaptations (*Chariots of Fire* (1981) is a good example). Nor do I think the heritage cinema label is only applicable to films made in the latter part of the twentieth century. Obviously hundreds of films were made before 1980 that in some way or other depicted the English past. And even if the particular way the heritage industry has developed in the 1980s and 1990s is different to what happened in previous decades, concerted efforts were still made in earlier decades to link films to other contemporary appropriations of the past and to conservative nationalist discourses.[8] The heritage cinema label can thus be used quite productively for films made in other periods.

GENRE AND THE INDUSTRY: PRODUCTION TRENDS

The concept of genre as it is understood in academic film studies has both an industrial and a critical dimension. Genres are seen as both means of organizing production and marketing, and ways of grouping films analytically, at the level of critical debate. But the film business itself doesn't as a rule adopt the terminology of genres. Tino Balio, in examining the output of the American film industry in the 1930s, proposes instead the terminology of production trends, suggesting that this is a better way to understand how cycles of similar films emerge within the industry. It is by definition a less rule-governed enterprise—precisely, a loose trend, rather than the hard and fast category that the term genre suggests.[9] Such trends emerge as producers attempt to repeat a success, or to exploit a current fashion. And, like genres, they can still be understood as playing off repetition (reworking a familiar and successful model) against difference (but not too different, not too original).

For the industry, working in this way is a means of ensuring a certain degree

---

[7] Steve Neale, *Genre and Hollywood* (London: Routledge, 2000), 43.

[8] See for instance my discussion of various silent British films: 'Heritage Discourses and British Cinema before 1920', in John Fullerton (ed.), *Celebrating 1895: Proceedings of the International Conference on Film before 1920* (Sydney: John Libbey, 1998), 182–9; 'The Victorious Re-cycling of National History: *Nelson*', in Karel Dibbets and Bert Hogenkamp (eds.), *Film and the First World War* (Amsterdam: Amsterdam University Press, 1995), 108–15; and the chapter on *Comin' thro' the Rye* (1923/4) in *Waving the Flag: Constructing a National Cinema in Britain* (Oxford: Oxford University Press, 1995), 26–97.

[9] See Tino Balio, *History of the American Cinema*, v. *Grand Design: Hollywood as a Modern Business Enterprise, 1930–1939* (New York: Charles Scribner's Sons, 1993).

of novelty while at the same time minimizing risks. And indeed if we look at the development of the heritage film over the 1980s and 1990s, we can see at times that producers are very much sticking with an established model. Merchant Ivory Productions, for instance, produced three adaptations of E. M. Forster novels with Edwardian settings in six years (and nine further quality literary adaptations with a period setting in the 1980s and 1990s—although they were not all British films nor did they all have English settings). On the other hand, certain producers have quite explicitly taken risks, breaking with convention in various ways. Derek Jarman's *Edward II* (1991) and Sally Potter's *Orlando* (1992), for instance, both drew on avant-garde practices, while Working Title's *Plunkett and Macleane* (1999) and *Elizabeth* blended the costume film with other more mainstream generic elements designed in part to attract younger male audiences.

Putting aside such variations for the moment, there can surely be no doubt that one of the key production trends in 'British' film-making of the 1980s and 1990s was the period film with an English, and sometimes a Scottish, or Welsh, or Irish setting. There is a world of difference between, say, the medievalism of mainstream American productions such as *Robin Hood: Prince of Thieves* and *Braveheart* (1995), and the polite decorum of low-budget art-house oriented films such as *A Room with a View* (1986) and *Mrs Dalloway* (1997). And yet for all their differences, such films have shared a surprising number of characteristics. These similarities are in part the consequence of decisions made at the level of production and marketing. In other words, the generic nature of the trend is in part the result of business decisions rather than the vagaries of critical debate. The success of one film facilitates and to some extent determines the production and marketing of subsequent films, and gradually a trend emerges. There is little evidence to suggest that the heritage film label has itself figured in production and marketing decisions. On the other hand, as will become clear, some companies undoubtedly identified the costume drama market as a niche worth exploiting, and they had their own labels for the sorts of films they were making—and in some cases, the sorts of films they didn't want to make. *Elizabeth*, for instance, was made as a costume drama, but one that would differ in various ways from the prevailing Merchant Ivory model—what producer Tim Bevan called the frock flick.[10]

Within the broad category of the English costume drama of the 1980s and 1990s, it is possible to identify a series of relatively self-contained cycles or tendencies, which yet overlap with each other in all sorts of ways. Going through some of these cycles will enable me to introduce the range of films I see as relevant to this study. The overall list of films I see as relevant is deliberately catholic (see the Filmography at the back of the book), and is thereby able to acknowledge the diversity of costume dramas with an English connection made in the period. Some are low-budget art-house films (*The Draughtsman's Contract* (1982), for instance), while others are much more mainstream productions (such as *Braveheart*). Some have a strong American connection, whether in their funding (*The English Patient*

---

[10] Quoted in the Press Book for *Elizabeth*.

(1996)) or their subject-matter (*The House of Mirth*), while others are European co-productions (*Orlando*). Many deal with the late Victorian and Edwardian periods, but others are set much earlier. I've already explained that I won't be dealing very much with films set during or after the Second World War—but it also seems important to acknowledge that some of those films—*Shadowlands* (1993, set in the 1950s), for instance, and even some films set more recently, like *Four Weddings and a Funeral* (1994)—share much with the other films I discuss.

The contemporary fascination with period drama, and especially costume drama about the English upper classes, was given a kick-start in 1981, when *Brideshead Revisited* on television and *Chariots of Fire* at the cinema caught the imagination of audiences, critics, and the judges at various awards ceremonies. Granada TV's *Brideshead Revisited* was a lavish serialized adaptation of Evelyn Waugh's lament about the decline of the English country house, its values, and its inhabitants. The serial was taken up as the embodiment of all that was best in British television. Its quality was visible in the casting, the adaptation, the locations and interiors, and the slow, expansive unfolding of the narrative: 'the truth is that *Brideshead Revisited* looks like the nearest thing to perfection that the television serial has managed in its entire history. It is an immense achievement'.[11] *Chariots of Fire*—a major success at the box office—also stirred up patriotic sentiments with its 1920s-set drama about class, ethnicity, national identity, and sporting achievement:

It puts you in direct touch with sentiments so long un-expressed publicly that you wonder if they ever existed—love of country, fear of God, loyalty to the team, unselfish pursuit of honour, becoming modesty in victory, and that doesn't by any means exhaust the list. I'd add it is a wholly English film . . . if that didn't seem in the circumstances like boastful bad form.[12]

Along with a handful of other period films released to critical acclaim in the early 1980s, these productions established that there was a market for quality English costume dramas that were in one way or another different from standard Hollywood fare. In *Screen International*'s end of year box-office chart for 1981, there were four quite distinct 'British' period films: *The Elephant Man* (1980) at number nine, *Tess* (1979) at number ten, *Chariots of Fire* at number twelve, and *Excalibur* (1981) at number sixteen.[13] But the market straddled television and art cinema as well as mainstream theatrical exhibition. On television, there was *Brideshead Revisited* and *The Jewel in the Crown* (1984). At the art-house there was Peter Greenaway's breakthrough success, *The Draughtsman's Contract*, and Cannes Film Festival prize-winner *Another Country* (1984). Crossing over into the mainstream theatrical market were two other literary adaptations with an art-house

---

[11] Chris Dunkley, '*Brideshead Revisited*' (review), *Financial Times* (14 Oct. 1981): cutting—no page given.
[12] Alexander Walker, 'Britain Back on the Tracks' (review of *Chariots of Fire*), *Evening Standard* (2 April 1981): cutting—no page given.
[13] End of year box-office chart, *Screen International* (19–26 Dec. 1981), 1.

cachet, *The French Lieutenant's Woman* (1981), and David Lean's much bigger budgeted *A Passage to India* (1984), along with Richard Attenborough's epic bio-pic, *Gandhi* (1982).

ADAPTING LITERATURE

Most of the costume dramas that followed in the footsteps of these illustrious trailblazers were adaptations of canonical English literature—unlike *Chariots*, *The Draughtsman's Contract*, and *Gandhi*, which were all made from original screenplays. Among the most prominent of the English costume drama cycles is the group of six adaptations produced in Britain by Merchant Ivory. These include the E. M. Forster adaptations, *A Room with a View*, *Maurice* (1987), and *Howards End* (1992), the Henry James adaptation *The Golden Bowl* (2000), and treatments of two much more recent novels, Ruth Prawer Jhabvala's *Heat and Dust* (1982) and Kazuo Ishiguro's *The Remains of the Day* (1993). The James and Forster adaptations are all set in turn-of-the-century or Edwardian England—although in two of them the protagonists also visit Italy; all four films deal with similar issues of class, inheritance, and national identity. The other two adaptations flit between two different time periods, with *Heat and Dust* looking at the English in India in the 1920s and the present, and *Remains* at an English country house and its various inhabitants, visitors, and servants during the 1930s and 1950s. Both then focus once more on Englishness, but ethnicity is stressed in the former and class in the latter. It is surely significant that the director of all these films, James Ivory, is American, as was Henry James, while the producer Ismail Merchant is Indian, Prawer Jhabvala (who also wrote the screenplays for most of the films) is of Polish Jewish extraction and Ishiguro was born in Japan. Despite these various identities, the Merchant Ivory films are celebrated for their tasteful, soft-edged, pictorial recreations of the English past. As the *Washington Post* put it, 'if Merchant Ivory . . . have anything to do with it, there'll always be an England'.[14]

It is surely also significant that of the 125 films in the Filmography, while Ivory made seven, only a handful of other individuals directed more than two films. There is no doubt, then, that Ivory, and his production company Merchant Ivory Productions, invested much in heritage cinema. Eleven directors worked on two films each, Richard Attenborough, Hugh Hudson, Derek Jarman, and Charles Sturridge on three, and Kenneth Branagh on four (all of them Shakespeare adaptations). The vast majority of directors worked on just one film each of those listed in the Filmography. The complexion would change slightly if we took into account films made during or after the Second World War. Mike Newell, for instance, besides directing *Enchanted April* (1991), set in the 1920s, also made *Dance with a Stranger* (1985, set in the 1950s), *An Awfully Big Adventure* (1994, set in the 1940s),

[14] Rita Kempley, ' "Howards End": Resplendent Return to Forster's England', *Washington Post* (24 Apr. 1992), D8.

1. James Ivory, Ruth Prawer Jhabvala, and Ismail Merchant: key players in the heritage film genre

and *Four Weddings and a Funeral* (set in the present, but sharing with English country house costume dramas much of the same iconography and many of the same character types). One conclusion we must draw is that the sense that Merchant Ivory films have played a major part in the development of the heritage film in the 1980s and 1990s is by no means misplaced or overemphasized. No other director or production company has been nearly so involved in such films.

Nor has the status of literature in this production trend been overplayed: three-quarters of the films listed in the Filmography are adaptations of one sort or other. Again, one can identify various cycles. Adaptations of Forster's novels in themselves constitute one key cycle. In addition to the three Merchant Ivory adaptations of Forster, a further two were made by other directors, David Lean's *A Passage to India* and Charles Sturridge's *Where Angels Fear to Tread* (1991). In the 1990s, three other canonical authors replaced Forster: Jane Austen, Henry James, and Thomas Hardy. There's a long tradition of serialized adaptations of Austen's novels on British television. Austenmania really hit the screens in the mid-1990s, however, with the enormously successful BBC serialization of *Pride and Prejudice* (1995), written by Andrew Davies. Davies also wrote a feature-length version of *Emma* (1996) for ITV. A big-screen version of *Emma*, starring Gwyneth Paltrow, appeared the same year, as did *Persuasion*, a BBC single drama that received theatrical distribution in the USA. Also released in 1996 was the Emma

Thompson-scripted film version of *Sense and Sensibility*.[15] A few years later, in 2000, a very racy version of *Mansfield Park* worried several self-appointed guardians of the literary heritage.[16]

Hardy was author of the moment in the late 1990s, with film versions of *Jude* (1996), *The Woodlanders* (1997), *The Scarlet Tunic* (1997, from a short story, *The Melancholy Hussar*), and—in an almost unrecognizable form—*The Mayor of Casterbridge*, which Michael Winterbottom reworked as *The Claim* (2000), a nineteenth-century drama set in the American West. There were also television serial versions of *Far from the Madding Crowd* and *Tess of the d'Urbervilles* (both 1998). The latter was also, much earlier, made as a film, *Tess* (1979). The James adaptations include *The Portrait of a Lady* (1996), *The Wings of the Dove*, and *The Golden Bowl*. Making much less impact were three mid-1990s adaptations from Joseph Conrad: *Victory* (1995), *The Secret Agent* (1996), and *Amy Foster* (1997).

Thanks especially to the tireless work of Kenneth Branagh, as both director and actor, and to the production company Renaissance Films, with which he was associated for some time, there was also a plethora of adaptations of the work of Shakespeare. Derek Jarman's *The Tempest* was produced in 1980, but the cycle really took off in 1989 with Branagh's *Henry V*. Shakespeare creates some problems of categorization, however. His work is clearly central to the English cultural heritage—but not all of it is about the English or has an English setting. Several of the adaptations of the 1990s—Christine Edzard's version of *As You Like It* (1992), Branagh's version of *In the Bleak Midwinter* (1995), and Michael Hoffman's version of *A Midsummer Night's Dream* (1999), for instance—were updated so that they are no longer strictly period films or costume dramas. I've decided to exclude these films from the Filmography, along with Franco Zeffirelli's version of *Hamlet* (1990), which is neither about the English nor has a British production link. Richard Loncraine's *Richard III* (1995) and Branagh's *Love's Labour's Lost* (2000), both updated to 1930s England, have to be included, as does Jeremy Freeston's *Macbeth* (1997), made very self-consciously as a Scottish film. I've also decided to include the following films, which all have a strong British dimension in the production set-up, even though none of them is strictly about the English: Peter Greenaway's *Prospero's Books* (1991), Branagh's *Much Ado About Nothing* (1993) and *Hamlet* (1996), Oliver Parker's *Othello* (1995), Trevor Nunn's *Twelfth Night* (1996), and Adrian Noble's *A Midsummer Night's Dream* (1996).

Other adaptations which deserve a mention, but which don't necessarily fit into any of the above cycles, include versions of several novels by 'classic' authors: Waugh's *A Handful of Dust* (1987), Charles Dickens's *Little Dorrit* (1987) and *The Mystery of Edwin Drood* (1993), D. H. Lawrence's *The Rainbow* (1988), George

---

[15] On the Austen boom, see Ros Ballaster, 'Adapting Jane Austen', *English Review* (Sept. 1996), 10–13; Roger Sales, *Jane Austen and Representations of Regency England* (London and New York: Routledge, revised edn., 1996), 227–39; and Julianne Pidduck, 'Of Windows and Country Walks: Frames of Space and Movement in 1990s Austen Adaptations', *Screen*, 39/4 (1998), 381–400.

[16] See for instance John Mullan, 'Fanny's Novel Predicament', *Guardian* (28 Mar. 2000): accessed from the *Guardian* website at www.guardian.co.uk.

Eliot's *Adam Bede* (1991), two Virginia Woolf novels, *Orlando* and *Mrs Dalloway*, Charlotte Brontë's *Jane Eyre* (1995), Emily Brontë's *Wuthering Heights*, Daniel Defoe's *Moll Flanders* (1995), Walter Scott's *Rob Roy* (1995), and George Orwell's *Keep the Aspidistra Flying* (1997). Adaptations of works by less canonical authors include Rebecca West's *The Return of the Soldier* (1982), Magdalen King-Hall's *The Life and Death of the Wicked Lady* (as with its 1945 predecessor, the film title was shortened to *The Wicked Lady* (1983)), Edgar Rice Burroughs's *Greystoke: The Legend of Tarzan, Lord of the Apes* (1984), John Galsworthy's *A Summer Story* (1987), Elizabeth von Arnim's *Enchanted April*, Bram Stoker's *Dracula* (1992), and H. E. Bates's *A Month by the Lake* (1994). There were also adaptations of several children's classics: Frances Hodgson Burnett's *Little Lord Fauntleroy* (1980) and *The Secret Garden* (1993), Anna Sewell's *Black Beauty* (1994), and Rudyard Kipling's *Jungle Book* (1994).

Many of the above novels were written as contemporary stories, and became period pieces only when they were adapted as films, with their original setting more or less maintained. There were also several adaptations of novels by more recent writers who conceived their works from the outset as period pieces. John Fowles's *The French Lieutenant's Woman*, Jean Rhys's *Quartet*, Prawer Jhabvala's *Heat and Dust*, William Trevor's *Fools of Fortune* (1982), Tom Hart's *The Innocent* (1984), Isabel Colegate's *The Shooting Party* (1984), James Fox's *White Mischief* (1987), J. L. Carr's *A Month in the Country* (1987), Bruce Chatwin's *On the Black Hill* (1987), Jennifer Johnston's *The Dawning* (1988), Maggie Hemingway's *The Bridge* (1990), Sam Hanna Bell's *December Bride* (1990), Stella Gibbons's *Cold Comfort Farm* (1995), A. S. Byatt's *Angels and Insects* (1995), Michael Ondaatje's *The English Patient*, Rose Tremain's *Restoration* (1996), Valerie Martin's *Mary Reilly* (1996), Peter Carey's *Oscar and Lucinda* (1997), and Pat Barker's *Regeneration* (1997). Many of these were prestigious stories from prize-winning writers. Adaptations of the work of more populist writers were much rarer, but included *The Lady and the Highwayman* (1988), from a story by Barbara Cartland.

Adaptations of successful contemporary plays with a period bent included *Another Country* from a play by Julian Mitchell, *Shadowlands* from William Nicholson's play, *Tom and Viv* (1994) from Michael Hastings's play, and *The Madness of King George* from Alan Bennett's play. There were also adaptations of Christopher Marlowe's *Edward II*, Terence Rattigan's *The Winslow Boy* (1998), George Coleman and David Garrick's *The Clandestine Marriage* (1999), and Oscar Wilde's *An Ideal Husband* (1999), as well as the films noted above based on the works of Shakespeare. The literary connection also figured in a series of bio-pics, including *Hedd Wyn* (1992, about the eponymous Welsh poet), *Shadowlands* (about C. S. Lewis), *Tom and Viv* (about T. S. Eliot's relationship with his wife), *Carrington* (1995, about the friendship between painter Dora Carrington and writer Lytton Strachey), *Wilde* (1997, about Oscar Wilde), and *Shakespeare in Love* (1998, a comic version of an imagined moment in Shakespeare's life). Earlier, Ken Russell's *Gothic* (1986) focused on a night Percy Bysshe Shelley, Mary Shelley, and Lord Byron famously spent telling stories to each other in Switzerland. Other films with an artistic connection included *The Bridge*, which embellishes incidents in the life of the painter Philip Wilson Steer, *Chaplin* (1992), a bio-pic of Charlie Chaplin, *Sirens* (1994), about the visit of an English couple to the Australian artist and poet Norman Lindsay, *Topsy-Turvy* (1999), exploring a passage in the illustrious careers of Gilbert and Sullivan, and *War Requiem* (1989), a reworking of Benjamin Britten's oratorio of the same name. A different sort of bio-pic was *The Fool* (1990), which was partly based on Henry Mayhew's mid-nineteenth-century documentary investigation, *London Labour and the London Poor*.

Literature and the process of writing is also very often something we see on screen, or hear as voice-over. There are novelists, dramatists, and other kinds of professional and amateur writers in *Angels and Insects, Mansfield Park, A Room with a View*, and *Shakespeare in Love*. There are letter-writers and diarists in *Chariots of Fire, The English Patient*, and *Mrs Brown*—and what they write occasionally fills in as voice-over narration. Stories and poems are read aloud in *A Handful of Dust, Orlando, A Room with a View*, and *Sense and Sensibility*. In one way or another, then, literature is vital to the appeal of these English costume dramas. The literary source material of so many of them functions as an important selling point, playing on the familiarity and/or cultural prestige of the particular novel or play, but also invoking the pleasures of other such quality literary adaptations and the status of a national cultural tradition. In the case of adaptations of canonical texts, the source text is as much on display as the past it seeks to reproduce. Lesser material may also be canonized when it is treated by film-makers in the same fashion, with the same modes of representation and marketing.

ADAPTING HISTORY

As should be clear by now, very few of the 'British' period films made in the 1980s and 1990s and set before the Second World War were developed as original screenplays, as opposed to adaptations from another source.[17] Several of them are what others would call historical films, since they deal with real historical figures in something approaching authentic settings, and almost all of them, in one way or another, are bio-pics. Several deal with folk heroes of more or less legendary status: *Excalibur*, about the Knights of the Round Table; *Robin Hood: Prince of Thieves*, and two other comic versions of the same story, *Robin Hood* (1990), and *Robin Hood: Men in Tights* (1993); *Braveheart*, about William Wallace leading the Scots against the English in the thirteenth century; *Plunkett and Macleane*, about two notorious highwaymen of the mid-eighteenth century; and *Comrades* (1986), about the Tolpuddle Martyrs of the 1830s. One might add to this list of folk heroes *Chariots of Fire*, about Britain's leading runners of the 1920s, *Topsy-Turvy*, the Gilbert and Sullivan film, and Richard Attenborough's two bio-pics of leading figures of the twentieth century, Charlie Chaplin, in *Chaplin*, and Mahatma

---

[17] Thirty-two such films are listed in the Filmography.

Gandhi, in *Gandhi*. Perhaps even David Lynch's eccentric film about a severely disabled late Victorian Briton, *The Elephant Man*, belongs in this list.

Most of the films could be categorized in other ways as well. *Gandhi*, for instance, was also part of what was dubbed 'the Raj revival' in the mid-1980s.[18] Other texts in this cycle exposing imperialist fantasies of national identity included *A Passage to India*, and the highly successful television serials *The Jewel in the Crown* and *The Far Pavilions* (1984).[19] Other films wholly or partly about the English abroad include *Heat and Dust*, *A Room with a View*, *White Mischief*, *The Deceivers* (1988), *Pascali's Island* (1988), *Where Angels Fear to Tread*, *Enchanted April*, *Orlando*, *The Englishman Who Went Up a Hill and Came Down a Mountain* (1994), *A Month by the Lake*, *Sirens*, *Rudyard Kipling's Jungle Book*, *Victory*, *The English Patient*, *Tea with Mussolini* (1998), and *The Last September* (1999).

One can also trace across the 1980s and 1990s a range of moving image appropriations of the royal family, including various television documentaries, interviews, and live broadcasts of weddings, jubilees, and funerals, but also fictionalized filmic accounts of the royal heritage, such as *Lady Jane* (1985), *Mrs Brown*, and *Elizabeth* (all original screenplays), and *Henry V*, *Edward II*, and *The Madness of King George* (all dramatic adaptations). It is noteworthy that a screening of *Emma* was slotted into the television schedule sensitively reorganized on the day of the funeral of Diana, Princess of Wales, in September 1997. This tasteful though not always reverential period drama, about a charismatic but insecure and less than perfect young upper-class heroine moving uncertainly towards a fairy-tale romantic closure, provided the happy ending that Diana's fairy tale did not have. That it did so with the cultural authority of Jane Austen meant that it could be deemed safe in the context of what many saw as a day of national mourning—but it was also both modern and traditional, like Diana herself.

Of the 125 films listed in the Filmography, that leaves just fourteen as yet unaccounted for either as literary adaptations or historical bio-pics. Several are based on true stories (*1871* (1989), *Fairytale A True Story* (1997), and *The Tichborne Claimant* (1998)) or are loosely autobiographical (*The Englishman Who Went Up a Hill . . .* and *Tea with Mussolini*). Several are works of fiction, in the sense that they are not strictly based on historically documented events, even if such events do occasionally figure in their narratives: *The Missionary* (1981), *The Draughtsman's Contract*, *Century* (1993), *Chasing the Deer* (1994), *Firelight* (1997), *The Governess* (1997), *Stiff Upper Lips* (1997), and *Solomon and Gaenor* (1998). Indeed, *The Missionary*, *The Draughtsman's Contract*, and *Stiff Upper Lips* are all comedies, the latter expressly parodying other period dramas. In each case, though, even if liberties are quite self-consciously taken for comic effect, efforts have been made to establish some sense of historical authenticity.

---

[18] Salman Rushdie, 'Outside the Whale', *Granta*, 11 (1984), 125–38; and Farrukh Dhondy, 'All the Raj', *New Socialist* (Mar./Apr. 1984), 46–7.

[19] For discussions of such films, see John Hill, *British Cinema in the 1980s: Issues and Themes* (Oxford: Clarendon Press, 1999), 99–123; and T. Muraleedharan, 'Imperial Migrations: Reading the Raj Cinema of the 1980s', in Monk and Sargeant (eds.), *British Historical Cinema*, 144–62.

Indeed, almost all the films listed make strenuous efforts to reproduce a period in all its fullness and authenticity—but a handful resists this sort of visual historicism. *The French Lieutenant's Woman*, *Heat and Dust*, Derek Jarman's *The Tempest* and *Edward II*, Sally Potter's *Orlando*, Ken McMullen's *1871*, and Peter Greenaway's *The Draughtsman's Contract* and *Prospero's Books* are all, in their way, period films with elements of costume drama. But they all also play with representation in a postmodernist fashion that challenges the realistic effect. *The French Lieutenant's Woman* and *Heat and Dust* move back and forth in time, between past and present (something similar happens in *The Remains of the Day*, although here the present is still the past, an immaculately recreated mid-1950s). The Jarman films refuse to reconstruct their period setting authentically, mixing costumes and other elements of the *mise-en-scène* from different historical periods. *Orlando* makes fun of the period costume genre in various ways, its central protagonist moving through several distinct historical epochs and living for 400 years. Like Jarman and Potter, Greenaway too has fun with period *mise-en-scène* in *The Draughtsman's Contract*, and plays with the image in even more complex ways in the multi-layered and experimental *Prospero's Books*.

GENERIC THEMES

In broad terms, the vast majority of the films under consideration are serious social dramas with a naturalistic quality and a period setting. Within this overarching framework, there are variations. Most of the dramas are drawn on an intimate rather than an epic scale, but some are clearly played as national epics—*Braveheart*, *Edward II*, *Elizabeth*, and *Henry V*, for instance. A handful blend in other more virile generic conventions—the thriller in *Elizabeth*, the sporting drama in *Chariots of Fire*, or the adventure film, in *Braveheart*, *Plunkett and Macleane*, and *Rob Roy*. *Greystoke*, interestingly, is played more as a serious social drama than as the adventure most Tarzan films have been. In some, a romance plot is foregrounded, inclining the film towards the woman's picture. Most of these films can still be seen as serious social dramas, however. Some of them are leavened with a comic sensibility—often in the vein of light romantic comedy (*Emma*, *An Ideal Husband*, *Much Ado About Nothing*, *Orlando*, and *Shakespeare in Love*, for instance). Only occasionally is the overarching naturalism of these films challenged by other modes, such as the absurdist humour of *The Draughtsman's Contract*, the parody of *Stiff Upper Lips* and *Robin Hood: Men in Tights*, or the touches of the gothic and the fantastic to be found in a handful of films. The self-consciously named *Gothic* falls into this category, of course, along with *Bram Stoker's Dracula*, *The Mystery of Edwin Drood*, *Mary Reilly*, *Fairytale A True Story*, and *Firelight*, while *The Elephant Man*, and even in parts *Elizabeth*, also draw on a gothic sensibility. But just as *Greystoke* colours the adventure film with historical realism, so *Mary Reilly*, a retelling of the gruesome Jekyll and Hyde story from

2. Female community in *Sense and Sensibility*

the maid's point of view, is played as much for the period authenticity of the quality costume drama as for its gothic qualities.

The connection with the classical woman's picture and a female point of view is important. As we shall see, the female audience is crucial to most of these costume films. Many of the films also foreground female protagonists, even in their titles: *Amy Foster*, (Dora) *Carrington*, *December Bride*, *Elizabeth*, *Emma*, *The Governess*, *Jane Eyre*, *Lady Jane*, *Little Dorrit*, *Mary Reilly*, *Mrs Brown*, *Mrs Dalloway*, *Moll Flanders*, *Tess*, *The Wicked Lady*—and more ambivalently, *The French Lieutenant's Woman*, *Oscar and Lucinda*, *Tom and Viv*, and *Orlando* (in which the eponymous character changes sex from a man to a woman mid-way through the film!). While a few of the heritage films may present grand national narratives or self-consciously public histories, many more present personal stories. In such films, there is a central romance plot, or an emphasis on the domestic, or the story provides space for the articulation of female voices and desires or the creation of a female community—as in *Elizabeth*, *Emma*, *Enchanted April*, *Sense and Sensibility* (Fig. 2), *Sirens*, and *Tea with Mussolini*.

It is worth noting too the number of women whose work has contributed significantly to the production process of the films (see the Table at the end of the book). Several of the films are adapted from novels by female authors as diverse as Jane Austen, Pat Barker, Barbara Cartland, Frances Hodgson Burnett, and Edith Wharton. Women were also often the screenwriters, with Ruth Prawer Jhabvala

3. Going against the grain: Stephen Fry as Oscar Wilde in *Wilde*

writing the screenplays for all but one of James Ivory's films, for instance, and Laura Jones writing both *Oscar and Lucinda* and *The Portrait of a Lady*. An impressive number of the films were either directed or produced by women, while several more drew on the services of female costume designers, production designers, art directors, and composers.

But if many of the costume dramas and period films of the 1980s and 1990s can be seen as woman's films, there are also quite a few that focus on male homosocial and sometimes homosexual communities. *Chariots of Fire* falls into the first category, as do *The Shooting Party, A Month in the Country, Much Ado About Nothing, Shadowlands, Regeneration,* and *Shakespeare in Love* (the joke here of course is that Gwyneth Paltrow as Viola has to pass as a man in order to belong to the all-male theatre community). In the second category, there are several depictions of homosexual communities, including *Another Country, Maurice, Edward II, Carrington,* and *Wilde* (Fig. 3). Indeed, when I first wrote in the early 1990s about English heritage films of the previous decade, it seemed to me that 'the national past and national identity emerge in these films not only as aristocratic, but also as male-centred'.[20] I had in mind such films as *Chariots of Fire, Another Country, A Handful of Dust,* and *Maurice,* the prominence of a small group of male actors (and white flannel trousers!), and the marked interest of gay audiences in such films. In these films, male desires seemed to outweigh female

---

[20] Higson, 'Re-presenting the National Past', 114.

desires—and even in *A Room with a View* Lucy Honeychurch (Helena Bonham Carter) could be seen as a pawn in a game of competing male egos. As other critics were quick to point out, however, and as I've acknowledged above, the cycle is just as effectively understood as a reworking of the classical woman's film.[21]

More generally, the extent to which these costume dramas of the 1980s and 1990s function as character studies rather than more action-oriented films can be seen in the number of films whose titles delineate characters rather than actions or events. We have already noted those which feature female characters in the titles. Others foregrounding male characters include *Adam Bede, Chaplin, Comrades, Edward II, The Elephant Man, The English Patient, The Englishman Who Went Up a Hill . . . , The Fool, Gandhi, Greystoke, Hamlet, Hedd Wyn, Henry V, An Ideal Husband, The Innocent, Jude, Little Lord Fauntleroy, Macbeth, The Madness of King George, Maurice, The Missionary, Pascali's Island, Plunkett and Macleane* (although this of course *is* an action film), *Prospero's Books, Shakespeare in Love, Wilde,* and *The Winslow Boy.*

Titles indicating action on the other hand are few and far between. The most obvious are *Braveheart, Robin Hood: Prince of Thieves,* and *Excalibur,* but then these are much more mainstream than all the others mentioned, and were all classified as solely American productions (as were another action-adventure film with a period setting, *Rob Roy,* and the Robin Hood parody, *Robin Hood: Men in Tights*). Other films whose titles indicate action perhaps include *Chariots of Fire,* although its version of the car chase or the shoot-out is a climactic running race between clean-cut men in the baggy shorts favoured by athletes in the 1920s; *The Lady and the Highwayman,* although it tempers the promise of action with the promise of romance; *The Secret Agent,* but this version is much more of a costume drama than a Hitchcock thriller; *The Shooting Party,* but it's a very class-specific sense of action; and *The Tempest,* although this is not a film about tornadoes, like *Twister* (1996), but a Shakespeare adaptation, with all the cultural kudos that implies.

ENGLISHNESS, CLASS, AND OTHER HERITAGES

Despite the number and diversity of films I've listed, the settings of the films also remain quite limited in terms of class milieu and period, and therefore of the heritages they depict. For a start—and this is of course the *raison d'être* of my Filmography—all of the films cited engage in one way or another with English heritage. That is to say, they all offer some version of the English past, or some representation of the history of Englishness or the English cultural heritage, whether at home or abroad, in literature or reality. Some of the Shakespeare adaptations—*Hamlet, Much Ado About Nothing, Prospero's Books, The Tempest,* and *Twelfth Night*—may not represent the English, but they play a huge part in the history of English culture. *The Claim* may be set in the USA, with no English

---

[21] See e.g. Claire Monk, 'The British Heritage Film and its Critics', *Critical Survey,* 7/2 (1995), 116–24.

characters, but it is loosely based on a Hardy novel. *The House of Mirth* too is set in the USA—but this time there is no British literary source, the film finding its way into my discussion because it is a British-American co-production which shares much stylistically and iconographically with costume dramas set in England and dealing with the English.

Quite a number of the films listed—more than a quarter—dwell on the exploits of the English upper classes and upper middle classes in the late Victorian period or in the early part of the twentieth century, between 1880 and 1940.[22] It is perhaps worth noting that this period is regarded by many as crucial in the formation of the dominant modern version of English national identity.[23] While there are just as many set in the nineteenth century, there are far fewer set in earlier periods (and of course some of the Shakespeare adaptations do not depict the English past at all, however much a part of the English cultural inheritance they are). One cluster worth noting is those films set in the Regency period (most of them Austen adaptations)—since the Regency is also frequently though not unproblematically appropriated as a key moment in and a vital representation of the national heritage.[24] Films set in earlier periods tend to focus on the making of the nation, whether the nation is England (*Henry V, Elizabeth*) or Scotland (*Braveheart*). In such films, the nation is hardly a settled place; on the contrary, its space and its sovereignty are contested, its future status is in the process of becoming.

Braveheart is by no means the only film of the period to deal with the Scottish past. Others include *Chariots of Fire, Chasing the Deer, Rob Roy, Macbeth, Mrs Brown*, and *My Life So Far* (1998). The Welsh past features in *Hedd Wyn, August* (1995, a reworking of Anton Chekhov's *Uncle Vanya* set in north Wales), *The Englishman Who Went Up a Hill . . .* , and *Solomon and Gaenor*. The Irish past is also explored in a number of 'British' films, including *The Dawning, Fools of Fortune, December Bride*, and *The Last September*.

The class focus of most of the films set before the nineteenth century is as circumscribed as those set in later periods. For the most part, they deal with monarchs, nobility, or aristocrats, and it is difficult to find films that step confidently away from the privileged classes. To identify as heritage cinema a body of films of dubious national identity, circulating a limited set of representations, is clearly to beg the question of whose heritage is being projected. In a multicultural society, there are many, often contradictory traditions competing for attention; yet so-called heritage cinema would seem to focus on a highly circumscribed set of traditions, those of the privileged, white, Anglo-Saxon community who inhabit lavish properties in a semi-rural southern England, within striking distance of

---

[22] *Another Country, Carrington, Chariots of Fire, Enchanted April, The English Patient, The Englishman Who Went up a Hill . . ., The Golden Bowl, Greystoke, A Handful of Dust, Howards End, An Ideal Husband, Maurice, Mrs Dalloway, A Passage to India, The Remains of the Day, A Room with a View, The Secret Garden, The Shooting Party, Sirens, Stiff Upper Lips, Tea with Mussolini, Tom and Viv, Where Angels Fear to Tread, Wilde, The Wings of the Dove, The Winslow Boy.*
[23] See e.g. Robert Colls and Philip Dodd, *Englishness: Culture and Politics, 1880–1920* (London: Croom Helm, 1986).
[24] Sales, *Jane Austen.*

the metropolitan seat of power. A few costume dramas deal with rural poverty in the nineteenth and early twentieth centuries, including *Comrades, December Bride, The Innocent, On the Black Hill, The Rainbow, Solomon and Gaenor,* and the Hardy adaptations (*Jude, Tess,* and *The Woodlanders*). Far fewer deal centrally with urban poverty—perhaps only the two Christine Edzard films, *Little Dorrit* and *The Fool.* Servants, governesses, and criminals feature in a number of films, but rarely take centre stage—although they do in *The Remains of the Day, Mary Reilly, Mrs Brown, Firelight, The Governess, Robin Hood: Prince of Thieves,* and *Plunkett and Macleane.*

Indeed the emphasis on the servants in a film like *Remains* reveals the work that goes into creating and maintaining the picturesque façade of the country house and the comfortable lifestyle of its inhabitants. As Roger Sales suggests, the presence of servants may also reveal the precarious position of the leisured classes, since they often witness the less salutary aspects of their employers' behaviour. In many more cases, however, servants seem to figure as little more than authentic period props, heritage decoration—and may in that respect underline the pleasures of the leisured classes they serve.[25]

Despite the caveats, then, most of the costume dramas cited seem fascinated by the private property, the culture, and the values of a very limited class fraction in each period depicted, those with inherited or accumulated wealth and cultural capital, and in close proximity to those with political power. The national past and national identity emerge in these films as very much bound to the upper and upper middle classes, while the nation itself is often reduced to the soft pastoral landscape of southern England, rarely tainted by the modernity of urbanization or industrialization—although we do see evidence of the latter in the Edzard films, *Howards End, Jude,* and *The Wings of the Dove,* for instance. Because from this perspective there are so few alternative visions on offer, it often seems as if the heritage of the upper classes has become the only or at least the most prominent face of the national heritage. In each instance, the quality of the films lends the representation of the past a certain cultural validity and respectability. But there is no escaping the reductiveness of the particular cultures and sets of traditions that stand in for the English national past. Private interest in effect becomes naturalized as in the public interest. Except, of course, that these are still films for a relatively privileged audience. As we will see, for all the success of quite a number of the films cited, most of the costume dramas in the Filmography are still relatively specialized products, whose core audience is more upscale than most mainstream films. Audiences who engage with these representations must in some degree negotiate their ideas of England and Englishness in relation to these representations. This does not mean that all audiences who engage with these representations automatically buy in to a particular mythology of the old country and national identity; but if they do not, then they must actively resist such representations and seek to create an alternative mythology.

[25] Roger Sales, 'In Face of All the Servants: Spectators and Spies in Austen', in Deidre Lynch (ed.), *Janeites: Austen's Disciples and Devotees* (Princeton: Princeton University Press, 2000), 188–205.

In so many ways, for all their elegance and allure, heritage films seem very often to deal with the last of England, or at least the last of old England. In films like *A Passage to India*, the focus is on the end of empire. Elsewhere, it is the death of liberal England (*Regeneration*), the betrayal of the nation (*Another Country*), the corrupt decadence and moral decay of the upper classes (*Angels and Insects, Another Country, A Handful of Dust, The Shooting Party, The Clandestine Marriage*), or the displacement of the aristocracy by a new meritocracy (*Chariots of Fire*).[26] The idea of heritage implies a sense of inheritance, but it is precisely that which is on the wane in these films. Several films thus focus on a crisis of inheritance among the privileged classes, or the threat of disinheritance. The problem is generally posed as a question: who is to inherit or, to put it more metaphorically, who is to occupy the centre ground?

Thus *Sense and Sensibility* sees the female members of a wealthy family disinherited, and thereby thrust into relative poverty. *Mansfield Park* compares the privileged lifestyle of one woman's family with the squalid and impecunious lifestyle of her sister's family. In *The House of Mirth*, a member of New York's high society is disinherited and forced to become a member of the working classes. In *The Wings of the Dove*, a young woman hangs grimly on to her place in English society, while having an affair with a working journalist and manœuvring to inherit the fortunes of a New York heiress. When the character of Orlando becomes a woman in *Orlando*, she is dispossessed of all her property. There can be no issue from the sexless and/or homosexual relationships of *Maurice* and *Another Country*. The family is torn asunder in *Wilde*. The son is killed in *A Handful of Dust*. All that Brideshead stands for is destroyed. In almost every case, there is a marked absence of strong father figures.

Looked at in this way, the films no longer seem so sure of the history of Englishness and its legacy for the present. We may also note that, if heritage films at one level play out dramas of the national elites, they also, and at the same time, find a central place for social figures often marginalized in mainstream cinema: women, gays and lesbians, ethnic or national others, the lower classes. On the one hand, heritage films seem to present a very conventional version of the national past, a view from above, conservative, upper-class, patriarchal; on the other hand, they very often seem to move marginalized social groups from the footnotes of history to the narrative centre. In the displaced form of the costume drama, the heritage film thus creates an important space for playing out contemporary anxieties and fantasies of national identity, sexuality, class, and power. Temporal displacement and cultural respectability license the exploration of difficult or taboo subjects such as the homoerotic passions of *Another Country, Maurice, Carrington*, or *Wilde*, the ethnic rivalries in *Chariots of Fire* or *The Deceivers*, or the class transgressions of *Mrs Brown* or *Howards End*.

That many of the films can thus seem interrogative and critical, exploring the underside of the often nostalgic vision, is perhaps not surprising since so many

---

[26] On *Chariots*, see Sheila Johnston, 'Charioteers and Ploughmen', in Martin Auty and Nick Roddick (eds.), *British Cinema Now* (London: British Film Institute, 1985), 99–110.

of the films are made not by upper middle-class English film-makers, but by directors and producers raised in other cultures. Inevitably, many such film-makers approach their subject-matter from a less than reverential position, from that of the outsider rather than the insider. We have already noted the ethnic and national identities of the Merchant–Ivory–Jhabvala triumvirate—but note too that several more films had American directors, including *The Elephant Man* (David Lynch), *Emma* (Douglas McGrath), *Restoration* (Michael Hoffman), and *The Winslow Boy* (David Mamet).

Jane Eyre and *Tea with Mussolini* were directed by an Italian (Franco Zeffirelli), *Sense and Sensibility* by a Taiwanese (Ang Lee), *Tess* and *The Secret Garden* by Poles (Roman Polanski and Agnieszka Holland respectively), *Mrs Dalloway* by a Dutch film-maker (Marleen Gorris), *Elizabeth* by an Indian (Shekhar Kapur), *Mansfield Park* by a Canadian (Patricia Rozema), and *Oscar and Lucinda* and *Sirens* by Australians (Gillian Armstrong and John Duigan respectively). Crews were often multinational too, such as those for *Orlando* and *The English Patient*. One might also note that the Scots Bill Douglas (*Comrades*) and Gillies MacKinnon (*Regeneration*), the Welshman Chris Monger (*The Englishman Who Went Up a Hill . . .*), the Irish directors Pat O'Connor (*A Month in the Country, Fools of Fortune*) and Thaddeus O'Sullivan (*December Bride*), and the Jewish film-maker Sandra Goldbacher (*The Governess*) all brought distinctive un-English, or at least non-mainstream English, perspectives to bear on the films they made.

On the one hand, then, we may conclude that heritage films frequently focus on poignant problems in the English past, on narratives of dissolution or on the marginal and displaced as much as the apparently privileged—and that they often do so from an un-English perspective. Such films, it seems, are capable of producing a sharp critique of the limits of past and present social and moral formations. On the other hand, and somewhat paradoxically, they also seem to offer decidedly conservative, nostalgic, and celebratory visions of the English past—and it is difficult to argue convincingly that the majority do not still, despite the evidence of the above, dwell on the privileged lifestyle and visible evidence of wealth of the leisured classes. These are issues to which we will need to return.

CASTING AND PERFORMANCE: STARS, CHARACTER ACTORS, AND ACTING STYLES

Another marked instance of the intertextuality of heritage films is in their casting. At its most extreme, the same actors play similar roles and class types in several different films, bringing a powerful sense of all the other heritage films, costume dramas, and literary adaptations to each new film. But there are also similar types of actors, performing similar types of characters, across many different texts. There are perhaps three different groups of actors, although the categories, and the boundaries between them, are by no means hard and fast.

First, there are established actors who specialize in character parts, and who bring with them all the qualities and connotations of the British theatre tradition.

4. Heritage star Helena Bonham Carter in *A Room with a View*

This group would include Denholm Elliott,[27] Judi Dench,[28] Maggie Smith,[29] Simon Callow,[30] Nigel Hawthorne,[31] Vanessa Redgrave,[32] John Gielgud,[33] and James Fox,[34] who all appeared in at least four of the films listed in the Filmography. Sometimes the character studies become central protagonists, stars—thus Judi Dench's role as Queen Victoria in *Mrs Brown*, several parts played by Emma Thompson[35] and Anthony Hopkins,[36] and Kenneth Branagh's Shakespearean roles.[37]

Secondly, there are various usually younger actors who seem virtually groomed for their parts in heritage films. Helena Bonham Carter (Figs. 4–5) is the

[27] *The Missionary, The Wicked Lady, A Room with a View, Maurice.*
[28] *A Room with a View, A Handful of Dust, Henry V, Hamlet, Shakespeare in Love, Tea with Mussolini.*
[29] *The Missionary, Quartet, A Room with a View, The Secret Garden, Tea with Mussolini, The Last September, Gosford Park* (2001).
[30] *A Room with a View, Maurice, Howards End, Shakespeare in Love.*
[31] *Gandhi, The Madness of King George, Twelfth Night, The Winslow Boy, The Clandestine Marriage.*
[32] *Comrades, Howards End, Mrs Dalloway, Wilde, A Month by the Lake.*
[33] *The Elephant Man, Chariots of Fire, Gandhi, The Wicked Lady, The Shooting Party, Prospero's Books, Hamlet, The Portrait of a Lady, Elizabeth.*
[34] *Greystoke, A Passage to India, Comrades, The Remains of the Day, The Golden Bowl.*
[35] *Howards End, Remains of the Day, Much Ado About Nothing, Carrington, Sense and Sensibility.*
[36] *The Elephant Man, Howards End, Bram Stoker's Dracula, Remains of the Day, Shadowlands, August.*
[37] *Henry V, Much Ado About Nothing, Othello, Hamlet, Love's Labour's Lost.*

5. Bonham Carter in *The Wings of the Dove*

quintessential model here, having become almost synonymous with Edwardian England with roles in *A Room with a View*, *Maurice*, *Where Angels Fear to Tread*, *Howards End*, and *The Wings of the Dove*—as well as other period parts in *Lady Jane*, *Keep the Aspidistra Flying*, and *Twelfth Night*. Other actors in this category include Rupert Graves,[38] Hugh Grant,[39] James Wilby,[40] and Jeremy Northam,[41] who all appeared in at least six of the films listed, and Kristin Scott Thomas[42] and Kate Winslet,[43] who each appeared in three. Clearly some of them go on to become stars who can inhabit roles from other genres—Kate Winslet, for instance, but also Hugh Grant and Helena Bonham Carter. Nigel Havers (*Chariots of Fire*, *A Passage to India*), Jeremy Irons (*Brideshead Revisited*, *French Lieutenant's Woman*), and Rupert Everett (*Another Country*—and later *The Madness of King George*, *An Ideal Husband*, and *Shakespeare in Love*), all made their names in such roles too.[44] Thirdly, there are several young actors, some British, some not,

[38] *A Room with a View*, *Maurice*, *A Handful of Dust*, *Where Angels Fear to Tread*, *The Madness of King George*, *Mrs Dalloway*.
[39] *Maurice*, *White Mischief*, *The Lady and the Highwayman*, *Remains of the Day*, *Sirens*, *The Englishman Who Went Up a Hill . . .*, *Sense and Sensibility*, *Restoration*.
[40] *Maurice*, *A Handful of Dust*, *A Summer Story*, *Adam Bede*, *Howards End*, *Regeneration*, *An Ideal Husband*.
[41] *Wuthering Heights*, *Carrington*, *Emma*, *An Ideal Husband*, *The Winslow Boy*, *The Golden Bowl*, *Gosford Park*.
[42] *A Handful of Dust*, *Angels and Insects*, *The English Patient*, as well as *Gosford Park*.
[43] *Jude*, *Sense and Sensibility*, *Hamlet*, as well as *Titanic*.
[44] See Julian Petley, 'Reaching for the Stars', for interesting comments on Jeremy Irons and Rupert Everett, in Auty and Roddick (eds.), *British Cinema Now*, 117, 119.

who are less typecast, yet who in building up their repertoire have included a number of period roles: Daniel Day-Lewis,[45] Tilda Swinton,[46] Gwyneth Paltrow,[47] Jonny Lee Miller,[48] Joseph Fiennes,[49] Christopher Eccleston,[50] Ralph Fiennes,[51] and Cate Blanchett[52] among them.

If the distinctions I've made between these three groups of actors are difficult to maintain—and I readily admit that they are—that is because most, if not all, of the roles they've played in English costume dramas have been character parts. And almost all of those films depended on ensemble casts and acting. That is to say, they are not star vehicles in the mainstream Hollywood sense, even if the presence of certain actors is crucial to both the raising of production funding and the marketability of the films. The key to the type of English acting that such roles call for is of course understatement and restraint, in which the tiniest of gestures can speak volumes, although careful diction counts for much too. There is thus a kind of performative overdetermination in many of these roles. On the one hand, many of them involve performing a highly circumscribed and conventional version of Englishness. The roles are class-bound, of course, and bring with them all the cultural requirements of reserve and repression, but also a superficial self-confidence and charisma. On the other hand, the sense of performance, the sense of masquerade, is paramount. Englishness, or rather a certain model of Englishness, is thus presented as a role, an act—a trope that is brought to the fore by the parody of *Stiff Upper Lips*, the masquerade of the butler as the gentleman in *The Remains of the Day*, and the construction of an English gentleman in *The Tichborne Claimant*.

MOVING TOWARDS THE PRESENT

I have of course deliberately left out another cycle of English period films and costume dramas: those that deal exclusively with the period from the 1940s to the present. Were we to include such films, we would find many more stories of ordinary people and far fewer central protagonists from the privileged classes.[53] Several such films were set in the Second World War: *Hope and Glory* (1988), *The Dressmaker* (1988), *Chicago Joe and the Showgirl* (1989), *Land Girls* (1998), and *Enigma* (2001), for instance. Several more were set between 1945 and 1960,

---

[45] *A Room with a View, The Age of Innocence, The Last of the Mohicans.*
[46] *War Requiem, Orlando, Edward II.*
[47] *Emma, Shakespeare in Love.*
[48] *Regeneration, Plunkett and Macleane, Mansfield Park.*
[49] *Elizabeth, Shakespeare in Love.*   [50] *Jude, Elizabeth.*
[51] *Wuthering Heights, Oscar and Lucinda, The English Patient.*
[52] *Oscar and Lucinda, Elizabeth, An Ideal Husband.*
[53] For interesting discussions of some of these films, see Phil Powrie, 'On the Threshold between Past and Present: "Alternative Heritage" ', in Justine Ashby and Andrew Higson (eds.), *British Cinema, Past and Present* (London: Routledge, 2000), 316–26; and Amy Sargeant, 'The Content and the Form: Invoking "Pastness" in Three Recent Retro Films', in Monk and Amy Sargeant (eds.), *British Historical Cinema.*

Modern recipes: No 21

Costume drama

1 *classic text*
1 *large tub whimsy*
3lb mixed anachronisms
1 *gross britches*
2 *gross frocks*
7 *tins potted ham*
1 *garden*
1 *Helena Bonham Carter*
(or own-brand
equivalent)

TAKE the classic text and age by the time-honoured process of using it to bore generations of schoolchildren. When thoroughly steeped in apathy, adapt it with a filleting knife and a lump hammer, taking care to discard all nuance, literary elegance and distinctive dialogue.

When only Mills & Boon plot is left, lard thoroughly with whimsy until gullet rises. Pepper with anachronisms, which should include at least 30 per cent psychobabble.

Carefully landscape the garden and fill with pathways. Fill the britches and frocks with ham and perambulate through the garden, turning every few minutes and basting with intrigue (ask your retailer for extra-insipid strength). For a slightly novel flavour, place the garden in South America or Africa, but don't stint on the britches and frocks.

Bake at gas mark $1/2$ until tepid. Garnish with Helena Bonham Carter. Serve to eager audience of former bored schoolchildren. Export leftovers to America.

As a complement to the meal, reissue classic text in shiny new cover featuring garden, pathways, britches, frocks, ham and Helena Bonham Carter. Decorate with sticker reading: "As seen on BBC1/ITV/ Sky Movies/The Nude Windsurfing Channel" (delete as appropriate).

David Bennun

ILLUSTRATIONS BY JASON FORD

6. How to make a costume drama: 'Modern recipes no. 21', from the *Guardian*, 1997

including *A Private Function* (1984), *Dance with a Stranger*, *84 Charing Cross Road* (1986), *Absolute Beginners* (1986), *Wish You Were Here* (1987), *Distant Voices, Still Lives* (1988), *Fellow Traveller* (1989), *The Long Day Closes* (1992), *Shadowlands*, and *An Awfully Big Adventure* (1994). The 1960s were depicted in *Personal Services* (1987), *Prick Up Your Ears* (1987), *Withnail and I* (1988), *Buster* (1988), *Scandal* (1989), *The Krays* (1990), *Backbeat* (1993), *The Young Poisoner's Handbook* (1994), *Small Faces* (1995), and *Love is the Devil* (1998), and the 1970s in *Sid and Nancy* (1986), *Young Soul Rebels* (1991), *Velvet Goldmine* (1998), and *East is East* (1999), amongst others.

Although these films deal with the relatively recent past, they are still period films and costume dramas, they still involve an element of historical reconstruction, and they still in various ways depict the English past. So why exclude them? As I've already indicated, the answer is partly down to pragmatism: I had to draw the limits somewhere. But there are other reasons too. One is that these films seem to me to engage with the past in different ways to most of those set before the Second World War. Rarely do they engage with the same elite heritage discourses as most of the other films I have mentioned, discourses which have accrued around themselves the aura of 'national tradition', and which have consequently played such a central role in defining England and Englishness (among the postwar films, *Shadowlands* is the obvious exception, and one of the reasons why I often return to it). Instead, these films about the recent past tend to deal much more with the everyday lives of ordinary people, often people from working-class backgrounds. Films set in earlier periods, such as *Jude*, *Little Dorrit*, *Comrades*— and even *Maurice*, *Howards End*, and *The Remains of the Day*—dealt with working people and with poverty. But the trend is less pervasive in the period before the Second World War. Many of the films set later than this also tend to build on the popular memory of media culture, drawing their stories from the headlines of newspapers, rather than from textbook history or from canonical literary culture, with its basis in formal education and middle-class leisure pursuits (again, *Shadowlands* stands out as an exception).

Even though the period films with earlier settings are the products of a modern media industry, the narratives themselves—even those depicting the 1920s and 1930s—seem to take place in an era that precedes, and indeed has no knowledge of, the mass media. Yes, there is a journalist in *The Wings of the Dove*; yes, the heroes of *Chariots of Fire* visit a cinema to watch themselves in a newsreel; and yes, there is another journalist in *The Remains of the Day*. But even in the latter film, newspapers are still in the 1930s ideally things that should be ironed by the butler before being delivered to the lord of the house on a silver tray! *Chaplin*, a bio-pic of a film star which undoubtedly does deal with the popular media, is then the exception that proves the rule. The films set in the 1940s and later are much more willing to engage with the mass media and popular culture, and to lift their stories from the pages of newspapers. Clearly such films still offer a version of the past, a cultural heritage, but it is a different way of grasping the past and a different heritage that is embraced, suggesting different narrative pleasures and identifications.

As such, the heritage cinema label has rarely been extended to such films—or if it has been, the label is generally modified to 'alternative heritage'.[54] To exclude such films from discussions of heritage is clearly problematic, since it implies that heritage always means elite heritage. It is as if the past lives, values, lifestyles, and living conditions of ordinary people are somehow irrelevant to the present. It is as if memories and representations of ordinary people, and the display of artefacts that yield insights into their lives, are somehow not part of the national heritage. Even the alternative heritage label suggests the elite heritage of the privileged classes is the *core* national heritage. But as Raphael Samuel has argued so persuasively, 'heritage' is in fact a very diverse term, applied to a whole range of cultural, political, and economic practices involving people from all walks of life. The national heritage is a rich, and richly hybrid, set of experiences and should not be reduced to the apparently singular experiences of elite, conservative patriotism; nor should it be reduced to the values of consumerism.[55]

Heritage is not simply an elite version of the national past; the past can be and has been appropriated in all sorts of ways, many of which are central facets of popular culture. Samuel also shows how ideas of heritage and the national past have been expanded, modernized, and democratized in the post-war period. Considerable amounts of energy are now invested in the active exploration of, for instance, local heritages, working-class heritages, industrial heritages, and the heritages of diasporic communities who have found a home in Britain—even by bodies such as English Heritage and the National Trust. It is worth noting, however, that, as Stephen Daniels puts it, while 'this has involved the restoration of alternative versions of English heritage, some . . . like parish pride, may overlap uncomfortably with conservative versions.'[56]

Films figure in this potentially democratizing development in various ways. On the one hand, we might see the box-office success of so many of the costume dramas set before the Second World War as in part a symptom of that development, rendering elite heritages accessible to millions of ordinary people. This is one way of interpreting the relative popularity of films like *Chariots of Fire*, *A Room With A View*, *Howards End*, *Sense and Sensibility*, *Elizabeth*, and *Shakespeare in Love*, all of which dwell on images of wealth and privilege, but all of which also did very well at the box office. On the other hand, we might want to dwell on the images of 'alternative heritage' in films from *Comrades*, *The Fool*, and *Jude* to *Wish You Were Here*, *Small Faces*, and *East is East*. The range of alternative traditions and ways of seeing that have found their way on to film and video can be extended further. Black Audio Films' *Handsworth Songs* (1986) and the BBC's 1998 *Windrush*

---

[54] Powrie, 'On the Threshold', 316–24.

[55] Raphael Samuel, *Theatres of Memory* (London and New York: Verso, 1994).

[56] Stephen Daniels, *Fields of Vision: Landscape Imagery and National Identity in England and the United States* (Cambridge: Polity Press, 1993), 4.

series explored some of the cultural traditions of black Britons whose families came from the Caribbean; Ken Loach's *Land and Freedom* (1995) offered a fictional account of British socialists fighting in the Spanish Civil War; and Derek Jarman's films frequently engaged with canonical English drama and other familiar heritage iconography in a very unfamiliar way, providing a queer take on core national traditions.

In noting such productions, the difficulty of drawing meaningful boundaries around distinct genres is once more made apparent. Indeed, while my concern here has been to delineate a certain trend in 'British' film production in the 1980s and 1990s, it seems at times as if the whole of the British film industry revolves around the heritage idea. Certainly it has proved central to attempts to define British cinema in this period. Of course not all the period films have the same relationship to the heritage industry. Indeed, Claire Monk suggests that, in the early 1990s, film-makers developed new ways of engaging with the past, in films like *Orlando* and *Carrington*, which she dubs post-heritage.[57] Of course too, it was by no means the case that all British films of the 1980s and 1990s were set in the past. *My Beautiful Laundrette* (1985), for instance, opened on the same day in New York as *A Room with a View*. *Trainspotting* (1996) appeared in cinemas across Britain in the same week that *Sense and Sensibility* was released. And *Elizabeth* followed *Lock, Stock and Two Smoking Barrels* (1998) around the multiplex circuits.

The seven biggest British box-office hits of the period 1990–2001 (indeed, of all time), included only two costume dramas, *Shakespeare in Love* and *The English Patient*. The others—in order of worldwide box-office takings, *Notting Hill* (1999), *The Full Monty* (1997), *Four Weddings and a Funeral*, *Bridget Jones's Diary* (2001), and *Bean* (1997)—were all contemporary dramas.[58] But of them, *Four Weddings*, with its country houses, olde-worlde inns, and upper class eccentrics, shares a great deal with heritage films like the Forster and Waugh adaptations. *Notting Hill* features Julia Roberts as an American film star who comes to England to appear in period costume in a Henry James adaptation. And *Bridget Jones's Diary* reworked parts of Jane Austen's *Pride and Prejudice*. Even *Trainspotting* could be discussed under the rubric of heritage. Thus Derek Malcolm suggested that 'you could call it an anti-heritage movie, except you can see a bit of Hogarth in it'.[59]

Heritage, alternative heritage, post-heritage, anti-heritage: the proliferation of terms indicates just how central the heritage idea became in contemporary cultural debate in general and British film culture in particular in the 1980s and 1990s. It also begins to suggest the extent of the disputes over the meaning and status of period drama and the costume film for British audiences in this period. I examine the nature of those disputes in the next chapter. In the remainder of this chapter, however, I chart the formal and pro-filmic qualities of the films: their main attrac-

---

[57] Claire Monk, 'Sexuality and the Heritage', *Sight and Sound*, 5/10 (1995), 33.

[58] For international box-office grosses, see the all-time box-office charts on the Internet Movie Database, at IMDb.com.

[59] Derek Malcolm, 'Just Say Yes (to the Movie)', *Guardian*, section 2 (22 Feb. 1996), 8.

tions and ingredients, the style of the films, the way they work as texts, and the claims that are made for them as texts.

FILM STYLE: THE AESTHETICS OF DISPLAY

The majority of films with which I'm concerned here are 'quality' films, as distinct from downmarket or mainstream populist fare. That is to say they occupy a particular niche in the marketplace, they depend upon particular ideas of good taste and aesthetic values, and they address particular audiences. Because I'm dealing with a production trend over a twenty-year period, there is, as we've already seen, a degree of variation among the films in question. Some, but not all of them, are literary adaptations. Some, but not all, deal with the English upper and upper middle classes at home and abroad. And so on. The same is true of the styles of narration and visual presentation that the films adopt: many of them share similar characteristics, but there are important exceptions. The films were made with different budgets and had different target audiences in mind. Some were decidedly specialized productions designed for art-house distribution and appreciation. Others were intended for wider release and by necessity had to appeal to a wider range of audiences—but most of the films in this latter category were conceived as crossover films, with a foot in both the mainstream and the art-house markets. In sketching in the stylistic parameters of these films, then, we must remember that these are not absolutes, but general tendencies, shared by a significant number of films, but with important exceptions. Many of the films are slow-paced, character-based films, for instance, but *Elizabeth*, made on a higher budget and intended to reach wider audiences than most, is much closer to a fast-paced action thriller. Along with other more self-consciously mainstream films such as *Emma, Sense and Sensibility*, and *The Wings of the Dove*, there are also many more close-ups than one finds in, say, the Merchant Ivory films— though such films are still more gently paced than most mainstream films.

The narratives of most of these films are typically slow-moving, episodic, and de-dramatized; that is to say, they do not normally adopt the efficient and economic causal development of the classical film, or its fast pace and narrative energy. They are also frequently organized around several central protagonists, which encourages both a more dispersed narrative structure than most hero-focused classical films, and an emphasis on ensemble performance. With dramatic, goal-directed action downplayed, this narrative structure typically creates a space in which character, place, atmosphere, and milieu can be explored.

I noted earlier that these concerns are generally played out within a naturalistic framework, consolidated by picturesque imagery and strong character acting, wherein authorship is marked in a subtle rather than ostentatious manner. Most of the films eschew overtly expressionist or symbolist narration, and even the comedies tend to be naturalistic in terms of their shooting style and modes of narration. Some of the Shakespeare adaptations—*Henry V* and *Much Ado About*

Nothing, for instance—deliberately adopt a more theatrical and less naturalistic mode of performance and address. There is also, as we've seen, a strand of the English period film that delights in the stylistic experimentation of modernist and postmodernist art cinema. Some of the literary adaptations, like their source novels, are organized around the restless play of memory and therefore adopt a more or less complex flashback structure—*The Remains of the Day, Mrs Dalloway*, and *The English Patient*, for instance. And the more obviously auteurist films of Derek Jarman, Peter Greenaway, Ken McMullen, and Sally Potter—*The Tempest, The Draughtsman's Contract, Edward II, Orlando, Prospero's Books, 1871*—are marked by a postmodern self-consciousness, by absurd anachronisms, and by game-playing.

Because so many of the English costume films of the 1980s and 1990s are character studies or dissections of specific milieux, and do not therefore feel the need to push the narrative relentlessly forward, their aesthetic is often different from mainstream Hollywood. The decoupage and the camerawork tend towards the languid. There is a preference for long takes and deep staging, for instance, and for long and medium shots, rather than for close-ups and rapid or dramatic cutting. The camera is characteristically fluid, but camera movement often seems dictated less by a desire to follow the movement of characters than by a desire to offer the spectator a more aesthetic angle on the period setting and the objects which fill it. Self-conscious crane shots and high-angle shots divorced from character point of view, for instance, are often used to display ostentatiously the seductive *mise-en-scène* of the films.

This is particularly clear in the Merchant Ivory films. Indeed, Ivory describes the strategy as 'a matter of showmanship. You can't be minimalist, you have to give people something. That's why it's larger than life . . . '[60] In *A Room with a View*, for instance, there is a typical interior shot of Lucy playing the piano at the Pensione Bertolini: Lucy, the ostensible focus of narrative interest, sits in the background, while artefacts and furnishings fill and frame the foreground; the camera gracefully, but without narrative motivation, tracks slowly round one splendid item of furniture to reveal it in all its glory. It is hardly of narrative significance that Mr Beebe is eventually revealed sitting on the far side of this item of furniture, watching Lucy play the piano; it is not as if the revelation of Mr Beebe has created suspense or mystery. Rather, the camera seems more concerned to play over the paintings on the wall, Lucy's dress, and the particular quality of light in the room.

In the same film, the shots of Florence are always offered direct to the spectator, unmediated by shots of characters within the diegesis looking at the view. Such shots, in fact, follow the views, rather than preceding and thus motivating them. Insert shots of Cambridge work similarly in *Maurice*, having only a minimal function as establishing shots. Such views are thus displayed for the cinema spectator alone. In this way, the heritage culture becomes the object of a public gaze, while the private gaze of the dramatis personae is reserved for romance: they

---

[60] James Ivory, quoted in Daniel S. Moore, 'Picture Perfect', *Variety* (28 Oct. 1996), 62.

almost never admire the quality of their surroundings. Heritage culture appears petrified, frozen in moments that virtually fall out of the narrative, existing only as adornments for the staging of a love story. Thus, from this point of view, historical narrative is transformed into spectacle; heritage becomes excess, not functional *mise-en-scène*, not something to be used narratively, but something to be admired.

All in all, the camera style is pictorialist, with all the connotations the term brings of art-photography, aesthetic refinement, and set-piece images.[61] Though narrative meaning and narrational clarity are rarely sacrificed, these shots, angles, and camera movements frequently seem to exceed narrative motivation. The effect is to transform narrative space into heritage space: that is, a space for the display of heritage properties rather than for the enactment of dramas. In this respect, therefore, this is not overwhelmingly a narrative cinema, a cinema of story-telling, but something more akin to that mode of early film-making that Tom Gunning calls the cinema of attractions.[62] In this case, the heritage films display their self-conscious artistry, their landscapes, their properties, their actors and their performance qualities, their clothes, and their often archaic dialogue. The gaze, therefore, is organized around props and settings—the look of the observer at the tableau image—as much as it is around character point of view. The use of flamboyantly designed intertitles in *A Room with a View*, while emphasizing the episodic nature of the narrative, suggests another affinity with very early cinema. It redundantly indicates narrative action before it takes place, and in so doing, interrupts the actual telling of the tale and highlights the artifice of the diegesis.

In describing the style of heritage films in this way, I certainly don't intend to imply that those films are aesthetically conservative, or that they are uncinematic, as some critics have suggested.[63] There is no reason why aesthetic differences from the mainstream should be perceived as either necessarily avant-garde or necessarily conservative. More important is to acknowledge that the aesthetic distinctiveness of heritage films is a sign of product differentiation, a sign that a specific sort of commodity has been produced for specific audiences, and that there are competing definitions of 'good cinema'.

The pictorialist museum aesthetic—the cinema of heritage attractions—provides the ideal showcase for the visual splendour and period richness of the carefully selected interiors and locations. In many cases, even the source novels and plays are in effect put on display as heritage originals. As Raphael Samuel remarks of *Little Dorrit*, 'the film resembles nothing so much as a series of cameos in which the chapters of the book are replayed as scenes'.[64] More generally, the *mise-en-scène*

---

[61] For a fuller discussion of pictorialism, see my *Waving the Flag*, 48–63.

[62] Tom Gunning, 'The Cinema of Attractions: Early Film, its Spectator and the Avant-Garde', in Thomas Elsaesser and Adam Barker (eds.), *Early Cinema: Space–Frame–Narrative* (London: British Film Institute, 1990), 56–62.

[63] See Monk, 'British Heritage-Film Debate', 178.

[64] Samuel, 'Docklands Dickens', in *Theatres of Memory*, 407.

of so many of these films is crammed with period artefacts plundered from the nation's heritage archives, which the distanced and slow-moving camera can linger over for the spectator's pleasure. Many of the films include set-piece cele-bratory events, lavish dinner parties or balls, for instance, which provide plenty of opportunities for filling the frame with splendid costumes and hair-dos, table-ware and food. Equally frequently, conversations take place against a backdrop of picturesque semi-rural southern English scenery, or the frontage of some mag-nificent castle, stately home, or quaint cottage, the types of ancient architectural and landscape properties conserved by the National Trust and English Heritage. Put the two together, and you have that recurrent image of an imposing country house seen in extreme long shot—sometimes an aerial shot—and set in a verdant landscape of gently rolling hills.

British cinema is often characterized as a cinema of restraint, a cinema that lacks visual interest. The production values and aesthetic concerns of the costume dramas of the 1980s and 1990s—and indeed, their many generic forebears—indi-cate that there is however a strong tradition of spectacle in British film-making. The emphasis on spectacle draws attention to the surface of things, and if spec-tators watch the films in this way, they may well experience what Fredric Jameson sees as a typically postmodern loss of emotional affect.[65] It is certainly possible to read the films in this way, whereby emotional engagement in the drama is dis-placed by the fascination with the heritage film's loving recreations of the past, their beautifully conserved and respectfully observed spectacles of past-ness. But it would be wrong to reduce the *mise-en-scène* of these films to heritage spec-tacle. Narrative function clearly cannot be absent from the visual plane, and what at one level operates as heritage spectacle may at another level function as the *mise-en-scène* of emotion, of desire and feeling, of romance and repression.

Most of the period films in question are organized around a romance plot of one sort or another, and many also include a fair share of narrative coincidence, fateful intervention, and obstacles thrown in the path of love. But if this is the stuff of melodrama, then emotions are underplayed, while sensationalism and contrivance are tastefully obscured—or turned into story events, as in *Wilde*. The excitements of the love story in a sense compete with the trappings of the period piece for the attention of the spectator. As Richard Dyer has argued, this does not mean that the films necessarily lack passion, or are skin deep; as he demonstrates, it is perfectly possible to see emotional depth in such films: many audiences would certainly testify to their power to move them emotionally.[66] As Dyer and others have suggested, British films will often deal very effectively with emotional repres-sion, the representation of which in itself can be a very moving experience. In such films, as Dyer puts it, 'feeling is expressed in what is not said or done, and/or in the suggestiveness of settings, music and situation'.[67]

The key point here is that heritage films are ambivalent enough to be read in

    [65] Fredric Jameson, 'Post-modernism, or the Cultural Logic of Late Capitalism', *New Left Review*, 146 (1984), 53–92.
    [66] Richard Dyer, 'Feeling English', *Sight and Sound*, 4/3 (1994), 17–19.
    [67] Ibid. 17.

different ways, even by the same viewer at a single viewing. Story-situations and character psychologies may cue emotional engagement, but the richly detailed and spectacular period *mise-en-scène* also cues the distanced and therefore more detached gaze of admiring spectatorship. This admiring gaze will often become entangled with the discourse of authenticity, especially at the level of production and promotion. For one of the central claims made on behalf of so many of the English costume dramas of the 1980s and 1990s is that their period trappings are not merely spectacular, but that they are authentic, or historically accurate. This discourse may often get in the way of the potential narrative meaningfulness of the *mise-en-scène*. With regard to the costumes, for instance, Stella Bruzzi argues that

Films such as *Howards End* [Fig. 7] or *Sense and Sensibility* look through clothes, as the major design effort is to signal the accuracy of the costumes and to submit them to the greater framework of historical and literary authenticity. Costume films that, conversely, choose to look at clothes create an alternative discourse, and one that usually counters or complicates the ostensible strategy of the overriding narrative.[68]

Her argument is thus that clothes do not function symbolically for the narrative, but only function diegetically, to symbolize the period correctly. The case is surely overstated, since clothes clearly do play a part in establishing character in these films. At the most basic level, they play some part in establishing the class, gender, age, nationality, wealth, and taste of the character they adorn. In *Sense and Sensibility*, for instance, the relative poverty of the Dashwood sisters is signified in part by the fact that the range of clothes they have at their disposal is limited, so that they frequently have to wear the same dress more than once. Bruzzi suggests that the more interesting costume dramas are those in which costume is eroticized, but that this does not typically happen in English heritage films. One might equally argue that the de-eroticization of clothing in the English heritage film is just as important in establishing the sexually repressed characters who are so vital to the genre, from *A Room with a View*, via *Sense and Sensibility*, to *The Winslow Boy*. Thus the 'pure, prim and high-necked' blouse that Helena Bonham Carter wears as Lucy in *A Room with a View* (and which Andy Medhurst finds so problematic) is actually an important signification of Lucy's character, and especially her buttoned-up attitude towards sexuality.[69]

Bruzzi compares the English heritage film to Martin Scorsese's *The Age of Innocence*, arguing that the latter works differently: in its representation of 'the exclusive milieu of late 1800s New York through an exquisite, close-up montage of accessories and sartorial detail, it is apparent that it is demanding a different level of engagement from its spectators than the traditionally disengaged heritage film'.[70] But is it that apparent? And cannot different audiences engage with the

---

[68] Stella Bruzzi, *Undressing Cinema: Clothing and Identity in the Movies* (London: Routledge, 1997), 36.

[69] See Andy Medhurst, 'Inside the British Wardrobe', *Sight and Sound*, 5/3 (1995), 17.

[70] Bruzzi, *Undressing Cinema*, 37.

film in different ways? Both types of film equally fetishize the clothes on display—and in both they can be read as signifiers of character and sensibility.

AUTHORSHIP, AUTHENTICITY, AND IRREVERENCE

Set against the intertextual, generic qualities of these films are the discourses of authorship and authenticity, which stress originality and uniqueness rather than similarity and repetition. These discourses work in various ways: many of the literary adaptations for instance strive to reproduce the tone that distinguishes the book, to respect the 'original' text and the 'original' authorship. Almost all the films cited seek to reproduce the surface qualities which define the past-ness of the particular period. Yet, at the same time, there is a foregrounding of filmic authorship, indicating the attempt to make a unique and original film. Each strategy is a means of stressing authorship, originality, authenticity—but the authenticities are not all of the same category, and each potentially pulls in a different direction, while the generic qualities potentially deny the sense of originality altogether. Paradoxically, the preoccupation with authorship, the display of good taste, and the self-consciously aesthetic sensibility are themselves generic qualities that bind the films together. Literary authorship, the process of writing itself, as I noted above, is foregrounded in the recurrent narrative episode of a character writing or reading a letter, a diary, or a book, either aloud or in voice-over, thus celebrating the purity of the word. Literary adaptations also, of course, foreground the authenticity of the 'original' by their effort to reproduce dialogue from the novel for characters in the film, or to transpose the narrative voice of the novel to the speech of those characters. There is also a studied reference to and reproduction of other art-objects and art-forms—classical paintings, statues, architecture, and music all add weight to the tasteful production values of these films.

The discourse of authenticity means that these references should be historically 'accurate', that the image of the past should not be anachronistic. While the vast majority of the films and television programmes cited above are presented as fiction, it is a fiction that the producers try to ensure has as strong a realist effect as possible. The discourse of authenticity, as we've seen, is central to the promotion of these texts, in terms of both the 'faithfulness' of adaptations to their source novels, and the 'correctness' of their historical reconstructions of place, costume, and interior design. What comes across is very often a fetishistic attitude towards surface impressions, a fascination with period detail, a reverence for source material—whether it is a novel or the historical past. But if the discourse of authenticity was prominent throughout the 1980s and 1990s, there was also a marked irreverence about some of the films of the 1990s, from *Edward II* and *Orlando* via some of the Austen adaptations of the mid-1990s to *Shakespeare in Love* and *Mansfield Park* at the end of the decade.[71]

---

[71] Several writers have addressed this issue: Monk, 'Sexuality and the Heritage'; Sales, *Jane Austen*; Pamela Church Gibson, 'Fewer Weddings and More Funerals: Changes in the Heritage Film', and Moya

As the conventions of the English costume drama became increasingly famil-iar, and as the marketability of the films became more readily accepted, so film-makers could begin to innovate. In particular, in the bid to reach wider audiences, producers often felt they could relax the fetishistic concern for getting the period details 'right' and address the film more obviously to contemporary sensibilities. Alternatively, as in *Stiff Upper Lips*, they might simply parody the conventions of previous period films. But it would be misleading to present this as a simple tra-jectory from reverence to irreverence, from authenticity to inauthenticity. After all, at the beginning of the 1980s, Derek Jarman and Peter Greenaway produced deliciously irreverent versions of Shakespeare on the one hand (*The Tempest*) and England in the 1790s on the other (*The Draughtsman's Contract*). Conversely, at the end of the 1990s, we can find James Ivory and Terence Davies producing fas-tidiously reverential versions of Henry James (*The Golden Bowl*) and Edith Wharton (*The House of Mirth*).

Few of the 'British' films go for the 'creative vandalism'[72] of *My Own Private Idaho* (1991), *William Shakespeare's Romeo + Juliet* (1996), or *Clueless*. *The Tempest* and *Edward II* may have a very anachronistic relationship to the past, but they have an equally idiosyncratic relation to the present: they are not contemporary-set dramas like the three American films. *The Claim* is undoubtedly a very radical adaptation of *The Mayor of Casterbridge*, but it is still set in the mid-nineteenth century. No, the irreverence of selected English costume dramas of the 1990s tends to be more subtle than this. As Roger Sales has remarked of the mid-1990s Austen adaptations, it is an acknowledgement on the part of the film-makers that the film versions of novels are precisely readings or interpretations, rather than 'faithful' transcriptions or reverential homages.[73] And frequently they are very knowing about the conventions established by their predecessors: their makers are only too aware of the conventions and are willing to play with them.

Several of the costume dramas of the late 1990s seemed to tap into the self-consciously modern and youthful culture of 'Cool Britannia' as much as they tapped into the past. As an American journalist commented,

England is still the place to film literary classics [like *Jude* and *Wings of the Dove*, but] even those classy adaptations are being made with a modern spin—*Wings* director Iain Softley saying his movie 'will focus on the elements that are timeless' and Kenneth Branagh assert-ing his . . . *Hamlet* is very much about a 'single family's lack of function'.[74]

Films like *Plunkett and Macleane* and *Elizabeth* seemed as conscious of *Trainspot-*

Luckett, 'Image and Nation in 1990s British Cinema', both in Robert Murphy (ed.), *British Cinema of the 90s* (London: British Film Institute, 2000), 115–24 and 88–99; Julianne Pidduck, '*Elizabeth* and *Shakespeare in Love*: Screening the Elizabethans', in Ginette Vincendeau (ed.), *Film/Literature/Heritage: A Sight and Sound Reader* (London: British Film Institute, 2001), 130–4; Church Gibson, 'From Dancing Queen to Plaster Virgin: *Elizabeth* and the End of English Heritage?', *Journal of Popular British Cinema*, 5(2002), 133–41.

[72] Jonathan Dollimore's phrase, cited in Susan Bennett, *Performing Nostalgia: Shifting Shakespeare and the Contemporary Past* (London: Routledge, 1996), 1–2.   [73] Sales, 'In Face of All the Servants'.

[74] David Finkle, 'Hope and Glory: The Unexpected Rebirth of British Cinema', *Village Voice* (6 Aug. 1996), 50.

7. Looking through costume or looking at costume? Heritage hats in *Howards End*

ting as a generic predecessor as they were of the Merchant Ivory frock flick. Indeed, in bidding for the 'youth audience' *Plunkett and Macleane* even starred Robert Carlyle and Jonny Lee Miller from *Trainspotting*. Such films boldly offered themselves as a modern take on the period film, both capitalizing on the success of the production trend and seeking to attract new audiences at the same time, thereby reinvigorating the production trend. It is worth noting too the shift from the proprieties of the Edwardian drawing-room to other increasingly vulgar and bawdy pasts—the low necklines of Regency England, the rude and lewd frankness of *Restoration*, *The Madness of King George*, and *Shakespeare in Love*, and the 'medievalism' of *Elizabeth*.

In particular, these films seem less chaste about sexual activity. Thus Sales notes a camp and frivolous emphasis on the 'period bosom' and Darcy's tight-fitting trousers in the 1995 television adaptation of *Pride and Prejudice*.[75] Claire Monk similarly notes 'a deep self-consciousness about how the past is represented' and an overt concern with 'transgressive sexual politics' in films like *Orlando* and *Carrington*, which she refers to as 'post-heritage'.[76] But as she goes on to note, 'paradoxically the post-heritage films revel in the visual pleasures of heritage, even as they seem to distance themselves'. In other words, there is no clear break between these films and, say, Merchant Ivory's Forster adaptations. Yes, *Wilde* confronts the 'scandal' of Oscar Wilde's homosexuality; yes, Helena Bonham Carter appears naked in *The Wings of the Dove*; and yes, the 1999 adaptation of

---

[75] Sales, *Jane Austen*, 238.   [76] Monk, 'Sexuality and the Heritage', 33.

Mansfield Park is decidedly racy for a Jane Austen tale. But then there was also a very lively gay sex scene in *Maurice* in 1987; *White Mischief*, made the same year, was self-consciously decadent, especially in terms of sexual activity; and Ken Russell's *Gothic*, made the previous year, was hardly genteel.

A CONCLUSIVE MAP?

My task in this chapter has been to map as thoroughly as possible the range of films that might be brought under the rubric of English heritage cinema in the 1980s and 1990s. But mapping is by definition initially an exploratory process and always an act of interpretation. The map produced can never be truly exhaustive or comprehensive, and the terrain is constantly changing. Other maps could be produced of the same terrain, emphasizing different features, displaying the same features in another way, or using a different scale. To strive for objectivity in this case would perhaps be foolish—not least because the costume dramas of the 1980s and 1990s have been the subject of much debate and contested interpretations. In the next chapter, I lay out some of the central terms of that debate.

2
Critical Reception: Heritage, Ambivalence, and Interpretation

The reception of English heritage films of the 1980s and 1990s has taken several different turns. In particular, critical debate about the films has proliferated in the last decade—and has at times become quite sharp. It has also tended to focus on a much narrower selection of films than described in the previous chapter. The titles that recur most frequently in critical debate include Merchant Ivory's 'English' films, the Austen, Forster, and James adaptations, and the bio-pics of monarchs and literary figures—one might say the films most concerned with class and cultural capital. Thanks to the relative popularity of such films and the intensity of critical debate about them, they now have a well-established place on the intellectual map of British cinema in the 1980s and 1990s. It has for instance become *de rigueur* for academic surveys of British cinema in this period to discuss the films and to comment on the nature of the debate about them.[1] Although such commentaries will frequently question the appropriateness of the term 'heritage cinema', they also inevitably establish the term more firmly on the intellectual map of British cinema simply by virtue of discussing it. The debate—and the use of the term—has also spilled over into discussions of other national cinemas, especially European cinemas.[2]

One strand of the debate about 'British' heritage films involves dismissing them on class grounds, from a leftist perspective: these are conservative films for middle-class audiences, and they function to maintain the values and interests of the most privileged social strata. According to such accounts, audiences are invited to escape from the cultural heterogeneity of contemporary Britain by celebrating a class and an ethnicity apparently secure in its self-knowledge and self-

---

[1] See for instance Sarah Street, *British National Cinema* (London: Routledge, 1997), 102–6; John Hill, *British Cinema in the 1980s* (Oxford: Clarendon Press, 1999), 73–130; Justine Ashby and Andrew Higson (eds.), *British Cinema, Past and Present* (London: Routledge, 2000), 299–351; Pamela Church Gibson, 'Fewer Weddings and More Funerals: Changes in the Heritage Film', in Robert Murphy (ed.), *British Cinema of the 90s* (London: British Film Institute, 2000), 115–24; Sheldon Hall, 'The Wrong Sort of Cinema: Re-fashioning the Heritage Film Debate', in Robert Murphy (ed.), *The British Cinema Book*, 2nd edn. (London: British Film Institute, 2001), 191–9; and Claire Monk, 'The British Heritage-Film Debate Revisited', in Claire Monk and Amy Sargeant (eds.), *British Historical Cinema* (London: Routledge, 2002), 176–98.

[2] See for instance Richard Dyer and Ginette Vincendeau, 'Introduction', in Dyer and Vincendeau (eds.), *Popular European Cinema* (London: Routledge, 1992), 6–8; Richard Dyer, 'Heritage Cinema in Europe', in Ginette Vincendeau (ed.), *The Encyclopaedia of European Cinema* (London: British Film Institute and Cassell, 1995), 204–5; Guy Austin, *Contemporary French Cinema: An Introduction* (Manchester: Manchester University Press, 1996), 142–70; and Ginette Vincendeau, *Film/Literature/Heritage: A Sight and Sound Reader* (London: British Film Institute, 2001).

sufficiency.[3] From a traditional, conservative perspective, however, the same films seem charming, precisely because they are traditional and conservative, precisely because that class and its culture are fascinating and worthy.[4]

Another strand to the debate treats the films less in terms of class politics and more in terms of sexual and gender politics. Some feminist and gay critics have thus been much more sympathetic to the films than those aligned with the leftist cultural critique, arguing that they found space for women and gay characters, and addressed their concerns and interests.[5] Some even see the films as quite liberal in terms of their class politics, even 'profoundly subversive'.[6] Others though see the films as sexually repressive, 'body-hating', and incapable of addressing popular sensibilities.[7] Questions of taste and the putative relationship of the films to popular culture are yet another source of contention.[8] Some see the leftist cultural critique of heritage films as patrician, an expression of anxiety about popular (middle-brow) cinema, and about heritage consumerism.[9] Certainly there are those who quite explicitly dismissed the films as too middle-brow, too far removed from anything that might be admitted as genuine cinematic artistry, 'a vulgarization and corruption of high culture'.[10]

[3] See Tana Wollen, 'Over our Shoulders: Nostalgic Screen Fictions for the Eighties', in John Corner and Sylvia Harvey (eds.), *Enterprise and Heritage: Crosscurrents of National Culture* (London: Routledge, 1991), 178–93; Cairns Craig, 'Rooms without a View', *Sight and Sound*, 1/2 (1991), 10–13; Paul Dave, 'The Bourgeois Paradigm and Heritage Cinema', *New Left Review*, 224 (1997), 111–26. My earlier publications on heritage cinema are also generally seen as belonging in this category—see Andrew Higson, 'Re-presenting the National Past: Nostalgia and Pastiche in the Heritage Film', in Lester Friedman (ed.), *Fires were Started: British Cinema and Thatcherism* (Minneapolis and London: University of Minnesota Press and UCL Press, 1993), 109–29; and 'The Heritage Film and British Cinema', in Andrew Higson (ed.), *Dissolving Views: Key Writings on British Cinema* (London: Cassell, 1996), 232–48.

[4] Norman Stone, 'Through a Lens Darkly', *Sunday Times* (10 Jan. 1988), C1–C2.

[5] See Pam Cook, *Fashioning the Nation: Costume and Identity in British Cinema* (London: British Film Institute, 1996), 1–9; Claire Monk, 'The British "Heritage Film" and its Critics', *Critical Survey*, 7/2 (1995), 116–24; Claire Monk, 'Sexuality and the Heritage', *Sight and Sound*, 5/10 (1995), 32–4; Claire Monk, 'The Heritage Film and Gendered Spectatorship', *Close Up: The Electronic Journal of British Cinema*, 1 (1996–7), at www.shu.ac.uk/services/lc/closeup/monk.htm; Julianne Pidduck, 'Of Windows and Country Walks: Frames of Space and Movement in 1990s Austen Adaptations', *Screen*, 39/4 (1998), 381–400; Church Gibson, 'Fewer Weddings and More Funerals'; Richard Dyer, 'Feeling English', *Sight and Sound*, 4/3 (1994), 16–19; Dyer, 'Heritage Cinema in Europe'; Richard Dyer, 'Nice Young Men Who Sell Antiques: Gay Men in Heritage Cinema', in Ginette Vincendeau (ed.), *Film/Literature/Heritage*, 43–8; and 'White Flannel', an episode of the television series *Out on Tuesday*, first transmitted on Channel 4 on 3 Apr. 1990.

[6] See Alison Light, 'Englishness', *Sight and Sound*, 1/3 (1991), 63; Street, *British National Cinema*, 104–5; Hall, 'The Wrong Sort of Cinema'; the quotation is from Jeffrey Richards, *Films and National Identity: From Dickens to Dad's Army* (Manchester: Manchester University Press, 1997), 169.

[7] The quotation is from Andy Medhurst, 'Inside the British Wardrobe', *Sight and Sound*, 5/3 (1995), 16–17; see also Stella Bruzzi, *Undressing Cinema: Clothing and Identity in the Movies* (London: Routledge, 1997), 35. The film-maker Alan Parker has frequently expressed similar views—see for instance his cartoon reproduced in *Making Movies: Cartoons by Alan Parker* (London: British Film Institute, 1998), 43.

[8] See Martin A. Hipsky, 'Anglophil(m)ia: Why does America Watch Merchant–Ivory Movies', *Journal of Popular Film and Television*, 22/3 (1994), 98–107.

[9] See Light, 'Englishness'; Raphael Samuel, *Theatres of Memory* (London: Verso, 1994); Pam Cook, 'Neither Here Nor There: National Identity in Gainsborough Costume Drama', in Higson (ed.), *Dissolving Views*, 56–9; and Cook, *Fashioning the Nation*, 1–9.

[10] Gary Crowdus, 'Editorial', *Cineaste*, 22/4 (1997), 1; from a slightly different perspective,

The ways in which the films reconstruct the past and represent history have also provoked debate. For many mainstream film reviewers, one of the great appeals of such films is the apparently authentic—and very often beautiful—vision of the past they offer. For the managers of the British tourist industry, the same films provide what often seems to be tailor-made promotional material for attracting visitors to heritage sites. From the perspective of the leftist cultural critique, on the other hand, both the nostalgic sensibility of the films and the ways in which they seem to become part of the heritage industry are deemed problematic. For other more sympathetic academic commentators, the historical masquerade of the costume drama provides an ideal space in which social, political, and cultural tensions and anxieties can be fruitfully explored.

Too often the debate about the meanings and values of heritage films has become polarized, as if one view was correct, and another incorrect. It is surely more productive to recognize that all these views are simply interpretations, that all interpretations betray the interests and perspective of the interpreter, and that the variety of interpretations is indicative of the vitality of the reception process and the richness of the films themselves. The process of interpretation is always negotiable, even if it is more difficult to formulate or maintain some positions rather than others. It is not, as Claire Monk suggests, that some readings of heritage films are 'wrong';[11] there is no absolute standard by which we can judge one interpretation as better or worse than another.

What we are faced with is a series of different and often competing readings, ways of engaging with the same text under different circumstances and from different perspectives. Producers, promoters, censors, critics, analysts, and audiences all try to fix the meanings of texts, to limit their ambivalence, but how specific audiences negotiate the meanings of a text, how they use that text, will always escape legislation, however formal and however rigorous. In my case studies of *Howards End* (1991) and *Elizabeth* (1998), I examine in detail the propensity of the two films to be taken up differently in different reception contexts or by different audiences. In this chapter, I look in more general terms at the critical debate about heritage films and the extent to which meanings and interpretations have proliferated around them. I begin by looking at the debate about heritage and the heritage industry, and the extent to which costume dramas draw on and contribute to the discourses and practices of heritage.

THE HERITAGE INDUSTRY

The tension outlined at the end of the previous chapter between reverence, propriety, and tradition on the one hand, and irreverence, youth, and sex on the other was in many ways symptomatic of wider tensions in Britain in the 1980s and 1990s.

compare David Bordwell, *On the History of Film Style* (Cambridge, Mass.: Harvard University Press, 1997), 44.

[11] Monk, 'The British "Heritage Film" and its Critics', 122.

Both Margaret Thatcher's New Right governments of the 1980s and Tony Blair's New Labour government of the late 1990s sought to establish the UK as a forward-looking, enterprising nation, without wanting to discard altogether established traditions, images, and identities. Both recognized that the UK was an old country but both, in Blair's terms, wanted to rebrand it as young and vibrant.[12] But brand images and established identities are hard to shake: 'When we think of England we do not picture crowded factories or rows of suburban villas, but our thoughts turn to rolling hills, green fields and stately trees, to cottage houses, picturesquely grouped round the village green beside the church and manor house. It is a green and pleasant land.'[13] Admittedly, these words were written in the 1940s—but many would adhere to them today, and heritage films of the 1980s and 1990s play an important role in maintaining such images in the public consciousness. It was thus a common complaint that,

As the twentieth century draws to its close, the image of Britain which is projected abroad (and at home) becomes ever more that of a Ruritanian theme park, a contrived fantasy of hype and heritage and, while the monarchy still occupies the starring part in this deluded pageant of self-indulgent historical backwardness, the cult of the country house follows very close behind.[14]

For much of the period under discussion, it was the heritage impulse that held sway, even as part of the enterprise culture. Cinema's engagement with heritage discourses is thus typical of cultural developments in postmodern Britain. As Gill Davies put it, 'the *zeitgeist* of the 1980s is an amalgamation and plundering of earlier identities'.[15] One might, with hindsight, add that this *zeitgeist* remained strong throughout the 1990s as well. Indeed, some have argued that 'the search for heritage is a defining characteristic of modernity'.[16] Consequently, as Raphael Samuel suggested, the heritage impulse became 'one of the most powerful imaginative constructs of our time'.[17] There is nothing new about a fascination with the past, of course, but there was something new in the emergence of 'heritage' as a keyword in contemporary British cultural debate, especially the debate about national identity. The term does not, for instance, appear in Raymond Williams's 1976 publication *Keywords*.[18] In 1985, David Lowenthal's magisterial exploration of changing attitudes towards the past was published, opening with the proclama-

---

[12] See e.g. Tony Blair, 'Britain can Remake it', *Guardian* (22 July 1997), 17.

[13] Arthur Gardner, *Britain's Mountain Heritage* (London: Batsford, 1942), 1, quoted in Malcolm Chase, 'This is No Claptrap: This is our Heritage', in Colin Shaw and Malcolm Chase (eds.), *The Imagined Past: History and Nostalgia* (Manchester: Manchester University Press, 1989), 128.

[14] David Cannadine, 'Beyond the Country House', in *Aspects of Aristocracy* (New Haven, Conn.: Yale University Press, 1994), 242.

[15] Gill Davies, 'The End of the Pier Show', *New Formations*, 5 (1988), 133.

[16] Celia Applegate, 'Heritage Thinking in Modern Germany', a paper delivered at 'The Idea of Heritage', a conference at London Guildhall University, 9 Sept. 1999.

[17] Raphael Samuel, 'Preface', in Samuel (ed.), *Patriotism: The Making and Unmaking of British National Identity*, i. *History and Politics* (London: Routledge, 1989), p. xii.

[18] Raymond Williams, *Keywords: A Vocabulary of Culture and Society* (Glasgow: Fontana, 1976); I am indebted to Sylvia Hardy, who pointed out this fact to me.

that 'the past is everywhere'; in 1989, an article in *New Statesman and Society* offered a reformulation: ' "heritage" is now everywhere'; in 1997, Lowenthal was in full agreement: 'all at once, heritage is everywhere—in the news, in the movies, in the market-place—in everything from galaxies to genes . . .'[19]

The standard dictionary definition of heritage is that which is received or inherited, that which is handed down to the present by previous generations. This implies that the receiver is an entirely passive partner, rather than someone who actively constructs their heritage, and there is surely always an active agency on the part of the present generation. From this point of view, heritage is a selective preoccupation with the past, it is what a particular individual or group takes from the past in order to define itself in the present, to give it an identity. It is what 'we' are happy to regard as '*our* heritage', enabling us to explain who we are by reference to the past. The heritage impulse is thus about seizing hold of selected aspects of the past and presenting them in a way that tallies with current sensibilities and needs—it is, in Lowenthal's terms, a declaration of faith in a particular way of seeing the past.[20] Indeed, it is important to recognize that heritage is as often invented or revised as it is conserved—hence the insistence on agency on the part of those who mobilize the past as heritage.

Mobilizing heritage involves asserting a sense of continuity with the past.[21] The construction of English national identity, for instance, is more often than not dependent on the recovery of heritage, the insertion of the present into the miasma of tradition. But if heritage has a temporal or historical dimension, it also has a spatial and geographical dimension: it is articulated as both exemplary narrative and traditional landscape.[22] When heritage culture is mobilized on a national scale ('our shared national heritage'), it is in this spatio-temporal grid that 'the nation' emerges as a unique, organic, meaningful community. The discourse of heritage ensures that the national community is bounded both temporally, by traditional historical narratives, and spatially, by the geographical vision of the nation. Heritage cinema plays a crucial role in this process of imagining English nationhood, by telling symbolic stories of class, gender, ethnicity, and identity, and staging them in the most picturesque landscapes and houses of the Old Country: filmic narratives must always, in a quite literal sense, *take place*; they must unfold in a narrative space. At the same time, that space insists on its attractiveness, the attraction of landscape.

For some commentators, it was not simply that heritage was everywhere, but that it was mobilized in particular ways. The cult of heritage as it developed in

---

[19] David Lowenthal, *The Past is a Foreign Country* (Cambridge: Cambridge University Press, 1985); Stephen Daniels and David Matless, 'The New Nostalgia', *New Statesman and Society* (19 May 1989), 40; David Lowenthal, *The Heritage Crusade and the Spoils of History* (London: Viking, 1997), p. ix.

[20] Lowenthal, *Heritage Crusade*.

[21] See e.g. Patrick Wright, *On Living in an Old Country: The National Past in Contemporary Britain* (London: Verso, 1985).

[22] See Stephen Daniels, *Fields of Vision: Landscape Imagery and National Identity in England and the United States* (Cambridge: Polity Press, 1983), 4–7.

the 1980s increasingly came to be understood as promoting a highly commercial-ized consumption of the past. The key texts in this debate were Patrick Wright's *On Living in an Old Country* and Robert Hewison's *The Heritage Industry*.[23] Both registered a profound concern from a left-wing point of view about the way in which our relation to the past seemed to have become a part of corporate consumerism, presented in terms of an institutionalized nostalgia. The past, they argued, was increasingly packaged as artefacts and images that could be sold to contemporary consumers, or experiences that could be bought into by tourists.

Hewison argued that 'the growth of the heritage industry took place against a background of perceived national distress and actual economic decline'; it thus represented a nostalgic and escapist flight from the present: 'we have turned to the past, both as an economic and a psychological resource'.[24] Britain's long-term decline as a world economic power coupled with the growth of multinational enterprises, involvement in the pan-national European Union, and the increasing acknowledgement of the multiracial and multicultural nature of British society inevitably disturbed traditional notions of national identity. What are at stake here are the effects of globalization, the blurring of political and economic boundaries, the aggressive global marketing of commodities, traditions, and identities. In this context, the cult of heritage was seen as an attempt to resist the sense of national dissolution by turning to past glories. But the cult was also an industry, and for Hewison, Wright, and others, the exploitation of heritage culture became the defining cultural and economic practice of Britain in the 1980s.

John Corner and Sylvia Harvey, for instance, argued that the Conservative gov-ernments of the 1980s responded to radical economic and social reconstruction by seeking new ways of managing the conflict between the old and the new, tra-dition and modernity. They identified the key concepts in this process as, on the one hand, 'heritage', with its connotations of continuity with the past, and the preservation of values and traditions, and, on the other hand, 'enterprise', with its connotations of change and innovation. The terms are vitally interconnected: 'what has come to be called "the heritage industry" is itself a major component of economic redevelopment, an "enterprise", both in terms of large-scale civic pro-grammes and the proliferation of private commercial activity around "the past" in one commodified form or another'.[25] Thus the Thatcherite project of recon-struction yoked the modernizing and transformative impulse of enterprise to the concern with tradition and continuity that we call heritage. This was not mere rhetoric, and the government gave heritage culture and the heritage industry the official seal of approval in the form of the National Heritage Acts of 1980 and 1983. These Acts brought into existence the National Heritage Memorial Fund, and an organization to oversee the state's interests in the past, English Heritage (estab-

---

[23] Wright, *On Living in an Old Country*; Robert Hewison, *The Heritage Industry: Britain in a Climate of Decline* (London: Methuen, 1987).

[24] Robert Hewison, 'The Heritage Industry Revisited', *Museums Journal*, 91/4 (1991), 23.

[25] John Corner and Sylvia Harvey, 'Mediating Tradition and Modernity: The Heritage/Enterprise Couplet', in Corner and Harvey (eds.), *Enterprise and Heritage*, 46.

lished in 1984). They also ensured that the number of listed buildings doubled during the Thatcher years.[26] Wright argues that the Acts also reworked concepts of public access and use in terms of commodification, exhibition, and display, encouraging the forthright marketing of the past within a thoroughly market-orientated heritage industry.[27] The concern was not about the fascination with the past in itself. The conservation and celebration of that which is deemed significant among the mass of material passed down to the present by previous generations has a long history. The concern was with the terms in which the interest in the past was expressed, the aspects of the past that were celebrated, and the intensity with which heritage culture was commercially exploited. History, it was argued, was being idealized, sanitized, and rendered harmless and unthreatening; it was being preserved in aspic.

It is difficult to deny that a heritage industry developed in the 1980s as a vital part of the contemporary leisure, tourism, and related service industries. But there were others on the left who interpreted these developments differently, notably Raphael Samuel, who argued his position at length in *Theatres of Memory*, published in 1994.[28] Samuel was prepared to admit that 'the decline of nationality in the present, and the growing uncertainty about its future, have been offset by an enlarged sense of the national past'.[29] But he was scathing about the critique of heritage activity developed by Hewison and Wright. He and others saw a worryingly Arnoldian streak, a fear of the popular, in the disparaging use of such terms as 'commercialization', 'commodification', 'vulgarization', 'trivialization', and 'superficiality' when describing cultural developments.[30] Samuel argues that aesthetes of the right and the left simply reveal their own difficulties with popular culture when they dismiss those versions of heritage which seem to package the past as tourist kitsch, as 'a Disneyfied version of history in place of the real thing'.[31] Like Arnold, Leavis, and Hoggart before them, Wright and Hewison seemed to uphold a moral concern that an educative mode of engaging with the past through genuine historical endeavour had been supplanted by a passive consumption of the past as heritage artefact, image, or entertainment experience. We have already noted that Samuel operates with a much enlarged, and much more democratic sense of the heritage impulse, and that he recognizes that people from many different backgrounds engage with the past in a variety of projects, both formal and informal, state-sponsored and commercial, public and private. What Samuel's work—and Lowenthal's—does so impressively is to demonstrate the richness and variety of heritage concerns—including a vibrant interest in working-class heritage, and a widespread popular curiosity about the past, not just in the UK but all over the world.

---

[26] Kenneth Powell, 'Heritage is a Thing of the Past', *Sunday Telegraph*, Sunday Review section (10 May 1998), 8.

[27] Wright, *On Living in an Old Country*, 42–8; see also Hewison, *Heritage Industry*.

[28] Samuel, *Theatres of Memory*.

[29] Raphael Samuel, 'Introduction: Exciting to be English', in Samuel, *Patriotism*, p. xlii.

[30] See Samuel, *Theatres of Memory*, esp. 259–73; also Davies, 'End of the Pier Show'.

[31] Samuel, *Theatres of Memory*, 259.

For Samuel, heritage is a form of *public* history, a non-academic and often extremely popular engagement with or consumption of the past. Lowenthal, on the other hand, sees heritage as a matter of faith rather than of historical fact—and it is a faith with a big following.[32] But the distinction frequently made between history and heritage is difficult to maintain. Richard Dyer summarizes the distinction thus: 'history is a discipline of enquiry into the past; heritage is an attitude towards the legacy of the past'.[33] According to such a perspective, where the discipline of history seeks to generate knowledge and understanding about the past, heritage as a discourse and practice is fascinated by artefacts, ideas, and the like inherited from the past. The discipline of history is conceived as systematic, objective, and authoritative; the discourse of heritage, on the other hand, is understood as valuing the 'evidence' of the past for its own sake. The heritage industry then showcases that evidence as something to be appreciated and enjoyed—for pleasure, it might be said, rather than for understanding. But the discipline of history can never be entirely objective and value-free; it is always both selective and authored. Indeed, history, like heritage, is always and necessarily an 'attitude towards the legacy of the past', dependent on the accumulation and display of evidence. Equally, heritage, like history, as Samuel and Lowenthal demonstrate, contributes to our knowledge of the past.

As Pam Cook has pointed out, in 'Re-presenting the National Past', the first piece I published on heritage films, I too was guilty of working through the same moral concerns that Samuel sees in the work of Hewison and Wright.[34] Both Cook and Samuel are surely correct in perceiving in such work an anxiety about 'mere entertainment', about dressing up, about spectacle, as well as an anxiety about history appearing as pastiche rather than as authentic, the real thing (as if history could ever be the real thing). I hope I've expunged some of those anxieties in this book—although they are anxieties to which we will need to return. But I don't want to lose sight altogether of the characterization of the cult of heritage as an industry. Nor do I want to suggest that the meaning of heritage is fixed, or that there is a right way of viewing heritage and a wrong way.

REBRANDING THE NATION

In 1991, as the Thatcher years drew to a close, even Hewison wondered whether 'the heritage boom'—the growth of the heritage industry in the 1970s and 1980s—was 'about to go bust'. In fact Thatcher's successor, John Major, actually went out of his way to try to renew the heritage effort. Most visibly, a new government ministry, the Department of National Heritage, was established in 1992 to create and

[32] Lowenthal, *The Heritage Crusade*.
[33] Dyer, 'Nice Young Men', 44.
[34] See Higson, 'Re-presenting the National Past'; Cook, 'Neither Here Nor There'; and Cook, *Fashioning the Nation*, 27–8.

maintain the infrastructure necessary to promote a conservative vision of national identity. Two years later, Major announced a 'crusade' to 'rekindle public confidence in Britain's greatness', asserting that, despite its entry into Europe, Britain would 'survive unamendable in all essentials'. This apparently meant 'old maids bicycling to Holy Communion through the morning mist', long shadows on county cricket grounds, and warm beer.[35]

But Hewison had been right to sense a new mood in the air, for a prominent market research report published around the same time strongly suggested that such a national self-image was problematic. The report confirmed that the UK was indeed seen from overseas in heritage terms, and argued that Britain was consequently 'a dated concept', difficult 'to reconcile with reality', with British identity entrenched in the past, and in the USA almost entirely 'fictionalised'.[36] As Wright commented, 'the image relies heavily on Merchant Ivory films, BBC dramatisations of 19th-century novels, and Helena Bonham Carter working overtime'.[37] This was the beginning of the debate about the rebranding of Britain that Blair was later to embrace, the search for a new national brand image that might exploit the design, fashion, marketing, and media industries, maximizing the 'inventiveness' that comes with the country's 'rich cultural diversity'.[38]

For the duration of Major's Conservative government, however, heritage was to remain very much on the agenda. In 1996, for instance, Virginia Bottomley, the Secretary of State at the Department of National Heritage 'provoked anger among British film-makers by arguing that they should become part of the heritage industry'. The film industry, she suggested,

should act as a standard-bearer to 'promote our country, our cultural heritage and our tourist trade . . . I am cautious about any edict, but part of my job is to encourage tourism and our great traditions . . . This is what films like Sense and Sensibility did as well as the BBC's Pride and Prejudice. If we have got the country houses and the landscapes, they should be shown off on film, particularly as we approach the millennium.'[39]

With the election of New Labour in 1997, the agenda inevitably changed more quickly. The emphasis on enterprise, on a modern, youthful, and energetic nation, remained, but no longer counterbalanced by quite such a conservative, elite notion of 'national heritage'. One of the first decisions to be made by the new government was to rename the Department of National Heritage the Department of Culture, Media and Sport. According to Blair, 'changing the name of the Department of Heritage . . . is not a gimmick. It is a symbol that we mean to look forward,

---

[35] John Major, quoted in Patrick Wright, 'Wrapped in the Tatters of the Flag', *Guardian* (31 Dec. 1994), 25.

[36] Anneke Elwes, *Nations for Sale* (London: DDB Needham, 1994), quoted in Wright, 'Wrapped in the Tatters of the Flag', 25.

[37] Wright, 'Wrapped in the Tatters of the Flag', 25.

[38] Elwes, *Nations for Sale*, quoted in Wright, 'Wrapped in the Tatters of the Flag', 25.

[39] Richard Brooks, quoting Virginia Bottomley, 'Bottomley Wants "Heritage" Films: Call for "Country House" Movies Fuels Row Over Lottery Cash Veto for "Arty" Projects', *Observer* (19 May 1996), 12.

not back.'[40] That desire to look forward was further symbolized in the mythology of 'Cool Britannia', and the celebration of the modern, youthful energy and enterprise of the contemporary design, fashion, music, and film industries.

The debate about Britain's national self-image was driven by big business as much as by politicians and cultural commentators. Within the business world, there were those who felt the image of Britain as an Old Country was the key to the export trade—but there were others who felt that being associated with Heritage Britain was a hindrance in the modern global economy. British Airways changed their brand image, for instance, 'when its marketing experts discovered that being British was a business handicap. This country, they discovered, is viewed as stern and starchy, arrogant and self-important—and therefore out of step with the preferences of international travellers.'[41]

Until then, British Airways had gone along with the Walpole Committee, which was set up to promote and exploit the 'quintessential Britishness' of their member companies, most of whom were luxury goods and service companies. They included the Savoy hotel group, the perfume business Penhaligon, the bags and belts company Mulberry, the jeweller Asprey, as well as multinational companies which still had the aura of Britishness about their goods, such as the Japanese-owned DAKS Simpson, the German-owned Land Rover, and the makers of Beefeater Gin, now part of Allied Domecq. The 'British' values these companies wanted to be associated with were 'customer care, craftsmanship, innovation and international appeal, . . . [and a] respect for tradition'. But in the mid-1990s, even the Walpole Committee was reconsidering its interest in Heritage Britain. At a Walpole Committee seminar, the sales and marketing director of Jaguar argued that it was now necessary to shift the image of Britishness away from the past:

He seriously believes that period dramas like Pride & Prejudice, . . . that Mr Darcy and his costume drama cronies, who enchant viewers worldwide, are hindering British industry's efforts to be viewed as innovative, leading edge producers. 'We do the past very well in this country, but how can we compete from a high-tech point of view when the rest of the world sees us dressed up in top hats and crinolines all the time?'[42]

The Prime Minister picked up the theme later the same year, when he launched a 'campaign to reshape Britain as a powerhouse of profit and the imagination' and to 'shed the image of being stuck in the past'.[43] He encouraged the British Tourist Authority 'to build on what they have done already in re-shaping Britain's image abroad', and businesses 'to look at how they are selling Britain':

Though I value the role of tradition in the tourist industry, I don't believe we have to rely on the cliched images that no longer reflect the people we are. We can show a fresh face to

---

[40] Blair, 'Britain can Remake it', 17.

[41] Julia Finch, 'Patriot Games', *Guardian* (14 June 1997), 30; see also Mike Wayne, 'The Re-invention of Tradition: British Cinema and International Image Markets in the 1990s', *EnterText*, 2/1 (2001/2), at http://www.brunel.ac.uk/faculty/arts/EnterText/issue_2_1.htm

[42] Finch, 'Patriot Games', 30, quoting Roger Putnam.

[43] James Meikle, 'Blair Calls for Pride and Profit Revolution', *Guardian*, G2 (18 Sept. 1997), 3.

the world. . . . When I talk about Britain as a 'Young Country', I mean an attitude of mind as much as anything. I mean we should think of ourselves as a country that cherishes its past, its traditions, and its unique cultural inheritance, but does not live in the past. A country that is not resting on past glories, but hungry for future success.[44]

The British Tourist Authority readily embraced this new vision, in which film was seen as playing a vital role. Indeed, film was central to the rhetoric of this new way of seeing the nation—the tourist authority's chairman, for instance, was quoted as saying that Britain was 'the Spice Girls as well as the Last Night of the Proms, Trainspotting as well as Pride and Prejudice, the Full Monty as well as Four Weddings and a Funeral'.[45] This rebranding exercise was effective enough for one Sunday paper to declare in 1998 not only that New Labour was 'profoundly indifferent' to heritage, but also that ' "heritage" is dead'.[46]

FILMS AND THE HERITAGE AND TOURISM INDUSTRIES

It is one of the basic premises of this book that costume dramas need to be seen as part of the heritage industry, even if this is not the only way they can be characterized. How then did this apparent cultural shift from conservative tradition to modernity affect the production and reception of English period costume dramas? First of all, it is worth noting that *The Winslow Boy*, *Elizabeth*, and *Shakespeare in Love* all appeared in 1998, *Plunkett and Macleane*, *An Ideal Husband*, *The Clandestine Marriage*, *Mansfield Park*, and *Topsy-Turvy* in 1999, and *The Golden Bowl* and *The House of Mirth* in 2000. Such a list hardly suggests that the moment of heritage had passed. In fact, I would argue that, far from having disappeared by the late 1990s, heritage cinema had been vigorously renewed, both culturally and economically, as the commercial and critical success of *Elizabeth* and *Shakespeare in Love* at the end of the decade surly confirms. Both films were major successes at the box office and both were taken up by and fed off the discourses and practices of the heritage industry and cultural tourism.

On the other hand, as we will see in subsequent chapters, *Mansfield Park*, *The Golden Bowl*, and *The House of Mirth* were all comparative box-office failures, despite quite substantial budgets, and the presence of American stars in the latter two. Those two films in many ways represent the more traditional strands of heritage film-making—one a Merchant Ivory production, both in many ways quite austere adaptations of canonical novels, both slow-moving and precise. But *Mansfield Park* was a self-conscious attempt to modernize the heritage film, and specifically Jane Austen, by packaging costume drama and literary culture for a more youthful and less reverential audience—yet it too failed with cinema audiences.

---

[44] Blair, 'Britain can Remake it', 17.
[45] David Quarmby, quoted in James Meikle, 'Tourist Chiefs Unveil New Brand Image for Britain', *Guardian* (23 Sept. 1997), 9.   [46] Powell, 'Heritage is a Thing of the Past', 8.

Taking the 1980s and 1990s as a whole, it is certainly useful to see the numerous English costume dramas produced in that period in relation to the heritage industry and the often very public mobilization of heritage discourses. I've already pointed out that there are other ways of making sense of the films as well, but that is not to deny that heritage culture was an important context for the production and reception of the films. In particular, as Amy Sargeant stresses, we should relate heritage films to 'the marketing and consumption of Britain's cultural heritage as a tourist attraction'.[47] As she points out, 'heritage is vital to the appeal of Britain as a tourist destination', and costume dramas have played a central part in keeping Heritage Britain in the public eye, both at home and abroad.[48] As a 1999 newspaper report put it, quoting Janet Anderson, then the Labour government's Tourism Minister, 'film tourism is an "exciting growth area" for the economy, combining two thriving industries and the leisure pursuits of the cinema and days out'.[49]

The tension I've outlined above between tradition and modernity was a particular feature of the British film industry in the 1980s and 1990s. A dying industry in the early 1980s, commercial enterprise and occasionally state support saw the modernizing of the cinema in the rise of the multiplex, the development of new sound, image, and editing technologies, and the production of many more British films by the end of the period. On the other hand, as we have seen, there was across the same period an insistent exploitation of the heritage film and its concern with tradition and the past—although even the heritage film was modernized in the late 1990s.

The emphasis in heritage cinema on picturesque landscapes and fine old buildings, and the public interest thereby generated, dovetails neatly with the work of heritage bodies like the National Trust and English Heritage. As the *Sunday Telegraph* reviewer suggested of the BBC's 1995 *Pride and Prejudice* adaptation, it was like 'a lovely day out in some National Trust property'.[50] Websites, books about the making of particular films and television programmes, gazetteers listing places that have appeared in films, and articles in the 'Travel' sections of newspapers and magazines will often detail the locations used in period dramas, and visits to those locations will often increase dramatically.[51]

---

[47] Amy Sargeant, 'Making and Selling Heritage Culture: Style and Authenticity in Historical Fictions on Film and Television', in Ashby and Higson (eds.), *British Cinema, Past and Present*, 301.

[48] Ibid. 308.

[49] James Meikle, 'Movies Redraw the Tourist Map: Visits to Locations Featured in Popular Films Provide Profitable New Dimension in the Travel Business', *Guardian* (16 June 1999), 12.

[50] 1 Oct. 1995, quoted in Roger Sales, *Jane Austen and Representations of Regency England* (London and New York: Routledge, revised edn., 1996), 237–8.

[51] See, for instance, Brian Pendreigh, *On Location: The Film Fan's Guide to Britain and Ireland* (Edinburgh and London: Mainstream, 1995); Allan Foster, *The Movie Traveller: A Film Fan's Travel Guide to the UK and Ireland* (Edinburgh: Polygon, 2000); John Pym, *Merchant Ivory's English Landscape: Rooms, Views and Anglo-Saxon Attitudes* (London: Pavilion, 1995); and the discussion of visits to Stamford, which stood in for Middlemarch in the 1994 BBC adaptation of Eliot's novel, in Jenny Rice and Carol Saunders, 'Consuming *Middlemarch*: The Construction and Consumption of Nostalgia in Stamford', in Deborah Cartmell *et al.* (eds.), *Pulping Fictions: Consuming Culture across the Literature/Media Divide* (London: Pluto Press, 1996), 85–98.

Following the success of *Brideshead Revisited* on television, according to one report, Castle Howard, which stood in for Brideshead, 'became one of the most frequently visited stately homes in Europe'.[52] In 1996, the British Tourist Board gave their top award to the BBC adaptation of *Pride and Prejudice* for its outstanding contribution to tourism.[53] Three major films with Scottish locations— *Rob Roy*, *Braveheart*, and *Loch Ness* (all 1995)—were estimated to have generated as much as £15 million in tourism revenue. Lyme Park in Disley, Cheshire, saw a 178 per cent increase in admissions after featuring in the BBC's *Pride and Prejudice*, while Saltram House in Devon, used for *Sense and Sensibility* (1996), was reported to have recorded a 57 per cent increase.[54] Osborne House, on the Isle of Wight, became a leading visitor attraction after the success of *Mrs Brown* (1997), much of which was set and shot there. Numbers of visitors had been falling for several years, but now went up by 25 per cent, with income from admissions and sales up by 20 per cent.[55]

In 1997, it was reported that 'English Heritage is enjoying a tourist boom at its historic properties', with the chairman of the organization giving 'the credit to the revival of the British film industry. Castles, abbeys, and stately homes used as locations in cinema and television films have seen visitor numbers soar.'[56] The Georgian city of Bath reckoned to have grossed £3 million by the summer of 1999 by setting up a film centre to celebrate Jane Austen novels filmed in the city.[57] Film- and television-related tourism is now big business, with the 2001 blockbuster *Harry Potter and the Philosopher's Stone*, for instance, enabling potentially extremely lucrative tie-ins—according to one newspaper report, 'British film mandarins went to extraordinary lengths to secure the work and the money that the Harry Potter movie franchise could bring to the country', hoping to exploit the mock-English heritage qualities of the books and films.[58]

Heritage cinema and television was also big business for the owners of period houses, who were often keen to have their properties used in films since the fees could help pay for upkeep. It's a well-organized business too, with companies such as Country House Locations, run by Sarah Greenwood, author of *Film and Photography for Historic Houses and Gardens*.[59] The Film Information National Database meanwhile carries details of around 20,000 film locations while the Historic Houses Association 'offers property owners advice, sample contracts and a guide to fees'.[60] Fees are impressive, with the historic village of Lacock in Wilt-

[52] Anon., 'Win a Grand Weekend', *Country Living* (Jan. 1999), 132.
[53] Amy Sargeant, 'The Darcy Effect: Regional Tourism and Costume Drama', *International Journal of Heritage Studies*, 4/3–4 (1998), 182.   [54] Meikle, 'Movies Redraw the Tourist Map', 12.
[55] Maev Kennedy, 'Films Bring Tourist Boom for Stately Homes', *Guardian* (26 Feb. 1998), 8.
[56] Kennedy, 'Films Bring Tourist Boom', 8.
[57] Patrick Wintour, 'Now you've Seen the Film, Don't Miss the Location', *Observer* (13 June 1999), from website (www.guardian.co.uk).
[58] See Gareth McLean, 'Hogwarts and All', *Guardian*, Friday Review (19 Oct. 2001), 2.
[59] Rachel Warren, 'When Home Movies Spell Hot Property', *Independent on Sunday*, Business section (4 Nov. 1990), 20.
[60] Dan Glaister, 'Film Locations Make Most of Period Charm', *Guardian* (21 May 1996), 11.

shire charging £20,000 per day to film there, and The George Inn, in Norton St Phillip, Somerset, used in *Pride and Prejudice*, charging £2,500. As a National Trust negotiator commented, 'We know the value of our places and we charge accordingly', defending this line by adding that 'We are committed to increasing public enjoyment of our properties. What better way than through the lens?'[61]

Tourism business developments such as these helped produce new ways of envisioning the nation—in part as an amalgam of local brand names: Thomas Hardy's Dorset, 1066 Country in East Sussex, Constable Country in Suffolk, Brontë Country, Shakespeare's Country, Robin Hood Country, and so on. 'Unnoticed by many natives, a new map of Britain has been drawn: a mixture of tradition, television, legend and literature, with splendidly unlikely neighbours united only in their hopes of securing tourist dosh. The past is now different Countries.'[62]

Another new map of the nation was the 'Movie Map' produced in 1998 by the British Tourist Authority: this was a map of the UK showing key film locations. More than 250,000 of these maps were sent to travel agencies in North America, the Far East, Australia, and Europe (Fig. 8).[63] While films with historical settings were by no means the only ones to feature, half the 1990s films on the map did in fact have pre-Second World War period settings, including *Howards End*, *The Madness of King George* (1995), *Mrs Brown*, *The Remains of the Day* (1993), *Sense and Sensibility*, *Wilde* (1997), and *Elizabeth*. Advertised on the back is the 'Great British Heritage Pass'. As the leaflet explained, 'Many of Britain's dramatic castles, beautiful stately homes and gardens, and medieval manor houses are featured on this Movie Map. And they are yours to discover with the Great British Heritage Pass—our invitation to the independent traveller to visit almost 600 of Britain's finest historic properties free of charge.' Tourism Minister Janet Anderson, launching the 'Movie Map', commented, 'Thanks to the success of our film and TV exports, many parts of Britain are now well known to people across the world.'[64]

Costume dramas are not infrequently used in the more general promotion of heritage culture, as the following random examples show. When *The Remains of the Day* came out, there was a full-page advertisement in the *Guardian* for a competition linked to the film, which was described as having 'a very English setting'. The main prizes were 'two luxurious weekend breaks to the elite, and very English, five star Hanbury Manor, . . . a restored Jacobean-style mansion built in 1890 and set in two hundred acres of Hertfordshire countryside, similar to the manor featured in *The Remains of the Day*'. The second prizes were 'ten hampers by Crabtree and Evelyn, including fine English biscuits, teas, preserves and other delicacies . . .'[65] The release of *Shadowlands* (1993) was the excuse for a long article, also in the *Guardian*, about American attitudes towards Englishness, illustrated with a large still of Anthony Hopkins in *Howards End*.[66] And an article in the travel

---

[61] Giles Clotworthy, quoted ibid.
[62] Charles Nevin, 'How to Make Money with the Country Practice', *Independent on Sunday* (11 Nov. 1990), 8.　　　　[63] Wintour, 'Now You've Seen the Film', from website (no page number).
[64] Ibid.　　[65] *Guardian* (22 Jan. 1994), 2.
[66] James Wood, 'An England in Shadow Land', *Guardian* (2 Mar. 1994), 22.

8. The British Tourist Authority's 'Movie Map'

section of the *Independent* about one of the 'luxurious country house hotels' owned by the Laura Ashley chain ran with the headline 'A Merchant Ivory setting and Edwardian service—the sepia-tinted appeal of Llangoed Hall'.[67]

There are numerous other formal and informal tie-ins, cross-promotions, spin-offs, and chance juxtapositions, encouraging the public to consume much more than simply a film or a television programme. Clothes stores such as Laura Ashley

---

[67] Ben Rogers, 'Here's Posh for You', *Independent* (15 Mar. 1997), 40.

exploit period costume fashions; upmarket lifestyle magazines promote period properties, interior designs, furnishings, and fabrics; and food outlets offer traditional fayre. Mompesson House admitted visitors at half price if they could produce a ticket stub from the Salisbury Odeon for a screening of *Sense and Sensibility*, which had used the house for some of its locations.[68] 'To celebrate the launch on video of the classic British drama series, *Brideshead Revisited*', the magazine *Country Living* ran a competition, the first prize for which was 'a weekend at the Wormsley Arms Hotel, Yorkshire, where Sir Laurence Olivier stayed during the filming of the series . . . plus an exclusive private tour of Castle Howard, the splendid stately home where *Brideshead Revisited* was set'.[69] A few years earlier, an auction of unwanted furniture and objets d'art from Castle Howard, some of which had been used in the television series, was reported to have done unexpectedly good business.[70]

Japanese travel companies frequently organized trips to the UK to experience the delights of the heritage settings featured in English costume dramas. One such company organized a seven-day package tour on the back of the release of *Mrs Dalloway* (1997), with publicity distributed at the specialized cinemas where the film was showing in Japan. The tour, which took in a manor house, flower arranging, tea at the Ritz, and some of the film locations, was advertised as enabling participants 'to experience the life of an English lady', to sample 'the atmosphere of the good old England where *Mrs Dalloway* is set', and to see 'the traditional lifestyle, the noble culture, and a Victorian town'.[71] In the USA, in the film magazine *Premiere*, *Shakespeare in Love* was promoted via a competition in which the first prize was a trip to the old country:

Miramax Films invites you on a romantic adventure for you and your true love to Shakespeare's England. . . . You'll have a chance to stroll along the same historic paths that the scribe himself walked upon. While on your romantic holiday, experience the charm of Oxfordshire, the picturesque villages of the Cotswolds, magnificent Blenheim Palace, and of course Shakespeare's birthplace, Stratford-upon-Avon.[72]

Then of course there is the literary tie-in. Publishers will often bring out new editions of adapted books, or create the book of the film or television series (Fig. 9). Canonical novels published under the Penguin Classics imprint might normally expect to sell 10,000 copies a year. In the late 1980s, it was estimated that that figure could be doubled within three months by a spin-off edition. As a commissioning editor at Penguin commented, 'even if 0.5 per cent of film-goers buy the book, that's a lot in publishing terms'.[73] Several heritage films are also adap-

---

[68] The National Trust Wessex Region News, 21 Feb. 1996, quoted in Sargeant, 'The Darcy Effect', 181.
[69] Anon., 'Win a Grand Weekend', 132.
[70] Dalya Alberge, ' "Brideshead" Jumble Sale Raises £1.2m', *Independent* (12 Nov. 1991), 3.
[71] 'English Lady Experience', travel brochure produced by HIS, Japan, 1998–9; my thanks to Shoko Otsuyama for the translation.
[72] '*Shakespeare in Love* Sweepstakes', *Premiere* (US), 11/4 (1998), 9–10.
[73] Sue Berger, quoted in Sheila Johnston, 'Read Any Good Films Lately?', *Independent*, Listings (14 Apr. 1989), 28.

9. The cover of Penguin's film tie-in edition of E. M. Forster's novel *Maurice*

tations of books that are A Level set texts. *Hamlet, Emma, Great Expectations, Wuthering Heights,* and *Jane Eyre,* for instance, were all listed as among the top fifteen A level set texts between 1951 and 1991, while *A Passage to India, Tess of the d'Urbervilles,* and *A Handful of Dust* were among the top fifteen works by twentieth-century authors used for A Level examinations.[74]

One way or another, then, images from heritage films circulate widely in middle-class culture, elite heritage discourses are frequently mobilized in discussions of the films themselves, and the films are tied in to other branches of the heritage, tourism, and leisure industries. The types of properties and landscapes on display in heritage films are themselves part of a much longer tradition of imagining England, through the work of bodies like the National Trust and

---

[74] Judith Judd, 'Novel Ideas Put Classics to the Test', *Independent on Sunday* (22 Sept. 1991), 8.

publications like the magazine *This England*. The heritage associations
films thus have a cultural resonance much wider than the films themselve,
prominence of the heritage impulse may influence how some audiences read t.
films—although other audiences may read them quite differently. The richness
and ambivalence of heritage cinema and the diverse ways in which different audiences engage with it make it impossible to pin down the meanings of particular
films. Even so, there is no denying the importance of heritage discourses in
enabling certain sorts of readings of those films.

AUTHENTICITY AND PASTICHE

There is another aspect of the representation of the past in heritage films that has
provoked debate. As we've seen, one of the central claims made about many heritage films is that they provide precise, authentic historical reconstructions—and
in the case of literary adaptations, particularly faithful renderings of the source
text. For mainstream film reviewers, and no doubt for many audiences, this is one
of the great attractions of heritage films. Within the terms of what I've called the
leftist cultural critique, however, the fetishizing of what is seen as a rose-tinted,
conservative vision of the past is one of the problems with the films, since it
renders that vision seductively attractive and at the same time blocks other historical readings. For those academic commentators with a more populist understanding of both the heritage industry and the historical film, the process of
historical reconstruction is regarded more sympathetically. For Richard Dyer, for
instance, the museum aesthetic is something to be valued, not worried over: 'The
fascination of the appearance of old things, a museum pleasure so consummately
reproduced in heritage movies, is a legitimate enough reason to go to the movies
. . .'[75] For others, the historical masquerade of the costume film is both a playful
and productive experience, and provides a space in which social and cultural identities can be explored.

What masquerades as the authentic in costume drama is always of course pastiche. In the case of the English heritage film, we are presented with an imagined
Englishness, an imagined national past: not the 'real thing', but a pot-pourri of
imitations, homages, gestures. Yet claims are still made in the name of authenticity, and it is the spectacle of heritage iconography that is frequently so compelling
in these films. In fact, the tension between narrative and spectacle in so many of
the films can be related to a tension in the wider heritage culture, between preservation and reconstruction. For many, 'our' heritage is something to be preserved.
But much of the heritage business is about reconstructing rather than simply pre-
serving the past, attempting to make it seem relevant to the present generation.
In effect, these are competing versions of authenticity, and the *mise-en-scène* of
heritage films draws on both versions. On the one hand, art directors and pro-

---

[75] Dyer, 'Feeling English', 18.

duction designers use what has been passed down from the past—'original' buildings, costumes, landscapes, and so on. On the other hand, they reconstruct a vision
of the past, animating it, bringing it to life. The latter tendency is heavily marked
in a film like *Elizabeth*, whose production team adopted a very cavalier relationship to the past. But it is also there in the much more exact and reverential production design of a film like *Howards End*, with its use of matte shots, and the
whole business of performance. As will become clear in the case studies that
follow, the difference is that, while *Elizabeth* still draws on and feeds off the discourse of authenticity, its production team was much more willing to explore the
discourse of licence and to depart from official history. Both films play off pastiche against authenticity, but in different ways and with different emphases.[76]

Pastiche has a double life in contemporary cultural theory. For Fredric Jameson,
pastiche is the sign of critical depthlessness in postmodern culture, precisely the
loss of an authentic sensibility, and thereby the villain of the piece.[77] For other
commentators, pastiche on the contrary is to be celebrated for its propensity to
challenge essentialism and reveal the extent to which traditions are constructed,
identities adopted. For those following in Jameson's footsteps, the problem with
the heritage industry is not simply that it transforms the past into a series of commodities for the leisure and entertainment market, but that in most cases the commodity on offer is an image, a spectacle, something to be gazed at. History, the
past, becomes, in Jameson's phrase, 'a vast collection of images' designed to delight
the modern-day tourist-historian.[78] In this version of history, a critical perspective is displaced by decoration and display, a fascination with surfaces, 'an obsessive accumulation of comfortably archival detail', where a concern for style
displaces the material dimensions of historical context.[79] The past is reproduced
as flat, depthless pastiche, where the reference point is not the past itself, but other
images, other texts. The evocation of past-ness is accomplished by a look, a style,
the loving recreation of period details. The image of the past becomes so naturalized that it stands removed from history. The past as referent is effaced, and all
that remains is a self-referential intertextuality.[80] As Andreas Huyssen points out,
however, there remains a felt need for a sense of past-ness and historicity, since
the search for tradition is such a vital feature of the contemporary response to the
felt failure of modernism.[81]

The strength of the pastiche, the self-conscious visual perfectionism of
the films, and their fetishization of period details, creates a fascinating but

---

[76] For an interesting discussion of authenticity and licence, see Kara McKechnie, 'Taking Liberties
with the Monarch: The Royal Bio-pic in the 1990s', in Monk and Sargeant (eds.), *British Historical
Cinema*, 215–36.

[77] Fredric Jameson, 'Post-modernism, or the Cultural Logic of Late Capitalism', *New Left Review*,
146 (1984).

[78] Ibid. 66; see also John Urry, *The Tourist Gaze* (London: Sage, 1990), chs. 5 and 6.

[79] Wright, *On Living in an Old Country*, 252.

[80] Jameson, 'Post-modernism', 60–2.

[81] Andreas Huyssen, 'The Search for Tradition: Avant-garde and Post-modernism in the 1970s', *New
German Critique*, 22 (1981), 23–40.

self-enclosed world. If on the one hand, from this point of view, this world seems cut off from the 'real' historical past, on the other hand, it also seems to have severed its connections with the present. The strength of the pastiche in effect imprisons the qualities of the past, holding them in place as something to be gazed at from a reverential distance, refusing the possibility of a dialogue or confrontation with the present. The films thus render history as spectacle, which can then seem quite separate from the viewer in the present, something over and done with, complete, achieved. Hence the sense of timelessness rather than historicity in relation to a national past which is 'purged of political tension' and so available for appreciation as visual display.[82] From the perspective of this leftist cultural critique, the heritage film as pastiche reduces each period of the national past through a process of re-iteration to an effortlessly reproducible, and attractively consumable, connotative style. As Cairns Craig suggests, this is 'film as conspicuous consumption'[83]—or rather, because it is only images being consumed, it is a fantasy of conspicuous consumption, a fantasy of historical Englishness, a fantasy of the national past.

This view of heritage films—the leftist cultural critique—has not gone down well in some quarters. Thus Pam Cook writes of 'the contempt in which recent "heritage" films are held by critics on the Left, who are fond of dismissing them as phoney, contaminated versions of history which mask the "true" account of our national past'.[84] Cook in fact cites my earlier work on heritage films as symptomatic of this problem, arguing that the position I adopted there was akin to the dismissal by middle-brow critics of the 1940s of the popular Gainsborough costume dramas of that period. In both cases, she argues that the critic has a problem with historical inauthenticity, that we dismiss the film versions of novels or of historical periods because they are not true to the original, that we cannot cope with populist rather than academic versions of history, that we are anxious about the way in which history is transformed into commodified spectacle.[85] As Cook notes, costume drama has traditionally been dismissed by mainstream male critics of the left and right as trivial, as feminine, as obsessed with mere decoration and display. Costume drama is also frequently seen as lacking the seriousness of real history, and dealing in images, which, it is purported, rarely have the authority of written scholarship.

While I admit that there is an anxiety about the popular running through my work, and while I've revised my earlier arguments in light of the criticisms of Cook and others, I think Cook's comments are overstated. In particular, I'm not persuaded that my discussion of heritage films of the 1980s and 1990s amounts to the same as the dismissal of Gainsborough costume dramas by mainstream British film critics of the 1940s. I agree that there is much about the leftist cultural critique that is problematic—but even in 'Re-presenting the National Past', I argued

---

[82] Wright, *On Living in an Old Country*, 69.
[83] Craig, 'Rooms without a View', 10.
[84] Cook, *Fashioning the Nation*, 7.
[85] Ibid.; and Cook, 'Neither Here Nor There', 57.

for the textual ambivalence of heritage films: if the visual spectacle of the films often seemed to reduce history to an alluring surface, narratively that history was once more reasserted.

But it is also the case that one of the key ways in which these films have been interpreted at the level of critical reception has been in terms of their trivialization of history, the presentation of history as decoration and display—and we cannot simply dismiss that view as wrong. Clearly, for many viewers, that is precisely how these films work for them, and why they don't like them. It is also important to acknowledge the extent to which heritage films are valorized in mainstream film criticism and by their producers and distributors in terms of the discourse of authenticity. This view in itself needs to be challenged: authenticity is always a construction; it is, precisely, not a 'true' account of our national past, however much the films may be promoted in these terms; it is always, simply, an account, which is marked as much by the concerns of the present as by the concerns of the past. It seems important to me that we puncture the balloon of authenticity, reveal how it is created, and establish an alternative reading of these films as precisely 'phoney, contaminated versions of history'.[86]

This does not mean that we should simply dismiss these films, since they are once again ambivalent texts, created and promoted as 'authentic', yet at the same time very often quite conscious of and playing up to their pastiche qualities. This can be seen especially in certain performances, such as those of Daniel Day-Lewis (Fig. 10) and Maggie Smith in *A Room with a View* (1986), Hugh Grant in *Maurice* (1987), Jonathan Pryce in *Carrington* (1995), or Helena Bonham Carter in *The Wings of the Dove* (1997). This performativeness is surely one of the great attractions of such films—while others delight in the eccentric, inauthentic qualities of pastiche. Thus *The Tempest* (1980), *Edward II* (1991), *Orlando* (1992), and *Shakespeare in Love* all play self-consciously on the possibilities and pleasures of pastiche.

Cook's critique of my earlier work on heritage films comes as part of a very interesting discussion of pastiche, costume drama, and national identity. She argues that costume drama is almost by definition a genre of pastiche, because of its indulgence in masquerade, in dressing up. 'It is pastiche,' she argues, 'that is the undoing of authentic identities. Pastiche suggests hybridity rather than purity.'[87] This allows Cook to view the costume drama as a vital space within which to explore the hybrid qualities of national identity, a vital space within which to highlight the impurity and the contamination of apparently authentic indigenous identities. This is a useful antidote to Jameson's critique of pastiche as the villain of postmodern culture. Thus, pastiche may to some audiences seem depthless and superficial. But it can also be fun, it can be playful, in the way it both implies a sense of authenticity yet at the same time acknowledges the conventionality and hybrid quality of the representation: 'it's only a story—enjoy it!'

---

[86] Cook, *Fashioning the Nation*, 7.
[87] Ibid. 5.

10. Pastiche and performativeness: Daniel Day-Lewis as Cecil Vyse in *A Room with a View*

Pastiche can enable the story-teller to establish a sense of location in history, in a real setting, by invoking the conventional signs for representing that historical location. But once that location is imagined, pastiche can then enable the story-teller to weave a narrative that can explore concerns that may have nothing to do with the implied historical setting, but everything to do with the moment in which the telling of the story unfolds. That is, it can enable the story-teller to explore concerns that may have everything to do with the present. Pastiche thus enables the anomalous and the perverse to be inserted into the apparently authentic historical location, it enables the past to be mixed with the present, it enables the fantastic to mingle with the realist. Although this is a line of analysis I shall explore further in my case study of *Howards End*, I don't imagine it will quite appease the populists, whose tastes and preferences are probably too firmly settled elsewhere. For Andy Medhurst, for instance, films like *Howards End* are too middle-brow, too caught up in 'that most reprehensible of tendencies, heritage mongering' (see also Alan Parker's widely quoted cartoon, reproduced as Fig. 11).[88] They are overly

[88] Andy Medhurst, 'The Mike-Ado', *Sight and Sound*, 10/3 (2000), 36.

11. Mistrusting the middle-brow: Alan Parker's 'Merchant Ivory as Laura Ashley' cartoon

"God, how I hate the Laura Ashley school of film making."

committed to purveying 'respectful, meticulous reconstructions of the past', in which 'dress functions primarily as distraction, where the careful period authenticity, sugary tourist-board visuals and just-right outfits act as guarantees of quality, material substance designed to hide the slightness of the narrative'.[89] Medhurst prefers those more rompish costume dramas that 'treat history as a great big dressing-up box': the popular traditions of Gainsborough and Hammer, Michael Powell and Ken Russell, Carry On and Morecambe and Wise.[90] Medhurst's argument is that the irreverence of such films towards costume and history enables them to imagine new and different identities for their audiences and to challenge 'official' views of the past in ways that 'the dreaded heritage movie' cannot.[91] Taste clearly plays a central role in such distinctions. Thus when Medhurst's favourite British film-maker, Mike Leigh, made *Topsy-Turvy* (2000), a period film about Gilbert and Sullivan which seemed dangerously close to the wrong sort of costume drama, he had to work hard to rescue the film by finding aspects that lent 'a dash of daring' to the 'usually ultra-conservative format' of heritage cinema.[92]

Other critics saw in the development of the English costume dramas of the

[89] Andy Medhurst, 'Dressing the Part', *Sight and Sound*, 6/6 (1996), 28, 29.
[90] Ibid. 28.
[91] The quotation is from Medhurst, 'The Mike-Ado', 36.
[92] Ibid. 37.

1990s a definite shift towards the more irreverential versions of history that Medhurst prefers. As we saw in Chapter 1, Claire Monk coined the term 'post-heritage' to describe 1990s' developments. Julianne Pidduck develops the argument to embrace two key films of the late 1990s, *Elizabeth* and *Shakespeare in Love*. Again, a contrast is made between 'the traditional, restrained stylistic frame of reference of British heritage cinema' and the 'unabashedly sexual', 'spontaneously ahistorical', and 'raucously unconventional' sensibilities of the two Elizabethan films.[93] Again, what Pidduck enjoys are the pleasures of pastiche and make-believe, the knowingly playful plundering of historical periods and referents, that allow room for the reimagination of the national past and the exploration of new identities. As with Medhurst, a distinction is made between those heritage films that apparently use the possibilities of dressing-up conservatively and those that use the drama of costumes in a more radical, questioning fashion. The problem with such an argument is that it leaves intact and unchallenged traditional heritage claims about authenticity—and their corollary, the denial of pastiche.

CONSERVATIVE OR LIBERAL?

The question of whether heritage films are conservative or liberal recurs throughout the critical debate about such films. The debate often depends upon contrasting films set in the present, dealing explicitly with contemporary social problems, with those set in the past, offering a very different vision of England. From this point of view, films such as *My Beautiful Laundrette* (1985), *Naked* (1993), *Bhaji on the Beach* (1993), *Trainspotting* (1996), *The Full Monty* (1997), and *Nil by Mouth* (1997) seem to address the state of the nation directly. Unlike the heritage films, they are set firmly in the present, away from the centres of power, in an unstable and socially divided, post-imperialist, and often working-class Britain inhabited by a frequently disenfranchised multicultural population whose identities are shifting and heterogeneous. Heritage films by contrast seem to provide a very different response to developments in modern Britain.

In 1988, the right-wing historian Norman Stone was asked by the equally conservative *Sunday Times* to comment on the current state of British cinema. He compared six 'worthless and insulting', even 'awful' and 'disgusting' recent films set in contemporary Britain and dealing with contemporary social issues, with 'some good, and even very good, films of a traditional kind', citing *A Room with a View*, *A Passage to India* (1984), and *Hope and Glory* (1987).[94] Stone was not alone in contrasting contemporary dramas with costume dramas, and he was not alone in regarding the costume dramas as the better sort of cinema: this was a fairly typical conservative middle-class viewpoint, embracing politics, morality, and

---

[93] Julianne Pidduck, '*Elizabeth* and *Shakespeare in Love*: Screening the Elizabethans', in Vincendeau (ed.), *Film/Literature/Heritage*, 131, 130, 132.
[94] Stone, 'Through a Lens Darkly', C1–2.

aesthetics. The aesthetic viewpoint was about lifting the heritage film out of the mire of popular culture, celebrating it as 'thoughtful and exquisitely crafted', valuing it for its 'visual beauty . . . and intelligent themes, but above all, for the intelligent casting and fine acting'.[95] The contrast might sometimes be directly with mainstream Hollywood cinema; commenting on the box-office success of *A Room with a View* in the United States, the *Daily Mail*, for instance, reported that 'An ivory-tower set of Edwardian exquisites is storming the fortress of Hollywood dross and violence by breaking cinema records across America'.[96] Craftsmanship rather than dross, intelligence rather than violence: this is the aesthetic promoted by the conservative celebrants of the heritage film.

But if some critics delighted in the apparent refusal of heritage films to wallow self-indulgently in the depths of contemporary social problems, others saw them as escapist, for the way in which they seemed to turn their backs on the iconography and values of postmodernity, post-industrialization, and multiculturalism. Thus many on the left disagreed with Stone's view of heritage films as the better sort of cinema. In one response, Derek Jarman argued that these films were, on the contrary, 'nostalgic, obsessed with the past . . . feeding illusions of stability in an unstable world'.[97] James Wood was equally dismissive of film-makers who fail 'to picture ourselves in the present', berating the heritage film for 'repeatedly turn[ing] away from our contemporary realities' and for equating Englishness with 'an idealised, bucolic past, with pastoral images' and 'a world of taste and order . . . dignified and refined'.[98]

For Tana Wollen, the nostalgia of the heritage film and its televisual equivalent, whose 'pasts were represented as entirely better places', is worrying because of its conservativeness.[99] For Cairns Craig, writing in 1991, 'the dominance and success of this particular brand of filmmaking in the past ten years is symptomatic of the crisis of identity through which England passed during the Thatcher years'.[100] The social, economic, and political uncertainties of the 1980s, argues Wollen, pushed film-makers into making these conservatively nostalgic connections with the past; Craig adds that 'the films also reflect the conflict of a nation committed to an international market place that diminishes the significance of Englishness and at the same time seek[s] to compensate by asserting "traditional" English values, whether Victorian or provincial'.[101] Wollen concludes: 'while it would be foolish to cast all the mainstream British screen fictions under discussion as entirely right-wing, their retrospection holds nationhood exclusively in its sights. Their nostalgia yearns for a nation in which social status is known and kept, and where

[95] From the dust jacket for Robert Emmet Long, *The Films of Merchant Ivory* (London: Viking, 1992).

[96] *Daily Mail* (14 Nov. 1986), 7.

[97] Derek Jarman, 'Freedom Fighter for a Vision of the Truth', *Sunday Times* (17 Jan. 1988), C9; see also Monk's discussion of other similar critical interventions of the period, in 'The British Heritage-Film Debate Revisited', 187–91.

[98] Wood, 'An England in Shadowland', 22.   [99] Wollen, 'Over our Shoulders', 186.

[100] Craig, 'Rooms without a View', 10.   [101] Ibid.

difference constitutes rather than fragments national unity.'[102] Craig too is in no doubt that 'for an English audience they gratify the need to find points of certainty within English culture . . . It is this secure world of an earlier Englishness—the antithesis of the fissiparous relativism of the present—that the films recreate.'[103] From such a perspective, '*Brideshead* for all its *noblesse oblige* is a truly Thatcherite text.'[104]

Once again, politics, morality, and aesthetics are at stake. Thus Hanif Kureishi is as horrified as the rest by what he sees as the heritage film's 'romanticised escapism', adding that this is 'the sort of soft-sore [*sic*] saccharine confection that Tory ladies and gentlemen think is Art'.[105] The implication is that, if you actually know anything about cinema, this is not in fact art. It is a view that has persisted, despite the revisionist attempts in the mid-1990s to win back heritage films for women and gay audiences. Thus Medhurst referred to 'this deadening, unforgivable oeuvre', using the blouse Helena Bonham Carter wears in *A Room with a View* as a metaphor for the genre as a whole: 'pure, prim and high-necked, it stands for all the starched, body-hating bookishness that makes this genre into film-for-people-who-hate-cinema'.[106] Given that millions of people have and continue to enjoy *Room*, it is clear that there are competing versions of cinema at issue here. Medhurst is in good company, however, since he can call on no less than David Bordwell as a witness in his defence: 'Even today, it is startling how many intellectuals identify film art with "quality cinema," the latest Shakespeare adaptation or Merchant Ivory vehicle, rather than with more vigorous and cinematically complex movies in popular genres'.[107]

The problem with such arguments is that an evaluative claim masquerades as an objective statement. The initial assumption is that good cinema can be defined unequivocally (in the case of Medhurst and Bordwell, it has something to do with popular cinema, but nothing to do with literary culture); there can be no room for alternative or competing views of what good cinema might be. Inverted snobbery thus promotes personal taste to a universal claim about film aesthetics, whereby good cinema is assumed to have nothing to do with the mainstream cultural preferences of the 'educated' middle classes. It is in effect a failure to recognize that there are competing filmic traditions for different audiences. The argument depends upon the assumption that there is a standard against which all other filmic traditions should be measured, a standard that is essentially cinematic. Difference from the standard is considered either progressive or, as in this case, retarded (a failure to understand the true cinematic potential of the material): it is never allowed to stand simply as *difference*. But what should be clear from the preceding discussion is that there are indeed different views of the value of heritage films, different assessments of their aesthetic and political worth.

[102] Wollen, 'Over our Shoulders', 181.
[103] Craig, 'Rooms without a View'.   [104] Wollen, 'Over our Shoulders', 183.
[105] Hanif Kureishi, 'England, Bloody England', *Guardian* (15 Jan. 1988), 19.
[106] Medhurst, 'Inside the British Wardrobe', 17.
[107] Bordwell, *On the History of Film Style*, 44.

FEMINIST SENSIBILITIES AND SEXUAL POLITICS

There are of course other more sympathetic appraisals of heritage cinema. If some critics saw the heritage films of the 1980s and early 1990s resonating, for better or worse, with the politics of Thatcherism, others saw in the same films a rather more liberal-humanist vision of social relations, arguing that the displaced territory of the period costume film allowed them to explore social taboos concerning desire, sexuality, the body, and identity. Such commentators sought not to criticize heritage films, nor to contrast them with contemporary dramas, but to understand and celebrate the pleasures they offered audiences, especially women and gay men. Central to this argument is the view that heritage films cannot be reduced to an elitist quality cinema addressed to the privileged classes. On the contrary, they should be seen as genuinely popular texts which thrive on their kinship with other popular literary and filmic cultural forms traditionally addressed to female audiences, and in particular the classical woman's film.

In a letter responding to Cairns Craig's disparaging assessment of heritage films of the 1980s, Alison Light argued that 'it is as romances that [these films] might be best understood, criticised, and (dare I say it?) enjoyed'.[108] Light links this approach to a directly political position, arguing that if we focus on the 'representation of sexuality' in these films, this might enable us to 'read the return to Edwardian England in the 80s as much as a rejection of Thatcherism and its ethics as a crude reflection of it'.[109] She thus aligns herself neither with those on the right, who would not want to see their chosen films as rejecting Thatcherism, nor with those on the left, who are worried precisely because the films seem to be Thatcherite. Instead, she argues that these films dramatize a vision of liberal-humanist values in a materialistic world: 'what the films . . . picked up on is the romantic longing within liberalism for making unions despite differences of nationality, sexuality, social class'.[110] For Light, then, the films are about the efforts of different social groups to connect with one another across cultural and social boundaries, thereby invoking the liberal consensus, reasserting the values of community, and offering a vision of a more inclusive, democratic, even multicultural England.

The argument is compelling, and many of the films do indeed seem to live out these values. Thus in *Howards End*, the ultimate inheritor of the house that symbolizes traditional England is the illegitimate son of the lower middle-class Leonard Bast and the upper middle-class Anglo-German Helen Schlegel. In *Another Country* (1984), *Maurice, Carrington, Mrs Dalloway*, and *Wilde* there are central and charismatic lesbian and gay relationships. In *A Room with a View, Maurice*, and *The Wings of the Dove*, the central relationships also transgress class boundaries, while in *Chariots of Fire* (1981) and *A Passage to India* there are powerful inter-ethnic friendships. *Chariots* also acknowledges the beginnings of a shift in power relations from aristocracy to meritocracy. And in *Howards End* and *The*

---

[108] Light, 'Englishness', 63.   [109] Ibid.   [110] Ibid.

Wings of the Dove it is the liberal-humanist focus on caring personal relationships which is valued over the efforts to secure inheritance and maintain social power. From this perspective, the films can seem culturally quite progressive.

This is clearly how James Ivory would like us to interpret his various 'English' films, which, he explains, were 'fired as much by skepticism and indignation as by affection and admiration'. He is therefore incensed by critics who view the Merchant Ivory films as reactionary, as nostalgic for a class-bound vision of the English past.[111] Claire Monk agrees, arguing that these are not conservative films, but films shot through with 'liberal pleasures',[112] focusing on the personal, on love, romance, and friendship, and on social transgression in one form or another. Some of the films, she suggests, work as satires or comedies of manners, demonstrating a sense of irony; others work as melodramas that expose social injustice.

The argument is taken up in different ways by different critics. Julianne Pidduck, analysing the various Austen adaptations of the 1990s, focuses on what she sees as the feminine structure of feeling that pervades such films and television programmes.[113] Jeffrey Richards, on the other hand, focuses on the way heritage films seem to challenge a deep-rooted, class-bound version of national identity. Such films, he argues, provide a 'comprehensive critique of the ethic of restraint, repression and the stiff upper lip, of the surrender of personal happiness to higher notions of duty and self-sacrifice, hitherto key elements of the national character'.[114] For Richard Dyer, one of the central pleasures of such films is their heightened emotionality—another staple of the woman's film. Like Richards, he relates the particular way in which this emotionality is handled to questions of national identity, arguing that the films deal very movingly with repression as an English character trait.[115]

Then there is the question of sexuality. Most commentators, left and right, have seen heritage films as chaste by comparison with the sexual explicitness of mainstream popular cinema (for those on the right, this is part of their charm, for those on the left, a symptom of their 'body-hating' repression). Monk sees things differently: 'That sexuality is central to their appeal has long been understood by those who ... enjoy them.'[116] According to Monk, women and gay men in particular enjoy these films and appreciate the star appeal of their mostly young male and female leads. Somewhat perversely, Monk sees *A Room with a View*, 'simmering with feminine, queer and ambiguous sexualities', as the most liberating film in this respect, rather than the more obviously sexually radical and explicit *Orlando* and *Carrington*.[117] This does seem perverse since *Room* had so enraptured

---

[111] James Ivory, 'Foreword', in Pym, *Merchant Ivory's English Landscape*, 9–12; the quotation is from p. 9.

[112] Monk, 'The British "Heritage Film" and its Critics', 122.

[113] Julianne Pidduck, 'Of Windows and Country Walks: Frames of Space and Movement in 1990s Austen Adaptations', *Screen*, 39/4 (1998).

[114] Richards, *Films and British National Identity*, 169.

[115] Dyer, 'Feeling English'.

[116] Monk, 'Sexuality and the Heritage', 34.   [117] Ibid.

conservative commentators—and should therefore be seen as yet another instance of the diversity of interpretations inspired by these films. More straightforward is Pidduck's observation that, at the end of the 1990s, *Elizabeth* and *Shakespeare in Love* played on the contrast between the finery of the costumes and the 'raw sexual energy' that lay underneath. The characters in these films were shown 'as creatures of passion . . . and bawdy worldliness'; the costumes were undoubtedly important to the appeal of the films—but just as importantly, 'in an affront to costume drama's tender sensibilities, the costumes *come off*'.[118]

Such arguments and interpretations would surely not have appealed to Norman Stone, although it was another right-wing historian, Andrew Roberts, who was mobilized by the *Daily Mail* to stem the flow of 'deviant sexuality' which seemed to have reached bursting point with *Carrington*.[119] For Monk, this film about the relationship between Dora Carrington and Bloomsbury group stalwart Lytton Strachey, shows 'an overt concern with sexuality and gender, particularly non-dominant gender and sexual identities: feminine, non-masculine, mutable, androgynous, ambiguous'.[120] For the *Daily Mail*, this was enough to make *Carrington* a bad object, which they used as an excuse to lambast the values of the Bloomsbury group: 'They hated the family, revered gay sex and loathed their country . . . we're still paying the price of the Bloomsbury set'.[121] If *Carrington* was the successor to *A Room with a View*, it was no longer the darling of the right.

Does this mark the souring of the conservative middle-class love affair with the heritage film? Or does it on the contrary draw attention once more to the diversity of texts I am mobilizing under the banner of heritage cinema? It would certainly seem to be the case that the market established in the 1980s for costume dramas and period literary adaptations enabled a rather more sexually explicit variant of the heritage film to emerge in the 1990s, from *Orlando* to *Carrington* to *The Wings of the Dove* to *Shakespeare in Love*, a variant which recognizes the range of potential audiences for this type of film. But it would be wrong to insist that *Carrington* was disowned by the *Daily Mail* simply because it was a different sort of film to *A Room with a View*. Again, it is questions of interpretation and reception on which we need to focus. After all, while *Room* could be celebrated by the right in terms of craftsmanship, good taste, and reticence about sexuality, Monk could still read it as a 'queered, gender-scrambled, deeply ambiguous celebration of female desire'. *Carrington* offers an equally seductive display of good taste in its *mise-en-scène*, yet the *Daily Mail* found its subject-matter immoral, while Monk thought it fell short 'of its radical sexual ambitions'.[122]

In their different ways, all these interpretations of the pleasures, politics, and aesthetics of heritage films propose that these are self-consciously nationalistic dramas, although precisely what that means will depend on the interpretation.

---

[118] Pidduck, 'Elizabeth and Shakespeare in Love', 135.
[119] Andrew Roberts, 'They Hated the Family . . . ', *Daily Mail* (9 June 1995), 20–1.
[120] Monk, 'Sexuality and the Heritage', 33.
[121] Roberts, 'They Hated the Family', 20–1.
[122] Monk, 'Sexuality and the Heritage', 34, 33.

For Norman Stone and those on the right, heritage films are to be celebrate their joyously patriotic take on a traditional, authentic, indigenous Englishn. .. For Tana Wollen and those on the left, that same nostalgic take is problematic for the way in which it promotes the out-moded and elite cultural values and social relationships of a country-house version of Englishness, 'a certain sense of Englishness that . . . should have no place in the future'.[123] On behalf of the revisionists, Richard Dyer depoliticizes the fine aesthetics of both the country house and the heritage film, promoting the sheer enjoyment of 'the appearance of old things', while Claire Monk takes the equally radical view that heritage films do not simply reproduce a traditional English identity, but provide 'spaces in which identities . . . are shifting, fluid and heterogeneous'.[124] In these films, she argues, 'Englishness is blatantly a *construct*, a product of cross-cultural masquerade, intrinsically impure'.[125] She might add that it is perfectly possible to read these films as decidedly ironic perspectives on traditional Englishness and the culture of privilege, rather than as straightlaced celebrations of those values.

REWORKING OLD ARGUMENTS

It would of course be entirely disingenuous of me were I to present this debate over the interpretation of heritage films without acknowledging my own interventions in the debate. In 'Re-presenting the National Past', I argued for the ambivalence of heritage films, acknowledging that they could be read *both* as conservative, nostalgic, escapist texts, *and* as much more liberal dramas.[126] In particular, I argued that the plots and *mise-en-scène* of 1980s' heritage films seemed to pull in different directions, the plots more liberal in intent, the visual display of heritage property much more conservative, apparently celebrating the culture of privilege and the architecture and landscapes of wealth. It's certainly possible, as Monk does, to read 'Re-presenting the National Past' as in the end favouring a reading of the films as conservative, nostalgic, escapist texts, even though, like her, my intention was to present the films as a 'mixture of conservatism *and* progressiveness'.[127]

Monk is undoubtedly correct to argue that my approach in this paper, primarily one of textual analysis, led me to imply a passive consumerist spectator of heritage films, 'helplessly in thrall to the spectacle of the text rather than an active producer of meaning'.[128] But I am less persuaded by her argument that 'Re-

---

[123] Anon., 'An English Inheritance' (editorial), *Sight and Sound*, 1/2 (1991), 3.

[124] Monk, 'Sexuality and the Heritage', 122.   [125] Ibid. 120.

[126] Higson, 'Re-presenting the National Past'; see also Higson, 'The Heritage Film and British Cinema'; John Hill, in *British Cinema in the 1980s*, argues a very similar position, sticking remarkably closely to the agenda established by the two pieces just cited. See also Andy Medhurst's discussions of *Restoration* (1996) and *Topsy-Turvy*, in 'Dressing the Part' and 'The Mike-Ado' respectively.

[127] Monk, 'Sexuality and the Heritage', 122.

[128] Monk, 'The Heritage Film and Gendered Spectatorship', 3.

presenting the National Past' 'allowed no space for the ambiguity and polysemy of heritage film texts'.[129] Given that one of my central arguments concerned what I called the ambivalence of the heritage film, even if I was not entirely consistent, it is surely a very reductive reading that can accuse me of such a monolithic view of heritage films. In fact, to be fair to Tana Wollen, whom I quoted above to illustrate a fairly uncomplicated leftist reading of heritage films, I should point out that she too acknowledges that 'there are strains in these fictions'. She too therefore allows a small space in her argument for ambivalence: 'Although these fictions are predominantly nostalgic, at the heart of their wistful sumptuousness there are occasional hints of something rotten . . .'[130]

In 'Re-presenting the National Past', I also argued that the term heritage cinema was appropriate because the culture of heritage conservation was so central to the way the films in question worked, overwhelming the narrative interest in liberal union, social change, and boundary transgression. At this stage, the key text for understanding heritage culture was Patrick Wright's *On Living in an Old Country*, whose arguments became central to the leftist cultural critique of heritage films.[131] In a later paper, 'The Heritage Film and British Cinema', published in 1996, I acknowledged that I had not allowed enough room for the revisionist and feminist readings advanced by Light, Monk, Dyer, and others.[132] By this stage, Wright's anxieties about the heritage industry had also been displaced by Raphael Samuel's much more positive appraisal of heritage culture in *Theatres of Memory*.[133] Even so, I concluded that films like *A Room with a View* and *Howards End* were still 'promoted and circulated within the culture precisely as heritage films, and not as woman's pictures or queer dramas'.[134] I went on to claim that 'both positive and negative critics of the films have treated them as paeans to a particular vision of England: this is the dominant view of them that has circulated in print and on television'.[135]

Looking back, this conclusion seems overstated. It is patently not the case that the costume dramas I had in mind were promoted primarily as heritage films rather than woman's pictures; indeed, the dominant promotional image for the vast majority of heritage films is precisely the sort of romantic image, often of a young heterosexual couple, that one associates with the classical woman's picture (Fig. 12). There is usually some element of heritage culture present too, but it is generally the romantic image that holds sway. The important point here is that the same film can circulate in different contexts, in which different senses may be made of its subject-matter and promotional packaging. The dominance of a particular reading will depend on the process of reception as much as the details of the film text or promotional copy—and the analyst's reading, mine or anyone else's, is just another reading.

---

[129] Monk, 'The Heritage Film and Gendered Spectatorship', 3.
[130] Wollen, 'Over our Shoulders', 185, 182.   [131] Wright, *On Living in an Old Country*.
[132] Higson, 'The Heritage Film and British Cinema'.
[133] Samuel, *Theatres of Memory*.
[134] Higson, 'The Heritage Film and British Cinema', 245.   [135] Ibid. 247.

MERCHANT IVORY PRODUCTIONS *for* GOLDCREST *Presents*

MAGGIE SMITH · DENHOLM ELLIOTT · JUDI DENCH · SIMON CALLOW
HELENA BONHAM CARTER · JULIAN SANDS · DANIEL DAY LEWIS

E. M. FORSTER'S

A Room with a View

Fabia Drake · Patrick Godfrey · Rupert Graves · Joan Henley and Rosemary Leach
Directed by James Ivory
Produced by Ismail Merchant
Screenplay by Ruth Prawer-Jhabvala · Photography by Tony Pierce-Roberts · Music by Richard Robbins · Edited by Humphrey Dixon

12. Foregrounding romance: the main promotional image used for *A Room with a View*

TEXTUAL AMBIVALENCE

To appreciate the meaningfulness of any text, I would argue, it is important to acknowledge its necessary ambivalence. Thus, although I've reworked my earlier arguments in various ways, I would still maintain that it is productive to view heritage films in terms of a tension between drama and *mise-en-scène*, between what they articulate narratively and what they present visually. This is not to deny that the films can be read in other ways too—that *mise-en-scène*, for instance, can be read as expressive of narrative themes. It is on the contrary to suggest that this is one way of responding to the potential meaningfulness of the films. At the level of the *image*, in so many costume dramas and period films, an exclusive, elite, English version of national heritage is displayed in all its well-tended finery. Visually, the impression is that England is a wonderful, desirable place of tradition and privilege. At the level of the *narrative*, as noted in the previous chapter, that heritage is often unstable, at risk, in disarray; social and cultural traditions are exposed as repressive; privilege is revealed as exploitation. So many of the films insistently scratch away at the idea of an essential England, noting the instability, the flux in identity, the hybrid quality of Englishness. Many of the films also dramatize the dissolution of a particular version of England and Englishness, the decay and the decadence of aristocratic life and its hold on the reins of power, or the loss of inheritance. In this sense, the narratives of the films seem much more radical, questioning the desirability of the lifestyle of those who inhabit these spaces.

But where the narratives often seem to encourage a critique of privilege and tradition, and to acknowledge cultural fluidity, impermanence, and change, the visuals equally often seem to encourage a nostalgic delight in images of wealth and antiquity. At the level of the image, narrative instability is frequently over-whelmed by the alluring spectacle of iconographic stability, permanence, and grandeur, providing an impression of an unchanging, traditional, and always delightful and desirable England. This is Heritage England, where social differ-ence, but also the possibility of making connections across social boundaries, is replaced by social deference, each person in their allotted place and transgression forbidden. The attention to visual pleasure, and to spectacular displays of the iconography of the past, can trouble even the most self-consciously liberal films, as Lizzie Francke points out in a review of *Orlando*: 'the overladen visual style per-versely turns the film into a celebration of the cultural heritage that Orlando in her liberated female state must reject'.[136]

Heritage films can also seem ambivalent in the way in which they appropriate both private and public space, both the local and the national. It is for this reason that they are sometimes referred to as intimate epics. As with the relation between narrative and spectacle, so the apparent tension between the intimate and the epic captures something of the complexity of the films, which itself encourages and enables diverse interpretations. While binary oppositions can often limit the play of meaning, I want to persevere with the opposition for a moment. On the one hand, as Light, Monk, and others suggest, these are intimate films, personal stories, private romances, which take place in domestic settings (Fig. 13). To that extent, they are woman's pictures, female-centred narratives, with a female point of view (or else they are male melodramas, or gay fictions, and may thus still be consid-ered *feminine* texts). They are films in which emotionality is stressed, films that, as Richard Dyer so persuasively demonstrates, make you cry.[137]

On the other hand, these narratives are played out in the official, public space of national history, in the stately homes and picturesque landscapes of the National Trust and English Heritage, the details authentically reproduced on an epic scale. This is what is alluded to by left- and right-wing critics alike, by both Tana Wollen and Norman Stone. Engaging with canonical literary culture, the (intimate) epic invokes the more masculine, educational values of the historical film as much as the feminine pleasures and playfulness of the costume drama. Their independent, strong-minded, and often rebellious protagonists in search of personal fulfilment are held in check by the repressiveness of the national char-acter, and their adherence to the traditions of duty, propriety, and public image; emotional expression is restrained by elegant decorum.

There is clearly a tension here, but it is a productive tension, since the heritage film draws on both tendencies, intermixes both strands. Thus on the one hand emotionality is always restrained (that is its poignancy in English cinema), and on the other hand, the epic quality, the public space of national history, is always

---

[136] Lizzie Francke, 'Orlando', *Sight and Sound*, 3/3 (1993), 48.   [137] Dyer, 'Feeling English'.

13. Romance in *Sense and Sensibility*

personalized. The overtly political is occluded in most of these films, appearing
only as an intrusion in what are at heart stories of thwarted love affairs (the arrest
of Lord Risley for soliciting a soldier in *Maurice*, the fascist sympathies of Lord
Darlington in *The Remains of the Day*, the memories of the First World War in
Mrs Dalloway). The emphasis on the pleasures of costume and interior design
ensures that political context is often reduced to decorative spectacle. On the other
hand, the desire for authenticity and the attention to historical detail requires the
camera to stand back from the love stories in order to show the bigger picture. If
at one level, these films are explorations of personal identity, the explorations
always take place in a national setting, of Englishness and its others; desire is
thus regulated by national convention, but convention must also respond to the
pressure of desire. It is precisely in this alignment of personal identity with
national experience that the latter becomes muddied and unstable, and therefore
open to transformation (a drama that is played out quite literally in *Chariots of
Fire*).

There is also a sense in which locality and setting themselves are caught up in
the interplay of the intimate and the epic. On the one hand, there is the (intimate)
regional specificity of semi-rural southern England, the primary location of so
many heritage films. On the other hand, there is the (epic) hegemonic regional-
ism of English history, in which the 'South Country' becomes the nation. But if
the local always seems overwhelmed by national tradition, the national is always
reduced to local tradition (the hunt at Hetton Hall in *A Handful of Dust* (1987),

the teeth in the tree in *Howards End*, the precision of the intertitle introducing Ham Spray House in *Carrington*).

NOSTALGIA AND ENGLISHNESS

Central to the leftist cultural critique of heritage films—and to my earlier work—was the argument that those films looked nostalgically to the past. The argument seemed particularly appropriate when applied to films about the upper and upper middle classes in the late nineteenth and early twentieth centuries. In the terms of the leftist cultural critique, nostalgia was a problem, indicating a flight from the present into a conservative vision of the past. The nostalgic vision, it was argued, imagined a time when England was great, and was peopled by lovable upper-class eccentrics. It was a privileged class vision of the national past, secured in images of exclusive and private heritage property. Erased from this vision, it was argued, were all the problems of class exploitation, patriarchy, and imperialism.

It is important to recognize, however, that the novels of Forster, James, Waugh, and others, which provide the sources for many of these films, have some edge to them of satire or ironic social critique, and the films in various ways try to reproduce this sensibility. But it seems equally clear that it is the pictorial qualities of the exotic period settings which have attracted the film-makers as much as the moral critiques implicit in their dramas. As a consequence, that which in the source narratives is abhorrent or problematic often becomes prettified, elegant, and seductive in the films. Even those films which develop an ironic narrative of the past often seem to end up celebrating and legitimating the spectacle of one class and one cultural tradition and identity at the expense of others through the discourse of authenticity, and the obsession with the visual splendours of period detail.

If we concentrate for a moment on E. M. Forster's novels, we should note first of all that they are centrally concerned with Englishness—but rarely is English identity framed as permanent and unchanging. On the contrary, Forster argues for a liberal-humanist refashioning of Englishness, rather than a simple assumption of an already formed national identity. The emphasis on the image and on period detail in the films of his novels can produce a very different effect, however. Thus, in *Maurice*, Forster savagely derides as sham the suburban middle-class Englishness of the Halls, yet their household in the film is rendered desirable in its accumulation of the antique collector's signs of Edwardian period style. As one critic put it, 'the society which Forster is criticising becomes almost involuntarily an object of veneration'.[138] This same shift in sensibility can be seen in many of the quality literary adaptations of the 1980s and 1990s. In the adaptation of Evelyn Waugh's *A Handful of Dust*, for instance, the owners of Hetton Hall constantly worry about the unfashionable qualities of their vast gothic pile, and the money

---

[138] Alan Hollinghurst, 'Suppressive Nostalgia', *Times Literary Supplement* (6 Nov. 1987), 1225.

it takes to maintain it, but in the film the hall is positively alluring and resplendent. As one reviewer commented, 'the Duke of Norfolk's country seat, Carlton Towers [which stood in for Hetton Hall] . . . is the star of stars'.[139] The pleasures of pictorialism thus seem to block the radical intentions of the narrative.

As I noted in Chapter 1, the desire for period authenticity in heritage films means that many of the literary adaptations transform contemporary social satires and comedies of manners into period pieces. It is often this transformation that sets the seductive images of period splendour at odds with the narrative ironies. Raphael Samuel argues that a similar process can be seen at work in the 1987 adaptation of Charles Dickens's *Little Dorrit*: 'the film's preoccupation with period effects is singularly at variance with Dickens himself, who was notoriously cavalier in his treatment of history and contemptuous of notions of heritage'.[140] Samuel goes on to claim that Dickens was not a period novelist, but drew ideas, images, and characterizations from different historical periods, self-consciously fabricating the fiction and creating 'a fantasy of Victorian England'.[141]

In 'Re-presenting the National Past', I explored the implications of this transformation of contemporary novels into period films by looking at the adaptations of some of Forster's novels. Although Forster is clearly a writer 'who manifests and is attentive to the social and historical context out of which he derives',[142] I argued that he is less a novelist of place than of ideas and manners. Place, setting, and *mise-en-scène* in Forster are dealt with in very general terms, rather than observed with the obsessively detailed eye of the art directors of the films adapted from his novels. The novels explore what lies beneath the surface of things, satirizing the pretentious and the superficial, and especially those who are overly concerned with keeping up appearances rather than acting according to the passions of the heart. The films, however, construct such a delightfully glossy visual surface that it is often much more difficult to attend to the ironic perspective and the narrative of social criticism.

A Room with a View, for instance, can be read as a satire on the repressions of the middle classes and a reaffirmation of generative, life-giving forces. As a critique of Victorian values, it may well be nostalgic for the emotional simplicity and libidinal spontaneity of the fairy-tale romance. But in the film, Maggie Smith plays the repressive life-denying figure of Catherine Bartlett so powerfully, so charismatically, that it becomes once more attractive. The film delights in her performance of Victorian primness, as it delights in the equally excessive performances of Simon Callow and Daniel Day-Lewis. Similarly in *Maurice*, Clive Durham, played by Hugh Grant, becomes for me a far more attractive and fascinating character than Maurice himself, partly because of Grant's boyish good looks and sublimely camp performance full of exaggerated gestures and mannerisms. Yet it is Maurice's sensibility that we are invited to share; indeed, the film purports to

---

[139] Alexander Walker, 'A Handful of Dust' (review), *Evening Standard* (9 June 1988), 32.
[140] Raphael Samuel, 'Docklands Dickens', in *Theatres of Memory*, 409.
[141] Ibid.
[142] Malcolm Bradbury, 'Introduction', in Malcolm Bradbury (ed.), *Forster: A Collection of Essays* (Englewood Cliffs, NJ: Prentice-Hall, 1966), 3.

criticize all that Clive eventually represents. Clive is, in the final analysis, horrified by Maurice's sexuality; he cannot confront it, preferring instead, like Catherine Bartlett, to save face, to maintain a respectable appearance, to look the part.

Forster's satirical impulse is also undercut in *A Room With a View*. On one level, it is there, for instance in George's description of Cecil to Lucy: '[Cecil] wants you for a possession, something to look at, like a painting or an ivory box, something to own and display. He doesn't want you to be real and to think and live . . .' But in the end, the film-makers adopt Cecil's pretensions, displaying the possessions (the props) they have accumulated and making every effort to fashion each image 'like a painting'. The film-makers want to criticize people who have a fear of being seen doing the wrong thing, encapsulated in Cecil's anxious, furtive looks about him before he kisses Lucy, his fiancée, for the first time. The other side of this fear is a love of being seen and admired by the right kind of people, as when Cecil looks around the gathered society at his mother's house for the nods of appreciation at his good taste as Lucy plays the piano. Yet arguably the film itself circulates in society in the same way, desperately wanting to be viewed by the right kinds of audiences, ceaselessly displaying the good taste of its producers in just as knowing a way as Cecil.

Sometimes the emphasis on the surface, on the image, can suggest exactly the superficiality of the characters their novelistic creators surely intended. Thus, in *A Handful of Dust*, the central protagonists indeed seem shallow, emotionally empty, and materialistic, desperate to maintain appearances. Except that all that these figures represent, and the spaces that they inhabit, are so lovingly, beautifully, and seductively laid out that they seem desirable and lovable. The effort to achieve period authenticity, the heritage impulse, frequently seems to recreate the past as the perfect nostalgic place. The satirical narrative on the other hand must disturb the sense of perfection, upset the pleasing heritage package.

Forster's novels were themselves of course nostalgic narratives, but the desire for period authenticity tends to refashion the nature of the nostalgia. Forster yearned for a mid-Victorian golden age rather than for the Edwardian present. His novels respond to a felt crisis in liberal-humanist values and play out a pastoral concern for a passing rural England, one encroached on by industrialization, suburbia, and London society. They demonstrate 'a profound, almost mystical, response to the English countryside and its living embodiment of the past [but] perceive it to be in the process of radical and destructive change'.[143] At the end of *Maurice*, as Maurice and Alec go off into the greenwood, Maurice realizes that 'they must live outside class. . . . But England belonged to them. That, besides companionship, was their reward. Her air and sky were theirs, not the timorous millions' who own stuffy little boxes, but never their own souls'.[144] England, in other words, is a pastoral scene without the trappings of class celebrated in the films, but the scene is already impaired by the spread of suburbia. The Forster

[143] Peter Widdowson, *E. M. Forster's 'Howards End': Fiction as History* (London: Sussex University Press and Chatto & Windus, 1977), 58.
[144] E. M. Forster, *Maurice* (London: Penguin, 1972; 1st publ. 1908), 208–9.

films, on the other hand, look back nostalgically to an Edwardian golden age. The greenwood of Merchant–Ivory's *Maurice* and the ruralism of their *A Room with a View*, the pastoral community of Summer Street, and the sincerity, companionship and moral support of the bourgeois family are offered as part and parcel of the period they depict; they have not yet become the lost objects of nostalgic desire. The pastoral of the films therefore invents a new golden age, one that the novels depict as already tainted and unstable.

In some films, the nostalgic perspective is built into the narrative itself, since the films purport to present to us the reminiscences of one of the protagonists as an older man or woman. This is true of the flashback narratives of *The Remains of the Day* and *Mrs Dalloway*—but in these cases, even the 'present' is firmly set in the past. In *Chariots of Fire* and *Another Country*, on the other hand, the main narrative is ostensibly remembered from the perspective of someone living in the 1980s, when the films were made. In *Another Country*, Guy Bennett, closeted in a dingy Moscow flat surrounded by the trappings of Englishness (a Harrods mug, a cricket ball, old school photographs), looks back on his last years at a highly privileged English public school during the 1930s. Here, as in *Maurice*, the nostalgic image of a perfect national past is deliberately set up, only to be destroyed by uncovering its shortcomings, especially its systematic exploitation and abuse of gay men. But at the same time, there is a lingering desire to celebrate that past in the loving recreation of the period piece. The film tries to contain this residual nostalgia by projecting the tale as Bennett's memory. But the vision of the past rapidly becomes the film's central diegesis, the range and scope of camera shots used suggesting that it is our vision rather than the partial vision of a character. Even before the possibility of a flashback is established, the title sequence creates a nostalgic perspective by cutting between a delightful English pastoral scene and the grey concrete of Bennett's Moscow apartment block. The tastefully melancholic music and the image of passing through a dark tunnel before being able to appreciate the full glory of the pastoral scene further underlines the sense of recalling a cherished but lost memory.

Narratives of nostalgia will very often return to a moment of stability and tranquillity as they themselves chart the process of decay, the fall from this utopian ideal. We are thus presented with both a narrative of loss, charting an imaginary historical trajectory from stability to instability, and at the same time a narrative of recovery, projecting the subject back into a comfortably closed past. *Another Country* illustrates just this complexity. At the end of the film, the journalist interviewing Bennett asks if he misses anything. Bennett hesitates; choral music fades in, and he replies, 'I miss the cricket!' End of film. The choral music here conjures up memories of the first scene of the flashback to the 1930s, a memorial service in the school quadrangle and the site of Bennett's first overdetermined gaze at his loved one, Harcourt, another boy at the school. Cricket also conjures up a specific memory, again of a particularly passionate exchange of looks between Bennett and Harcourt on the cricket field. If only those perfect scenes could have lasted forever, the system in place, homosexual desire able to live a secure, passionate, if closeted life! If only the past in all its perfection could have remained in place, unimpaired. But the film goes on to show that this image of perfection is indeed already impaired, the product of a militarily authoritarian system that is openly corrupt and exploitative.

In these films, however, the sense of impending narrative-historical loss is so often offset by the experience of spectacular visual pleasure. Their reconstructions of the national past feast on the spectacle of authentic objects, clothing, and other signs of an apparently secure heritage, contrasted with the often-fearful exoticism of other cultures. Thus even a film like *A Passage to India*, which purports to criticize British imperialism, shows the cinematic spectacle of the British in power. The theatricality of the Raj, and the epic sweep of the camera over an equally epic landscape and social class, is utterly seductive, potentially undermining all sense of critical distance and restoring the pomp of Englishness felt to be lacking in the present. Similarly, *Another Country*'s critique of the details of class power, and the whole system of privilege, inheritance, and tradition, is frequently almost smothered by the welter of period detail. As Cairns Craig puts it, 'the death of inheritance . . . is counteracted by the seeming permanence of the architecture, landscape and possessions that fill the screen'.[145] In *Maurice*, Forster describes Clive Durham's country house as on the verge of decay, rather than magnificent ('it struck [Maurice] once more how derelict it was, how unfit to set standards or control the future'[146]). In the film, the outhouses are decrepit, ladders are everywhere because the house is being repaired, and the sitting-room ceiling is leaking ('why is my house falling down?', asks Clive), but the crumbling inheritance is never foregrounded as much as the remaining magnificence of the house: the splendour of the society in place seems to me to undercut images of the last of England. Visual effect, the complete spectacle of the past, becomes an autonomous attraction in itself, once more displacing the narrational qualities of the *mise-en-scène*.

'The national past', argues Patrick Wright, 'is capable of finding splendour in old styles of political domination and of making an alluring romance out of atrocious colonial exploitation'.[147] The heritage film often seems to work in this way too, as it weaves its (often upper-class) romances around authentic period details. The *mise-en-scène* of power, the spectacle of privilege: so many of these films construct a fantasy of extravagance, decadence, promiscuity, and passion. Class, gender, and race relations, and the values of the ruling elites, are in effect re-presented as just so much *mise-en-scène*, elegantly displayed in splendid costumes, language, gestures, and all the props (the properties) of the everyday life of one or another class. The history of exploitation is effaced by spectacular presentation. The past becomes once more unproblematic, a haven from the difficulties of the present.

[145] Craig, 'Rooms without a View', 11.
[146] Forster, *Maurice*, 209.
[147] Wright, *On Living in an Old Country*, 254.

THE DEBATE CONTINUES

Throughout this chapter, I have insisted that there are different ways of making sense of heritage films. The argument I've just outlined is essentially that the films themselves are structured in such a way that they invite competing readings from their audiences, one appropriate to the image track, the other to the narrative line. If this is the case, no wonder then that some read the films as conservative (concentrating above all on the iconography) and others read them as liberal (foregrounding the narrative concerns of the film). Some critics are less than happy with this way of reading heritage films. Claire Monk, for instance, argues that the *mise-en-scène* of these films, far from challenging their narrative lines, or establishing a separate discourse of scenic display, actually plays its part in promoting the narrative concerns.[148] It is indeed possible to read the *mise-en-scène* of these films as narratively meaningful, indicating character traits and sensibilities, expressing the emotional intensity of the scene. From this point of view, props act not as spokespersons for the heritage industry but as symbolic indications of the inner life of the characters. Indeed, it seems to me perfectly feasible to argue that the films are ambivalent enough to be read in both ways, perhaps even at the same time.

The argument that heritage films provide a conservative flight away from the multicultural present, a nostalgic journey into the past, has also had its critics. It's certainly important to acknowledge that the nostalgic sensibility is itself profoundly ambivalent, involving as it does a dialogue between the imagined past and a vision of the present. It never simply talks about the past, and is always in effect a critique of the present, which is seen as lacking something desirable situated out of reach in the past. Nostalgia always implies there is something wrong with the present, but it doesn't necessarily speak from the point of view of right-wing conservatism. It can of course be used to flee from the troubled present into the imaginary stability and grandeur of the past. But it can also be used to comment on the inadequacies of the present from a more radical perspective.

The debates about heritage films will continue, because the films, like all texts, are capable of being read in different ways, and because different audiences will bring different values and interests into play when reading the films. I'll return to the richness of the reception process in my two case studies of *Howards End* and *Elizabeth*. Before I do that, however, I want to examine over the next two chapters the production context that enabled so many English heritage films and costume dramas to be made in the 1980s and 1990s, the ways in which the films were funded and marketed, and the audiences they reached.

---

[148] Claire Monk, 'Sex, Politics and the Past: Merchant–Ivory, the Heritage Film and its Critics in 1980s and 1990s Britain', unpublished MA dissertation, British Film Institute and Birkbeck College, 1994.

3
The Commercial Context of the
Heritage Film: Home Affairs

In spite of armloads of prizes and Austenmania, 'British cinema' doesn't really amount to much more than a niche-servicing industry and a precarious network of boutique producers, who are all heavily dependent on either Hollywood or European media empires for serious funding, and on UK television for small-scale investment. British cinema, with the best will in the world, is more a carefully contrived illusion than a serious industry.[1]

This chapter and the next deal with the commercial context of English costume dramas, the conditions under which those films were funded, produced, distributed, and exhibited, and the audiences they attracted in the 1980s and 1990s. My task is not to produce a comprehensive history of the British film industry in this period; instead, I'll be concentrating on those aspects of the industry that are pertinent to understanding the delicate economy of the heritage film.

Few would describe the production sector in these years as particularly viable or healthy, despite occasional critical and box-office successes, and periods in which a good number of films have been made. On the contrary, the production sector is best characterized as impoverished and highly fragmented, a cottage industry, with producers experiencing enormous difficulties in putting together workable budgets and appropriate distribution deals for the films they want to make. Compare this to the American film industry, which is distribution-led, by large, integrated companies, which are able to plough distribution revenue back into production. The impoverishment of the British production sector can be explained in terms of the disinterest of the UK financial sector in high-risk investment and the lack of corporate or equity funding; the relative smallness of the UK domestic market, making it difficult for British producers to recoup costs locally; the unintegrated structure of the production, distribution, and exhibition sectors in the UK; the dominance of the Hollywood majors both locally and globally and the consequent difficulty in securing adequate distribution for British films; and government policies incapable of reversing the situation.

1981 was a particularly low point, with no more than twenty-four British films being produced that year (about a tenth of the films released in the USA in the same year). Despite all the problems, however, the situation did improve noticeably over the next couple of decades. During the 1980s, the average number of

[1] Ian Christie, 'Will Lottery Money Assure the British Film Industry?', *New Statesman* (20 June 1997), 38.

films produced each year was around forty-six (despite a fall off in 1989); by the latter half of the 1990s, this had risen to around 100 films a year (although again there were marked dips in 1992 and 1998). Overall, almost twice as many films were made in the 1990s as in the 1980s. True, the average budget size in the 1990s (£4.95 million) was not much higher than the average in the 1980s (£4.12 million)—indeed, if prices are adjusted for inflation, then the average amount spent on each British film actually fell, from £7.28 million to £5.25 million. And if one would need to go back to the early 1960s to find as many films being made per year in the UK as were made in the late 1990s, 100 films a year is still only about one-fifth of the number of films released in the USA. Even so, more than 1,200 British feature films of one sort or another were produced across the two decades, and there were several identifiable and significant production trends and cycles.[2] What these statistics suggest is that, if we undoubtedly need to recognize the problems facing British film-makers across these two decades, we also need to understand what made it possible for this many films to be made and for the various identifiable production trends to emerge.

As we've seen, one of the most visible production trends in British film-making in this period was the quality costume drama, which did good business at the box office in the specialist and crossover markets, in the UK, but also in other territories, especially the USA. In other words, a good few productions that might be classed as heritage films were developed, and were seen by sometimes quite considerable audiences. Of course, such films constitute a niche market, but it is a market none the less. So while I want to look at the problems facing British producers, I also want to look at the solutions that enabled heritage films to be made and to reach a meaningful market. What exactly were the conditions under which this particular production trend emerged? And what was the nature of the economic base that supported this cultural development? One of the reasons why this particular production trend emerged, and was marked by identifiable cycles, was of course that occasional individual films were extremely successful given the size of their budget, inspiring others to put together similar packages that might exploit this proven market. So what sorts of funds were available for those who wanted to make such films? How were such films distributed, marketed, and exhibited? What sorts of releases were they given? And to what sorts of audiences were they addressed, who actually watched them, and how did those audiences compare with audiences for mainstream films?

One of the keys to understanding the relative longevity and success of this particular niche or production trend is the involvement of specialist American distributors. In other words, rather than constituting an obstacle to British film production, American distributors in this instance have been vital to its well-being. Rather than fighting clear of American involvement, British producers have

---

[2] Eddie Dyja (ed.), *BFI Film and Television Handbook 2002* (London: British Film Institute, 2001), table 1, 23; American statistics from MPAA Worldwide Market Research, '2000 US Economic Review', 9, on the Motion Picture Association of America website, at http://www.mpaa.org/useconomicreview.

been eager to secure their interest as early as possible in the packaging process, since such interest secures access to the world's most lucrative film market, and makes it easier to raise additional funds from other sources. Why then were American distributors interested in funding and distributing 'culturally English' costume dramas? In part, the answer to this question is that they recognized that some American audiences were interested in watching such films. More complexly, the answer to this question is bound up with the development of the mainstream and the specialized or art-house markets in the UK and the USA, and the recognition that, with proper handling, modestly budgeted films might cross over from the specialized to the mainstream market and produce sizeable profits for their distributors.

It is not just that a particular market has developed. More generally, audiences in the UK have grown quite dramatically since the mid-1980s, which has of course to some extent benefited all film-makers. In the early 1980s, cinema admissions continued their dramatic post-war decline, falling from 101 million in 1980 to 54 million in 1984. But from then on they picked up considerably, rising back to 100 million by 1991, and 142.5 million by 2000.[3] This increase in audience size has been attributed to the development of purpose-built multiplexes as much as anything else. Thus although there is little difference in the number of cinema sites between 1984 and 1999 (660 to 692), the number of actual screens has increased dramatically, from 1,271 to 2,758 (at the same time, it's worth noting that there are now over 37,000 screens in the USA!).[4] Although these screens are dominated by mainstream American fare, there is inevitably some pay-off for English costume dramas.

The interest of American companies in such films also needs to be seen in the context of global developments in the media industries. The American major Time-Warner's annual report for 1989 stated: 'No serious competitor could hope for any long-term success unless, building on a secure home base, it achieved a major presence in all of the world's important markets.'[5] Film historian Tino Balio explains that, 'In practice, this meant that [American] companies upgraded international operations to a privileged position by expanding "horizontally" to tap emerging markets worldwide, by expanding "vertically" to form alliances with independent producers to enlarge their rosters, and by "partnering" with foreign investors to secure new sources of funding.'[6] American investment in relatively modest English costume dramas is just one small strand to such developments in the media economy.

    [3] Dyja (ed.), *BFI Handbook 2002*, table 13, 37.

    [4] Ibid., table 15, 38; US figure from MPAA, '2000 US Economic Review', 21.

    [5] Time Warner, *1989 Annual Report* (New York: Time Warner Inc., 1989), 1, quoted in Tino Balio, 'Adjusting to the New Global Economy: Hollywood in the 1990s', in Albert Moran (ed.), *Film Policy: International, National and Regional Perspectives* (London: Routledge, 1996), 23.

    [6] Tino Balio, '"A Major Presence in All the World's Important Markets": The Globalization of Hollywood in the 1990s', in Steve Neale and Murray Smith (eds.), *Contemporary Hollywood Cinema* (London: Routledge, 1998), 58.

Another key factor in sustaining the costume drama production trend has been the relative availability of state subsidies of one sort or another for modestly budgeted films with a British or European base. While some argue that subsidies limit the horizons of film-makers, it is undeniably the case that a number of the costume dramas produced in the 1980s and 1990s benefited from such funding. The growth of so-called ancillary markets—video, cable, satellite, terrestrial television, and so on—and the development of pre-sales fund-raising has also been important in creating a reasonably viable funding base and market for modestly budgeted, specialized films. The financial interest of UK terrestrial broadcasters in such films has of course been crucial to this sector of the production industry, with Channel 4 paving the way in the early 1980s. A tiny handful of British-based companies—such as Goldcrest in the 1980s, PolyGram Filmed Entertainment in the mid-1990s, and the three lottery-funded franchises in the late 1990s—have occasionally managed to establish a sufficient capital base to build up something resembling a production schedule rather than a series of one-off packages. Then there have been a series of much smaller independent production companies that have either specialized in or at least developed a number of English costume dramas, including Merchant Ivory Productions, Renaissance Films, and Working Title. But most producers have struggled from one production to the next, unable to plan for a slate of films to play off against each other, each film having to stand on its own terms. Such instability has dogged British film production throughout the period in question.

My investigation of these issues is split between this chapter, which concentrates mainly though not exclusively on the British end of things, and the next chapter, which concentrates on American involvement and interest in the English heritage film.

THE CROSSOVER FILM: BETWEEN THE MAINSTREAM AND THE ART-HOUSE

As far as the Hollywood-oriented film business is concerned, there are today three basic categories of film production and distribution. At one extreme is the mainstream studio film, produced primarily by the Hollywood majors, with big budgets and big stars, and addressed to what the industry likes to think of as its core 15- to 24-year-old cinemagoing audience. At the other extreme is the low-budget, specialized or art-house film, produced by small independent companies, addressed to what the film trade perceives as niche audiences. In between, and drawing on both, there is the crossover film. The traditional view of the Hollywood studios is that only the mainstream film makes economic sense, since it responds to the laws of supply and demand. To that extent, the mainstream film is understood as commercial, or as market-driven, since it is deemed to be based on a secure understanding of the sorts of films that the most frequent cinemagoers desire and that will therefore generate the most profit.

The specialized or art-house film on the other hand is generally characterized as being driven by a cultural imperative rather than the logic of the market, operating according to a European model in which greater emphasis is placed on cultural value than on market performance. Such films have been dependent on subsidies introduced as a means of shoring up national film production in the face of American cultural imperialism and market dominance.[7] They are traditionally thought of as too 'difficult' for mainstream distribution, while their audience is thought of as more educated, more sophisticated, and more adult than the mainstream. Traditionally, this is a market in which the majors are uninterested and which they don't serve well—not least because the profit margins are seen as too small. More recently, however, the industry as a whole has increasingly recognized that the specialized film market can be commercially viable. Thus in the late 1970s and early 1980s, some of the American majors ran 'classics' divisions to exploit this particular niche. After a lull, they moved again in the mid-1990s to establish their own in-house 'specialty labels', though primarily to chase the crossover market rather than strictly the specialized or art-house market. I shall explore these developments in more detail in the next chapter.

Traditionally, art cinema has been defined in cultural terms, in terms of film form, film style, and subject-matter, but also in terms of estimations of cultural worth—as a *Sight and Sound* editorial put it, the art film constitutes 'more intelligent adult fare'.[8] But it is clear that the difference of the art-house or specialized film from the mainstream film can also be defined in economic terms. In this case, we might focus on the size of a film's budget, the scale of its production values, and the amount of profit it achieves or is expected to achieve. Equally, we might focus on the way a film is marketed, who its target audience is deemed to be, and the type of release it is given (how many prints, what sorts of venues, wide or narrow release, and so on—thus for *Variety*, in a statement that will surprise many, 'an arthouse pic may be defined as any indie specialty title that opens on fewer than 600 screens [in the USA]'[9]). Then again, we might look at the actual audiences the film reached and the way it was received and made sense of by critics and others. Authorship and agency play a part too. This might be in cultural terms, where the director is thought of as an auteur or artist, who can stamp his or her authorial signature on the film. Or it might be in economic terms, since particular production companies, distributors, and exhibitors concentrate on the specialized or art-house film.

But if there are clear differences between the mainstream film and the specialized film, there has always been something in between, which draws on aspects of both. Hollywood has always produced the occasional middle-brow prestige film

---

[7] Nick Roddick, 'If the United States Spoke Spanish, We would have an Industry . . .', in Martin Auty and Nick Roddick (eds.), *British Cinema Now* (London: British Film Institute, 1985), 3–18; Thomas Elsaesser, *New German Cinema: A History* (London: Macmillan, 1989).

[8] Anon., 'Distributing in the Dark', *Sight and Sound*, 10/11 (2000), 3.

[9] Dan Cox and Jonathan Bing, 'Art Pic Overkill?', *Varietyextra online*, at Variety.com, updated 4 Oct. 2000.

that is designed to succeed commercially while at the same time cloaking itself in cultural value. In the 1980s, medium-budget prestige films like *A Passage to India* (1984) and *Gandhi* (1982), both backed by major British and American corporations, fell into this category. In the 1990s, it is what have come to be termed crossover films, productions such as *Howards End* (1992), *The English Patient* (1996), and *Shakespeare in Love* (1998), all of which achieved significant box-office success in the North American market. Such films are driven by both the commercialism and the market imperative of the mainstream studio film and the cultural imperative and artistic values of the specialized film. Their budgets fall between the two stools too, and they frequently draw on funding sources associated with both sectors. And crucially, they are designed to be distributed on both the low-budget, often subsidized, art-house circuit and the mainstream, multiplex circuits, and to appeal to their different audiences.

Thus, according to one trade analyst, where the specialist film appeals 'mostly to older audiences . . . and [the] mainstream [film] . . . mostly to the young cinemagoers who form the bulk of the cinema audience', the crossover film appeals to 'mixed audiences', drawn from both the other sectors.[10] But even then there is a niche element, since 'crossover films tend to appeal to slightly older audiences, bringing together the older element of the mainstream audience with the art-house audience'.[11] In the 1980s and 1990s, the majority of British films were low-budget productions with limited market appeal. The most successful in commercial terms were those that crossed over between the two sectors, 'mid-budget productions that appealed to mixed audiences comprised of both art-house and mainstream elements'.[12] It makes eminent sense for British film-makers to concentrate on such fare and thereby to address audiences that are not normally addressed by the mainstream film: here is a good example of product differentiation, of carving out a niche market relatively untouched by the majors—at least until recently.

What this characterization of the industry as split between mainstream, crossover, and specialized production takes no account of is the low-budget indigenous genre film. Once the staple of most national cinemas, neither the USA nor the UK any longer has much room for such activity. If such fare is still made in the USA or the UK, it is destined for television or straight-to-video release. In the case of the UK, the fragmentation of the production sector and the relative smallness of the domestic theatrical market militate against such film-making: it is no longer perceived as commercially viable to make low-budget genre films since they will no longer be able to recoup their costs in the domestic market. It might be argued that the cycle of gangster films that followed in the wake of *Lock, Stock and Two Smoking Barrels* (1998) represented a rebirth of the genre film— except that such films also have to be able to succeed internationally, where they

---

[10] Terry Ilott, *Budgets and Markets: A Study of the Budgeting and Marketing of European Films* (London: Routledge, 1996), 37.
[11] Ibid. 39   [12] Ibid. 19, 28.

can be sold less as genre films than as quirky British films, playing on the national cinema label.

While there has always been something in between the mainstream and the specialized film, since the mid-1980s an industry designed to exploit the potential of the crossover film has developed. This too has situated itself somewhere between the majors and the small independents. In the mid-1980s, the mini-major emerged, with companies like Orion in the USA, and Goldcrest in the UK. In the late 1980s and early 1990s, it was the aggressive independents like Miramax that caught the eye and played the market most successfully. In the mid-1990s, the majors moved in, either establishing their own niche distribution outfits, like Sony Classics, or buying up the most successful independents and maintaining them as in-house 'designer labels', as in the case of Disney buying Miramax. The UK equivalent would be the relationship PolyGram established with smaller independent production companies such as Working Title and Revolution.[13]

English heritage films of the 1980s and 1990s are best understood precisely as crossover films. On the one hand, some intellectuals routinely dismiss them as middle-brow because they typically fall between the populist studio film and the high-brow art-house film, becoming neither one thing nor the other. On the other hand, industrially, they fit perfectly into the model of the crossover film identified above. Clearly, their budgets and their aspirations vary. At one end, there are the comparatively large budgets of films like *A Passage to India* ($15 million), *Shadowlands* (1993, £15 million), *Rob Roy* (1995, £16 million), *Braveheart* (1995, £35 million), *The English Patient* ($27 million), *Hamlet* (1996, £11.1 million), *Elizabeth* (1998, £13 million), *Shakespeare in Love* (£15 million), *Topsy-Turvy* (1999, £13.5 million), and *The Claim* (2000, £12.5 million), much more clearly addressed to the mainstream, but in most cases still finding a place in art-houses.[14] At the other end are films with much smaller budgets, and a greater attachment to art-house production values and sensibilities, films like *The Draughtsman's Contract* (1982, £300,000), *Another Country* (1984, £1.6 million), *A Room with a View* (1986, £2.3 million), *Enchanted April* (1991, £1.1 million), *Edward II* (1991, £850,000), *Mrs Brown* (1997, £1 million), and *Mrs Dalloway* (1997, £2.6 million).[15] In the middle are such films as *Chariots of Fire* (1981), *The Madness of King George* (1995), *Where Angels Fear to Tread* (1991), all costing £3–4 million; *Howards End* (£4 million);

[13] Alice Rawsthorn, 'Put to the Screen Test', *Financial Times* (30 Aug. 1997), 7.

[14] Marjorie Bilbow, 'Thorn EMI Proves the Key to Critical and Commercial Success of Lean's India', *Screen International* (16 Mar. 1985), 24; Nick Thomas (ed.), *BFI Film and Television Handbook 1995* (London: British Film Institute, 1994), 29; Eddie Dyja (ed.), *BFI Film and Television Handbook 1996* (London: British Film Institute, 1995), 29; showbizdata.com; Dyja (ed.), *BFI Film and Television Handbook 1998* (London: British Film Institute, 1997), 26; Dyja (ed.), *BFI Film and Television Handbook 1999* (London: British Film Institute, 1998), 41, 18; Dyja (ed.), *BFI Film and Television Handbook 2000* (London: British Film Institute, 1999), 20, 22.

[15] Robert Brown, 'From a View to a Death', *Monthly Film Bulletin*, 49/586 (1982), 255; Jake Eberts and Terry Ilott, *My Indecision is Final: The Rise and Fall of Goldcrest Films* (London: Faber & Faber, 1990), 132, 571; David Leafe (ed.), *BFI Film and Television Handbook 1993* (London: British Film Institute, 1992), 22, 23; Dyja (ed.), *BFI Handbook 1998*, 20, 26; Dyja (ed.), *BFI Handbook 2002*, 27.

Jude (1996, £5.7 million); *The Remains of the Day* (1993), *Emma* (1996), *Orlando* (1992), *Wilde* (1997), *An Ideal Husband* (1999), and *Mansfield Park* (1999), all costing £6–7 million; *The House of Mirth* (2000, £7.5 million); *The Wings of the Dove* (1997, £8.7 million); and *Sense and Sensibility* (1996), *Plunkett and Macleane* (1999), and *The Golden Bowl* (2000), all costing around £9.5 million.[16] It is worth noting that fewer low-budget but more mid-budget costume dramas were made in the late 1990s—and that even £9 million could be seen by the industry as a low budget.[17]

Regardless of budget, most of the films discussed in this book were marketed in such a way that they might break out of the art-house into the multiplex, or at least achieve a wider release than the specialized film with specifically limited appeal. The success of films that make up this production trend has been their ability to take certain attributes of the specialized sector and to market them to a wider audience: this is precisely the crossover strategy. The two most significant achievements in these terms in the 1980s were *Chariots of Fire* and *A Room with a View*, both at the lower end of the production budget list, but major successes at the box office, reaping considerable dividends in the USA; both were multiple Oscar winners too. *Chariots* took over $62 million in the American market, making it the highest grossing English-language film imported from Europe until the 1990s (Fig. 14).[18] As Jake Eberts of Goldcrest, who provided development money for the film, recalled,

The success of *Chariots* . . . was to be enormously important in raising the profile of the film industry in Britain and was to make it a lot easier for producers to secure funds from hitherto sceptical financial institutions. It also helped raise the profile of British films abroad, especially in the United States, and was to open many doors for us that had previously been closed. *Chariots* was a breakthrough—that much was not media hype.[19]

A Room with a View was the tenth highest grossing English-language European film in the 1980s, taking $25 million in the USA, and more than $68 million worldwide. It too 'boost[ed] confidence in the UK production industry'.[20] Other English costume dramas grossing over £20 million in the USA and over £3 million in the UK in the 1980s include *Tess*, *The Elephant Man*, *The French Lieutenant's Woman*, and *A Passage to India*. Even more impressive were *Gandhi*, which took $52.8 million in the USA and £7.7 million in the UK, and Hugh Hudson's follow-up to

---

[16] Anthony Smith, 'Where Chariots should Lead', *Sunday Times* (4 April 1982), cutting; Leafe (ed.), *BFI Handbook 1993*, 39; David Leafe and Terry Ilott (eds.), *BFI Film and Television Handbook 1994* (London: British Film Institute, 1993), 23, 38; Thomas (ed.), *BFI Handbook 1995*, 38; Dyja (ed.), *BFI Handbook 1996*, 24, 26; Dyja (ed.), *BFI Film and Television Handbook 1997* (London: British Film Institute, 1996), 24, 27; Dyja (ed.), *BFI Handbook 1998*, 26; Eddie Dyja (ed.), *BFI Film and Television Handbook 2001* (London: British Film Institute, 2000), 24, 37, 26; Dyja (ed.), *BFI Handbook 2002*, 32.

[17] See e.g. Colin Brown, 'Big Spenders Eye Small Rewards', *Screen International* (12 Apr. 1996), 1.

[18] Anon., 'Eurochamps Stateside', *Variety* (18 May 1992), 85.

[19] Eberts and Ilott, *My Indecision is Final*, 36.

[20] Anon., 'Eurochamps Stateside', 85; *Screen International* (9 Aug. 1986), 22; Bernard Weinraub, 'Disney Signs up Merchant and Ivory', *New York Times* (27 July 1992), C15; Daniel S. Moore, 'Novel Scribe', *Variety* (28 Oct. 1962).

14. The heritage film as box-office hit: setting the pace with *Chariots of Fire*

Chariots, Greystoke: The Legend of Tarzan, Lord of the Apes, which took $45.9 million in the USA, but only £2.6 million in the UK.[21] Such figures were extraordinary, and far from typical. For instance, *Maurice* (1987), Merchant Ivory's next film after *Room*, took only $2.3 million in the USA and £504,000 in the UK,[22] while *A Handful of Dust* took just $1.6 million in the USA. Another prominent quality costume drama, Kenneth Branagh's *Henry V* (1989), was a little more impressive, taking $10 million in the USA and $7 million in Europe—but it was still a long way off the successes of *Chariots* and *Room*.[23]

In the 1990s, in terms of hard box-office takings, the most successful 'British' costume dramas were *Howards End*, *Much Ado About Nothing* (1993), *The Remains of the Day*, *Shadowlands*, *Emma*, *Sense and Sensibility*, *The English Patient*, *Elizabeth*, and *Shakespeare in Love*, which all took over $20 million at the American box office, in some cases much more—*Shakespeare in Love*, for instance, took $100.3 million. Most of these films were from the higher end of the budget range, though two other films at the expensive end of the list were comparative box-office failures, *Hamlet* and *Restoration* (1996). *Howards End*, on the other hand, was from the lower end of the budget range—and it was its success as a crossover film, as much as that of any other film, which producers and distributors tried to emulate in the 1990s. Among other box-office notables in the 1990s were

---

[21] Box-office statistics from A. C. Nielsen EDI Ltd., 2001.
[22] Showbizdata.com; *Screen International Film and TV Yearbook* (1988), 20 and (1989), 17.
[23] Showbizdata.com.

Enchanted April, The Madness of King George, The Wings of the Dove, and *An Ideal Husband,* which all took $13–18 million. Even *Orlando* took over $5 million and *Mrs Dalloway* over $3 million.

When revenue from other markets is factored in, and budget sizes are taken into account, all of these results look impressive.[24] To keep the figures in perspective, however, it's worth noting that, on average, over thirty-five films a year throughout the 1990s grossed more than $20 million at the American box office, while in the same period twenty-two films in total took over $200 million.[25]

PATTERNS OF EXHIBITION

In 1984, the ABC and Odeon circuits between them dominated exhibition in the UK with 523 of the 660 cinema sites. By 1999, the multiplex dominated, with UGC, Odeon, Showcase, UCI, and Warner Village all running more than 200 screens.[26] In the mid-1980s, there were around sixty cinemas in the UK showing specialist films, thirty-seven of them supported by the British Film Institute (BFI) as Regional Film Theatres.[27] In the same period, there were also some twenty-two independent cinemas, including both repertory and first-run houses, in London.[28] These specialized and often very small-scale cinemas constituted the 'only significant (in trade terms) public exhibition alternatives to mainstream programming'.[29] By the end of the 1990s, the sector was even smaller, with some twenty or so cinemas still supported by the BFI and another twenty-five or so other independent, art-house cinemas.[30] The greatest concentration of cinemas and cinemagoing throughout the period was in London, with more than a quarter of UK admissions there between 1993 and 1997.[31]

Theatrical releases for films fall into the same categories as for production. As one UK distributor put it, 'The key is to recognise that there are two different markets, one for the majors and one for the independents', although 'every year there are two or three films that crossover'.[32] At the top end of the scale, the mainstream film will receive a wide release, with anywhere from 100 to 400 prints in circulation in the UK at one time. Blockbusters in particular will receive a

---

[24] Ibid.

[25] MPAA, '2000 US Economic Review', 8; all-time box-office charts on Internet Movie Database, at www.imdb.com.

[26] Dyja (ed.), *BFI Handbook 2001,* tables 14 and 26, 35 and 46.

[27] David Docherty, David Morrison, and Michael Tracey, *The Last Picture Show? Britain's Changing Film Audiences* (London: British Film Institute 1987), 53–4.

[28] Archie Tait, 'Distributing the Product', in Auty and Roddick, *British Cinema Now,* 79.

[29] Barry Edson, 'Film Distribution and Exhibition in the UK', in Mundy Ellis (ed.), *British Film Institute Film and TV Yearbook 1983* (London: British Film Institute, 1983), 142.

[30] See Dyja (ed.), *BFI Handbook 2001,* 145–72; and Dodona Research, *Cinemagoing 8* (Leicester: Dodona Research, 2000), 63.

[31] *Screen International* (23 Oct. 1998), 52.

[32] Rupert Preston, President of Metrodome, quoted in Anon., 'Whose Money is it Anyway?', *Guardian,* G2 (24 July 1997), 6.

saturation release, with the maximum amount of prints. The practice was developed initially in the USA for exploitation films, but adopted for mainstream releases there in the 1970s. By the early 1980s, saturation releases were standard in the USA for mainstream films, which routinely show on 1,500 to 3,000 screens for their opening weekend.[33] Although by the early 1980s blockbusters were given saturation releases in the UK, the typical release in the UK for a non-blockbuster mainstream release adopted the traditional cascade model. A West End opening would be followed by screenings in other London cinemas, then key regional cities, then circuit cinemas in other towns, and finally independents and second-run screenings.[34]

Mainstream films are heavily advertised, using television and other media, and the opening weekend is crucial: that is what the distributors concentrate on. This increases costs enormously. Hundreds, or in the USA, thousands, of prints of each film have to made, and the opening weekend has to be prepared for with a nation-wide advertising campaign using television, radio, large advertisements in newspapers and magazines and on billboards, and, in the late 1990s, dedicated websites. In 1990, the average cost of studio films was put at $26.8 million, with another $12 million spent on prints and advertising. By 2000, the figures had gone up to $54.8 million and $27.3 million respectively.[35] The budgets for prints and advertising for mainstream films thus exceed the production budgets for many English costume dramas.

If the mainstream film with a wide release is at the top end of the exhibition scale, in the middle of the scale is the crossover release; in the UK, this means there would typically be twenty to a hundred prints in circulation. Such films are often platformed, where the film will start on a limited number of screens, usually one or two in London's West End, and then slowly build up as it moves to higher platforms—perhaps specialist cinemas in other metropolitan centres, followed by a wider release in selected multiplexes. At the bottom end of the scale is the specialized or art-house release, which might involve as few as just one or two prints, or as many as twenty in the UK.[36]

Chariots of Fire and *A Room with a View* provide perfect illustrations of the crossover release in the 1980s. Although the term was not then in common currency, the sentiments were in place. *Chariots* was described in a trade paper as 'a film with a great deal to offer to the discriminating and to those middle-of-the-roaders who belong to the silent majority'. It was identified as an excellent booking for 'selected cinemas; but not being an impulse buyer's movie, needing time for word of mouth recommendations to do the necessary.'[37] A Hollywood journalist

[33] A. D. Murphy, 'What does Average Per Screen Mean?', *Variety* (7 July 1982), 1; Tino Balio, 'The Art Film Market in the New Hollywood', in Geoffrey Nowell-Smith and Steven Ricci (eds.), *Hollywood and Europe: Economics, Culture, National Identity 1945–95* (London: British Film Institute, 1998), 64.

[34] Edson, 'Film Distribution and Exhibition in the UK', 141.

[35] MPAA, '2000 US Economic Review', 14, 16.

[36] I am grateful to David Litchfield, Director of Cinema City, Norwich, for discussing these issues with me; see also Balio, 'The Art Film Market'.

[37] Marjorie Bilbow, 'The New Films', *Screen International* (11 Apr. 1981), 19.

15. Period romance as good box-office material: George and Lucy in *A Room with a View*

described *Room* more succinctly yet equally aptly as 'an art-house blockbuster'.[38] *Chariots* opened in April 1981 in the UK, and in September in the USA. Showing at just a few cinemas initially, it generated outstanding press reviews and average takings per screen, built up good word of mouth, then slowly rolled out on to more screens. In the USA, it was decided not to book the film in art-houses, but to focus on first-run cinemas that attracted a cross-section of viewers because of where the cinemas were located. On the other hand, each booking was initially an exclusive, single-cinema run, so the film did not show anywhere else in the same city. Gradually, more cinemas and more prints were added to the release, as it built up from one platform to the next, until by the time of the 1982 Oscars, it was on over 800 cinemas nationwide.[39]

A *Room with a View* (Fig. 15) opened in April 1986 on just one screen in London's West End, the Curzon Mayfair, where it did record-breaking business—and stayed for over seven months! It went straight to number five in the London box-office chart, despite the fact that every other film in the top ten was playing in far more than just one cinema, and stayed in the London top ten for more than

---

[38] Jack Mathews, 'The Little Film that Could', *Los Angeles Times* (30 Mar. 1987), part VI, 5.
[39] B. J. Franklin, 'How "Chariots" Caught Fire', *Screen International* (15 May 1982), 8.

a year.[40] In its second week, òne more screen was added, in Glasgow. In its third week, it did excellent business in provincial art-houses, as well as showing for a week in selected ABCs (one of the two mainstream circuits at the time).[41] From week seven, it was playing on around twenty screens nationally, and had reached number one in the London box-office chart and number five nationally. The other top grossing films during this period were all playing on more than fifty screens, with *Down and Out in Beverly Hills* (1985) on 186, and *The Jewel on the Nile* (1985) on 290.[42] Significantly, this was during the school summer term, a traditionally quiet period for the box office, with the blockbusters reserved for the summer holidays. *Room* initially circulated with around twenty prints; a further ten were added after six months. By then it was regarded as 'one of the most successful British films at the box-office for years', having benefited from 'some clever booking schedules' and lasting 'far beyond industry expectations'.[43] It enjoyed long runs in cinemas in Brighton, Bristol, Edinburgh, and Nottingham, as well as London, and was still showing around the country in the autumn of 1986. Having 'proved itself to be much more than a select audience film', it was being prepared for a wider release in the new year, when critics would publish their 'ten best films of the year' lists, and the awards season started.[44] It eventually took around £3 million at the UK box office, which was considered 'exceptional for this type of film'.[45]

The American release was very similar. It opened on just one screen (the Paris Theater in New York) in March 1986, building up to seventy-eight screens by week 10, when it entered the box-office charts at number seven, and 'play[ed] in cities where no Merchant–Ivory film has played before'. It went up to 130 screens in week 14 and was still in the top twenty after six months. It was back on 150 screens for the Oscars—the widest release it received throughout its long run—and re-appeared in the top twenty, a year after it opened.[46] As I noted above, it eventually took $25 million in the American market, a staggering figure for a £2.3 million production 'that figured to appeal largely to the film buff and literary audiences. . . . But it attracted some of the mainstream crowd even before the Oscar nominations.'[47] Even so, according to its distributors, 'There was no way that "Room" was going to break through to really general audiences'. On the contrary, 'it was going to make its money from a long play before sophisticated audiences'. There were never more than 200 prints in circulation, and 'even with all the good reviews and word of mouth, the film has still not done well in many smaller cities'. The

---

[40] *Screen International* (19 Apr. 1986), 81.

[41] Ibid. (3 May 1986), 341.

[42] See weekly box-office charts in *Screen International* for May to July 1986.

[43] *Screen International* (16 Aug. 1986), 66.

[44] Ibid. (13 Dec. 1986), 25.

[45] Ibid. (9 August 1986), 22.

[46] See *Screen International* and *Variety* box-office charts for 1986–7; the quotation is from Aljean Harmetz, 'Merchant and Ivory Strike Gold', *New York Times* (5 July 1986), cutting.

[47] Dennis Hunt, ' "Room with a View" for Rent', *Los Angeles Times* (27 Mar. 1987), cutting.

distributors resisted buying more prints even when it received eight Oscar nominations: 'Even with nominations, it is a movie with a limited audience.'[48]

Among 'British' costume dramas of the 1990s, some were kept pretty much within the art-house circuits. Thus *Edward II* opened on two screens in the USA and never went on to more than sixteen; *Where Angels Fear to Tread*, *Orlando*, and *Wilde* opened on two, three, and seven screens respectively and never went on to more than thirty-five, seventy-eight, and sixty screens respectively. (Given the cost of *Wilde*, this must be regarded as a failure.) Among platformed crossover releases, *Much Ado About Nothing*, *Shadowlands*, *The Madness of King George*, *Emma*, and *Mrs Brown* were typical. All opened on between two and nine screens in the USA. *Much Ado*, *Madness*, and *Mrs Brown* gradually built up to between 350 and 470 screens, *Emma* to 848 and *Shadowlands* (by far the most expensive of the group) to 1,023. *Shakespeare in Love* also opened on only eight screens; after five weeks, it was up to 632 screens; after ten weeks, it was on 2,000 screens, enabling it to gross more than $54 million in the USA alone. For the British release, a different strategy was used. The film had already become a hit in the USA, and when it was released in the UK it opened wide, on 314 screens, taking it straight to the number one spot in the UK box-office chart.[49]

With such releases, overheads have to be kept to a minimum, even in the USA, and advertising is less important than reviews. As Archie Tait, a distributor, observed in the mid-1980s,

Instead of taking the film to the audience through the channel of a chain of local cinemas whose running costs must be maintained, the distributor and exhibitor will . . . combine forces to attract the audience to the film, wherever it is playing, and undertake only a single cinema overhead. The crucial means of doing this is the local and national press, not so much through advertising, as through editorial coverage . . . [since] the British film press consistently wields its influence in favour of independently produced and distributed films. It is perfectly possible to release a film successfully in Britain with one print, in one cinema, on an advertising budget of £1,000, simply on the basis of positive reviews in the key papers—*The Times*, *Sunday Times*, *Guardian*, *Daily* and *Sunday Telegraph*, *Financial Times* and *Observer*, together with London weekly listings magazines *Time Out* and *City Limits*.[50]

The situation remained very similar throughout the 1980s and 1990s, with reviews and word-of-mouth playing the key role in creating interest around a specialist film. Marketing, or promotion, in one form or another, is of course vital for all films if they are to reach their intended audience. Marketing is about catching the audience's attention, attempting 'to marry the product to the consumer through a series of carefully targeted advertising and positioning strategies'.[51] As cinemagoing has moved from a frequent and routine pastime to a special occasion

---

[48] Ira Deutchman of Cinecom, quoted in Mathews, 'Little Film that Could', 5.

[49] Showbizdata.com.

[50] Tait, 'Distributing the Product', 78.

[51] Nick Roddick, 'Shotguns and Weddings', *Mediawatch '99*, special supplement to *Sight and Sound* (Mar. 1999), 10.

for many people—even to some extent for regular cinemagoers (who fill cinemas at the weekend)—so the purpose of much marketing has been to create the 'event' film, the 'want-to-see' phenomenon. This is the case for the blockbuster, but also, in a more modest way, for the much lower budgeted heritage film: marketing tries to present the heritage film as a special event for its target audience. There is much more to say about the marketing of specialized and crossover films, however, and I shall return to the topic later in the chapter.

The creation of an event and of 'want-to-see' also characterizes the relationship between theatrical releases and small-screen dissemination (whether on video or television, terrestrial, cable, or satellite). The theatrical release in effect provides a high-profile shop-window 'event' for the product, which creates market expectation for the small-screen version. As Tait explains, 'the electronic media rely heavily on the existence of the old distribution/exhibition infrastructure to create the audience for the films they transmit, sell and rent, and to create the market and the word-of-mouth values of those films'.[52] This is true of a major box-office success like *Chariots of Fire* being screened on television for the first time, reaping the benefits of the enormous amount of publicity the film had generated after its Oscar successes. It's also true of a much smaller film like *The Draughtsman's Contract*, which drew 'considerable benefit from the "buzz" that accompanied the film's theatrical release in London and provincial art houses' when it was first shown on television.[53]

If television has found a place for 'small' films, what of the multiplex? There had been hopes that the multiplex would create greater diversity in film programming at mainstream cinemas, creating more spaces for independent or otherwise specialist films. The standard view is that this hasn't happened, that minority audiences are not better catered for and that multiplexes simply show more of the same. The view of mainstream distributors and exhibitors more or less confirms this impression. One exhibitor, for instance, argues that, 'If you mix [art-house product] into a commercial cinema, you get confusion. If you look at your consumer, it's your popcorn-and-chips brigade that goes to the commercial cinema, the coffee and cake brigade that goes to the arthouse. They are different markets'.[54] Chris Bailey, then head of theatrical distribution at PolyGram, argues that it is not the fault of the multiplexes or the big distributors that small films don't get shown: 'A film must have commercial merit as well as artistic merit. The prime concern is the bottom line. Independent producers say they don't get representation on screens, but I would say: "you aren't making the right films."'[55]

What these views seem to overlook is the development of the crossover film, which, if it is to succeed, must show both at the independent and art-house

[52] Tait, 'Distributing the Product', 72.

[53] Martin Auty, 'But is it Cinema?', in Auty and Roddick, *British Cinema Now*, 60–1.

[54] Mike Ross of Ster-Kinekor, owner of the Ster Century chain, quoted in Melanie Clulow, 'A Tear-jerker at the Movies', *Independent on Sunday*, business section (5 Apr. 1998), 3.

[55] Quoted in Clulow, 'A Tear-jerker at the Movies', 3.

cinemas and at selected multiplexes belonging to the main circuits.[56] It must also then to some extent attract the 'coffee and cake brigade' into the multiplex environment. Of course by doing this, it also makes things difficult for the independent or art-house exhibitor, for whom such films are vital to box-office success. On the one hand, the crossover film markets the potentially specialist film to a wider audience; on the other hand, it takes potential audiences away from the art-house.

CINEMA AUDIENCES: WHO WATCHES WHICH FILMS?

The audience for heritage films is generally perceived as relatively middle-aged. As far as the mainstream film industry is concerned, such audiences constitute 'a niche older audience'.[57] This is because it perceives its core audience as the 15–24 year olds which statistics confirm are the most frequent cinemagoers in terms of the proportion of that age group who attend the cinema once a month or more. In fact, 15–24 year olds are a much smaller proportion of the total UK population than those aged 35 and over—but those aged 35 and over go to the cinema much less frequently. So although there are more cinemagoers aged 35 and over than aged 15–24, most of them are infrequent cinemagoers. In 1994, for instance, only about one-fifth of total admissions were from those aged 35 and over.[58] What those statistics can't tell us, of course, is whether a greater proportion of 15–24 year olds visit the cinema more frequently than other age groups simply because the majority of films are designed with them in mind and then carefully targeted at them.

There is certainly no denying that film audiences are divided according to age, class, gender, and taste. For instance, in the early 1980s, two-thirds of the audience in the UK for *Superman III* (1983) were from C2DE social categories, while for *Gandhi* the trend was the opposite, with two-thirds of the audience from ABC1s.[59] In the mid-1990s, 49 per cent of the audience for *Shadowlands* was aged 45 or over, but only 30 per cent aged 24 or under. For *Mrs Doubtfire* (1993), on the other hand, only 17 per cent was aged 45 or over, with 43 per cent aged 24 or under.[60] Indeed, research carried out on behalf of the cinema, advertising, and video industries in 1994 demonstrates several significant characteristics of audiences favouring period dramas. While films such as *Shadowlands*, *The Remains of the Day*, and *The Age*

[56] Alex Ben Block, 'Entering New "Golden Age," Specialty Films Cash In', *Hollywood Reporter online*, at www.hollywoodreporter.com, 12 Mar. 1993.

[57] Martin Dale, *The Movie Game: The Film Business in Britain, Europe and America* (London: Cassell, 1997), 5.

[58] See the annual breakdown of frequency of cinemagoing in the *BFI Handbook*, which draws on statistics from Screen Finance and CAVIAR; the 1994 figure is given in Dyja (ed.), *BFI Handbook 1996*, 36.

[59] Docherty *et al.*, *The Last Picture Show?*, 50, drawing on an unidentified CAVIAR report.

[60] Cinema and Video Industry Audience Research (CAVIAR), *Caviar 12, vol. 1: Computer Tabulations: Cinema, Television, Readership, Leisure* (London: CAVIAR/BMRB International Ltd., 1995), tables 23/1 and 23/2, 86–7.

of Innocence (1993) were not seen by more than 4 per cent of the sample interviewed, they and other period dramas were overwhelmingly favoured by women, by older cinemagoers, and by more upmarket cinemagoers.[61] Mainstream films with a contemporary setting, on the other hand, tend to attract much younger audiences.

In the mid-1980s, according to David Docherty and his colleagues, even within the middle classes, there were significant taste differences: 'around half those in middle-class occupations attended "mass" entertainment films, rather than "art" films. Within the middle class it seems that teachers, lecturers, social workers and others in the caring professions prefer art house films, whereas middle management in commercial companies prefer straightforward commercial films.'[62] Education is a key factor here: 'Over one-third of the [Regional Film Theatre] audience is in full-time education, and if we add in the number of lecturers and teachers then over half of the audience are connected to full-time education.'[63] Cultural leanings are clear: Regional Film Theatre audiences are broadsheet (especially *Guardian*) newspaper readers rather than tabloid readers, and Radio 4 rather than Radio 2 listeners, and they frequent classical concerts, theatres, and art galleries. (Heritage films rather neatly tap into all of these interests and tastes, with their 'seriousness' as opposed to 'escapism', and their frequent references to or uses of classical music, art and literature.[64])

Art-house films are then unquestionably specialist products in the sense that they reach much smaller audiences than most films, as a glance at box-office admissions statistics will confirm, while the social formation of those audiences was quite distinct from what is regarded as the mainstream audience. In a 1991 survey carried out for the industry, 'less than 2% of the sample claimed to see any film of this type; in 1992, this proportion effectively doubled, largely due to the success of *Howards End*, and in 1993 it increased again to 5%. This was explained by [the] relatively wide appeal of the top film, *The Crying Game* (1992), with a measured audience of 1.4 million.'[65] The crossover film thus plays a key role in broadening the appeal of the art-house sector. The same market researchers point out that 'the Art House film market has always had a distinctly upmarket bias'. In 1994, for instance, 44 per cent of the art house audience was made up of ABs.[66] The art-house sector also 'tends to have a slightly older appeal than mainstream cinema', with 38 per cent of the art-house audience in 1994 aged 35 or over, and 27 per cent aged 45 or over.[67] Audiences at my local art-house cinema confirm these general trends: around 65 per cent of audiences are ABC1s, and around 58

---

[61] CAVIAR, *Caviar 12, vol. 1*, tables 6/2, 6/6, 23/2, 23/3, 23/8, and 23/9, pp. 20, 24, 87, 88, 93, and 94; see also Claire Monk, 'Heritage Films and the British Cinema Audience in the 1990s', *Journal of Popular British Cinema*, 2 (1999), 22–38.

[62] Docherty *et al.*, *The Last Picture Show?*, 50–1.

[63] Ibid. 54–5.   [64] Ibid. 56–9.

[65] CAVIAR, *Caviar 12, vol. 3: Report of Findings*, 39.

[66] Ibid. *vol. 3*, 40; and *vol. 1*, table 23/11, 96.

[67] Ibid. *vol. 3*, 41; and *vol. 1*, table 23/11, 96.

per cent are aged 35 or over.[68] It's worth noting in addition that, while period dramas tend to attract the same socio-economic class of audiences as for most art-house films, the audiences for period dramas tend to be older and to include more women.

Since the early 1980s, by comparison with earlier decades, there has in fact been an increasing embourgeoisement of the cinema audience generally, with statistics revealing a slight upmarket trend in cinemagoing in the UK. In the mid-1980s, industry commentators noted 'the opening up of the audience which was enticed back to the cinema by films such as *A Passage to India . . . Amadeus* [and *A Room with a View*]—people outside the recognised major cinema audience age-group (15–24 years) and those whose interests include literature or the arts in general were drawn back to the cinema'.[69] By 1999, there was little difference between the proportions of ABC1s and C2DEs visiting the cinema.[70] Audiences are also slowly ageing, so that by 1999 there was little difference between the numbers (as opposed to the proportion) of 15–24 year olds and those aged 35 and over who were regular cinemagoers in the UK. Indeed the numbers of people aged 35 and over who went to the cinema at all, regardless of frequency, actually outweigh the numbers of those aged 15–34, and were more than double the numbers of 15–24 year olds. The proportion of 15–24 year olds who visited the cinema once a month or more may still have been higher than any other social category, but the actual numbers of people in that social category were relatively small.[71] As the UK industry's market researchers had noted in 1995, cinema was appealing to a progressively wider age-range and more upmarket audiences.[72]

The gender balance of audiences seems to have become more even too. In the late 1980s, statistics suggested that more men than women attended the cinema. In the 1990s, though, audiences as a whole seem not to be weighted one way or the other.[73] Part of the reason for these changes may be that multiplexes are attracting audiences in the UK for which they were not specifically designed. Thus in 1989, the proportion of women attending multiplexes was greater than the proportion of women attending traditional cinemas (56 per cent of audiences in multiplexes, but only 38 per cent in traditional cinemas). Multiplexes also seemed to be attracting more older people, with 27 per cent of their audiences aged 35 or over, compared to 19 per cent in traditional cinemas, a trend which was maintained throughout the 1990s.[74]

[68] Statistics courtesy of David Litchfield, Director of Cinema City, Norwich.

[69] Tina McFarling, 'Media Interest Justifies Merchant's Room Hopes', *Screen International* (15 Mar. 1986), cutting.

[70] Docherty *et al.*, *The Last Picture Show?*, 30–1; CAVIAR, *Caviar 12*; Dyja (ed.), *BFI Handbook 2001*, table 15, 35.

[71] See Dyja (ed.), *BFI Handbook 2001*, table 15, 35.

[72] CAVIAR, *Caviar 12, vol. 3*, 22–3.

[73] Monk, 'Heritage Films and the British Cinema Audience'; Anon., *MSI Databrief: Cinema: UK* (London: Marketing Strategies for Industry [UK] Ltd., 1991); Ilott, *Budgets and Markets*, 23; Dyja (ed.), *BFI Handbook 2001*, table 15, 35, all drawing on CAVIAR reports.

[74] Andrew Feist and Robert Hutchinson, *Cultural Trends 1990*, 6 (London: Policy Studies Institute, London, 1990), 18; Dodona Research, *Cinemagoing 8*, 27.

The same trends are evident in the USA too:

The overall composition of movie-goers has . . . changed over the last decade—with those in the 40+ age group accounting for 40% of total moviegoers in 2000, compared to only 32% in 1990. . . . At the beginning of the decade, 12 to 24 year olds accounted for almost half of total frequent movie-goers. In contrast, frequent attendees came from a more even mix of ages in 2000.[75]

Indeed, those aged 40 and over made up nearly one-third of frequent moviegoers in 2000, while the rise in cinema attendance overall was attributed to the increase in cinemagoing by adults. However, where around a half of the teenage population attended the cinema frequently, only about a quarter of all adults attended regularly. It is presumably this tendency that continues to hold the thrall of American industry executives: even though the overall number of teenage Americans is far smaller than the overall number of adult Americans, the teenage audience remains the prime target for mainstream films. Although a breakdown of audiences by class is not readily available, it is worth noting that, in broad terms, the more highly educated a person is, the more likely that person is to attend the cinema regularly. As in the UK, there is little difference in the patterns of attendance by gender, although a lower proportion of women are classified as frequent cinemagoers than men.[76]

Despite these demographic changes in the cinema audience in the UK and the USA, mainstream films still seem to be predominantly targeted at the 15–24 age group, to appeal in particular to young males, and to be aimed relatively downmarket. If this is cinema's 'mass audience', it is a very specific sort of mass. Indeed, as Claire Monk points out, young male cinemagoers might be better understood as constituting a niche market rather than the mainstream market—but it is of course to this niche that most mainstream films are addressed.[77] Monk argues persuasively that addressing young, male frequent cinemagoers as the mainstream in effect marginalizes or renders insignificant female cinemagoers and older cinemagoers, who in fact statistically represent a significant proportion of the cinemagoing population as a whole.

If most mainstream films still seem to be addressed to this demographic—and therefore in some ways seem to be out of touch with the broader demographic shifts—then Peter Krämer suggests that the core business of the media conglomerates since the late 1970s has in fact been family entertainment. That is to say, most of the biggest box-office successes of the 1980s and 1990s have succeeded with family audiences, and have allowed extremely lucrative multimedia merchandising (the film itself, but also videos, books, toys, theme park rides, and so

[75] MPA Research Department, '2000 Motion Picture Attendance Survey', table of contents, on the Motion Picture Association of America website, at http://www.mpaa.org/useconomicreview /2000AttendanceStudy/index.htm.
[76] Ibid., table of contents and table 4.
[77] Monk, 'Heritage Films and the British Cinema Audience'.

on).[78] If we focus on such films—that is, on the majority of the biggest box-office hits of this period—we must conclude that they succeed not by addressing only young, male frequent cinemagoers but by reaching as many different niches as possible. As Tino Balio points out, since the 1960s, the film industry has increasingly targeted specific audience segments.[79] To this extent, the 'mass audience' is necessarily an agglomerate of niches, while the goal of the blockbuster is to become a 'must-see' event that even the most irregular cinemagoers will want to attend.

To see heritage films as specialist films is thus to identify them as addressing a different market segment to so-called mainstream films. There is no denying that even the most successful heritage film is in fact seen by smaller audiences than most successful mainstream films, but that is partly because they are not as heavily marketed and there are fewer prints in circulation. As Monk notes, industry statistics also confirm that heritage films attract a mainly middle-class audience, and one that is older than the mainstream—but if the heritage film audience is more middle class than the mainstream, it is also less middle class than for most arthouse films.[80] Heritage films thus tend to reach a wider range of people than most mainstream films and most art-house films, and to appeal more to infrequent cinemagoers than mainstream films—and marketing is designed to exploit this phenomenon. If they are to succeed as crossover films, then they must in part appeal to the relatively youthful audience that constitutes the mainstream core, as well as encouraging less regular cinemagoers and older cinemagoers to visit the cinema.

As one market research organization put it, '20 blockbusters a year is not enough to sustain the industry, it needs other films to cater to the most regular and frequent filmgoers and to audience segments which might not be attracted primarily to these blockbuster movies.'[81] On the one hand, then, the industry as a whole likes occasional films that can pull in audiences not usually attracted by mainstream fare. This is one of the reasons why heritage films appeal to the cinema, video, and television industries. As another market research report notes, 'one of the major concerns of the cinema industry is the lack of a strong franchise among the older generation', and one of the key ways of reaching that audience is 'through more serious or literary film titles such as *Schindler's List* and *Shadowlands* [and *The Piano*]'.[82] On the other hand, a large proportion of exhibitors' income is generated by concession stands selling popcorn, soft drinks, ice cream, and the like—but it is the under-25 frequent cinemagoing audiences that are most attractive in this respect, since they spend the most money at concession stands.

---

[78] Peter Krämer, 'Would You Take your Child to See This Film? The Cultural and Social Work of the Family-Adventure Movie', in Neale and Smith (eds.), *Contemporary Hollywood Cinema*.

[79] Tino Balio, 'Introduction to Part I', in Balio (ed.), *Hollywood in the Age of Television* (Boston and London: Unwin Hyman, 1990), 28.

[80] Monk, 'Heritage Films and the British Cinema Audience'.

[81] Dodona Research, *Cinemagoing 8*, 29.

[82] CAVIAR, *Caviar 12*, 7, 36.

Thus it is important to maintain what the industry regards as its core audience, but it is also important to diversify, especially since the overall number of people aged under 25 has been shrinking since the 1980s.[83]

It is also worth noting that 'the inherent biases of a medium will directly influence the film as it is released to that medium. Films tend to take on an older and more downmarket profile as they move from cinema to video to TV.'[84] It should come as no surprise then that downmarket tabloid newspapers will often be quite sniffy about quality costume dramas when they are reviewed for theatrical release, but much more complimentary about them when they appear on television. More generally, we might note that the slight ageing of both the cinema audience and the population as a whole, the evening out of the numbers of males and females visiting the cinema, and the slight upmarket trend in audiences across the 1990s will have had a positive impact on the audiences for heritage films, since they are addressed primarily to older, more female, and more upmarket audiences.

A COTTAGE INDUSTRY: THE PRODUCTION SECTOR IN THE 1980S AND 1990S

In 1992, more than half the money spent by consumers globally on films at the cinema, on video, and on pay television was spent in the USA. The European market attracted around a quarter of global consumer spending, of which the British contribution was itself around a quarter. Put in these terms, it is no surprise that British producers looked to the American market, and indeed the UK is Europe's most successful exporter of films to the USA.[85] Given that the domestic market—especially the specialist or art-house market—is too small to cover the costs of any but the most low-budget films (and even that is often difficult), as one industry commentator put it, 'For UK cinema, export success is not a bonus, it is a necessity'.[86]

If we take *The Wings of the Dove* as a typical film from the middle of the budget range, we find that while it cost £8.7 million to make, and was the seventh best-performing British film at the UK box office the year it was released, it took only £2.1 million (whereas in the American market, it took $13.7 million). Several other key costume dramas of the 1990s failed to take more than £3 million at the UK box office, including *Mrs Brown, Wilde, An Ideal Husband, Topsy-Turvy*, and *The Golden Bowl*. *Shakespeare in Love*, the most successful 'British' costume drama ever in terms of box-office takings, racked up £20.8 million; but since this figure is gross, and the exhibitors take a cut before redistributing the money, even this princely sum is unlikely to have covered the £15 million production costs. *Howards*

[83] CAVIAR, 26–7.   [84] Ibid. 10.

[85] Ilott, *Budgets and Markets*, 9; Christine Ogan, 'The Audience for Foreign Film in the United States', *Journal of Communication*, 40/4 (1990), table 1, 64–5.

[86] Ilott, *Budgets and Markets*, 15.

End, Remains of the Day, The Secret Garden (1993), and *The Madness of King George* were all deemed considerable successes for this type of film at the UK box office, but all took between £3.5 million and £4.6 million. More impressive were *Much Ado About Nothing* (£5.4 million), *Braveheart* (£11.3 million), and *The English Patient* (£12.7 million)—but again, production costs were not covered. At the lower end of the budget scale, *Mrs Dalloway* cost £2.6 million, and took only £240,000 at the UK box office ($3.3 million in the USA). *Edward II*, made for an even smaller budget (£850,000), took only £64,000 in the UK, but over a million dollars in the USA. But several much more costly films also took less than £1 million at the UK box office, including *Hamlet, Keep the Aspidistra Flying* (1997), *Mansfield Park, The House of Mirth*, and *The Golden Bowl.*[87]

Given these sorts of figures, it is hardly surprising that British producers looked to the export market, and especially the huge American market. But look at the market from the other direction and a different picture emerges. In 1980, 30 per cent of the revenue of the American film industry came from foreign markets; by 1989 it was 38 per cent; by 1994, overseas rentals for American films were greater than domestic rentals. Put in these terms, it is no surprise that American distributors sought to maximize the potential of foreign markets, including the British market.[88] American distributors have long dominated the British market, a situation that prevailed throughout the 1980s and 1990s. In 1987, for instance, forty-five of the top fifty films at the UK box office were American, while in 1998, the five major American distributors held 83.5 per cent of the UK market.[89] The mainstream cinema circuits in the UK are thus geared above all to screening mainstream American films. At the beginning of the 1980s, two 'British' multinational corporations, Rank and Thorn-EMI, also had a stake in distribution, as well as owning the major exhibition circuits. By the end of the 1990s, both companies had withdrawn from distribution, while the new generation of American multiplex owners dominated exhibition.

Already in the early 1980s, the two British majors had more or less withdrawn from production activity. As John Hill has pointed out, this means that for the whole of the period in question, the concerns of film producers in the UK were quite different to the concerns of those who owned and controlled distribution and exhibition, a situation only exacerbated by the increase in American ownership of the leading cinema chains.[90] No companies offered the security of an integrated studio and distribution outfit, although for a while, in the mid-1990s, PolyGram provided both corporate funding and guaranteed distribution for its satellite producers. For the most part, though, the production sector was extremely fragmented and insecure, a cottage industry living from hand to mouth.

[87] Box-office statistics from *BFI Handbooks 1993–2002*; Beverly Gray, 'The Reel Deal', *Hollywood Reporter* (11 Aug. 1998), 10; showbizdata.com; A. C. Nielsen EDI Ltd., 2001.

[88] Geraldine Fabrikant, 'When World Raves, Studios Jump', *New York Times* (7 Mar. 1990), D1, D8; Leonard Klady, 'Earth to H'wood: You Win', *Variety* (13 Feb. 1995), 1, 63.

[89] Derek Malcolm, 'One Smoking Barrel', *Guardian*, G2 (29 December 1998), 11.

[90] John Hill, *British Cinema in the 1980s: Issues and Themes* (Oxford: Clarendon Press, 1999), 49.

In the 1980s, for instance, 342 companies were involved in film production, of which 250 were set up for or involved in one-off projects. Only five companies were involved in more than ten films: Handmade, Goldcrest, Enigma, Zenith, and Palace.[91] This was a cinema of auteurs and enterprising producers rather than of studios and genres, and it was best fitted to exploit the margins of the market, the specialist sectors as yet uncolonized by the majors. There were few opportunities to draw on in-house funding and it was difficult to secure anything more than a limited release in the UK for domestically produced films. Just over a third of the British films produced between 1984 and 1998, for instance, were shown on less than thirty screens within a year of production, mainly in art-house cinemas or in the West End only. Just under a third of British films in the same period remained unreleased a year after production.[92]

Various efforts were made to create a more stable production environment in the 1980s and 1990s. On the one hand there were corporate efforts to produce well-capitalized companies that might provide an umbrella for a range of independent film-makers. On the other hand, the state attempted to establish the sort of infrastructure that might foster stability and commercial viability in the production sector, especially in the late 1990s. The two key corporate efforts were Goldcrest in the 1980s and PolyGram Filmed Entertainment (PFE) in the 1990s. Both significantly had the backing of a major media conglomerate—Pearson Longman in the case of Goldcrest, and PolyGram in the case of PFE. Although Goldcrest lacked its own distribution facility, it was still able to establish a reputation as one of the leading independent film companies in the world and was widely associated with the so-called renaissance in British film production in the early and mid-1980s.[93] The company exploited to the maximum the capital allowances scheme of the early 1980s in order to attract city investment. Gradually, it built up a reputation for producing films that appealed 'to a middle-brow, middle-class audience', 'the kind of thoughtful, adult films . . . that had become rare in a Hollywood in thrall to the teenage audience and obsessed with special effects'.[94] This was a deliberate strategy of differentiating its product from the Hollywood majors; its policy was thus to 'stay distinctive . . . by stressing the uniqueness and excellence of its output' and to 'produce films for both mass and specialized audiences'.[95] Thus it sought to 'produce both major films and classics (i.e. art movies and low-budget movies with high-brow themes or literary subject matter) in the hope that now and again a classic would break into the mass market'.[96]

[91] R. Lewis, *Review of the UK Film Industry: Report to BSAC* (London: British Screen Advisory Council, 1990), quoted in John Hill, 'Government Policy and the British Film Industry 1979–90', *European Journal of Communication*, 8 (1993), 217.

[92] Dyja (ed.), *BFI Handbook 2001*, table 8, 28.

[93] On Goldcrest, see Eberts and Ilott, *My Indecision is Final*.

[94] Ibid. 231, 152.　　　[95] Ibid. 296, 369.

[96] Ibid. 296.

PFE inherited Goldcrest's mantle in the 1990s, developing a long-term strategy to turn itself into a European major, 'a large multinational corporation that was prepared (and able) to sustain short-term losses in the interests of [the] longer-term strategy'.[97] PFE, like Goldcrest before it, had 'deep pockets', with its parent company investing profits from its music division in the film side of the corporation; crucially, it also built up a worldwide distribution network, in the hope that this would give it 'the clout of a major studio'.[98] Among its assets was part-ownership of the American distributor, Gramercy—for, as Michael Kuhn, chairman of PFE, put it, 'You can't be in this business seriously unless you're in US distribution'.[99] With 11 per cent of the UK market in 1997,[100] and some of the most successful British films of the 1990s on its books (including *Four Weddings and a Funeral* (1994), *Trainspotting* (1996), *Bean* (1997), and *Lock, Stock and Two Smoking Barrels*), it was indeed up there with the American majors. But PFE also began to think like a major too, not least in order to provide films for its American distribution arm. Thus, for Kuhn, the company's goal was 'the $40 billion annual world cinema market; making small cultural films is not the way to reach it'.[101] For Kuhn, the debate about what makes a British film was irrelevant; more important was simply to attract production funds and activity to Britain, and more generally to Europe, and to keep the profits in-house by building up a distribution network. 'There are two businesses in film,' Kuhn argued; 'there are cultural films and there are Hollywood films, and the business is really Hollywood films.'[102]

Both Goldcrest and PFE gathered a satellite group of independent producers around them (one of the key figures associated with Goldcrest was David Puttnam, while Working Title was the most successful of PFE's satellite companies). The strategy is similar to the one Rank developed in the 1940s, in its links with Two Cities, Independent Producers Ltd., and Ealing Studios.[103] In all three instances, the producers retained a degree of autonomy and independence while enjoying the security of regular funding.

The fortunes of neither Goldcrest nor PFE were to last, however. Goldcrest crashed in the late 1980s, having overstretched itself badly. Its fall, coupled with the removal of the capital allowances scheme at around the same time, led to a loss of confidence in film production on the part of finance houses, and investment in the sector tailed off dramatically in the late 1980s.[104] A little over a decade later, PolyGram was sold off by its (Dutch) parent company, Phillips, to the

---

[97] Hill, *British Cinema in the 1980s*, 46; see also Rawsthorn, 'Put to the Screen Test', 7.

[98] Rachel Halliburton and Peter Guttridge, 'Best of British', *Independent*, Film section (27 Mar. 1997), 8–9.

[99] Rawsthorn, 'Put to the Screen Test', 7.

[100] See Dyja (ed.), *BFI Handbook 1999*, table 23, p. 39.

[101] Raymond Snoddy, 'Think Big, Think Hollywood, Then Add a Dash of British Expertise', *The Times* (28 Nov. 1997), 41.   [102] Ibid.

[103] See Geoffrey Macnab, *J. Arthur Rank and the British Film Industry* (London: Routledge, 1993), 82–120.

[104] Terry Ilott, 'UK: Commentary', in Peter Noble (ed.), *Screen International Film and TV Yearbook 87–88* (London: King Publications, 1987), 227; Hill, *British Cinema in the 1980s*, 43.

Canadian conglomerate Seagram's, who already owned one of the Hollywood majors, Universal.[105] This dealt a severe blow both to the company itself and to the collective ambitions of the European film industry, many of whose protagonists had come to depend on it as a key player in European production and distribution. As an editorial in the British trade paper *Screen International* pointed out, 'over the past seven years, PolyGram ha[d] spent about $1bn creating Europe's only serious answer to the Hollywood studio system', thereby playing a key role in 'propelling the renaissance of local cinema into the next millennium'. Urging the European Community to help mount a rescue bid to save PFE for Europe, the editorial argued that 'the survival of a vibrant PFE [would] have a greater impact on Europe's film production and distribution sectors than anything the EC could ever hope to achieve'.[106] No such rescue bid was forthcoming and PFE was effectively absorbed by Hollywood, merging into Universal.

It is generally argued that, until the late 1990s, the state either had little interest or made little headway in establishing a viable production infrastructure. The Thatcherite policy of deregulation meant that subsidies and other supports were few and far between in the 1980s. The government dismantled the post-war subsidy system, replacing it with privatized initiatives—notably British Screen— and what were intended as incentives to competition, efficiency, self-sufficiency, and enterprise, rather than state support. The introduction of lottery funding and European support mechanisms in the mid-1990s began to make some difference, especially the decision in 1997 to establish three lottery-funded production consortia, DNA, Pathe Productions, and The Film Consortium. Each was awarded a six-year franchise worth around £30 million pounds by the Arts Council of England (ACE).

In so doing, ACE sought to establish 'a guaranteed stream of revenue to the franchises to invest over a slate of films' in an effort to 'break the boom-or-bust cycle that has plagued Britain's film producers for so long and [thereby to] provide an infrastructure to their fragmented industry'.[107] The goal was to move away from the *ad hoc*, 'project-by-project, cottage-industry approach', where small production companies had been forced to start from scratch with each new project, and instead to allow for forward planning on the basis of a carefully considered production strategy.[108] Charles Denton, chairman of ACE's Advisory Panel on Film, explained that in awarding the franchises,

We were looking for commitment, enthusiasm and imagination as well as business sense and an eye to the boxoffice, because we want the lottery funding to be recouped. We looked

---

[105] In 2001, Seagram's itself became part of Vivendi, a French-based multinational media and leisure corporation.

[106] Unattributed editorial, 'A Price Worth Paying', *Screen International* (16 Oct. 1998), 12.

[107] Louise Bateman, 'British Film Bid Advisers Sure Winners of Lottery', *Hollywood Reporter online*, at www.hollywoodreporter.com, 4 Mar. 1997.

[108] Nick Thomas, 'UK Film, Television and Video: Overview', in Dyja (ed.), *BFI Handbook 1999*, 28.

for track records that showed a history of high-quality productions. We wanted to be certain that Lottery funding would be used to attract private sector investment, not substitute for it, and to be sure that franchise holders would reinvest profits in more British films.[109]

Each consortium brought together producers, production companies, sales agents, and others, in effect creating three mini-studios on the Hollywood model, with their own reasonably substantial funds and links to major distributors.[110]

These efforts to revitalize the British film industry were given further impetus by the election of the new Labour government in 1997. One of the government's policies was to promote a modernized film industry in the UK, presenting it as one of the most enterprising aspects of the British creative industries. In part fulfilment of this aim, they established the Film Policy Review Group (FPRG), which was mandated to take 'a more global perspective',[111] to create the basis for a more competitive production sector, and to encourage foreign investment. The goal was to ensure that British films were more successful at the box office, matched to audiences, and appropriately marketed—in effect, to encourage a distribution-led industry rather than a production-led one.[112]

Planning for this shift from a fragmented, production-led industry to a better capitalized and more integrated distribution-led industry was central to the FPRG's report. Commercial viability—what the market was deemed capable of supporting—rather than cultural worth was to be the key. If the report also called for 'a new definition of a culturally-British film' this was for marketing purposes above all else.[113] Funds were to be channelled into training, script development, marketing, and distribution, as well as production. At the same time, the various state responsibilities for the film industry were to be brought under one umbrella organization, the Film Council, established in 2000. Under the chairmanship of Alan Parker, the latter has attempted to create the conditions for a more commercially viable production sector in the UK, with reasonably substantial production funds, and a policy of working with the American studios and

---

[109] Quoted in Cathy Dunkley, '3 Franchises Hit the Jackpot in U.K. Lottery', *Hollywood Reporter online*, at www.hollywoodreporter.com, 18 May 1997, 16.

[110] Ibid.; Louise Bateman, 'British Trio Form Lottery Ticket', *Hollywood Reporter online*, at www. hollywoodreporter.com, 27 Feb. 1997; Cathy Dunkley, 'Consortium Hits $48 Mil Lottery', *Hollywood Reporter online*, at www.hollywoodreporter.com, 16 Sept. 1997; Cathy Dunkley, 'UIP in Talks to Distribute Film Consortium', *Hollywood Reporter online*, at www.hollywoodreporter.com, 30 Jan. 1998; Anon., 'Whose Money is it Anyway?', *Guardian*, G2 (24 July 1997), 6; Cathy Dunkley, 'On New Pathe to Film Prod'n', *Hollywood Reporter*, at www.hollywoodreporter.com, 28 Jan. 1998.

[111] Stewart Till, head of Polygram International, and co-chair of the Film Policy Review Group, quoted in press release DCMS 54/98, 25 Mar. 1998.

[112] See Film Policy Review Group (FPRG), *A Bigger Picture: The Report of the Film Policy Review Group* (London: Department of Culture, Media and Sport, Mar. 1998); Stephen Pratten and Simon Deakin, 'Competitiveness Policy and Economic Organization: The Case of the British Film Industry', *Screen*, 41/2 (2000), 217–37.

[113] (FPRG), *A Bigger Picture*, 7.

European co-producers to produce higher budgeted and more populist films than have hitherto been supported by the state. The goal is to produce films that will work in multiplexes, and so to move beyond what Parker called the 'little Englander mentality' of 'the cottage industry that we all currently work in'.[114]

There is one other development of the 1980s and 1990s that demands attention here, and that is the involvement of Channel 4 Television in film production. Channel 4 in effect straddles the public and the private sectors and by the end of the 1990s was the organization with the longest-lasting commitment to British film production, dating back to 1982, when it first went on air. As a film producer, it has gone through various phases, including sole funding of low-budget films, co-funding more expensive films, and establishing its own marketing and distribution divisions and its own film channel for cable and satellite. As such, it has had a significant impact on low- and medium-budget independent film-making, both nationally and internationally. In 1998, when it set up Film Four Ltd., bringing together production, distribution, and sales in one company as a sort of vertically integrated subsidiary of Channel 4, Michael Jackson, then Chief Executive of Channel 4, proclaimed that 'our goal is to create Britain's foremost film studio'.[115]

To date, the various efforts to provide some stability in the British production sector, whether the result of capitalist enterprise or state initiative, have been insufficient to enable 'British' film production to become a significant long-term force in the global media industry. Yet those developments have created the space for several modest production cycles of low-budget independent films, including the various heritage films. As with most 'British' production in the period, these heritage films were spread across numerous independent companies, some reasonably well-capitalized, some much smaller. Goldcrest, for instance, provided funding of one sort or another in the 1980s for *Chariots of Fire*, *Gandhi*, *Another Country*, *A Room with a View*, and *White Mischief* (1987). In the 1990s, Working Title was involved with or produced *Fools of Fortune* (1990), *Edward II*, *Four Weddings and a Funeral*, *Plunkett and Macleane*, and *Elizabeth*. Of these, PolyGram funded all but *Edward II*, as well as *Jude*, *The Portrait of a Lady* (1996), and *Photographing Fairies*. One of the lottery-funded franchises, Pathe Productions, was involved with *The Woodlanders* (1997), *An Ideal Husband*, *The Claim*, and *Love's Labour's Lost* (2000). Merchant Ivory Productions produced *Heat and Dust* (1982), *A Room with a View*, *Maurice*, *The Deceivers* (1988), *Howards End*, *The Remains of the Day*, and *The Golden Bowl* (as well as several other literary adaptations and period films which fall outside the boundaries of this discussion). Renaissance Films produced *Henry V*, *Much Ado About Nothing*, *Twelfth Night* (1996), and *The Wings of the Dove*. Many more companies produced or were put together for just one or two such films.

---

[114] Fiachra Gibbons, 'Help for Film Makers Taking on Hollywood', *Guardian* (2 May 2000), 5; and Gibbons, 'New Film Council to "Shamelessly" Back British Blockbusters', *Guardian* (3 May 2000), 5.
[115] Quoted in Dan Glaister, 'Film Four Leads British Charge', *Guardian* (16 Apr. 1998), 23.

FUNDING BRITISH FILMS IN THE 1980S AND 1990S

Unlike American studio productions, few 'British' films made in the 1980s and 1990s were funded from just one source. On the contrary, most budgets have to be cobbled together from a variety of sources. Given the complex funding packages that producers have to put together, the national identity of a film frequently becomes blurred and most packages are best regarded as multinational co-productions. The most important sources of funding have been pre-sales to overseas distributors and ancillary markets (video, cable, satellite, and terrestrial television), television in its own right, and various forms of state subsidy. Since the early 1980s, pre-selling—selling distribution rights, or video or TV rights, before the film has been made—has become increasingly significant as a means of funding films. In terms of theatrical distribution, British producers have looked to both the American and the European markets—even, in some cases, the Japanese market. The involvement of American distributors has been particularly important, and in the 1990s has increasingly moved from pre-selling to capital funding, which gives the distributor some control over the production process itself. In terms of ancillary markets, 'the new electronic means of distributing and exhibiting films' became increasingly significant sources of revenue in the 1980s—as one report put it, 'in these multimedia days a low-budget film's success needn't depend on its big-screen showing'.[116] The development of Channel 4 in the UK and, in the USA, cable stations like Home Box Office (HBO), was important. So too was the growth of VCR ownership and the video rental and sales market. Between 1981 and 1986, for instance, the percentage of UK homes with VCRs rose from 7 to 51, with a greater penetration in middle-class households.[117]

Quality costume dramas and literary adaptations were ideal material for public service broadcasters to pick up, and seasons, or scheduling slots, like Channel 4's 'Film on Four', were crucial in providing outlets for specialized or art-house films. The involvement of television in the UK, as elsewhere in Europe, has often involved much more than simply pre-selling the right to broadcast the film, however, since several broadcasters, but notably Channel 4 and the BBC, have become involved in genuine production funding, providing capital upfront. Almost half the films produced in Britain at the end of the 1980s, for instance, involved some form of television funding.[118] Across the 1980s and 1990s, Channel 4 and the BBC between them were involved one way or another in an impressive array of 'British' costume films. Channel 4's slate included *The Draughtsman's Contract, Another Country, A Room with a View, Comrades* (1986), *Maurice, A Month in the Country* (1987), *On the Black Hill* (1987), *The Deceivers, Pascali's Island* (1988), *The Bridge* (1990), *Fools of Fortune, December Bride* (1990), *The Fool* (1990), *Prospero's Books* (1991), *Howards End, Four Weddings . . . , Angels and Insects*

---

[116] Tait, 'Distributing the Product', 71; Halliburton and Guttridge, 'Best of British', 8–9.
[117] British Videogramme Association figures cited in Docherty *et al.*, *The Last Picture Show?*, 62, 63.
[118] Hill, 'Government Policy', 214.

(1995), *August* (1995), *A Midsummer Night's Dream*, *The Madness of King George*, *Elizabeth*, *The Woodlanders* and *The House of Mirth*. The BBC's slate included *White Mischief*, *Henry V*, *War Requiem* (1989), *Edward II*, *Adam Bede* (1991), *Enchanted April*, *Jude*, *Mrs Brown*, *Mrs Dalloway*, *Much Ado About Nothing*, *Cold Comfort Farm*, *Persuasion* (1996, released theatrically in the USA), *Regeneration* (1997), *Photographing Fairies*, *Twelfth Night*, *Wilde*, *The Governess* (1997), *The Claim*, and *The House of Mirth*. Other television companies also funded such films, including London Weekend Television (*A Handful of Dust* and *Where Angels Fear to Tread*), Granada (*August*, *The House of Mirth*), S4C (*Hedd Wyn*, 1992), Grampian (*Macbeth*, 1997), and the American Mobil Masterpiece Theatre (*Mrs Brown*).

State subsidies for 'British' film production have come in various guises, including national subsidies as well as European funding, loans and tax concessions as well as straight capital funding, lottery money as well as money raised through taxes, and funds for developing projects before they go into production as well as funds for production itself. In effect, television funding is also a form of subsidy, given the public service commitments of the terrestrial broadcasters, the funding of the BBC through the licence fee, and the semi-protected status of Channel 4 for much of the period in question.

Several of the 'British' costume dramas of the 1980s and 1990s benefited from some form of state subsidy. From 1979 to 1986, the capital allowance tax write-off scheme enabled finance houses to write off 100 per cent of film production costs in the first year. Such concessions provided crucial fiscal incentives to investors to put money into films, with companies able to set pre-tax profits against film production investment.[119] *Chariots of Fire* and *Another Country* both benefited from these tax concessions.[120] The removal of tax breaks from 1986 was one of the factors leading to a dramatic fall-off in investment in British film production in the late 1980s,[121] although similar benefits were reintroduced by the Labour government in 1997, with *Shakespeare in Love*, for instance, benefiting from a bank sale-leaseback deal.[122]

Another Country and *A Room with a View* received the help of the National Film Finance Corporation (NFFC), a sort of nationalized film bank, which made loans to producers for films deemed commercially viable. The NFFC also administered the National Film Development Fund, which provided script development funding to *Another Country*, *The Innocent* (1984), and *Tom and Viv* (1994). The NFFC was effectively privatized by the Thatcher government, with its role taken over by British Screen, with some funds from the government, and the rest from the industry. British Screen became the main source of British production funding

---

[119] See Matthew Silverstone, 'Finding the Money', in Auty and Roddick, *British Cinema Now*, 37–40.
[120] See Graham Wade, *Film, Video and Television: Market Forces, Fragmentation and Technological Advance* (London: Comedia, 1985), 10.
[121] Ilott, 'Commentary', 227; Hill, *British Cinema in the 1980s*, 37.
[122] Andrew Pulver, 'Bard to Worse at the Multiplex', *Guardian* (5 Feb. 1999), 19; Marie Woolf, 'Why the Next English Patient will be British', *Independent on Sunday* (20 Dec. 1998), 9.

for the latter half of the 1980s and the first half of the 1990s.[123] However, as Simon Relph, then Chief Executive, put it in the company report in 1986, 'we are not a subsidising body. British Screen will be run on commercial lines because, by seeking a real return on money, it is hoped we will be able to increase investments in the future.'[124] Typically supporting around ten to twelve films a year, 'British' costume dramas it assisted included *Comrades, On the Black Hill, White Mischief, The Bridge, December Bride, The Fool, Edward II, Orlando, Sirens* (1994), *Tom and Viv, Rob Roy, Victory, Richard III, Photographing Fairies, Amy Foster, Wilde, The Governess,* and *The Last September* (1999). The British Film Institute also had a small fund for production, again provided by the government, through which it financed *The Draughtsman's Contract* and *On the Black Hill,* among others.

From 1994, when it was founded, the National Lottery Film Funding Programme provided production funding on a more ambitious scale than hitherto seen. The scheme, administered by the Arts Council of England, and its equivalents in Scotland, Wales, and Northern Ireland (though since taken over by the Film Council), had a dramatic impact on the number of films being made. In 1996, for instance, 64 per cent more films went into production than the previous year, and by 1999, more than £100 million had been disbursed to over 200 projects.[125] There was a serious downside, however, with critics pointing to three major difficulties, claiming that few of the films deserved funding, too few found their way into distribution, and of those that did, too many were failures at the box office. The implication was that expansion had been at the expense of quality. Whatever one's views of the films, lottery funding undoubtedly fuelled the costume drama production trend. Thus the Arts Council of England awarded funding to *A Midsummer Night's Dream, Keep the Aspidistra Flying, Photographing Fairies, Amy Foster, Wilde, Plunkett and Macleane, The Governess, The Woodlanders, An Ideal Husband, Topsy-Turvy, The Claim, The House of Mirth, Mansfield Park,* and *Love's Labour's Lost,* while the Scottish Arts Council Lottery Fund supported *Regeneration,* and the Film Council *Gosford Park* (2001).

Several 'British' costume dramas also received European funding, although the UK was late in entering such schemes. *Orlando* (Fig. 16), *Prospero's Books, Carrington* (1995), and *Mrs Dalloway* were all officially co-productions, and benefited from the European Co-production Fund, administered at the time by British Screen. *Orlando, The Englishman Who Went Up a Hill . . .* (1994), *Victory, Rob Roy, Wilde, Photographing Fairies,* and *The Wings of the Dove* were supported by the European Script Fund and *Prospero's Books* and *Jane Eyre* (1995) by Eurimages, while *Rob Roy, Elizabeth, The Last September,* and *The House of Mirth* received assistance from the MEDIA Programme.

The task of the producer is to put together a viable budget from these diverse sources, which means juggling several balls at once if deals are to be struck. The

---

[123] Hill, 'Government Policy', 209.

[124] Simon Relph, in British Screen Finance Ltd, *British Screen Company Report and Accounts for the Year Ended 31 December 1986.*

[125] Pulver, 'Bard to Worse', 19; Dyja (ed.), *BFI Handbook 2001,* 31.

16. Queer queens and fine frocks in *Orlando*, a notable beneficiary of European funding

funding of *A Room with a View* was typical of the struggle for funding for low-budget films in such a complex and impoverished environment. The film was a seven-way co-production between Merchant Ivory Films, the NFFC, Channel 4, Goldcrest, the British distributors Curzon, the American distributors Cinecom, and Embassy Home Video. Merchant Ivory had also received script development money from the National Film Development Fund.[126] Thus there were state subsidies, television funding, and corporate finance, as well as pre-sales to theatrical distributors, television, and video—all to put together a budget of less than £3 million for a film that went on to take more than $60 million at the box office worldwide (at a time when the average mainstream studio film cost $17 million).

Subsidies and the support of television clearly provide some sort of safety net for those working in the production sector. State subsidies are an acknowledgement that, in the present global media economy, it is very difficult for British producers to survive on a commercial footing. European support mechanisms on the other hand recognize that the problem is not restricted to particular nation-states. Both depend on the view that local cultural production brings both economic and cultural benefits to that particular locale. The state in effect provides what one

---

[126] John Francis Lane, 'Merchant–Ivory's "Room"', *Screen International* (8 June 1985), 24; McFarling, 'Media Interest Justifies Merchant's Room Hopes', cutting.

producer calls 'money with a cultural mission',[127] where that mission is in part to protect and promote national cultures in a climate increasingly geared to what is perceived as an undifferentiated global culture.

Not all agree with such views. Some recent economic analyses of the film industry have contrasted the financial health of the Hollywood mainstream with what they see as the financially limited horizons of those working in the publicly subsidized sector. Martin Dale, for instance, writes of what he calls the 'subsidy trap', arguing that 'quotas and subsidies have herded European cinema into a cultural ghetto', in which considerations of cultural worth and public service override the need to establish a market for films.[128] Or as Colin Hoskins and his colleagues put it, 'Financial discipline, imposed by the market, forces Hollywood creators to tailor their films to the desires of the movie-going public; independent producers able to draw on public funds are much better placed to pursue artistic and creative agendas unrelated to what moviegoers wish to see.'[129]

There are at least two problems with this perspective. First, clearly some moviegoers do want to see the sort of specialized films that subsidies make possible: there is a market there, albeit a niche market. Secondly, such a perspective hardly takes into account the aspirations of the crossover film. Indeed what happened in the 1990s was that the niche market became recognized as significant in its own right, even by the majors, and the crossover film was developed as a compromise middle-brow product that could exploit the space between the mass market and the specialized arena. Dale's view, on the other hand, is that subsidies, far from simply enabling certain films to be made that would otherwise not be made, actually encourage a particular type of film-making. Or, to put it another way, subsidies *limit* film-making to that type, thereby pushing European film-making to 'the margins of society' and confirming 'its economic dependence'.[130] As he puts it, 'for subsidy-driven films . . . most filmmakers have to prove that their project isn't "commercial" in order to secure funding, and as a consequence they usually find it impossible to achieve any market impact.'[131] In effect, Dale sees no space for genuine product differentiation or innovation, no reason to make films that the Hollywood majors are not interested in, no purpose in making films for audiences that the mainstream product is not designed for.

Terry Ilott takes a similar view with regard to television funding, arguing that the more dependent European films have become on television funding, the smaller their budgets have become. In other words, he suggests that television involvement tends actually to drive budgets down, rather than simply to support low-budget film-making.[132] Again, however, there is a sound marketing logic for non-mainstream film-makers to seek television support, since they are more likely

---

[127] German producer Wieland Schulz-Kiel, quoted in Dale, *The Movie Game*, 117.
[128] Dale, *The Movie Game*, pp. xi, x.
[129] Colin Hoskins, Stuart McFadyen, and Adam Finn, *Global Television and Film: An Introduction to the Economics of the Business* (Oxford: Oxford University Press, 1997), 59.
[130] Dale, *The Movie Game*, 183.   [131] Ibid. 226.
[132] Ilott, *Budgets and Markets*, ch. 5.

to reach the older audiences to whom their films are targeted via television than through a theatrical release.

The relative poverty of budgets for 'British' films can be explained at least in part by the role of Hollywood in the global film industry. On the other hand, far fewer English heritage films would have been made in the 1980s and 1990s if it hadn't been for the involvement of American distributors. In the next chapter, then, I go on to examine the other side of this story about the commercial context of the heritage film, namely the interest of American distributors in the English heritage film.

4

American Commercial Interests in the Heritage Film

THE IMPACT OF GLOBALIZATION

The American market was vital for quality 'British' costume dramas in the 1980s and 1990s. Box-office success in that market, and the links with American distributors that made such box-office results possible, have probably been as important as anything else in ensuring the relative longevity of this particular production trend. Two questions immediately arise. First, why has the American market been so important for the producers of quality 'British' costume dramas? And, secondly, why should American companies have been interested in investing in or buying the rights for what often seem small-scale, specialized films with a markedly indigenous flavour—films usually made in Britain with self-consciously British subject-matter?

The key to answering the first question, as we've seen, is the size of the American market and the potential box-office revenue that it offers—especially when compared to the far smaller UK market. In 1980, the American trade paper *Hollywood Reporter* declared that it was 'virtually impossible for a film to make its money back at the UK box-office alone, unless it was made for less than $2 million'.[1] On the one hand, that explains why so much British film-making falls into the low-budget category, since that is all that the domestic market can support. On the other hand, it indicates why anyone wanting to make a more ambitious film has to look to overseas markets, and especially the American market. As one British film executive was reported as saying, 'it was just possible to make small-budget pictures on British subjects and get your money back in the UK, but that was a defeatist approach when it was possible to make bigger films for a world-wide audience'.[2] This suggests that 'British' films made on a larger budget will necessarily lose their indigenous qualities. Arguably, however, what the producers of heritage films have done over the years is to find ways of making self-consciously 'British' subject-matter marketable in the American market and elsewhere.

One way of explaining why there was so much American interest in small 'British' films is to see that interest as one of the by-products of the globalization

[1] Kenelm Jenour, 'British Film Industry Execs Cite Struggle to Compete with US', *Hollywood Reporter* (1 Apr. 1980), 29.
[2] Barry Spikings of Thorn-EMI, paraphrased ibid.

of the media industries. The conventional assessment of globalization is that it only works in favour of the multinational corporations, the majors. As Tino Balio puts it, while 'every year, a few offbeat pictures and smaller art films . . . win wide critical acclaim and enjoy significant box-office success . . . Hollywood neverthe-less remains committed to megapics and saturation booking, which have the combined effect of dominating most of the important screens around the world to the detriment of national film industries.'[3] These were the sorts of issues explored in the debate about the media during the GATT negotiations in 1993. As a French producer put it, 'the real battle at the moment is over who is going to be allowed to control the world's images, and so sell a certain life style, a certain culture, certain products and certain ideas'.[4] The French in particular argued that European culture needed to be defended against 'a marauding commercialism from Hollywood intent on standardizing the world's tastes at the level of *Jurassic Park* or the techno-thrills of Sylvester Stallone in *Cliffhanger*'.[5]

Yet what could be more national than the English heritage film, the 'British' costume drama? And did they not form a consistent production trend through the 1980s and 1990s, not least because of American financial support and distrib-ution? Does this really suggest that cultural diversity and the richness and coher-ence of local cultures has been squeezed out by global cultural phenomena such as MacDonald's, Coca Cola, *Star Wars*, and Disney? Or does it on the contrary suggest that there is still a space for the local even in the reign of Hollywood? As one journalist put it, 'international financing is sophisticated enough nowadays to support . . . fiercely localised work'.[6]

Whether one agrees or not, it is certainly the case that the growing market for American films abroad is, as one industry commentator noted, 'encouraging American studios to pay closer attention to foreign moviegoers'.[7] This develop-ment has taken various forms. First, distributors need to be sure that their films are going to work with different national audiences—which some have argued has contributed to 'a kind of Europeanizing of Hollywood'.[8] One might equally argue that there has at the same time been a kind of 'Asianizing' of Hollywood too. Secondly, the American majors have begun to invest in so-called 'indigenous' productions that are designed first and foremost for local markets—in Hollywood terms, niche markets. As one industry executive put it,

Our belief is the domestic [i.e. American] market, if not saturated, has at least enough films being made and seen . . . The pendulum is swinging the other way towards a greater

---

[3] Tino Balio, ' "A Major Presence in All the World's Important Markets": The Globalization of Hollywood in the 1990s', in Steve Neale and Murray Smith (eds.), *Contemporary Hollywood Cinema* (London: Routledge, 1998), 70.
[4] Marin Karmitz, quoted in Roger Cohen, 'Aux Armes! France Rallies to Battle Sly and T. Rex', *New York Times*, section 2 (2 Jan. 1994), 1.
[5] Cohen, 'Aux Armes!', 1.
[6] Andrew Pulver, 'Bard to Worse at the Multiplex', *Guardian* (5 Feb. 1999), 19.
[7] Geraldine Fabrikant, 'When World Raves, Studios Jump', *New York Times* (7 Mar. 1990), D1.
[8] British film director Michael Apted, quoted in Adam Dawtrey, 'Eurobucks Back Megapix', *Variety* (7 Mar. 1994), 2.

predisposition to getting more profits outside the US. . . . We are looking for films that are profitable without playing in the US . . . We then hope they play in the US, as long as we find the right way to release them in the US, appropriate to their [local] success so that all their profits are not lost on marketing.[9]

The argument is that 'local production for audiences locally and beyond cannot be ignored in the hunt for worldwide revenues'. In other words, given the nature of the global market, it makes sense in some cases that the majors are 'targeting local and international audiences and looking on the US market as a bonus'.[10]

At the same time, American companies wanted to create the sort of local market conditions that would best enable them to exploit those films. That meant in part investing for the long term by helping to build up and modernize foreign markets, whether those markets were theatrical or ancillary. The UK in fact became a testing ground in this respect, with American companies investing heavily in cinema-building, creating space for more bookings for American films, and helping audiences to grow once more.[11] By 1994, as noted above, overseas rentals for American films were greater than domestic rentals. The corollary was that locally made product had a poor year in its own domestic markets. In this context, 'US players have seized upon marketplace weakness to forge international ties that have assured access and favorable trading practices for US product.'[12] The benefits were not always perceived in such one-dimensional terms, however, since at the same time the British government was specifically encouraging foreign and especially American production activity and investment in the UK because it created jobs for British workers. There may be cultural benefits too. An article in the *New York Times* suggested that the result of the GATT negotiations was that 'Europeans can rest assured that their heritage is safe for now from limitless *Dukes of Hazzard* reruns'.[13] But one might equally argue that European heritage is often only brought to European screens with the help of American finance or distribution.

It is also important to recognize that *European* companies are buying into the global market, a trend that works on different levels. At one level is the attempt to attract American investment in small-scale and self-consciously indigenous 'British' films. At a second level is the production of films carefully designed for and targeted at the American market, as in the case of Goldcrest and Palace in the mid- and late 1980s. At a third level is multinational corporate development. As one report put it, citing PolyGram as an example, 'while Europe's national film

[9] Gareth Wigan, Columbia TriStar Films co-vice chairman, quoted in Adam Minns, 'What Dreams may Still Come?', *Screen International* (23 Oct. 1998), 32.

[10] Minns, 'What Dreams may Still Come?', 32.

[11] Fabrikant, 'When World Raves', D1, D8, first quote from D1; Geraldine Fabrikant, 'Hollywood Takes More Cues from Overseas', *New York Times* (25 June 1990), A1, D14, second quote from D14; Richard Gold, 'US Pix Tighten Global Grip', *Variety* (22 Aug. 1990), 1, 96; Terry Ilott, 'Yank Pix Flex Pecs in New Euro Arena', *Variety* (19 Aug. 1991), 1, 60; Leonard Klady, 'Earth to H'wood: You Win', *Variety* (13 Feb. 1995), 1, 63.

[12] Klady, 'Earth to H'wood: You Win', 1.

[13] Richard W. Stevenson, 'Lights! Camera! Europe!', *New York Times*, section 3 (6 Feb. 1994), 1.

cultures buckle before the industrial might of Hollywood, European money and talent nonetheless are carving out an increasingly prominent role in the international movie business'.[14] The problem for 'Euro politicos and filmmakers worried about Hollywood's influence on their local cultures, is whether Euro financing will bring any flavor of Europe to the films they back'.[15]

As the same report goes on to note, while some companies are using European finance to bolster traditional studio films, 'others are trying to discover the right creative and financial blend for a viable European alternative'. In this case, the goal is 'to combine Europe's tradition of personal movie-making on serious artistic subjects with Hollywood's production gloss and marketing savvy'. This combination was in part about 'attempting to unlock the elusive but potentially lucrative arthouse crossover market—which only Merchant Ivory has cracked with any consistency'. PolyGram was again cited as exemplary, especially in its involvement with production companies like Working Title.[16] But, as we shall see, American companies too were developing the same strategy, having realized that one way of responding to improved foreign markets was 'to make more low-budget "art films"'.[17] If such films could also be exploited as crossover products in the American market, then American companies were on to a winner. Thus while there is nothing very new about British production companies trying to break into the American market, less typical was that some American distributors were actively encouraging them to do so, but only once they had ensured that they would have a considerable share of any profits thereby accrued.

A succession of modestly budgeted foreign films—several of them costume dramas—became 'unexpected' crossover box-office successes in the 1980s and 1990s, including *Chariots of Fire* (1981), *The Kiss of the Spider Woman* (1985), *A Room with a View* (1986), *Cinema Paradiso* (1989), *Like Water for Chocolate* (1991), *Howards End* (1992), *The Crying Game* (1992), *The Piano* (1993), *The Postman* [*Il Postino*] (1994), *Four Weddings and a Funeral* (1994), *The English Patient* (1996), *The Full Monty* (1997), *Elizabeth* (1998), *Shakespeare in Love* (1998), and *Notting Hill* (1999). It is the desire to have a share of the profits generated by such films that has driven American companies into this market, spreading the risks across a number of films in the hope of at least one of them coming up trumps. As a Miramax executive explained, 'a "risky proposition" is worth it to them. The "key" is a low budget'.[18]

The international box-office success of home-grown 'riskier fare' like *Driving Miss Daisy* (1989) and *Dances with Wolves* (1990) also inspired the majors to explore international co-financing and presale deals as a way of buying into such projects at an early stage. Previously, such projects—'period pieces, theatrical adaptations—in other words, hard to develop films that are even harder to

[14] Dawtrey, 'Eurobucks Back Megapix', 1.   [15] Ibid.   [16] Ibid. 1–2.
[17] Fabrikant, 'Hollywood Takes More Cues from Overseas', D14; see also Balio, ' "A Major Presence" ', 65–6.
[18] Paul Webster, head of production at Miramax, quoted in David Finkle, 'Hope and Glory: The Unexpected Rebirth of British Cinema', *Village Voice* (6 Aug. 1996), 51.

market'—had been considered too risky for the majors on their own.[19] Co-financing was developed as a way of spreading the risk and maximizing available production funding, in part by making sure that American companies could tap into local subsidies.[20] Co-financing modestly budgeted 'indigenous' or specialized films also added product to a company's overall distribution roster—and allowed films that wouldn't otherwise see the light of day to move into production: 'ironically, it's precisely those projects that become runaway hits or win Oscars . . . precisely because they *are* different'.[21] Thus, once again, it seems that the tendency towards globalization can create the space for diversity and innovation. Even the majors recognize this fact, as the following statement from the president of Fox Films underlines: 'If everything is an event picture, nothing stands out as being unique, innovative or exceptional. You need different types of pictures, and all kinds of pictures have worked successfully.'[22]

One type of picture that had produced its fair share of crossover hits was the English costume drama. By the time of *Elizabeth*, at the end of the 1990s, this had become, in the words of one trade journalist, 'a safe genre',[23] a niche consumer phenomenon which the industry could buy into and exploit. The goal was to build on the success of the production trend, to maintain its established, core audience, but at the same time to lift it out of the specialized art-house circuit, insert it into the multiplexes and attract new audiences, more mainstream cinemagoers. These were not films that would usually compete with solidly mainstream fare—certainly not with the blockbuster; on the contrary, they would run alongside the mainstream film in the crossover market. Just occasionally, of course, one of the higher budgeted costume films would compete with the blockbusters: *Shakespeare in Love*, *The English Patient*, and *Braveheart* (1995) (which cost more than twice as much as the other two films) all grossed more than $200 million worldwide, a figure which no more than 200 films have ever achieved.[24] Once more, the film industry reveals itself capable of catering for difference.

DEVELOPING THE CROSSOVER MARKET IN THE USA

The identification within the film business of a distinct crossover market is the result of a series of modestly budgeted, specialized films breaking out of the

[19] Richard Natale, 'Risky Pix Get a Global Fix', *Variety* (28 Sept. 1992), 1, 97; quotation from 97; see also Peter Hlavacek, 'New Indies on a (Bank) Roll', *Variety* (24 Jan. 1990), 1; Lawrence Cohn, 'Majors are Relying on Indies in a Major Way', *Variety* (27 Apr. 1992), 3.

[20] See Balio, ' "A Major Presence" ', 64; and Dawtrey, 'Eurobucks Back Megapix', 1.

[21] An unnamed former studio head, quoted in Natale, 'Risky Pix Get a Global Fix', 97.

[22] Bill Mechanic, president of Fox Films, quoted in Leonard Klady, 'Why Mega-flicks Click', *Variety* (25 Nov. 1996), 87.

[23] Minns, 'What Dreams may Still Come?', 32; for another account of how British costume dramas fared in the American market in the 1980s and 1990s, see Sarah Street, *Transatlantic Crossings: British Feature Films in the USA* (London: Continuum, 2002), ch. 8.

[24] See the all-time box-office charts on the Internet Movie Database, at imdb.com.

art-house and crossing over successfully into the mainstream cinemas. Its base, though, is in the art-house market. Art cinema became well established as a niche market in the USA in the post-war period, 'appealing to high-income, well-educated Americans . . . as an addition to the traditional modes of "high art"— literature, music, and drama'.[25] In the early 1950s, there were some 470 art-house theatres; by the late 1960s, there were over a thousand, most of them in the well-off areas of large cities and in university towns.[26] Middle-brow British films— sophisticated literary adaptations and offbeat fare—were often shown successfully in such contexts. The mid-1960s proved to be the high point in this niche market development—even some of the major film companies became interested. But from the late 1960s onwards, art cinema went into decline as an American exhibition business: 'by 1980, the universe of theatres in the United States that regularly ran foreign films was down to less than one hundred'.[27]

With the rise of home video from the early 1980s, the art-house or repertory cinema became 'an extremely rare commodity'.[28] It is now confined for the most part to university towns and major cities, and to museums, non-profit organizations, and independently owned cinemas, such as the small Landmark Theaters chain, which became part of the Goldwyn company in the 1990s. Such cinemas traditionally showed mainly foreign-language films and English-language films produced outside the USA, without American backing. A small niche market, distinct from the mainstream, valuing art over commerce, it catered for what *Variety* called the 'lost audience': 'mature, adult, sophisticated people who read good books and magazines, who attend lectures and concerts, who are politically and socially aware and alert. . . . These people have been literally driven out of the motion picture theatre by the industry's insistence on aiming most of its product at the lowest level'.[29]

In the late 1970s and early 1980s, several low-budget quality films broke through to larger audiences than the usual art-house release could deliver, effectively attracting some of that 'lost audience' back into mainstream cinemas. Two particular successes, both 'British' costume dramas, were *Chariots of Fire* and *Gandhi* (1982), respectively the highest and second highest grossing English-language European imports to the USA ($62 million and $52 million) until the 1990s.[30] In an effort to exploit this market, and in the hope that the prestige associated with such films might rub off on them, some of the major studios established

---

[25] Douglas Gomery, *Shared Pleasures: A History of Movie Presentation in the United States* (London: British Film Institute, 1992), 180.

[26] Ibid. 181.　　[27] Ibid. 193.

[28] Christine Ogan, 'The Audience for Foreign Film in the United States', *Journal of Communication*, 40/4 (1990), 58; see also Alex Ben Block, 'Entering New "Golden Age," Specialty Films Cash in', *Hollywood Reporter online*, at www.hollywoodreporter.com, 12 Mar. 1993.

[29] Alfred Starr, 'The Lost Audience is Still Lost', *Variety* (16 Jan. 1954), 61, quoted in Tino Balio, 'Introduction to Part I', in Balio (ed.), *Hollywood in the Age of Television* (Boston and London: Unwin Hyman, 1990), 7.

[30] Lawrence Cohn, ' "Chariots of Fire" Becomes Top Import Pic in U.S. B.O. History', *Variety* (7 July 1982), 1; Anon., 'Eurochamps Stateside', *Variety* (18 May 1992), 85.

small-profit 'classics' divisions, such as Triumph Films at Columbia and Twentieth Century Fox International Classics. Distribution of the films, however, was left to the same people that handled the mainstream releases, and they failed to give the films the special attention they needed if they were to succeed. As independent distributor Ira Deutchman explains, the 'classics' divisions were 'quickly abandoned when it became clear that prestige was higher than profits and that there wasn't enough quality product around to feed them all'.[31]

This intervention on the part of the majors echoed their production of prestige films in the 1930s. While these films were different in that they were big-budget productions, with big stars, in other respects, they had qualities associated in the later period with 'classics'. Thus they were typically based on pre-sold properties, often canonical nineteenth-century literature or Shakespeare, or they were biopics or historical subjects, often with a European dimension. Once produced, they were frequently given road-show releases, which have some parallels with the slow roll-out of the crossover film. Some of the productions were loss leaders, made to garner prestige as much as generate box office—though many were top box-office hits.[32] It was this mix of prestige and profits that the majors sought to establish with their short-lived 'classics' divisions.

When the majors withdrew from the 'classics' market in the mid-1980s, their place was taken by a new breed of independent distributors, which specialized in handling upscale art-house products: Orion Classics, Miramax, New Line, and Goldwyn. The success of these companies owed much to the flowering of the various ancillary markets in the USA in the early 1980s (especially pay cable, home video, and syndicated television) and the development of the practice of pre-sales. As Balio points out, 'such ancillary income for a low-budget picture might make the difference between profit and loss'.[33] The video market in particular seemed a godsend, especially with the extremely favourable deals offered in the early days when video labels desperately needed new material. As a result, 'numerous small independent distributors (Cinecom, Avenue, Island, Aries, etc.) mushroomed into existence in order to service these deals, with the understanding that a theatrical release increased the value of the video titles'.[34] Cinecom then had an enormous success in 1986 with *A Room with a View*, although they were unable to repeat that success on a consistent basis (*Maurice* (1987), which they also distributed, was much less successful, as we've seen).

---

[31] Ira Deutchman, 'Independent Distribution and Marketing', in Jason E. Squire (ed.), *The Movie Business Book* (New York: Fireside, 1992), 322; see also Justin Wyatt, 'The Formation of the "Major Independents": Miramax, New Line and the New Hollywood', in Neale and Smith, *Contemporary Hollywood Cinema*, 84; and William Grimes, 'Little Movies Trying to be Bigger Movies', *New York Times* (30 July 1992), C13–14.

[32] See Tino Balio, *The History of the American Cinema*, v. *Grand Design: Hollywood as a Modern Business Enterprise, 1930–1939* (New York: Scribners, 1993), 179–211.

[33] Tino Balio, 'Introduction to Part II', in Balio, *Hollywood in the Age of Television*, 280; see also Wyatt, 'The Formation of the "Major Independents"'; and Balio, '"A Major Presence"'.

[34] James Schamus, 'To The Rear of the Back End: The Economics of Independent Cinema', in Neale and Smith, *Contemporary Hollywood Cinema*, 94; see also Hlavacek, 'New Indies on a (Bank) Roll', 1.

As Robert Murphy noted in 1985,

British films seem to have secured a small but permanent place in the American market. Distributors like the Goldwyn company have shown that the art-house market can be a lucrative one and that British films, particularly those like *Chariots of Fire, Betrayal* and *Educating Rita*, which are ostentatiously British, are as acceptable there as traditional European art movies.[35]

Had Murphy been writing a year or two later, *A Room with a View* and Cinecom would undoubtedly have been in that list. Other indie distributors that handled English costume dramas in this period include New Line with *A Handful of Dust* (1987), while Goldwyn also handled *Henry V* (1989). The problem was that the buoyancy of the mid-1980s could not be maintained by the American independents, with the cable, television, and video markets settling down, and the specialist film market becoming more and more competitive and eventually saturated with too many films. As the indies suffered, so too did British producers, with American investment in British production falling off from £176 million in 1986 to £67 million in 1988.[36] With the collapse of Goldcrest and the withdrawal of the capital allowances scheme, finding production funding in the UK became more and more difficult.

In the UK and the USA in the late 1980s, there were too many independent companies working in the same market, all competing for the same sources of funding, the same films, and the same audiences. And although the market had grown, it hadn't grown sufficiently for all the specialist films to reap box-office takings on the scale of *Chariots, Gandhi,* or *A Room with a View*: 'The independent sector was overcrowded and smaller companies too often found themselves producing films that got no more than a token theatrical release.'[37] By 1989, there were signs of a resurgence among surviving American independent distributors, mainly thanks to better exploitation of foreign markets, both theatrical and video.[38] The companies left in the market after the shakeout of the late 1980s were also more careful with their acquisitions, sticking to high-quality, low-budget films 'rooted in national cultural identity'.[39] Fine Line, established by mini-major New Line in 1990, was typical of the new breed of company. In the words of their president, Ira Deutchman, formerly of Cinecom, they would handle 'classics' films with limited potential, but crucially they would also distribute films that 'take a little more immediate special attention to launch them into the market-place, a

---

[35] Robert Murphy, 'Three Companies: Boyd's Co., HandMade and Goldcrest', in Martin Auty and Nick Roddick (eds.), *British Cinema Now* (London: British Film Institute, 1985), 56.

[36] John Hill, 'Government Policy and the British Film Industry 1979–90', *European Journal of Communication*, 8 (1993), 212.

[37] Jake Eberts and Terry Ilott, *My Indecision is Final: The Rise and Fall of Goldcrest Films* (London: Faber & Faber, 1990), 449; see also 231–2.

[38] See Tom Bierbaum, 'Captains of Video Cruise into LA . . .', *Variety* (22 Feb. 1989), 21; Hlavacek, 'New Indies on a (Bank) Roll', 1.

[39] Deborah Young, 'Attempting to Figure out the Market for Arthouse Films', *Variety* (18 May 1992), 85).

little more time to find their audience, but that have more market, more crossover potential than classics-oriented films'.[40]

Inspired by the success of companies like Fine Line, Miramax, and Goldwyn, the really significant development of the 1990s was the various and on the whole successful attempts by the majors to move back into the specialized and crossover markets, though it was really the crossovers that the majors were interested in. The majors achieved this primarily by absorbing the successful independents as relatively autonomous units within their overall operations, or establishing their own distinctive in-house 'designer labels'. Either way, the new units were intended to reach the niche audiences, and especially the upscale, educated audience, that were out of reach of their mainstream distribution arms. Thus the executive team from Orion Classics moved over to establish Sony Classics; Miramax became a subsidiary of Disney; New Line and Fine Line became part of Turner Broadcasting, which then itself became part of the Time-Warner empire; Goldwyn was acquired by MGM; Twentieth Century Fox established Fox Searchlight, and Universal acquired October and at the same time ran Gramercy with Poly-Gram (both were later sold to USA Networks, another developing multimedia corporation, in the aftermath of the merging of Universal and PolyGram[41]).

Some of the traditional terminology consequently had to be revised, since 'an indie distributor no longer means independent ownership, but rather a company which caters for specialty product'.[42] On the other hand, there is a remarkably consistent—and very revealing—set of terms used in the industry when discussing such operations. The films are 'specialized', 'art-house', 'adult oriented', 'high-quality', 'classics'; they are made by 'prestigious' and 'innovative' teams, 'quality filmmakers'; the finished products require 'special handling', they have to be 'nurtured'; even the distributors are 'sophisticated, highly literate', and 'have a wonderful creative sensibility'—indeed, 'their emphasis on quality, taste and a truly global view of filmmaking is a model for our entire motion picture business'.[43]

[40] Claudia Eller, 'New Line Forms New Label for Specialty Releases', *Variety* (10 Dec. 1990), 5.

[41] Martin Peers and Benedict Carver, 'Swap Meet Feels the Heat', *Variety* (12 Apr. 1999), 1, 78–9.

[42] Martin Dale, *The Movie Game: The Film Business in Britain, Europe and America* (London: Cassell, 1997), 56.

[43] Such terminology can be found throughout the trade press, but all of the terms quoted are used in the following: Eller, 'New Line Forms New Label', 5; Kirk Honeycutt, 'BV to Distribute Merchant Ivory', *Hollywood Reporter online*, at www.hollywoodreporter.com, 29 July 1992; Claudia Eller and John Evan Frook, 'Mickey Munches on Miramax', *Variety* (3 May 1993), 1; Richard Natale, 'Gramercy to the Rescue of Smaller Pix', *Variety* (25 May 1992), 7; Joseph Steuer and Kirk Honeycutt, 'Barker, Bloom, Bernard Still Sony Classics', *Hollywood Reporter online*, at www.hollywoodreporter.com, 27 Jan. 1997; Klady, 'Why Mega-flicks Click', 1, 87; John Calley, President of Sony Picture Entertainments, quoted in Joseph Steuer, 'Sony's Classic Trio Inks, Plans to Get Aggressive', *Hollywood Reporter online*, at www.hollywoodreporter.com, 31 Jan.–2 Feb. 1997.

That final phrase—'a model for our entire motion picture business'—is particularly interesting!

The move by the majors into the specialized market represented a sea change in Hollywood, 'as studios and independents increasingly align[ed] to battle booming marketing and production costs, capture fragmented audiences and scramble for bigger market shares'.[44] The move provided a new arm to the majors' revenue-generating activities. Their partnerships with the independents enabled them to build up their distribution rosters and to establish relationships with new creative talent. What the majors recognized was that, in the globalized multimedia market, audiences were increasingly fragmented, and there was a profit to be made by addressing specialized niches. It might not be a *Titanic*-sized profit, but it was a profit worth exploiting all the same.

By 1994, with specialized distributors like Miramax, Fine Line, and Goldwyn all looking to invest in 'British' productions, with audiences still on the rise, and with the introduction of lottery funding and European subsidies, the British production sector was looking much more buoyant.[45] Costume dramas in particular benefited from American involvement in the 1990s. Miramax, for instance, was involved with *Enchanted April* (1991), *A Month by the Lake* (1994), *The English Patient, Emma* (1996), *Restoration* (1996), *The Wings of the Dove* (1997), *Mrs Brown* (1997), *Shakespeare in Love, An Ideal Husband* (1999), *Mansfield Park* (1999), *Love's Labour's Lost* (2000), and *The Golden Bowl* (2000). The Samuel Goldwyn Company was involved with *Henry V, Much Ado About Nothing* (1993), *Angels and Insects* (1995), and *The Madness of King George* (1995). Sony Classics were involved with *Howards End, Orlando* (1992), *Hamlet* (1996), *Persuasion* (1996), and *Wilde* (1997). Fine Line/New Line were involved with *Where Angels Fear to Tread* (1991), *Edward II* (1991), and *Twelfth Night* (1996). Gramercy handled *Carrington* (1995), *Jude* (1996), and *Elizabeth*. First Look—'one of the last remaining true independents'[46]—was involved with *Keep the Aspidistra Flying* (1997; *A Merry War* in the USA) and *Mrs Dalloway* (1997). Savoy, only on the scene from 1992 to 1995, was involved with *Shadowlands* (1993). And among the majors, Columbia (part of Sony), who in the 1980s had backed *A Passage to India* (1984) and *White Mischief* (1987), financed and released *The Remains of the Day* (1993), *Mary Reilly*, and *Sense and Sensibility* (1996), Paramount financed *Wuthering Heights* (1992) (they had also backed *Lady Jane* (1985)), Warners financed *Black Beauty* (1994), MGM backed *Moll Flanders* (1995), and Fox Searchlight backed *The Secret Agent* (1996).

1992 in particular was an important year. Universal set up Gramercy with PolyGram; Savoy started operations; New Line/Fine Line and Castle Rock became

---

[44] Eller and Frook, 'Mickey Munches on Miramax', 1; see also Tino Balio, 'The Art Film Market in the New Hollywood', in Geoffrey Nowell-Smith and Steven Ricci (eds.), *Hollywood and Europe: Economics, Culture, National Identity 1945–95* (London: British Film Institute, 1998), 63–73.

[45] See Edwin Riddell and Alex Clarke, 'Brits Energize Film Production', *Hollywood Reporter online*, at www.hollywoodreporter.com, 9 Feb. 1994.

[46] Beverly Gray, 'The Reel Deal', *Hollywood Reporter* (11 Aug. 1998), 10.

part of the Turner company; Merchant Ivory Productions formed a partnership with Disney; and Sony Picture Classics was established at Sony. The first film Sony Classics handled was Merchant Ivory's *Howards End* (prior to the Disney deal)— which they nurtured into a huge box-office success as a crossover film. Other small films 'crossed over' successfully that year too, films that would once have circulated solely in the art-house market. Thus the *Variety* box-office chart for the first week of August of 1992 shows *Howards End, Enchanted April, Where Angels Fear to Tread*, and *Edward II* all in the American top 60 (along with *Delicatessen* (1990), *Mediterraneo* (1991), *Fried Green Tomatoes* (1991), and *The Player* (1992)).[47] As the *Hollywood Reporter* noted, 'a spate of films for grown-ups . . . have broken out of the art-house ghetto over the past year at a record pace . . . [These] high-flying hits . . . have given new life to the specialty film market.'[48] The president of the small independent cinema chain, Landmark Theaters, commented: 'The specialized film business has hit a new plateau . . . It's almost like a golden age. You have to go back to the '60s when all the Italian films hit to see anything like this.' His view was that the buoyancy of the market was due in part to the enormous success of *Howards End* and in part to the ageing of the population: 'That's a lot of audience for films like these.'[49]

Both *Howards End* and *Enchanted April* (Fig. 17) were major box-office successes as crossover films. The former is discussed in a separate chapter. The latter was made as a low-budget television film shot on 16 mm for the BBC for £1.1 million, when more substantial funds had proved impossible to source. It was picked up midway through production by Miramax, who bought worldwide distribution rights, paid for it to be blown up to 35 mm, gave it an advertising budget and released it theatrically in the USA. In the end, more was spent on prints and advertising in the USA than had been put into its production in the first place. Opening on five screens, it gradually built up to 324 screens after seven weeks, and was still doing well after thirty weeks. It went on to gross around $15 million in the USA alone and to receive two Oscar nominations. In the UK, having attracted the attention of the London Film Festival, which presented it as their opening film, it was hurriedly given a theatrical release with almost no advertising, and inevitably hardly made a mark, taking only £64,000.[50]

Where Angels Fear to Tread and *Edward II* also did well with audiences given their art-house production values, but their box-office takings were much more modest. *Where Angels*, as another Forster adaptation, was able to benefit from the publicity surrounding *Howards End* and was deliberately released in the USA at the same time as the Merchant Ivory film. It opened in two cinemas and then gradually widened, but never showed on more than thirty-five screens in one

---

[47] *Variety* (10 Aug. 1992), 8.

[48] Block, 'Entering New "Golden Age" ', from website.

[49] Stephen Gilula, quoted ibid.

[50] See Terry Ilott, *Budgets and Markets: A Study of the Budgeting and Marketing of European Films* (London: Routledge, 1996), 87–94; and David Leafe (ed.), *BFI Film and Television Handbook 1993* (London: British Film Institute, 1992), 38.

17. A British television drama, an American box-office hit: the video sleeve for *Enchanted April*

week, though it was still doing the rounds after twenty-three weeks. *Edward II* was also released in the USA around the same time, again on two screens, though it never built up to more than sixteen screens. Even so, high average takings per screen meant it was still in the American box-office top 60 after nineteen weeks.

The shake-up of independent or specialized distribution in the mid-1990s in the USA produced

an entire new generation of entities that look like indies and act like indies but have the financing and marketing prowess of majors behind them. . . . 'It's no longer a case of majors versus independents but rather the option of going mainstream or specialised' . . . [with] the studios being increasingly receptive to non-mainstream ventures. . . . 'What's been happening is that more and more films like *Remains of the Day* and *In the Name of the Father* are coming from the majors and their boutique arms'.[51]

One result of this sort of development is that 'the line between arthouse pics and mainstream releases has increasingly blurred'.[52] The first sign that the major

---

[51] Leonard Klady, 'New Studio Inroads are Irking the Indies', *Variety* (13 Dec. 1993), 91, quoting Jonathan Dana of Triton Pictures and Bert Manzari of Landmark Theaters.
[52] Lawrence Cohn, 'Shiny New Imports Rev up for B.O. Race', *Variety* (21 Oct. 1991), 3.

studios were 'starting to think small' was the establishment of Gramercy at Universal as 'a boutique operation . . . to handle the kind of specialised films the majors often have trouble releasing'. The key here was that the studio established a separate outfit to distribute such films, rather than relying on their mainstream distribution division. The response of the indies was to question whether 'major studios can ever really nurture such films, even via in-house labels', arguing that they had too many films on their books to be able to take on individualized marketing, to 'give smaller films the care and feeding needed to survive'.[53]

This was the problem that had thrown the majors when they first established classics divisions in the late 1970s and early 1980s—and other majors were initially very wary of Universal's move. As one studio executive was quoted as saying, 'If you want to be in a business that makes $3 m a year, then you're okay', but for some, the lack of what seemed like significant revenue in the majors' terms did not suggest this was a worthwhile market.[54] Used to spending vast amounts on advertising on television, in print, and on billboards—'we're always looking for the home run, the blockbuster'—the prospect of making $2–3 million hardly seemed viable.[55] On the other hand, if profits were small, losses were never enormous either, and for the small, dedicated in-house label, dealing with ten films a year, those small profits slowly add up. As Fine Line's Deutchman explained, 'The studios are poised to think in the macro. We think in the micro, working each market separately . . . It's not just a matter of spending less money, but how you spend that money'.[56] Or as *Variety* put it, the studios prefer 'to gamble big than make $1 billion a dollar at a time'.[57] This is because their mainstream distribution divisions are geared to accommodate blockbusters, not to nurture specialized films.

On the face of it, perhaps the most surprising deals of the 1990s were those made between Disney and two of the most successful independent companies of the previous decade, one a producer (Merchant Ivory Productions) and the other a distributor (Miramax). In fact, Disney, the consummate family-oriented studio, had for some time been diversifying, having earlier established Touchstone to make more adult fare. Their interest in well made but more modestly budgeted films that had the potential to break out of the art-house and cross over into the mainstream market tied in with studio head Jeffrey Katzenberg's call for restraint on inflated costs in the industry.[58] It also allowed Disney to spread its risks across 'an eclectic slate of projects', to produce a range of films suited to different parts

[53] Natale, 'Gramercy to the Rescue of Smaller Pix', 5.

[54] Unnamed studio executive, quoted ibid. 7.

[55] Tom Pollock, head of MCA-Universal motion picture group, quoted in Natale, 'Gramercy to the Rescue of Smaller Pix', 7.

[56] Ira Deutchman, president of Fine Line, quoted in Natale, 'Gramercy to the Rescue of Smaller Pix', 7; see also Gray, 'The Reel Deal', 10; and Aljean Harmetz, 'Sam Goldwyn's Little Studio that Could', *New York Times*, section 2 (18 Oct. 1992), 13.

[57] Klady, 'Why Mega-flicks Click', 87.

[58] Laurence Earle, 'Rushes', *Independent* (7 Aug. 1992), 14.

of the increasingly fragmented market.[59] By 1992, when the deal with Disney was announced, Merchant Ivory had a formidable reputation as the producers of *A Room with a View* and *Howards End*, two of the most visible crossover successes of the previous few years. Through the deal with Disney, they gained production financing and guaranteed distribution in the USA and elsewhere. Disney on the other hand acquired the kudos of a deal with 'prestigious film makers', which would guarantee them 'serious films aimed at adults', at relatively little financial cost—'the kind of film we, frankly, will be very proud to be associated with'.[60]

For the *New York Times*, this was still a very odd match because Disney and Merchant Ivory seemed to be on 'such opposite sides of the creative spectrum' and to have 'entirely different tastes and styles: relentlessly commercial versus relentlessly highbrow'.[61] The merging of these two sets of values is of course precisely what makes up the crossover film—and clearly that is what both parties were aiming for. Thus, on the one hand, Katzenberg said 'We don't want Merchant Ivory to . . . make the kinds of movies that we do . . . They have a unique quality and distinctiveness'; on the other hand, he recognized that the deal 'takes them out of the more limited art house world that they began in': 'I think their films are well-suited to a much broader audience . . . I don't see them as small, limited (audience) movies'.[62] Ismail Merchant for his part suggested that 'they are part of the mainstream and so are we'.[63]

The acquisition of the 'fiercely non-conformist' Miramax by the 'thoroughly mainstream' Disney worked in a very similar way. As *Variety* noted, both have that 'rarest of qualities in Hollywood: brand identity'. The deal gave Miramax much more secure funding and far better access to ancillary markets, especially home video and pay television. Disney again secured access to 'high-quality, lower-budgeted independent movies', 'highbrow, artistic movies'—both those that Miramax would develop or acquire and those that already made up their prestigious back library of more than 200 films.[64] Miramax would operate as a fully autonomous division within Disney, as a sort of in-house designer label. The goal though was for Disney and Miramax to converge, in the sense that Miramax would concentrate on the crossover market, midway between the mainstream and the art-house, 'marketing and targeting audiences beyond a narrow art house niche'.[65]

[59] Peter Bart, 'A Year to Dwarf All Others', *Variety* (19 July 1993), 5.

[60] Bernard Weinraub, 'Disney Signs up Merchant and Ivory', *New York Times* (27 July 1992), C15; Jeffrey Katzenberg, Chairman of Walt Disney Studios, quoted in Honeycutt, 'BV to Distribute Merchant Ivory', from website; see also Balio, ' "A Major Presence" ', 66; and Balio, 'The Art Film Market', 71.

[61] Weinraub, 'Disney Signs up Merchant and Ivory', C15.

[62] Quoted ibid., C17; and Honeycutt, 'BV to Distribute Merchant Ivory', from website.

[63] Quoted in Weinraub, 'Disney Signs up Merchant and Ivory', C17.

[64] All quotations from Eller and Frook, 'Mickey Munches on Miramax', 1; see also Claudia Eller, 'On-screen Chemistry', *LA Times* (1 Dec. 1995), D1, D5; and Betsy Sharkey, 'The Brothers Miramax', *New York Times*, section 2 (24 Apr. 1994), 1.

[65] Wyatt, 'The Formation of the "Major Independents" ', 76.

For much of the 1990s, these new alliances in the American film industry enabled a good few 'British' costume dramas to see the light of day and to reach often quite large audiences in the USA. Several American companies actually set up offices in London, while others announced deals with British producers. Miramax, for instance, backed HAL Films with substantial funds, which enabled them to make *Mansfield Park*, among other films. HAL is an interesting case, since it was run by two former senior executives from Channel 4 Films and one from Miramax. As *Mansfield Park* also received lottery funding, the company effectively brought together the three most significant developments in British production in recent years—television, an American independent, and lottery money.[66]

PROMOTING AND RELEASING SPECIALIZED AND CROSSOVER FILMS

The *New York Times* described the opening weekend release of mainstream films, with thousands of prints and millions of pounds spent on advertising, as a blitzkrieg, where 'small, independent films must wage guerrilla warfare'.[67] The analogy is appropriate. Given the huge budgets for prints and advertising, the distribution strategy for the mainstream film is quite different to the specialized release, although just as carefully planned, especially as regards release dates and launch dates for the publicity. The film will open on thousands of screens, backed up by a national advertising campaign that requires little effort at the local level. The aim is to recoup as much as possible of the production cost on the opening weekend. But if blockbuster releases 'do not require a lot of finesse: they work or fail from the very first matinee', more specialized films (*Emma* is among those cited) require 'special handling' and even then at best rarely generate profits greater than $10 million.[68] Distribution for specialized films is seen as more creative, building up, as we've already noted, from an exclusive opening on a very small number of screens to an increasingly wider release, with audiences and revenue slowly developing over time. The goal is to exploit those markets tradi-tionally ignored by the majors, and to emphasize the difference of the specialized film from the mainstream release. But, if the film is to become a crossover success, the strategy must be twofold. Initially, its difference from the mainstream will be stressed, but as the release widens, so its similarity to the mainstream must be acknowledged.

Distributing the film via a slow rollout helps to generate a sense of exclusivity, as opposed to buying into the ultra-consumerist hype of the Hollywood block-buster. The specialized film is something you wait patiently for, not consume with

---

[66] See Cathy Dunkley, 'Rough Crossing', *Hollywood Reporter* (Independent Producers and Distributors Special Issue, 11 Aug. 1998), 30.
[67] Grimes, 'Little Movies Trying to be Bigger Movies', C13.
[68] Klady, 'Why Mega-flicks Click', 87.

the masses on the opening weekend! This was precisely what Sony Classics tried to achieve with *Howards End*: 'We did not want to saturate any market-place and use it up. We preferred to have long lines in front of our theaters . . . You didn't have to hurry up and see it.'[69] The slow rollout, city by city, is in some ways akin to a touring theatre production, or the roadshow release used for large-scale prestige films from *The Birth of a Nation* (1915) onwards.[70] There is a limited window in each city and the audience has to wait for the film to arrive. When it does arrive, it's a special event, although clearly as an event movie it's on a different scale to the latest blockbuster. The opening weekend mentality is avoided—as the distributors said of *Howards End*, 'there wasn't that kind of immediate need to see the picture, but there was a want-to-see'—and it was the task of the distributors to create that 'want-to-see' through their marketing.[71]

The 'studio marketing machine simply doesn't have the time to nurture such films, to support a slow, deliberate rollout'.[72] Specialized and crossover films require more attention, with more time and energy spent on promotional work and publicity rather than on advertising—to which end, specialized distributors usually work with specialist public relations firms.[73] Since the films are not released nationwide but tend to roll out slowly, gradually building up from just one or two screens on a platformed basis, marketing costs are kept far lower than for mainstream films. Such films are rarely advertised on television. On the contrary, as industry insider Mark Litwak explains, 'the distributor places much more reliance on benefit screenings, free publicity, festival showings, critical reviews, and other methods designed to spread positive word-of-mouth'.[74] For *Chariots of Fire* (Fig. 18), for instance, special screenings were organized for opinion leaders in religion, education, sports, music, fashion, community affairs, and government, who were courted to aid in publicizing the film. The film was also shown at festivals in New York and Toronto, while the film's principal actors, the producer, and the director made personal appearances in key cities. Vangelis's soundtrack was released as a record, with special displays sent out to music stores and radio stations, and free ticket competitions organized. The costumes used in the film were also heavily promoted by sending story material billing the film as 'Fashion Movie of the Year' to fashion columnists on local and national newspapers.[75] Building up publicity in this way, often territory by territory, is an intensive process, and the publicity departments of major studios, in the words of one

---

[69] Tom Bernard of Sony Classics, quoted in Martin A. Grove, '*Howards End* Driven Theatrically, Not by Video', *Hollywood Reporter* (1 Mar. 1993), 2.

[70] See Sheldon Hall, 'Hard Ticket Giants: Hollywood Blockbusters in the Widescreen Era', unpublished Ph.D. thesis, University of East Anglia, Norwich, 1999.

[71] Michael Barker of Sony Classics quoted in Grove, '*Howards End* Driven Theatrically', 2.

[72] Natale, 'Gramercy to the Rescue of Smaller Pix', 7.

[73] Grimes, 'Little Movies Trying to be Bigger Movies', C14.

[74] Mark Litwak, 'Foreword', in Tiiu Lukk, *Movie Marketing: Opening the Picture and Giving it Legs* (Los Angeles: Silman-James Press, 1997), p. xiii; see also Jeffrey Daniels, 'Specialty Strategies Shared', *Hollywood Reporter online*, at www.hollywoodreporter.com, 12 Mar. 1993.

[75] B. J. Franklin, 'How "Chariots" Caught Fire', *Screen International* (15 May 1982), 8.

18. The pleasures of Englishness: period precision in *Chariots of Fire*

marketing executive, are 'not staffed to take people away from a major release to work every day for six months nurturing a small movie'.[76] This is exactly how the specialized distributors work, whether they are independents or niche in-house labels at one of the majors. As an executive at Goldwyn suggested, 'It's the difference between a mass production factory and a crafts cottage where things are made by hand'.[77]

A Room with a View, another key crossover film of the 1980s, had a 'relatively paltry ad budget', which was spent on small advertisements in local newspapers, spots on radio stations with classical music formats, promotional material circulated via bookstores, a tie-in paperback edition of Forster's novel, a soundtrack album, a study guide sent to high school and college English and film teachers— and even a special screening for academics at the annual Modern Languages Association conference.[78] The task was to reach the film's perceived target audience. As one Hollywood journalist put it, 'there are only so many people in each market who are potential customers for a film with literary pretensions. They are not the

---

[76] Unnamed executive, quoted in Natale, 'Gramercy to the Rescue of Smaller Pix', 7.

[77] Tom Rothman of Goldwyn, quoted in Natale, 'Gramercy to the Rescue of Smaller Pix', 7.

[78] See Aljean Harmetz, 'Merchant and Ivory Strike Gold', *New York Times* (5 July 1986), cutting; and Jack Mathews, 'The Little Film that Could', *Los Angeles Times* (30 Mar. 1987), part VI, 5.

people who rush out to see any movie on opening weekend.'[79] The marketing strategy for a specialist film depends on building up good local contacts with the print and broadcast media, with schools, colleges, and universities, and with special interest groups. With the media, it is reviews and other editorial material that the distributors are after, not paid-for advertisements. It is generally accepted that 'films of mass appeal are relatively impervious to "critics"', partly because of the huge amount of money spent on advertising, and partly because audiences of mainstream films are assumed to be less than avid readers of the print media.[80] (Television review shows are another matter, hence the clips distributors release to the television companies, designed to show off the film's attractions at their best.) For smaller films aimed at more upscale audiences, however, reviews in the right print media are crucial: 'Reviews matter to filmgoers who patronize specialty films, because they read reviews and can be influenced by them, unlike the people who patronize major studio films, who are less affected by reviews.'[81]

If the opening weekend does not have the same aura for smaller, more specialized films, release strategies are still very carefully planned. Distributors aim to open their films when few other films are being released, so they avoid the early summer months, Thanksgiving and Christmas in the USA, which is when the blockbusters are delivered. At times like these, vast amounts of money have to be spent on advertising simply to get noticed. But there are no hard and fast rules, so that Sony Classics could deliberately—and very successfully—open *Orlando* on the same weekend as *Jurassic Park* (1993), advertising it as a distinct alternative. They also knew that few other films would open that weekend, so there would be room to get a serious film widely discussed in the press.[82] In general, though, American releases for specialized films are much more likely to take place between January and March or between August and October—dates which tie in well with the awards season in the new year, building up to the Oscars in February/March. Distributors will also try to open their films on a weekend when there are no other films opening with the same target demographic audience. But it's not just the opening weekend that is important with a slow rollout or a platformed release, and distributors will continue to open their films on non-competitive dates for each new market in which the film is released. The focus is thus much more on the local and regional than on the national, on the micro rather than the macro, on the niche rather than the mass.[83]

The platformed, slow rollout release of *Howards End* in 1992 became a benchmark for other speciality films with crossover potential (the release is discussed in much more detail in the next chapter).[84] Sony Classics opened it in one upscale Manhattan cinema, then slowly rolled it out territory by territory. The number of screens on which it was showing peaked during the awards period, with its widest

[79] Mathews, 'The Little Film that Could', 5.
[80] Industry analyst, A. D. Murphy, quoted in Dale, *The Movie Game*, 4.
[81] Mark Litwak, quoted in Lukk, *Movie Marketing*, 120.
[82] Lukk, *Movie Marketing*, 122.
[83] Ibid. 3, 20, 125.   [84] Ibid. 128.

release in the run-up to the Oscars. The same release pattern was subsequently used for similar films with similar crossover potential, such as *The Remains of the Day*, *Sense and Sensibility*, and *Elizabeth*. The Oscar tie-in could prove particularly lucrative: *The Remains of the Day* took $2.7 million dollars between the announcement of the Oscar nominations and the awards ceremony itself, *Sense and Sensibility* $14.7 million, and *The English Patient* $21.1 million.[85] The particular release strategy wasn't new, however: Columbia, for instance, had adopted a very similar campaign for *Gandhi* a decade earlier in 1982 (as had Cinecom with *A Room with a View*). *Gandhi* had been delivered to Columbia in the May of 1982, but they deliberately kept it back, well away from that summer's blockbusters (*ET*, *The Raiders of the Lost Ark*, and *Poltergeist*). During the summer months, they organized hundreds of special screenings for invited audiences of potential opinion leaders, until the film was eventually released at the end of November.

There were in fact two tiers to the release strategy. On the one hand, the film was released simultaneously in as many territories worldwide as possible, because Columbia expected it to generate a great deal of publicity and news, given its subject-matter, and wanted to exploit that publicity to the maximum. Thus they organized gala premieres in Delhi, London, Washington, New York, Toronto, and Los Angeles, all within the space of seven days. But within each territory, the film only opened in a few showcase cinemas (in North America, for instance, it initially opened in New York, Washington, Los Angeles, and Toronto) and then gradually widened. The aim was for 'word-of-mouth' to create 'want-to-see'—and given that the film had no stars, and could hardly be classed as a high concept film, 'want-to-see' had to be worked on. The widening of the release was timed from the outset to coincide with the build-up to the Oscars—a wise move, since the film received eleven nominations and eight Oscars, bringing it enormous amounts of free publicity.[86] The film was thus in effect played as a crossover film, although the concept had not been coined at the time. The logic was the same, however: 'We knew that *Gandhi* was not the sort of film immediately to attract the young people who account for 80 per cent of the cinema-going public. In fact it was a film for an audience that no longer goes to the cinema very often.'[87]

Releasing a film via a slow rollout may not generate a higher audience than if it had been given a wide release and heavy advertising from the start, but the net profits will be much greater. The key is to maximize the amount of money the film takes for each screen at which it is showing. Successful specialist and crossover films tend to achieve much higher average takings than mainstream films for each screen on which the films show, and to do so for a much longer period of time. As producer James Schamus points out, a film with a high per-screen average takes far more than the theatre owners' share of the gross. A saturation release will often only just, if that, pay the theatre owners' share of the payout. With a specialized

---

[85] Anon., 'Best Picture Nomination: What it Can Do at the Box-Office', *Screen International* (19 Feb. 1999), 30.
[86] Eberts and Ilott, *My Indecision is Final*, 133–7, 139, 145.   [87] Ibid. 138.

release, films play on relatively few screens, which means relatively few theatre owners have to be paid; at the same time, each screen ideally yields high takings. With a saturation release, of course, distributors have to pay cinema owners for huge numbers of screens, and their per-screen averages are usually much lower.[88]

Studios can afford to do this with blockbusters since theatre exhibition is in effect little more than a showcase for the ancillary markets and tie-ins. Mainstream releases are driven not by revenue generated directly by the theatrical release, but by revenue from video and the various kinds of television outlet. They have 'long-term video or cable obligations to satisfy . . . Those deals protect the studios' downside, but also contractually obligate them to a faster release pattern and an expensive ad campaign to give the film visibility. The studios must continually feed the voracious appetites of those two markets.'[89] Hence blanket opening weekend releases and short theatrical outlets, with the video appearing within six months, and the theatrical release having to be out of the way by then. The logic is that the distributor reaps as much benefit as possible as quickly as possible from the national advertising campaign, the costs of which often more or less cancel out the revenue generated by theatrical rentals. Audiences are maximized as near to the start of the film's release as possible, so that they can get the film out on video and into other ancillary markets while that publicity is still relatively fresh, so freeing up the income from those markets.

The relationship of specialized films to the video market is different. Although the emergence of the video market was a vital factor in the development of the specialized or independent sector in the 1980s, and although many specialized films eventually go on to video, the market for such films is theatrically driven, not video driven. As Schamus puts it, art-house films tend to be 'ancillary-resistant', and producers look to the distributor likely to adopt the most creative strategy for a release in cinemas.[90] Unlike the majors, such companies do not have long-term video or cable obligations. The lack of pressure to release on video as quickly as possible means that a slow rollout is feasible, as in the case of Sony Classics' release of *Howards End*: 'we were in no great hurry to meet any video window . . . We did not have to be out in video in six months to get our video cash to feed the company.'[91] On the contrary, they sought to squeeze every possible benefit out of the theatrical release.

'AN EXTREMELY SATURATED MARKETPLACE'[92]

By the late 1990s, the marketplace for specialized and crossover films had become increasingly crowded once more and 'the significant adult audience that . . . led

[88] Schamus, 'To the Rear of the Back End', 92–5.
[89] Natale, 'Gramercy to the Rescue of Smaller Pix', 7.
[90] Schamus, 'To the Rear of the Back End', 95.
[91] Tom Bernard, quoted in Grove, '*Howards End* Driven Theatrically, Not by Video', 2.
[92] Trimark executive vice president Cami Winikoff, quoted in Thom Grier, 'Indies' Hopes

almost all the studios to open specialty labels appear[ed] to have fractured among more releases than ever before'. According to the *Hollywood Reporter*, there were no major successes in 1998 that 'stirred audience passion and became must-sees for the art house crowd', while few of the films released in this sector were 'drawing young filmgoers to art houses'. The result was that 'the audience for specialized fare . . . remained static or even diminished'.[93] The overriding problem was that there were too many films on release, too many films all opening on the same weekend, all competing for the same specialized screens, the same window of opportunity, the same audience. As the same trade paper put it, '73 arties hit the screen this summer [1998] as compared to 30 last summer' (and only a handful more than that in 1995).[94] While more films grossed over a million dollars than had even been released the previous year, for instance, fewer were significant box-office successes by the standards of the sector.[95] In 2000, the art-house box office was again down, this time by 15 per cent against the previous year, with the market still saturated with too many films from too many distributors. Between 1990 and 2000, the market had dropped by 31 per cent, even after taking inflation into account. (In 1990, 171 films had taken $262 million; in 2000, 250 films took $185 million.[96]) Audiences were thus spread relatively thinly across the increased number of specialized films on release. As Schamus explains,

Not long ago, sophisticated viewers had each week a choice between a large number of Hollywood films and one, maybe two, new art house releases. Choosing the art film was a matter of simply asserting one's identity as an upscale viewer. Recently, there were many weeks in which four, five, six, sometimes seven 'speciality' films opened simultaneously in the major markets. How to choose? You will probably veer towards the newest, 'hottest' indie title, the one reviewed in your morning paper, the one with the biggest ad.[97]

The problem was that the involvement of the major studios in the specialized and crossover markets had inevitably brought with it studio thinking about how to handle art-house films, in the process squeezing the traditional art-house distributors out of the market. While the majors were in the market partly for prestige, Oscars, and the occasional freak hit, they were also constantly seeking to maximize revenues. The sheer numbers of mainstream multiplexes meant an increased demand for low-budget films with crossover potential. Everyone wanted a part of the next *Full Monty*, but distributors became 'overly ambitious in their release plans . . . Those lofty expectations are ruining it for indies that were happy with more modest B.O. . . . What once was a vibrant but sparsely populated business sector marked by alternative approaches to filmmaking and distribution has

for Hits Broken by Fractured Audiences', *Hollywood Reporter online*, *Year end wrap 98*, at www.hollywoodreporter.com, 7 Jan. 1999.

[93] Grier, 'Indies' Hopes for Hits', from website.

[94] Gray, 'The Reel Deal', 10; Grier, 'Indies' Hopes for Hits', from website.

[95] Grier, 'Indies' Hopes for Hits', from website.

[96] Dan Cox and Jonathan Bing, 'Art Pic Overkill?', *Varietyextra online*, at Variety.com, updated 4 Oct. 2000.

[97] Schamus, 'To the Rear of the Back End', 104.

become an arena flush with studio cash and heavily influenced by studio sensibilities.'[98] Even the logic of the 'opening weekend' had found its way into specialized distribution, as had the assumption that if you handle a dozen or so films,
one is bound to become a success and pay for all the rest, whereas indie thinking
was that you had to carefully nurture every film for it to make a profit.[99] Advertising costs had gone up dramatically, which small companies handling small films
could hardly afford—yet at the same time, everyone was 'reaching for broader
audiences'.[100] Schamus again:

> The independent cinema has quickly become a victim of its own success, a success that has
> made the independent film game look more and more like a microcosm of the studio busi-
> ness. . . . Six years ago a distributor might have hit the $2 million mark by cycling 20 or so
> prints of a film on a continuous, long-term roll-out that would, over the course of as many
> as sixty weeks, see the film play in as many as 300 markets. Today [1997], even a small film
> might open on six to twenty prints within its first two weeks, breaking to ten or twenty
> cities within a month. And this faster, wider release will of necessity require a significant
> advertising budget in order to reach out to the film's core audience. That core audience will
> have to start talking fast, spreading the proverbial word-of-mouth to a larger, cross-over
> audience within a month's time, so that the distributor can justify an increasingly costly
> marketing campaign (including TV or cable spots, radio advertising, and national print
> media) which in turn will convince the larger exhibitors to book the film nationally on
> upwards of 200 to 400 screens.
>   Five years ago *Howards End* (1992) broke the $20 million mark and played on screens in
> North America for over a year, sometimes playing in a single cinema for nearly that entire
> time. Today, it would probably need to hit that box-office mark within twenty weeks, sup-
> ported by a marketing campaign exponentially more expensive, before being thrown off
> its screens by the next 'indie hit' to come along.[101]

The new practices had been pioneered by companies like Miramax, in its
Disney-subsidiary phase, and Columbia, the mainstream distribution division of
Sony. They deliberately sought to occupy the middle ground and did so by selecting films they thought had crossover potential, then giving them a release somewhere between specialty and mainstream. But they increasingly released the films
not via a slow rollout, but via a relatively wide opening weekend release. In the
USA, this meant 100 prints, rather than the ten traditionally associated with specialized films, or the 1,000-plus prints of the mainstream release.[102] This was a
much more costly operation than a slow rollout, with greater risks involved. Such
costs and risks were only possible for those companies that were able to draw on
the resources of one of the majors. Columbia released both *The Remains of the
Day* and *Sense and Sensibility* in this way. *Remains* opened on ninety-four screens,

---

[98]   Cox and Bing, 'Art Pic Overkill?', from website.
[99]   Ibid.; Gray, 'The Reel Deal', 10.
[100] Grier, 'Indies' Hopes for Hits', from website.
[101] Schamus, 'To the Rear of the Back End', 103.
[102] Robert Laemmle, 'The Independent Exhibitor', in Squire, *The Movie Business Book*, 361.

and went straight to number thirteen in the American box-office charts. *Sense and Sensibility* opened on seventy screens, which took it to eleventh place in the charts. Both films were then platformed, the former eventually showing on more than 500 screens, the latter on more than 1,000. After reaching their peaks, they gradually wound down again, although both widened briefly once more for the Oscar season. The strategy enabled *Remains* to gross $23 million in the USA, *Sense and Sensibility* $43 million (significantly, *Sense and Sensibility* had also cost about twice as much as *Remains* to make).[103]

For British producers, despite the improved funding situation in the mid- and late 1990s, and the box-office success of films like *The Full Monty, Bean* (1997), *Sliding Doors* (1998), and *Notting Hill*, there was increased competition for scripts, directors, actors, and audiences.[104] David Aukin of HAL Films, and formerly head of Channel 4 Films, described the situation as follows:

> The good news is that everyone is interested in looking at the British film market and acquiring British films, because of the track record they have established over the past three years. But the sheer number of films now being produced in the U.K. means there is a huge choice for distributors—and only a few get successful U.S. distribution or any U.S. distribution at all. The dilemma is that although it is easier to finance films at different budget levels than at any time over the past decade, this is not always linked to distribution, which is the strength of the U.S. marketplace.[105]

The involvement of the majors in the specialized film had left its mark—for it was not really the specialized market they were interested in, as we've seen, but the crossover potential. This had various consequences. According to Simon Perry, chief executive of British Screen, 'the U.S. buyers want higher-concept films and better elements—often a known director and festival prizes—which add to [a film's] profile'. Guy East, head of film funder Intermedia, concurred: 'Unless you have a very clear marketing hook, it is very difficult to presell films anywhere at the moment'.[106] The availability of lottery funding meant in many cases that producers no longer needed a pre-sale to an American distributor to cover their production costs. But this meant that films that wouldn't otherwise have been made were now being made without any guarantee of distribution in the vital American market.[107] Even when an American distributor had been secured, things were not easy. According to the *Hollywood Reporter*, 'overall, the market is so competitive, the indies really have to squeeze in there between the big blockbusters . . . If one film is really dominating the marketplace, it makes it harder for the smaller ones to get noticed'.[108]

---

[103] Showbizdata.com.
[104] Dunkley, 'Rough Crossing', 30.
[105] Quoted ibid.
[106] Both quoted ibid.
[107] Ibid.; see also Cathy Dunkley, 'Sharp Knife for U.K. Film Funds', *Hollywood Reporter online*, at www.hollywoodreporter.com, 15 Dec. 1998; and Cathy Dunkley, 'Britain's Film Biz Takes Pounding, Braces for More', *Hollywood Reporter online*, at www.hollywoodreporter.com, 29 Dec. 1998.
[108] Grier, 'Indies' Hopes for Hits', from website.

CONCLUSION

Small films have of course always had to squeeze in between the bigger, better capitalized, more intensively marketed ones. And the film business has passed through many cycles in its time, cycles of boom and bust, expansion and contraction. Cycles develop as the industry seeks to exploit a particular cultural phenomenon that has proved successful or a market opportunity that has arisen as a result of demographic shifts, investing in that phenomenon or market until there is no more money to be made from it. In the late 1980s, it seemed as if the market for small, distinctive, independent films had outgrown its potential, distributors having overmilked its profitability, but it revived. Its form gradually changed through the 1990s, however, as the majors bought into this particular niche, actively engineered the crossover film as an entity rather than a possibility, and developed increasingly costly ways of marketing it. In the late 1990s, this particular consumer-oriented trend itself seemed to have been developed beyond its capacities. Will the market revive this time?

As audience figures seemed to confirm the potential profitability of the 'British' costume drama, so production and marketing budgets went up. Fewer low-budget costume dramas have been made recently—and for the medium-budget films that have been made, the American connection has become more and more important. I've described the crossover film as a compromise product, a compromise between the art-house and the mainstream market—and it is that which has enabled it to become successful. But what else is being compromised? In my Introduction, I asked whether the 'British' heritage film could really be considered British. The conclusion was twofold: first, that it is very difficult to know what Britishness is; and, secondly, that the label 'British' is in fact a useful way of branding a film, giving it a marketable label. The problem is, what does that label promise, what are the characteristics of that brand? Or, to put it another way, to what extent is the brand compromised by being tailored for particular markets and particular consumer trends and tastes? On the one hand, the brand is tailored to an upscale audience, and so must to some extent detach itself from popular culture. On the other hand, the brand is made as much for overseas audiences, and especially American audiences, as it is for domestic audiences, and so must be tailored in such a way that it meets their understanding of Britishness. To some extent, this is a business about selling particular images of Britishness to foreign consumers.

In this respect, as Paul Swann notes, exporting quality dramas about English heritage belongs to a well-established tradition: 'British producers have historically reached out to American consumers but, significantly, their products—Rolls-Royces, Scotch whiskey, Saville Row tailoring, and motion pictures—were aimed at an elite audience'. Rather than competing in the 'mass' market, British producers 'emphasize[d] expensive handcrafted items' which they 'sold on the basis of prestige'.[109] Crucial to this strategy is the national label, 'a British film'. It is a means of identifying and marketing a particular type of commodity. But it's important to acknowledge that, given the transnational arrangements of the media business and the globalization of culture, as Swann puts it, 'the label no longer "belongs" in any simple way to Britain'.[110]

Is it surprising then that so many of the heritage films can be, and have been, characterized as conservative and traditional (even if those labels are contested)? Is it surprising that such films present established 'British' stereotypes, where Britishness is reduced to upper-middle-class and upper-class Englishness, an Englishness that is rooted in the past and made anew for export? But that point is important too: heritage images are made anew. Throughout the 1980s and 1990s, as we've seen, under the governments of Thatcher, Major, and Blair, heritage and enterprise have been developed hand in hand. Tradition has not been divorced from modernity—indeed, the heritage film is by definition a modernized representation of tradition, using the modern technology of cinema to retell old stories. And the heritage film itself was modernized in the late 1990s, tailored increasingly for a wider, more youthful audience—the best examples here are *Elizabeth* and *Shakespeare in Love*. This is hardly breaking with tradition, more a sense of presenting it with a modern face.

The other way in which heritage films are tailored for American audiences is by inserting 'America' into the films themselves. American characters—and the actors that play them—perform important roles in *Orlando*, *The Remains of the Day*, *Shadowlands*, *The Wings of the Dove*, and *The Golden Bowl*. American actors also play important roles in non-American parts: Gwyneth Paltrow in *Emma* and *Shakespeare in Love* (the latter of which also featured Ben Affleck), Keanu Reeves (actually Canadian) and Denzel Washington in *Much Ado About Nothing*, Liv Tyler in *Plunkett and Macleane* (1999), and Uma Thurman in *The Golden Bowl*, for instance. The idea of 'America' as a goal or a threat appears in *Orlando*, *The Madness of King George*, and *Shakespeare in Love*. *The Age of Innocence* (1993) and *The House of Mirth* (2000), both set in the USA, do for the American author Edith Wharton what other films set in England have done for E. M. Forster, Jane Austen, Thomas Hardy, and Henry James.

Various combinations of national (state-sponsored) capital and transnational (corporate or EU) capital have enabled such films to be made. One key source of such funding has been the Hollywood studios, in one guise or another. On the one hand, as the above suggests, Hollywood has 'Americanized' the 'British' heritage film. On the other, those films are still recognizably 'British' ('English') in a cultural sense, and distinct in all sorts of ways from the mainstream film. Hollywood is not a monolithic enterprise, and indeed has developed a business struc-

[109] Paul Swann, 'The British Culture Industries and the Mythology of the American Market: Cultural Policy and Cultural Exports in the 1940s and 1990s', *Cinema Journal*, 39/4 (2000), 29, 30.
[110] Ibid. 39.

19. Addressing the multiplex audience: *Mansfield Park*

ture that allows it to cater for different audiences, different tastes, different markets. The key here is that the niche, the special interest group, is to some extent catered for.

But has the bubble burst? Three films from the end of the 1990s, each of which seemed typical of the way the English costume drama production trend developed, were comparative flops: *Mansfield Park* (Fig. 19), *The House of Mirth*, and *The Golden Bowl*. None of them were cheap productions, their budgets ranging between £6 million and £9.5 million, suggesting they were conceived as crossover films. They seemed to have everything going for them. *The Golden Bowl* was a Merchant Ivory production; *Mansfield Park* was a Miramax film; all three films were adaptations of classic works by canonical authors; both *The Golden Bowl* and *The House of Mirth* had strong American strands in their casting and storyline; all three films had something that was thought suitable for the under-35 audience (Uma Thurman, star of *Pulp Fiction*, in *The Golden Bowl*, Gillian Anderson, star of *The X Files*, in *The House of Mirth*, an irreverential and sexy version of Austen in *Mansfield Park*). Yet all failed at the box office, despite a platform release in multiplexes as well as an art-house run. None of them took more than £710,000 in the UK or more than $4.8 million in the USA.[111] Two different strategies were tried for *Mansfield Park*. In the USA, it opened on eight screens, moving up to

---

[111] A. C. Nielsen EDI Ltd., 2001.

thirty in week two, and 148 in week seven, from when it gradually tailed off. This platform release yielded only $3.9 million. In the UK, the film already began quite wide on its opening weekend, on seventy-six screens—and when it failed to take off, was almost as immediately pulled, falling out of the charts immediately.[112] None of the films were given the sort of careful handling and the slow rollout that had succeeded at the beginning of the 1990s with *Howards End*. But the newer production and release strategies that these three films each in their own way embodied seemed to have failed.

[112] See weekly box-office charts in *Screen International* (Jan.–Apr. 2000).

5
Case Study I: *Howards End*

Howards End stands, in a sense, for everything that is settled and honourable about England.[1]

Howards End, one of the best known and most commercially successful heritage films, was released in 1992, at the tail-end of the Thatcherite period, a year after Margaret Thatcher's downfall. Directed by James Ivory, produced by Ismail Merchant, and scripted by Ruth Prawer Jhabvala for Merchant Ivory Productions, it's a very tasteful adaptation of Forster's novel about Englishness, class, tradition, and modernity. There had of course been three other Forster adaptations in the previous few years. David Lean's *A Passage to India* had appeared in 1984. The other two were both Merchant Ivory productions, *A Room with a View* (1986) and *Maurice* (1987); as we've already noted, the former proved an immense critical and box-office success for a low-budget literary adaptation. A fourth Forster adaptation, Charles Sturridge's *Where Angels Fear to Tread* (1991), was released in Britain while *Howards End* was in production (it was released in the USA at the same time as the Merchant Ivory film), prompting cries of 'Forstermania'.[2] In each case, while Forster had set the novel in what for him was the present day, the film became a period piece, set in the past.

Widely applauded by critics on its release, *Howards End* went on to win numerous awards and, like *A Room with a View*, to do extremely good business at the box office for a modestly budgeted independent film—indeed, for one commentator, it was 'a landmark in . . . specialized film distribution'.[3] Because of its cultural prominence, it also became the most visible marker of a particular kind of film-making deemed to be safe, respectable, and properly British. Thus, when the Foreign and Commonwealth Office refused to cover the costs involved in sending a raft of films by Black British and British Asian film-makers to a festival in Tunisia, the reasons they gave were that the films were 'not likely to be representative of British cinema' and would 'possibly give a bad image of Britain to outsiders . . . after all, they're not exactly *Howards End*'.[4] When the Conservative government published its White Paper, *The British Film Industry*, in 1995, the

---

[1] John Pym, *Merchant Ivory's English Landscape: Rooms, Views and Anglo-Saxon Attitudes* (London: Pavilion, 1995), 77.

[2] See *Variety* (12 Nov. 1990), 22; and Terry Pristin, 'Old Novels, New Screenplays', *LA Times*, Calendar section (26 Apr. 1992), 4.

[3] Tom Bernard, quoted in Tiiu Lukk, *Movie Marketing: Opening the Picture and Giving it Legs* (Los Angeles: Silman-James Press, 1997), 128.

[4] Derek Malcolm, 'Not Quite Howards End', *Guardian*, section 2 (21 Oct. 1992), 5.

Introduction was graced with a still from *Howards End*.[5] In 1998, publicity for *The Acid House*, an adaptation of a novel by *Trainspotting* author Irvine Welsh, included the claims that *The Acid House* 'makes *Trainspotting* look like *Howards End*', 'a Women's Institute tea-party', or 'a tourism commercial'.[6] *Howards End* could also stand in as a pictorial signifier of everything that the heritage industry represented. In 1995, the *Sunday Times* reviewed Raphael Samuel's book *Theatres of Memory*, a lengthy discussion of heritage and related ideas and practices. The review was illustrated with a large still from *Howards End*, with the caption 'Sentimentalizing the past? Helena Bonham Carter as Helen Schlegel in *Howards End*'; neither the review, nor the book, it should be noted, mentions the film.

The purpose of this case study is to explore in rather more detail than I've been able to do so far some of the issues that have arisen in previous chapters, by focusing on an exemplary heritage film, or at least an extremely successful one. One way of summarizing this chapter is to say that it is concerned with how a film—in this case *Howards End*—becomes meaningful. What meanings can be attributed to the film, and what status do we then give to those attributions? Answering these questions will involve looking at the film itself, the way it is put together, its attractions, and its thematic resonances. It will also involve examining the production, distribution, and exhibition of the film, but especially the way that it was marketed, and to whom. Finally, it will involve an assessment of the critical reception of the film, and the way that it was taken up in wider discourses, especially those to do with the heritage industry and cultural tourism. I will begin by considering some of the film's themes and the ways in which it might be thought to work politically.

READING THE FILM: CONSERVATIVE OR LIBERAL?

With its attention to period detail, its self-consciously artistic production values, its relatively conventional story-telling style, its avoidance of irony, and its slow-moving and gentle narrative about English elites of the Edwardian period, *Howards End* can seem a very conservative film. Its central characters, landscapes, and cultural co-ordinates seem to embody a very traditional version of national identity. Reviewers, after all, described it as a 'terribly English production',[7] 'quintessentially British',[8] 'one of the better kinds of British film',[9] and 'an instant national treasure . . . a country-house classic . . . an immediate part of the British heritage'.[10] Some audiences certainly saw the film as nostalgic—and some

[5] Department of National Heritage, *The British Film Industry* (Cm 2884, London: HMSO, June 1995), 4.

[6] See advertisement in *Time Out* (16–30 Dec. 1998), 116; the quotations are from reviews in the *Scotsman*, the *Daily Telegraph*, and the *Edinburgh Evening News*.

[7] Angie Errigo, 'Howards End', *Empire*, 36 (1992), 24.

[8] Victoria Mather, 'Another Round of Forster's', *GQ* (May 1992), 47.

[9] Shaun Usher, 'Fine Probe into Past Prejudices', *Daily Mail* (1 May 1992), 34.

[10] Tom Hutchinson, 'Period Piece Making its own History', *Mail on Sunday* (3 May 1992), 39.

delighted in it for that very reason, while others were horrified by the way it seemed to recreate an ideal, prelapsarian England as seen through rose-tinted spectacles. Its ideal audience would seem to be elite cultural connoisseurs, for here is a film that seems proud of its seriousness, sophistication, and refinement, and its aesthetic attachments to high culture. Here too is a film that is much less willing to acknowledge its debt to popular culture—though it is there all the same in both source novel and film, in the touches of melodrama, the narrative coincidences, and the romance structures and set-pieces.

This reading of the film as a paean to conservatism would seem to be confirmed by the stunningly picturesque images in the closing sequence of the film, its final four minutes. The sequence opens on a high-angle long shot of the house at the centre of the story, Howards End. This is a charming, sprawling cottage set in a country garden fronted by a rich green lawn. The camera gently cranes down to ground level. Cut to an interior, where Henry Wilcox is addressing his family about the conditions of their inheritance. The decor is fine, the colours warm, the speech delivered in the familiar tones of upper middle-class southern English. The meeting over, we move outside to see the family leave in a highly polished vintage car. They are watched from the garden by Henry and his second wife, Margaret (née Schlegel), and in the distance by Margaret's sister, Helen, and Helen's illegitimate son. Helen and the boy are in a field across the road, in which a horse-drawn mower is cutting the long grass. The camera cranes back and up from the scene, leaving us with a final Constable-like image of a green landscape bordered by trees and the ancient cottage—'a Merchant-Ivory landscape', as one reviewer described it.[11]

Here, then, is surely a conservative, nostalgic representation of the old country, defined in terms of pastoral, in the style of Constable, one of England's most iconic painters: the small-country-house-cum-large-cottage, the garden, the horse-drawn mower, the charming people in the equally charming semi-rural, heart-of-England setting—threatened only by the antiquated modernity of the highly polished vintage car. As one reviewer suggested, 'Howards End, the enchanting country estate which is the subject of romantic nostalgia and ruthless power play, stands as a symbol of English endurance'[12] Here, then, is a timeless, traditional England in which the house can be read as the vessel of the core English identity, the homeland that must be conserved. Here, then, is 'our' heritage. And of course the question of inheritance is central to the scene. Who is to inherit Howards End? And therefore, who is to inherit England?

There is a mythic quality to the scene, yet at the same time we are encouraged to see it as authentic, as a faithful and accurate representation of the way things were. The discourse of authenticity was frequently mobilized around the film, whether it was to celebrate the 'authentic Edwardian interiors',[13] to proclaim the

---

[11] Anthony Lane, 'End to the Ivory Trade in Whimsy: Howards End', *Independent on Sunday* (3 May 1992), 19.

[12] David McGillivray, 'Homes and Gardens', *What's on* (29 Apr. 1992), 61.

[13] Nicole Swengley, 'And Now, an Oscar for the Wallpaper', *The Times*, Life and Times section (30 Mar. 1992), 5.

'absolute fidelity' of the film to the source novel,[14] or to explain the choice of film stock in terms of its perceived ability to create 'a more realistic look'.[15] This discourse of authenticity, this aura of reverence, is vital to the cultural status of films like *Howards End*. But as Pam Cook points out, costume drama, with its indulgence in masquerade, in dressing up, is almost by definition a genre of *pastiche*— and *Howards End*, whatever its producers may think, is still a costume drama, a frock flick. As we noted earlier, Cook goes on to argue that pastiche 'is the undoing of authentic identities. Pastiche suggests hybridity rather than purity'.[16]

What would happen if we read *Howards End* in terms of this 'undoing of authentic identities', rather than as a celebration of a traditional, pure, and authentic English national identity? If we return to the closing sequence of the film in this spirit, we might read it in rather more liberal terms, as a representation of changing times, with a *crisis* of inheritance at its centre, rather than a simple handover of property. For what Henry Wilcox announces is that the house Howards End is to be passed from his own family, the Wilcoxes, via his second wife, Margaret, to the Schlegel family. The house had in fact initially belonged to the first Mrs Wilcox, so what Henry's announcement reveals is that the house is to continue to pass down a female line of inheritance. Margaret has further made it clear that the house will eventually be passed on to her sister's son, the illegitimate offspring of Helen's transgressive cross-class liaison with Leonard Bast, an unemployed insurance clerk.

If we follow this line of thought, concentrating more on the narrative discourse than the visual discourse, and keeping an ear cocked for the slightly disturbing tones in the music that accompanies the sequence, it becomes possible to read the film, like the novel before it, as an exploration of social change and shifting identities. Thus visually, the sequence might suggest permanence, timelessness, and a stable English identity; narratively, though, things seem to be much more in flux. The old country may still look more or less the same, but it is inhabited by a new social formation. Thanks to a crisis of inheritance, it belongs now to a population whose identities are complex and fluid. Englishness no long seems quite so secure, quite so certain. As with so many of the heritage films, it is this ambivalence that fascinates me, this tension between the *narrative* critique of established national traditions, social formations, and identities, and the *visual* celebration of elite culture and a mythic landscape. On the one hand, the various characters in *Howards End* are played as solid English types, reproducing a certain notion of Englishness, apparently stable, confident, and secure in its identity. On the other hand, the story explores tensions and slippages in this identity, it explores identity crises, by probing beneath the mannered surface and throwing characters from different backgrounds into confrontation with each other. England thus

---

[14] Pat Anderson, 'Howards End', *Films In Review*, 43/3–4 (1992), 117.

[15] Tony Pierce-Roberts, 'What's in a Look?' (interview), *In Camera* (Autumn 1991), 4.

[16] Pam Cook, *Fashioning the Nation: Costume and Identity in British Cinema* (London: British Film Institute, 1996), 5.

becomes a seething mass of tensions, in which no one's identity seems pure or stable or authentic.

Most obviously, the Schlegels, who seem to inhabit a quintessential upper middle-class Englishness, are in fact part German. Further, the identities of the sisters shift in the film. Thus Helen becomes progressively less decorous, more obsessive, more hysterical, more gothic in her appearance—as if Helena Bonham Carter were preparing for her role in *Mary Shelley's Frankenstein* (1994)! Finally, she adopts a new identity as a sort of Pre-Raphaelite pastoral single parent, quite at home in the old country. Her sister Margaret's identity is equally fluid, as she moves from radical New Woman, independent, intelligent, and philanthropic, to devoted wife, reasonable, respectable, tolerant, and understanding, with none of the excesses of those around her.

Then there is the Wilcox family. Henry owns several houses, including an ancestral home with a ruined castle in the grounds and a gallery of portraits of the ancestors. But the house has not been inherited, it has been purchased, along with the portraits of the previous owners' family. To this extent, as Lizzie Francke has remarked, *Howards End* is *about* the heritage industry of which it is itself a part.[17] The Wilcoxes themselves have acquired a new identity, not inherited an old one: they are nouveaux riches, not aristocracy, and the wonderfully mannered performances of Anthony Hopkins, as the father, Henry Wilcox, and to a lesser extent James Wilby, as his son Charles, suggest the element of masquerade involved in their adoption of the persona of the pure, essential Englishman. The source of their wealth is also foreign, since it results from the exploitation of the colonies.

The Basts occupy an equally fluid class position in the film. It is tempting to identify them as working class. But in fact if we place Leonard according to his initial occupation, then he needs to be seen as a member of the emergent middle class. Leonard is a white-collar worker, initially a clerk in an insurance company, a component of the new lower middle class. But his position is highly tenuous, highly insecure. The situation of the Basts' house, backing on to a railway line in a run-down area of London, suggests something much more proletarian than membership of the emergent middle class, and he is in fact very much on the verge of poverty, especially when he is made redundant. But he also aspires to cultural betterment and social mobility in the other direction, for he seeks to 'improve' himself through literature and music, to adopt a new cultural identity. Samuel West's perversely uncharismatic performance as Leonard perfectly catches this very insecurity of character.

By the end of the film, a new, national community has been imagined, potentially consensual, but clearly a hybrid intermixing of different social groups. New class liaisons have been established, and new social groups have been invited into the centre of this community, to inhabit and inherit Howards End—and England. Other social groups, previously central, have been marginalized. Thus the errant

[17] Lizzie Francke, 'Howards End', *Sight and Sound*, 2/1 (1992), 53.

sister, now a single parent, is in, as is her illegitimate son from her union with the lower class Leonard Bast. Leonard himself remains outside, literally removed from the narrative by his death. But the grotesquely inhumane and hypocritical businessman Charles Wilcox has also been literally removed by his imprisonment for killing Leonard—while the aristocracy have already been removed from view before the narrative starts, their ancestral homes now the property of nouveaux riches capitalists like Henry Wilcox.

The new England has been Europeanized and feminized by the promotion of the Schlegel sisters and their modified values. But if their values have been modified, they have still had their influence on the characters of those around them. Margaret, in particular, holds a real power within the community established at the end of the film. In the final sequence of the film, as Henry speaks of leaving the house to Margaret, the camera tracks towards her, while all the other characters have been kept distant from the camera. It is as if she holds the centre of the film's hybrid drama. And when she and her husband go into the garden to bid farewell to his children, she grasps him as if to prevent him falling over: literally, she enables him to remain upright. This conclusion to the film in many ways struggles to establish a stable closure, but the tensions remain, suggesting the instability and insecurity, the heterogeneity and impurity, the plurality rather than singularity, of the national community. England itself is equally unstable and insecure, as the film explores tensions between country and city, tradition and modernity, organic development and grasping acquisition ('This place is not really the country and . . . well, it's certainly not the town', says Paul Wilcox). Thus the glistening vintage car in which the family drive off is an icon of both antiquity (for modern-day audiences) and modernity (for those in the film)—and for all its positive virtues in terms of revolutionizing communication and travel, it belches vile fumes into the pastoral green landscape that the camera so lovingly captures. (This of course was Forster's perspective in the novel.)

From this perspective, it no longer seems so productive to read the film as a conservative drama celebrating the lifestyles, values, and property of the traditional national elites. Instead, the film appears quite liberal in its muted critique of capitalism and its social effects, its promotion of feminist principles, and its celebration of multiculturalism. In repeatedly cutting back and forth between the fortunes of the impoverished Basts, on the one hand, and those of the much more wealthy and privileged Schlegels and Wilcoxes on the other, the film is able to draw attention to class difference. At the same time, political and economic power comes to seem less important in this film, less desirable than emotional energy and personal contact ('only connect', in Forster's famous words). Thus it is the humanity of the Schlegels, and of Mrs Wilcox, which wins out over the bombastic confidence of class, the self-satisfied sense of importance, and the entrepreneurial capitalism of Henry Wilcox and his offspring. Thus too, the connections the Schlegels make with the Basts come to seem as significant as the gulf that lies between them.

THE FILM AS PASTICHE

Thus far, I've not really said anything about the film that hasn't already been said about the novel, which might lead one to draw the conclusion that it's precisely a faithful adaptation of the novel. But there is more to say about the film, and I want to concentrate now on those elements of it that 'go beyond' the novel. First of all, we should remember that the characters in the film are performances. The fact that these are actors, playing roles, underlines the constructedness of the English nation narrated by *Howards End*. These people are not the real thing: their performance of a particular cultural identity is precisely a performance, a pastiche.

The element of pastiche is there in the style of the film too. The locations in which the various scenes of the film are set are cobbled together to create an imaginary geography, for instance. That geography is paraded as authentic, but its purpose is in part to reproduce an already fictional space, as created by Forster in the source novel. As a headline in one newspaper discussion of the film put it, making the film involved 'finding realities to fit a film's illusions'.[18] Thus some of the exteriors were created through matte work. Wickham Place, for instance, the Schlegels' house in London, is played by a Georgian square behind Buckingham Palace, but, as the cinematographer reveals, 'to suggest it being encroached upon by huge blocks of flats, they're matting in other buildings from other parts of London onto our prime location'.[19]

The generic identity of the film is also a pastiche of styles, mixing the 'absurd' coincidences of melodrama and the 'frothy' romantic liaisons of the woman's picture with the 'good taste' of the reverential literary adaptation. The aesthetics of heritage display also coexist with an almost parodic version of working-class realism for the presentation of the Basts' home and milieu, while psychological realism is interspersed with the mannered acting and stylized gestures of the English theatrical tradition.

The title sequence of the film is also very interesting in this respect, in particular two images incorporated into the sequence: the painting which precedes the title, and the lettering and design of the title itself. These should be seen as agenda-setting devices, invitations to read the film in a particular way. The first image we see, after the production company credits, is a painting from 1906, *La Danse*, by André Derain. Derain was one of the leading French avant-gardists of the Edwardian period, one of the so-called Fauvistes, experimenting with formal rather than representational aspects of colour—as with the intense, luminous colours of *La Danse*. As is clear from this painting, the Fauvistes also drew on primitive art: here, a series of women, some of them naked, dancing in a garden of serpents. This uninhibited use of colour and the wild cavortings of the women,

---

[18] Janet Maslin, 'Finding Realities to Fit a Film's Illusions', *New York Times*, Home section (12 Mar. 1992), C1.

[19] Pierce-Roberts, 'What's in a Look?', 4.

painted by a continental avant-gardist, hardly signals a conservative Englishness, or invites one to adopt that frame of mind while settling down to watch the film.

Why then is the painting there? What function does it have? What sorts of connotations might it set in play for the attentive spectator? I want to suggest three possible readings here. First, we can read the presence of the painting in terms of art-historical realism. There is a certain period fidelity, a certain authenticity about the painting, in that Derain was more or less a contemporary of the Wilcoxes and the Schlegels (and he did in fact do a series of London scenes at about the time *La Danse* was painted). The Schlegels are certainly presented as being aware of modern movements in art, although James Ivory wonders whether Derain might have been too radical for them (his paintings were after all seen by many at the time as transgressive, degenerate, even shocking)![20] Secondly, the painting might be seen as establishing a certain cultural credibility. In effect, it says 'this is Art', and invites a sense of connoisseurship: to appreciate this image, the spectator must be in possession of elite cultural capital; to recognize it and be able to place it indicates a well-educated spectator of good taste. And at the same time that the spectator is as it were applauded for their connoisseurship, so that sense of good taste and great art might rub off on the film itself.

Thirdly, we might read the presence in the film of this pictorially rich, modernist painting in terms of its connotations of visual luxury and cultural exoticism. In this sense, Forster and Englishness are situated in the culturally exotic context of European modernism. In the same way that Forster takes a basically melodramatic story and subjects it to a modernist treatment, so James Herbert argues that in Derain's painting we can see a similar process, a hybrid of classical and modernist tropes. Thus the classical tradition of the pastoral—nudes posed in a generalized landscape—has been infected by modern styles, especially the vibrant use of paint and colour, by knowing, even parodic, intertextual references to Gauguin and others, and by an exotic primitivism.[21] Even so, the prefacing of *Howards End* by an image of such primitivist sensibility, celebrating wild, unabashed passions, is surprising, for the film seems so refined, so concerned to keep those passions in check. Yet of course there is a current of passion running through the film, primarily in the character of Helen Schlegel.

The second image of the film is the title itself, with art nouveau lettering and a leafy scroll underneath, which grows almost organically on the screen. This time, Englishness seems more secure in the lettering and design of the title, given the roots of art nouveau in the English Arts and Crafts movement—except that in art nouveau too we can see the Europeanization of English arts and crafts. The image is certainly more tame, less disturbing, than Derain's Fauvism, although there is still a tension between formality, reason, convention, and manners on the one hand, and untamed nature, and organic growth, on the other. As the title

---

[20] See Pym, *Merchant Ivory's English Landscape*, 78; and James D. Herbert, *Fauve Painting: The Making of Cultural Politics* (New Haven, Conn., and London: Yale University Press, 1992), 135–9.

[21] Herbert, *Fauve Painting*, 135–9.

disappears, to be replaced by the first diegetic image, piano music is heard on the soundtrack. It is Percy Grainger's *Bridal Lullaby*, which draws on the English folk-song tradition, again suggesting the organic nature of indigenous folk traditions. But as with the art nouveau reference, there's more to be said about this than period fidelity and the connotations of pastoral Englishness. Both art nouveau and Grainger's music were reactions to the academic arts of the nineteenth century. Both were strikingly innovative—Grainger in particular, in his efforts to establish a musical democracy both in his folk populism and in what he called his free music. (Grainger was in fact an Australian, who studied in Germany, then settled in Britain, although by 1916, when he composed *Bridal Lullaby*, he had emigrated to the USA.)

What this title sequence suggests is that there are disturbances and hybrid formations in the text right from the outset. The self-consciously intense decorativeness of these opening images may signal the cultural capital, the tastefulness, the artistry of the film-makers and their ideal audiences. It may also be the authentic arts, crafts, and music of the period on display. But it is not easily reduced to Englishness, and certainly not to a pure, untainted, traditional Englishness. On the contrary, these opening images suggest a rich heterogeneity, a complex, challenging, hybrid cultural formation. Then, of course, this pastiche of inauthentic identities and masquerades has been carefully, lovingly crafted by a heterogeneous, cosmopolitan production team: an American director, an Indian producer, and a scriptwriter of Polish-Jewish extraction, engaged in what Merchant himself refers to as a very productive 'cross-cultural manœuvring'.[22] One might even see the three cavorting women in the painting standing in symbolically for the exotic cultural identities of James Ivory, Ruth Prawer Jhabvala, and Ismail Merchant!

THE STATUS OF INTERPRETATION

Here, then, in broad terms, are two readings of *Howards End*. One treats the film as a conservative, nostalgic representation of a traditional, elite English identity. The other treats it as a much more culturally and politically liberal text, which explores multiple and hybrid English identities. This more liberal reading suggests that the film does not simply reproduce an already formed, stable national identity but worries over crucial questions of class, gender, and ethnicity as they relate to Englishness, in the 1990s as much as the 1910s. According to this reading, the film refuses the essentialism of pure, authentic identities and foregrounds the unfixity and instability of identity. But what is the status of these readings? They are of course simply readings, interpretations, and there is nothing absolute about them. One conclusion that we might legitimately draw is that *Howards End* is an ambivalent text, which can be read in different ways by different audiences. What

---

[22] Ismail Merchant, quoted in Mansel Stimpson, 'A Truly Flourishing Plant', *What's On in London* (29 Apr. 1992), 17.

are the political implications of such a relativist stance? Texts, it is argued, narrate the nation. *Howards End*, according to my more liberal reading, narrates England as a hybrid space and Englishness as made up of various composite, constructed identities. But is it legitimate to read the text in this way, when from other perspectives it seems so centrist, when it seems to promote such a conservative, essentialist image of Englishness, a core identity? Is it really productive to read such a film in terms of a discourse developed for analysing post-colonial, diasporic texts which much more self-consciously deal with the peripheral and the transient, the marginal and the blatantly hybrid? To be more precise, can an apparently centrist text like *Howards End* be as 'progressive' as a self-consciously 'peripheralist' text like, say, *Orlando* (1992), or *Bhaji on the Beach* (1993), both produced around the same time?

My response is once again to resort to relativism: this is simply a reading. And of course it may be just as problematic to construct *Howards End* as a centrist text, to allow it to stand in for core English identities and values. What the liberal reading demonstrates, I hope, is that even what can be seen from one perspective as the most traditional, fixed, and essentialist identity can from another perspective be seen as unstable and shifting. Is there any legitimacy in privileging one reading over another? Can we identify a preferred reading? Or does this simply beg the question of who prefers that reading—producers, distributors, critics, audiences? Is there a dominant reading, which the majority of audiences have adopted? Or is that quest for the meaning of a text always bound to confront the possibility that different audiences will respond to the same text in different ways, according to circumstances? To explore some of these questions, we will need to change tack, and look at how the film was promoted, and to which audiences, how it was taken up by critics, how it figured in wider discourses, and how it fared at the box office. I'll start by looking at how the film was funded, distributed, and marketed—and how it fared at the box office as a result.

PUTTING THE PACKAGE TOGETHER

As with most small independent films, especially those made in Europe, the budget for *Howards End* was an enormous struggle to put together and came from a complex variety of sources. Distributors put money up front—but both the original distributors for the UK and the USA (Palace Pictures and Orion Classics respectively) went bankrupt and had to be replaced at the last minute by Mayfair Entertainments and Sony Picture Classics. Distribution advances also came from Italy, Germany, and France. Channel 4 put in money, as did the city merchant bank Guinness Mahon, while Film Finances Ltd. provided a completion guarantee.[23] More unusual was the funding received from a Japanese company, Nippon

---

[23] Gary Leboff, 'Howards Way', *Empire*, 47 (1993), 56–8.

Film Development and Finance, and its investment partners Sumitomo Corporation, Imagica Corporation, Cinema Ten Corporation, JSB Japan Jatellite Broadcasting Inc., and Ide Productions. Japanese media corporations and investment banks were at that time looking for European media partners and investment opportunities, having become dissatisfied with the low profits that ensued from their various deals with American media companies in the 1980s. British productions had the added attraction of being tailored to the large global English-language market, and English period dramas in general and Merchant Ivory's previous 'English' films in particular had gone down well with certain Japanese audiences. The Japanese investment in *Howards End* needs to be seen in this context.[24] It also underlines the extent to which even the economic base on which this 'English' film's superstructure was built was transnational and cosmopolitan, cobbled together from a variety of sources.

Most reports put the cost of the film at around £4 million—at a time when the average budget for a Hollywood film was $26.1 million.[25] The budget for prints and advertising was also low by industry standards, with some $4 million dollars being spent in the USA.[26] Clearly the investment was worthwhile. *Howards End* was the second highest grossing British film at the UK box office in 1992 (though only the thirty-seventh highest grossing film overall) and by the end of its run had taken £3.7 million.[27] Revenue in the larger American market was inevitably much more impressive, with takings of $25 million recorded. Only two other British-made films (*The Crying Game* (1992) and *The Lawnmower Man* (1992)) grossed more in the USA in the same year.[28] According to one estimate, the film was on target to gross more than $70 million worldwide—although to put that in perspective, it is worth noting that twenty-five films grossed more than $98 million during that same period, with *Basic Instinct* (1991) grossing $328 million![29]

'A SLOW, SLOW ROLL-OUT':[30] EXHIBITING THE FILM IN THE UK AND THE USA

After Palace's financial difficulties, the film was eventually distributed in the UK by Mayfair Entertainment, who also owned the Curzon Mayfair cinema where the film opened in early May 1992. Business was outstanding from the outset, with an

[24] Nick Bell and Mark Schilling, 'European Watershed?', *Screen International*, 819 (2 Aug. 1991), 14, 16.

[25] David Leafe (ed.), *BFI Film and Television Handbook 1993* (London: British Film Institute, 1992), 22; Richard C. Morais, 'A Reverence for the Theater', *Forbes* (7 Dec. 1992), 42.

[26] Bernard, quoted in Lukk, *Movie Marketing*, 128.

[27] *Screen International* (29 Jan. 1993), 13; David Leafe (ed.), *BFI Film and Television Handbook 1994* (London: British Film Institute, 1994), 38.

[28] Leafe (ed.), *BFI Handbook 1994*, 41.

[29] Bernard Weinraub, 'Disney Signs up Merchant and Ivory', *New York Times* (27 July 1992), C15; Anon., 'Top International Performers of 1992', *Screen International* (8 Jan. 1993), 9.

[30] William Grimes, 'Little Movies Trying to be Bigger Movies', *New York Times* (30 July 1992), C13.

opening weekend gross of £27,900, which 'shattered' the Curzon house record.[31] More significant is the fact that the film opened in a single art-house venue, rather than in the hundreds of cinemas nationwide which is the norm for a Hollywood film. Gradually over the next few months, the film moved to more and more cinemas in an expanded release. Thus twenty-four prints were in circulation by mid-May, though still mainly at well-established art-house venues, as well as upmarket screens in London. This enabled the film to reach number four in the London box-office charts, and number seven for the UK as a whole that month. By late June, the film was on forty-three screens, and altogether it stayed in the list of UK top ten box-office successes for ten weeks (and in the London top ten until late September), eventually being seen at the cinema by an estimated one million people.[32] By mainstream standards, having forty-three prints in circulation and reaching only a million cinemagoers made it a very small film—significantly, it wasn't even one of the top thirty films at the UK box office for 1992; but by the standards of a small, independent quality film, the figures were impressive.

The goal had been to establish *Howards End* as a crossover film, one that would move out of the confines of the art-house circuit and into the major cinema chains, thereby hopefully attracting a larger, younger, more male audience and a more even spread among the different social classes. The distributors would have expected the film to get a good airing in the broadsheet newspapers that catered for its core audience. But what they also needed was more populist publications like *Empire* to suggest, as they did, that 'this very handsome, intelligent, witty piece of work' was 'deserving of a wider audience than the few folk unlikely to be put off by the combination of Foster [sic], Merchant-Ivory, and a handful of British luvvies'.[33] The doubt that *Howards End* might not in fact reach that wider audience was shared by the British trade paper *Screen International*:

The Merchant Ivory name and the all-star cast will ensure an impressive opening at the UK turnstiles and guarantee a solid performance ... with sophisticated audiences. Mainstream potential is less certain as the film's intimate nature is unlikely to score many points with the average cinema-goer accustomed to the high-tech wizardry of big-budget blockbusters.[34]

Industry analyses of the UK audiences for *Howards End* suggest that around 2 per cent of the UK population over 7 years old saw the film, where the most popular box-office successes of the year were seen by between 6 and 11 per cent of the population.[35] On the other hand, the majority of art-house releases were seen by less than 1 per cent of the population, suggesting that in terms of the size

---

[31] *Screen International* (8 May 1992), 1.
[32] Box-office statistics from *Screen International* weekly box-office charts, and from Cinema and Video Industry Audience Research (CAVIAR), *Caviar 10, vol. 1: Computer Tabulations: Cinema, Television, Readership, Leisure Expenditure* (London: BMRB International Ltd., 1993), table 12/11.
[33] Errigo, 'Howards End', 24.
[34] Patricia Dobson, 'Howards End', *Screen International* (13 Mar. 1992), 23.
[35] CAVIAR, *Caviar 10, vol. 1*, tables 12/1 and 12/2, 38–9.

of the audience, the film was in fact reasonably successful as a crossover film.[36] As might be expected, a greater proportion of *Howards End*'s audiences were middle class than were audiences for the most popular box-office successes—but the film also seemed to attract more middle-class audiences than for the majority of art-house releases.[37]

As Claire Monk demonstrates, if *Howards End*'s audiences are compared with those for other period films, art-house films, and popular successes for the period 1992–4, however, there is evidence that the film did in fact win over more than its expected core 'sophisticated' audience. If it did well with middle-class audiences, it was less reliant on them than several art-house films and other period dramas released in 1994, attracting more spectators from the C1 and C2 social categories, with its overall audience much less skewed towards ABs. Indeed, the only social categories with which it fared less well than the most popular box-office successes of the period were Ds and Es—semiskilled, unskilled, and unemployed workers. The breakdown of the audience by gender suggests that around 51 per cent of the audience were female, 49 per cent male. This is virtually the same as the breakdown for cinema audiences in the UK as a whole, but less skewed towards female audiences than for period dramas as a whole in the early 1990s.[38]

Thus in terms of the overall size of the audience, and its class and gender breakdown, there is some evidence that the film achieved the sort of crossover success that the distributors had aimed for. In terms of age, however, there was less evidence of crossover appeal. A significantly greater percentage of the audience for *Howards End* was aged 25 or over than for either the top box-office hits or for other art-house films of 1992, with the percentage of the audience aged 45 or over particularly impressive.[39]

In broad terms, the distribution strategy adopted in the USA by Sony Pictures Classics was very similar to the UK model, but the scale was rather different. Again, the film opened on just one screen and then very slowly rolled out to more and more cinemas over the next year. It was in fact the first film to be distributed by Sony Classics, the 'specialized marketing and distribution arm' of Sony Pictures Entertainment.[40] Until very shortly before the premiere, Merchant Ivory were still in negotiation with the financially struggling Orion Classics, eventually buying the film back from them. As Merchant put it, 'I was unconvinced that Orion could

---

[36] CAVIAR, *Caviar 10, vol. 1*, table 12/5, 42.

[37] Ibid., table 12/11, 48: 37% of *Howards End*'s audiences were estimated to be from social category AB, and another 37% from C1, while for art-house films as a whole, the figures were 32% and 33% respectively; note these figures are different to those Claire Monk gives in table 4 of her 'Heritage Films and the British Cinema Audience in the 1990s', *Journal of Popular British Cinema*, 2 (1999), 36, because she conflates evidence from reports for different years (CAVIAR, *Caviar 10*, and *Caviar 12* (London: BMRB International Ltd., 1995)); it is also worth noting that CAVIAR classified *Howards End* as an art-house film.

[38] See table 4 in Monk, 'Heritage Films and the British Cinema Audience', 36.

[39] Of *Howards End*'s audiences 31% were aged 45 and over, 75% aged 25 and over; CAVIAR, *Caviar 10, vol. 1*, table 12/5, 42.

[40] John Evan Frook, 'Sony Unit's "Howard" Slow Rollout Pays Off', *Variety* (11 Jan. 1993), 16.

give it the special attention that it needs'.[41] Sony Classics was in fact set up by former Orion Classics executives Michael Barker, Tom Bernard, and Marcie Bloom—and it was they who had originally bought the distribution rights to *Howards End* for Orion. They bought them for a second time when Merchant Ivory pulled out of the Orion deal.[42] At Orion, Barker, Bernard, and Bloom had established a reputation for working with 'strictly specialized films [which] were marketed slowly and economically by relying on their quality, good reviews, and word of mouth'.[43] This was the plan for *Howards End*. What they bought, quite knowingly, was a niche product—'a must-see picture for class audiences'[44]—but one which potentially had a much broader appeal, although it would have to be handled carefully if its potential profitability were to be maximized. High-quality production values were considered the key: 'The thing that's significant for us is the quality of the picture,' proclaimed Bernard. 'To see a picture made for (a little more than) \$7.5 m that looks like a \$20 m picture to us was just astounding.'[45]

The film had its world premiere on 27 February 1992, at the Lincoln Center in New York. It opened a fortnight later on 70 mm at Loews Fine Arts Theater, in Manhattan, New York—as in the UK, it thus began life on a single art-house screen, and was still playing there three months later. Its opening weekend was 'spectacular', with takings of \$52,000, which enabled it immediately to reach ninth place in the chart of independent releases.[46] The film stayed on this single screen for five weeks, after which it was introduced to eleven more cinemas. Extremely high average takings per screen enabled it to move into the main box-office chart, at number 26, despite still being on only twelve screens. By comparison, the top five films in the chart were on more than 1,800 screens, the top fifteen were all on more than 1,200 screens, and most of the other films in the top thirty were on more than 200 screens.[47] For the first eight weeks of its release, *Howards End* was averaging around \$20,000 per screen, when most of the other films in the top 60 had averages of less than \$2,000. In *Variety*'s words, such performances were 'world-beating' and 'torrid'.[48] At this stage, the distributors were picking cinemas 'in upscale neighborhoods', concentrating on what was deemed to be the film's core audience.[49]

It wasn't until mid-June that the film was on more than 100 screens. By mid-September, it was on more than 200 screens, although as the number of screens increased, so the average takings per screen decreased. Even so, it still managed to register as one of the top twenty highest grossing films in the USA for several

[41] Quoted in Michael Fleming, ' "Howards" Ends up at Sony Classics', *Variety* (2 Mar. 1992), 31.

[42] Ibid.

[43] Anne Thompson, 'A Classics Tale: From Orion to Sony—to Oscar?', *LA Weekly* (17 Apr. 1992), cutting.

[44] Lawrence Cohn, 'Howards End', *Variety* (24 Feb. 1992), 247.

[45] Tom Bernard, quoted in Martin A. Grove, ' "Howards End" Good Sony Classics Beginning', *Hollywood Reporter* (26 Feb. 1993), 14.

[46] *Variety* (23 Mar. 1992), 8.

[47] *Screen International* (24 Apr. 1992), 20.

[48] *Variety* (11 May 1992), 8; (18 May 1992), 6.   [49] Lukk, *Movie Marketing*, 127.

weeks. From September 1992 until January 1993, the number of screens it was playing on slowly went down, although it was still on seventy-five screens after forty-six weeks. In February and March, a year after the film first opened, there was a dramatic change in the exhibition pattern. Following the Oscar nominations, as well as successes in other end of year 'best ten films' lists and awards from the National Board of Review and the Golden Globes, the number of screens it was playing on went up to 282 in late February, and then a week later to 402, which put it once more back in the list of the twenty highest grossing films of the week.[50] In the week that the Oscars were actually announced, it achieved its highest market share, appearing on 547 screens. It didn't disappear from *Variety*'s list of the sixty highest grossing films of the week until the middle of July 1993, some sixteen months after it opened. Even then, it was still on eleven screens. In total, it was on release for seventy weeks.[51]

This was no haphazard attempt to milk *Howards End*, but a deliberate strategy that was from the outset devised to keep the film on release for over a year, and that slowly increased the number of prints in circulation as word of mouth and reviews had time to circulate.[52] The plan was to lend the film an aura of exclusivity, to make it a special event rather than part of the routine cinemagoing fare. Bookings for all venues were open-ended, so the film could stay at a screen until audiences began to tail off. There was thus no need to rush to see the film on its opening weekend, and the distributors could maximize the film's theatrical life.[53] Tom Bernard of Sony Classics explained that they did not want to saturate the marketplace at the outset: 'We preferred to have long lines in front of our theaters with everyone learning that there was going to be a theater in that town where "Howards End" would be playing for a long time.'[54] As one newspaper headline put it, 'You Don't Understand—They Want You to Stand in Line for "*Howards End*".'[55] The article went on:

If there was a bad review for 'Howards End', it was pretty hard to find. . . . [C]ritics . . . positively drooled [over the film] . . . not that many people have seen it. . . . The fact that the picture isn't playing in many theaters and isn't expected soon at your local multiplex— and even if it *is* playing within driving distance, is drawing long lines once you get there— has actually contributed to its success. And it's all very intentional. 'If you make it a little difficult . . . , it is more attractive,' said Merchant, the film's producer.[56]

It was the exclusivity of the film, and the queues that ensued, that created the high average takings per screen. Since fewer prints were used than for most studio films, and less money was spent on advertising, this ensured that profit levels were

[50] Lukk, *Movie Marketing*, 127.

[51] Box-office statistics from weekly charts in *Variety* and *Screen International* for 1992 and 1993.

[52] Martin A. Grove, ' "Howards End" Driven Theatrically, Not by Video', *Hollywood Reporter* (1 Mar. 1993), 2.

[53] Jane Galbraith, 'You don't Understand: They Want You to Stand in Line for "*Howards End*" ', *Los Angeles Times* (14 June 1992), cutting.

[54] Tom Bernard, quoted in Grove, ' "Howards End" Driven Theatrically', 2.

[55] Galbraith, 'You don't Understand'.   [56] Ibid.

kept high. In fact, rather than spending huge amounts of money on advertising, the distributors relied on reviews and word-of-mouth. They knew in advance that a Merchant Ivory production would generate good reviews and plenty of critical attention, and the quality of the film ensured that they were not disappointed. They did not of course eschew other forms of publicity, and employed a specialist public relations firm, Samantha Dean and Associates, to help make *Howards End* 'the latest film to make a successful leap from cult status into a broader market'.[57] Publicity was provided at strategic intervals throughout its planned year-long run. The film's stars, for instance, were deployed in publicity tours across country, while displays in theatre lobbies and bookshops linked the film to Forster's novels and to the thirtieth anniversary of the Merchant–Ivory partnership, 'celebrated in a recent coffee table book' (Robert Emmet Long's *The Films of Merchant Ivory*).[58]

Such tie-ins and publicity stunts were seen as vital ways of maximizing audience awareness, especially among cultural elites who were not necessarily regular cinemagoers. Thus theatre managers were encouraged to distribute flyers 'in record stores, bookstores, high schools, colleges, [and] cafes and . . . to people standing in line for tickets to cultural events'. They were also encouraged to 'make sure that the local classical radio plays the soundtrack on the air and mentions the opening date of the film in [the local] theatre . . . [and] to advertise in college newspapers [and] alternative newspapers'.[59] Benefit preview screenings in local theatres, organized in conjunction with high-profile organizations, and with community leaders and local celebrities present, were seen as another crucial way of increasing the hype around the film: 'You must make this an event, something everyone will talk about, word-of-mouth brings about box-office!'[60] It was also suggested that

there will be a considerable amount of interest in the film on the part of high schools and colleges. Group sales programs should be set up in advance. The way to do this is to invite to the advance screening all teachers and department heads of the schools in your area. Please focus on ENGLISH, DRAMA, HISTORY and LITERATURE departments.[61]

A similar strategy had been adopted in the UK, where a special and quite extensive Study Guide on the film had been produced by Film Education, a film industry sponsored body whose aims are 'to promote the use of film in the school curriculum and to further the use of cinemas by schools'. The Study Guide itself was sponsored by the British Academy of Film and Television Arts and Shell UK, 'as part of their joint-venture to promote British film and television'.[62] The guide,

---

[57] Anon., 'A Tale of "Howards End": Shuttling the Stars around', *New York Times* (30 July 1992); cutting, C18.

[58] Ibid.; Robert Emmet Long, *The Films of Merchant Ivory* (London: Viking, 1992).

[59] Howards End Advertising and Publicity Guide, distributed by Sony Pictures Classics, 1992.

[60] Ibid.   [61] Ibid.

[62] Ian F. Kelly, *Howards End Study Guide* (London: Film Education, undated, 1992?); quotations from p. 9.

intellectually serious and well put together, is aimed quite clearly at teachers of A-level English literature, while the distributor informed theatre managers that Film Education would provide 'lists of your local schools' addresses'.[63] There are clear benefits all round: teachers received a free teaching resource, Shell UK and the film industry were associated with a genuine educational venture, and another plank in the promotion of the film was put in place.

The key was to ensure that the very specific attractions of the film were exploited appropriately for publicity purposes. In the case of the American publicity strategy,

The lush locations and period costumes allowed Ms Dean [the publicist] to tap some unusual publicity outlets, like Victoria magazine, Country Accents and Country Life, as well as airline magazines. The strategy called for a public relations event every two months 'to remind people in big cities that it's around and people in small cities that it's coming,' said Michael Barker, a co-president of Sony Pictures Classics. . . . 'We want the audience to say, 'It's finally here,' rather than: 'Where did it go? I heard it was a good movie.'[64]

Another crucial plank in the exhibition strategy was the timing of the release in relation to the following year's Academy Awards ceremony. The Oscars generate enormous amounts of publicity for both nominated films and those that actually receive awards. Being nominated for Best Picture, as well as for other high-profile awards, gave the film a significantly broader audience potential, which was duly exploited by rapidly increasing the number of screens on which the film was appearing, a year after its initial release.[65] Again, the strategy was in place from the beginning, as Michael Barker explained:

It was important . . . for us to keep the profile high on the picture for the entire year so that at the year-end it would be a picture to which everyone compared other pictures. The fact that it has got a high profile—it's now in its 50th week—is what gave it that special distinction that caused the Academy to consider it so seriously in all these areas.[66]

Orion Classics, the original distributors, had actually booked the 13 March North American release date even before the film had started shooting the previous April—in the midst of the 1992 Oscar 'season', in fact, when the ballyhoo about *Silence of the Lambs* (1990) meant that Anthony Hopkins was very much in the public eye. 'We strategically set the picture to open during the Oscar campaign,' explained Tom Bernard, 'knowing speculation about Hopkins would help the profile of the film.'[67]

The distributors were thus playing a carefully orchestrated and double-handed game. On the one hand, they were nurturing the film's core niche audience—

[63] Publicity sheet for *Howards End* issued by Mayfair Entertainments UK Ltd.
[64] Anon., 'A Tale of "Howards End"', C18.
[65] Grove, ' "Howards End" Good Sony Classics Beginning', 14.
[66] Quoted ibid.; see also Thompson, 'A Classics Tale', cutting, in which Bernard explains the campaign in advance!
[67] Thompson, 'A Classics Tale', cutting.

essentially the art-house audience. On the other hand, they were trying to reach a wider audience. The Advertising and Publicity Guide issued by the distributors thus insisted to theatre managers that 'not unlike films such as AMADEUS, GANDHI, TESS, CHARIOTS OF FIRE and A ROOM WITH A VIEW, HOWARDS END has a wide commercial appeal'. They consequently encouraged exhibitors to 'increase mainstream awareness on this film. The regular art film oriented public WILL go see the film anyway, we want you to help us get the more commercial film audience in your theatre. . . . HOWARDS END is a truly wonderful film and deserves all the attention and exposure of any mainstream film.' To help theatre managers achieve this goal, the distributors produced 'a poignant and entertaining trailer which appeals to a wide audience. Trailers should be up and early and attached to both commercial and art films'.[68]

In this respect, the marketing and distribution strategy was based on that for *A Room with a View* (1986). The links with *Room* were important, but also the differences, and they were immediately picked up by critics reviewing the film in the trade press: 'The art house crowd is certain to be enraptured by this gem. Many of the same ingredients that made "A Room with a View" such a popular success are present here, though "Howards End" ultimately is more downbeat. Still, there is potential to gain a wider, more mainstream audience.'[69] Some commentators did wonder if that 'downbeat' quality would make it difficult to market *Howards End* successfully with the same strategy that had worked for *Room*. Where the earlier film 'was essentially a romance set to operatic music against the backdrop of turn-of-the-century Florence, "Howards End" is less a love story than an eloquent Edwardian saga of families in conflict, so it is questionable whether it will have the kind of crossover appeal to teens its predecessor did'. As a distribution executive admitted, 'It's not as much a date film.'[70] That didn't stop the publicists trying to present it as such, and the key promotional image, used in most posters and advertisements, prominently featured a romantic moment between two of the film's younger cast members, Helena Bonham Carter and Samuel West (Fig. 20).

As I noted in an earlier chapter, the financial motivation for most studio films is not what their theatrical releases yield, but the income from video rental and sales, and the various kinds of television outlet. The theatrical release thus functions as a shop window for these ancillary markets and the revenue-generating potential of that window needs to be maximized as soon as possible so the film can move into the next stage of its life as a video release. Most films appear on video within six months, so the theatrical release has to be out of the way by then—hence the effort and money put into the opening weekend. This was not the case with *Howards End*. Tom Bernard recalled:

[68] Howards End Advertising and Publicity Guide.
[69] Jeff Menell, 'Howards End', *Hollywood Reporter* (13 Mar. 1992), 34.
[70] Quoted in Galbraith, 'You don't Understand', cutting.

20. The key romantic image used in publicity for *Howards End*

We were in no great hurry to meet any video window or cable window or ancillary demands like most of the films out there. We did not have to be out in video in six months to get our video cash to feed the company. We felt it was important to get every theatrical dollar out of this film. We wanted every town in the country to say, 'Where is "Howards End?" ' And when it got there they'd say, 'Gee, it's finally here. We're so excited.' As opposed to saying, 'Oh, it already came and went. I guess I'll wait for the videocassette,' which is the norm.[71]

With *Howards End*, print and advertising costs were kept 'extraordinarily low', where most distributors spend enormous amounts on such things, often more or less cancelling out the revenue generated by film rentals. There was consequently little pressure on the distributors to release the video of *Howards End* as soon as possible and it was not in fact released until a year or more after the film's theatrical opening.[72] The timing was deliberate, with the video release designed to maximize the 'free' publicity generated by the Oscars. Not that other ancillary markets were left untapped, since Sony exploited the film in the hotel and airline markets, outlets not usually explored by small independent companies handling niche products. In this case, however, the specialized distribution arm of one of the Hollywood majors was making the most of its corporate links.[73]

[71] Bernard, quoted in Grove, ' "Howards End" Driven Theatrically', 2.
[72] Frook, 'Sony Unit's "Howard" ', 16.   [73] Ibid. 18.

NICHE PRODUCTS, THE MEDIA ECONOMY, AND MEANING

Howards End thus provides a perfect illustration of a key development in the media economy, whereby major corporations were buying into the low-profit specialized market and milking the products they acquired as thoroughly as possible. On the one hand, this gave independent producers like Merchant Ivory a certain buoyancy. On the other hand, it raised fears about the 'mainstreaming' of independent film. What is clear is that the niche markets were increasingly identified by the majors as worth exploiting, and that the specialized distribution of 'artistic' films like *Howards End* is still very much a business, in which profit is the goal. It may operate differently to the Hollywood mainstream, but it is still a business, in which artistic values are among the selling points for a commodity—and the ultimate goal of the distributors is to enable a film like *Howards End* to cross over into the margins of the mainstream market. Even with the crossover element, the niche market still remains a niche, which means that in terms of sheer numbers of people seeing the film, the figures were not high by comparison with the most successful box-office hits. As one cynical American commentator put it:

> Virtually no-one in America has seen *Howards End*. It has had no impact on the consciousness of the country. It just happens to be English, and so we figure it must be very tasteful. Just like *Masterpiece Theatre* which we all pretend to watch. . . . Don't believe me, look at the money: after 374 days on release, *Howards End* made $21 million. . . . *Teenage Ninja Turtles* made $13 million in 5 days.[74]

Even if comparative box-office returns do not impress on this basis, $21 million is still an immense amount of money, while the comments about taste indicate the ways in which commodities like *Howards End* do in fact have an impact on public consciousness. The relative success of films like *Howards End* thus helps to reinforce well-established cultural hierarchies based around taste and national identity. The success of *Howards End*, on the back of *A Room with a View*, certainly transformed Merchant Ivory's fortunes, enabling them to establish much closer links with Hollywood majors. Thus by December 1992, it could be announced that Columbia Pictures were backing *The Remains of the Day* (1993), with $11.5 million; that Walt Disney Studios had paid $3.7 million for the North American rights to *Jefferson in Paris* (1995), and were working on four more projects with Merchant Ivory (Jeffrey Katzenberg, chairman of Walt Disney Studios, described *Howards End* as 'the best movie of the year'); and that Warner Bros. had signed to back Merchant Ivory's *Surviving Picasso* (1996).[75]

How does this economy and this marketing strategy affect the debate about the meaning of the film? One conclusion we must draw is that, at the level of production, distribution, and exhibition, the politics of the film were simply not an issue. On the one hand, it was enough that the film was perceived by many as a

---

[74] Cynthia Heimel, 'Your Oscar is No Big Deal', *Independent on Sunday* (28 Mar. 1993), 43.
[75] Morais, 'A Reverence for the Theater', 42.

21. Young love, heritage style: the poster used in the UK for *Howards End*

great work of art. On the other hand, it was a commodity which needed to be sold to as many consumers as possible, in as many different markets as possible. This effectively meant opening up the film to a range of audiences and a range of readings, not closing it down to one particular reading. There is, however, a great deal more to be said about the promotion of the film.

PROMOTING THE FILM: YOUTHFUL ROMANCE IN A
HERITAGE LANDSCAPE

Promotional material invites audiences to engage with a film in particular ways—an invitation that is once more extended, as we've seen, in the title sequence of the film itself. In the case of *Howards End*, again as we've seen, there are in effect multiple invitations to different audiences, different sensibilities, and different taste groups. Once more, the film is constructed in terms of ambivalence and polysemy—to open it up to a range of readings is more profitable than closing it down to one particular reading. As far as publicity material was concerned, as I've already noted, one key image was widely used in posters and advertisements (Fig. 21). This shows Samuel West as Leonard Bast kissing the palm of Helena Bonham Carter/Helen Schlegel's outstretched hand as she embraces him. It is an image of young heterosexual love, and for many may well have invoked Merchant Ivory's earlier Forster adaptation, *A Room with a View*. The widespread use of this image, in both the UK and the USA, indicates the extent to which the film was sold as a romance—that is, as a film about the affairs of the heart, not about class and national identity. One of the key audiences that this image addresses is the audience that is assumed to most enjoy costume dramas, namely the female audience; but the image also addresses a youthful audience. Significantly, it is the romance between the film's young couple that is foregrounded, not the relationship between Helen's older sister Margaret, played by Emma Thompson, and the much older Henry Wilcox, played by Anthony Hopkins—even though the latter consumes far more story-time.

Taking such images into account, as Claire Monk and others have pointed out, it becomes very clear that what I call the heritage film could equally be classed as a modern variant of the woman's picture.[76] Audiences who read such films in terms of youthful romantic love may simply not consider those films in terms of debates about heritage, tradition, and the national past. The relative popularity of such texts does not necessarily indicate that audiences are buying in to a fantasy of the national past, or an international mythology of Englishness. It may on the contrary be that audiences are engaging with the films as dramas of romance and desire. Of course, the woman's film may also be read in terms of sexual politics, and *Howards End* is by no means unique in featuring strong-willed, independent women, and exploring their interests, outlooks, and desires. Nor is it unique in telling a tale about sexual transgression and the crisis of inheritance. It would be difficult, however, to suggest that this more politicized reading is encouraged by the central promotional image for *Howards End*.

The trappings of heritage, on the other hand, are much more prevalent. For this romantic image of the film's young stars rarely appeared on its own and was generally situated in a broader promotional context, made up of other images, as well as carefully chosen words. Images first: in many but not all advertisements, postcards, and posters, the cottage, Howards End, can be seen behind the couple, fronted by an old stone wall and a meadow of wild flowers. It is an idyllic and alluring vision (especially when the image is presented in colour) of semi-rural, traditional England, ancient, but in good shape. The couple is superimposed on this background image, their bright white shirts making them stand out—an effect reinforced by the fact that the couple is sepia-tinted, while the background is in full colour. The couple is of course in period costume. On the one hand, these details are simply the trappings of romance, the *mise-en-scène* of desire. On the other hand, for those spectators to whom such images appeal, there is no doubt that this is a gentle and tasteful period film, set in a heritage landscape: the *mise-en-scène* of desire is also the *mise-en-scène* of heritage, the sense of pastness conveyed by the sepia image. Indeed, even the representation of desire suggests genteel manners and restrained passions rather than acres of naked flesh and close-ups

---

[76] See e.g. Claire Monk, 'The British Heritage Film and its Critics', *Critical Survey*, 7/2 (1995), 116–24.

of the sexual act. The image of the young couple is thus a far cry from the ecstasy of both the women in Derain's *La Danse*, the painting that prefaces the film, and the couples we see having sex in the *Basic Instinct*, the biggest box-office attraction the year *Howards End* was released.

Two relatively distinct readings of the film are thus offered in this image—one presenting it as a woman's film, the other as a tasteful period drama. It is perhaps worth noting that the image is composite, obviously constructed from several different photographs, and that the central image of the romantic clinch does not actually appear in the film in this precise form. This underlines once again the extent to which the film works as pastiche, the extent to which it is a hybrid creature, but also the extent to which the image has been staged precisely to attract an audience. The potential attractions of the film are opened up in other ways too. Thus while the young couple—and Helena Bonham Carter in particular—are foregrounded, so are the film's other stars, both by listing them prominently above the title of the film, and, in some cases, by superimposing much smaller images of Emma Thompson, Anthony Hopkins, and Vanessa Redgrave (who plays the first Mrs Wilcox). This is in part then a star vehicle, with different stars appealing to different audiences. Then there are the quotations lifted from reviews to help sell the film. The British poster selected a range of refined superlatives—'breathtaking beauty and imagination' (*Radio Times*), 'elegant and powerful . . . Merchant Ivory's finest film' (*Time Magazine*): this is still clearly promotional material, but it's neither the language of the street nor typical of the rhetoric used to sell most Hollywood studio films. But it's worth noting again the range of sources drawn on: the middle-brow *Radio Times*, the more upmarket and serious *Time* magazine, but also, interestingly, the men's magazine *GQ* (whose selected superlative is perhaps more masculine, and certainly more racy: 'terrific'!). If this was a film that it was assumed would appeal mostly to female audiences, little touches such as this were perhaps intended to ensure male audiences didn't feel left out.[77]

When the film opened in New York, and while it was showing exclusively at Loews Fine Arts, less effort was made to broaden the appeal of the film, with the quotations clearly selected to attract the core art-house audience: 'A crowning achievement . . . a masterpiece' (David Ansen, *Newsweek*); 'A comedy of character, expertly realized in performances that match any on the screen now or in the recent past. A great pleasure' (Vincent Canby, *New York Times*); 'A grand piece of moviemaking' (David Denby, *New York Magazine*).[78] When the film was first released on video in the UK, the choice of superlatives on the video sleeve again suggested the film was being sold primarily as a quality film for an 'educated', middle-class audience: 'sheer class triumphs' (Derek Malcolm, *The Guardian*); 'an instant national treasure, a great movie' (Tom Hutchinson, *Mail on Sunday*); 'style, atmosphere . . . a masterful film' (Iain Johnstone, *Sunday Times*); and again 'a film

---

[77] See the poster advertised on the publicity leaflet distributed by Mayfair Entertainments UK Ltd.
[78] See the advertisement in the *New York Times* (22 Mar. 1992), 20.

of breathtaking beauty and imagination' (*Radio Times*). The blurb on the video sleeve reinforces the aura of quality cinema, describing the film-makers as an 'artistic team', and the film as 'embellished with . . . polished skill'.[79] A video trade magazine confirms this view of the market: 'should be able to woo the upmarket renter'.[80]

While all of these verbal efforts to sell the film as a quality product of interest to art-house audiences were accompanied by the image of youthful romantic love in a heritage setting, a slightly different line of attack was used in promoting the American video. This time it was the middle-aged couple, Anthony Hopkins/Henry Wilcox and Emma Thompson/Margaret Schlegel, that was foregrounded, looking much more formal and much less romantic or passionate (Fig. 22). This attempt to address an older audience was echoed in a trailer used for a UK television screening of the film on Channel 4. The voice-over in the trailer was delivered in a very slow, elegant, and elegiac manner by an older-sounding woman, who laid great stress on the film as an adaptation of a canonical novel ('E. M. Forster's *classic* tale of passion and companionship'), while writing on the screen proclaimed the film as 'E. M. Forster's *Howards End*', rather than Merchant Ivory's *Howards End*. Over a montage of images from the film, the voice-over also tells us that 'love and devotion can take many forms', suggesting that the film will therefore appeal to a range of different audiences and sensibilities.

THE TEXT ITSELF: FILM STYLE AND ICONOGRAPHY

The attractions of both high-quality production values and youthful romantic love are of course mobilized in various ways in the film itself. I've already noted the ways in which the title sequence of the film situates it in relation to prestigious art and craft movements. There are other culturally specific links made to both classical literature and theatre in this sequence as well. Thus the art nouveau title card is followed by one establishing Forster's authorship ('based upon the novel by . . .'), which itself then parts in the middle and draws to either side to reveal the diegesis, like a curtain pulling back at the start of a stage play. Mrs Wilcox is seen meandering slowly through the garden at Howards End at twilight, her dress trailing in the long grass. She wanders past the windows of the house and looks in to see her family playing a board game and the maids clearing the dining table. Although almost nothing happens, it is a highly charged sequence, with its display of charming period costumes and the picturesque rural setting of the house. It is a very languid sequence too, making full use of long takes (the first three shots last for two minutes eighteen seconds), a moving camera, deep focus, and dissolves between shots. In the fourth shot of the film, in another long take

---

[79] Sleeve for *Howards End*, a Curzon Video Release, distributed by Fox Video, CV 0024, 1993.
[80] Anon., 'Howards End', *Video Home Entertainment* (6 Mar. 1993), 20.

22. Old romantics: the DVD sleeve used in the USA for *Howards End*

discreetly shot from a distance, we see Helen Schlegel and the younger Wilcox son steal out of the house and into the garden, where they embrace and kiss.

This is the trigger for the narrative to unfold, although it is hardly a conventional Hollywood narrative. When Helen's family hear of her liaison with the

Wilcox boy, there is a certain haste in trying to deal with the issue, but the narrative as a whole is far too slow-moving and episodic to engage most audiences attuned to the Hollywood action film, or even most modern variants of the woman's film or romantic comedy. While certain narrative expectations and lines of development are set in motion by these early events, the goal that the film reaches at its closure is hardly one that could be envisaged at the outset. On the contrary, the film is less goal-driven or organized around the causal logic of action sequences than it is driven by a desire to explore character and ambience, period detail and manners. Of course, there is still a strong romantic sensibility, but it is dispersed across several different characters and couplings rather than restricted to a single narrative line or central protagonist. The episodicism of the narrative means that there are often quite abrupt or under-motivated transitions to new scenes. The use of music underlines these abrupt transitions, since it often bursts out, without warning and unexpectedly loud, as a new scene starts. On several occasions, ellipses between, and sometimes within, scenes are heavily marked by a fade to black and then a fade up again to action. This highly self-conscious marking of the passing of time is also evident in the occasional use of intertitles between sequences ('A few months later').

The slowness of the film is in part a function of its realism, and the film-makers' bid for authenticity. Thus the plot could not be changed too much from that developed originally by Forster because the film-makers were playing on a sense of fidelity to the source novel. What some regard as longueurs in the film—'Screenwriter Ruth Prawer Jhabvala fails yet again to be sufficiently strict with her source material: the opening 45 minutes could usefully have been compressed into 30'[81]— were thus justified by their presence in the novel. Equally the realism of the *mise-en-scène* slows the film down. The desire to provide as full a diegesis and as convincing a setting as possible produces an obsessive attention to period detail and to the details of performance. Since there is also a desire to display that detail, the camera will often stay with a scene longer than might be strictly necessary for the purposes of presenting a narrative action or event. There are for instance several meal scenes in the film, which give plenty of scope for period detail: the clothes of the characters; the props that fill the well-stocked tables, as well as any sideboards, dressers, or mantelpieces in the room; even the paintings on the walls. To capture all of this detail, the camera must inevitably stay back from the action, going no closer than a medium shot, and often going for long takes as well. The film also explores the subjective reality of one of its characters, Leonard Bast, with the camera showing his reveries, as he inserts himself into the literature he reads, or dreams of meeting Helen all over again. The surface realism achieved through the attention to period detail is thus matched by the psychological realism achieved in these subjective sequences, and indeed in the general emphasis on character rather than action.

[81] Christopher Tookey, 'Christopher Tookey on "Howards End", "Grand Canyon" and "Mobsters"', *Sunday Telegraph* (3 May 1992), p. no. unclear on cutting.

The look of the film is dominated by the attention to period detail, with the *mise-en-scène* positively littered with heritage properties. This heritage presence is enhanced by the visual style that the film-makers have adopted, what I've called the aesthetics of display—that is, a particular use of the camera and a particular way of editing that works superbly to display as spectacle this range of heritage properties. Thus the film is characterized by long shots and medium shots rather than close-ups—indeed, I would say there's not a single shot in the film that would normally be described as a close-up. The emphasis visually is thus as much on the period detail in the background, the space and setting of the narrative, as it is on the characters that inhabit that space. The film is also characterized by relatively long takes, producing an average shot length of 8.92 seconds—which makes it seem very leisurely for contemporary cinema. (Barry Salt suggests that most commercial American films in the 1980s had an average shot length of around five to seven seconds, with a significant number much faster than that.[82] Surprisingly, *Howards End* is not slow by comparison with classical Hollywood, for at least in the 1930s and 1940s the typical average shot length for American films was around nine to ten seconds, according to Salt.[83]) Combined with the slow pace of the narrative and the relative lack of action, this allows the camera to linger on the settings, to give full rein to the display of heritage properties, a fact to which we will need to come back in due course. It is a highly pictorialist use of the camera. Thus while the image clearly does have a narrational function, conveying information necessary to our understanding of the story, it also insists on its presence precisely as image, as picture. It is both an image that grants the spectator access to splendid views of heritage iconography, and an image that is a carefully composed aesthetic object in its own right.

The look of the camera at such iconography is sometimes self-consciously detached from character point of view and from the functions of the establishing shot. In formalist terms, such shots might be described as narratively unmotivated—or perhaps better, in David Bordwell's terms, as artistically rather than narratively motivated.[84] Of course, the *mise-en-scène* could be absorbed into the narrative, read literally as setting or symbolically as the externalization of character psychology. Yet the difference of some of the shots also invites a reading of them as exceeding narrative requirement. This difference, this potential narrative excess, is achieved by the length of time they are on the screen, the spectacular vantage point from which many of them are framed, or their detachment from the classical conventions for marking establishing shots and point of view shots. This gap between narrative requirement and the attraction of the *mise-en-scène* thus allows the image to come to the fore precisely as image, as spectacle, as the

---

[82] Barry Salt, *Film Style and Technology: History and Analysis* (London: Starword, 2nd edn., 1992), 296.
[83] Barry Salt, *Film Style and Technology: History and Analysis* (London: Starword, 1983), 306–7 and *passim*; Salt concludes that this was the *mean* average shot length in the 1930s and 1940s.
[84] See David Bordwell, *Narration in the Fiction Film* (London: Methuen, 1985), 36 and *passim*.

unfettered display of heritage properties. It is a trope constantly remarked on by reviewers discussing the visual splendour of such films, as we shall see.

To take a few examples, shots of grand buildings in London, or of Oxford colleges, are often shot from a high angle or low angle position which seems to serve no narrative purpose, but shows off the buildings wonderfully. On one visit to Oxford, Margaret is seen outside with her brother Tibby; the shot is carefully framed in order to capture as much of the architectural splendour as possible—even though it again serves no narrative purpose. On another occasion, while touring Henry Wilcox's latest property acquisition, the spectator is treated to a montage of paintings, which only retrospectively is anchored in the narrative by a subsequent shot of Margaret Schlegel looking at the paintings.

Consider too a brief scene set in the hospital where the first Mrs Wilcox is dying. How are we to read it? After a shot of Margaret Schlegel giving some flowers to Mrs Wilcox as she lies in her hospital bed, we move to a wide long shot from a high camera position of the exterior of the hospital, a splendid period façade, beautifully framed by the cinematographer. The camera very slowly pulls back and pans slightly, to reveal Charles Wilcox and his wife looking out of a window, but in the opposite direction to the view with which we have just been presented (the shot is on screen for all of twenty seconds). Gradually the scene picks up from here, with a further two shots.[85] If we stay with the central shot, rather than moving on, we might ask, 'for whom is this splendid view of the building?' This brief fragment from a scene, with its narratively unmotivated view of the hospital building, and its narratively unmotivated camera movement, could be read in a variety of ways. It could be read as a slightly unconventional establishing shot, but it doesn't work very effectively as such, since there is little visually that actually establishes that we are in a hospital. Nor is the view seen by the characters (they are looking in the opposite direction), so we cannot really read it as a point of view shot, even though structurally it seems to be set up in this way (with the camera pulling back to reveal the gazing couple). The unconventionality of the shot (the lack of narrative motivation, the fluid camera movement) could be read as a mark of art-cinema style. It could be read symbolically, as an elegiac expression of the concern of the characters for Mrs Wilcox's health, an indication of their inner feelings, their emotions. But it is also possible to conclude that the view is solely for the camera—or, to put it another way, that the shot is designed to display a unique heritage property (the building), to offer a view for the enjoyment and appreciation of the spectator.

There is no fixed way in which spectators must read this scene, and of course most will not notice the details I've laid out. But they are there, and in one way or another, while watching the film, the spectator must make sense of the cues, must draw some conclusions, however implicitly, about how to comprehend the details. Different spectators will read the same scene in different ways, and of

---

[85] My thanks to Sheldon Hall for pointing out that I had on an earlier occasion described these shots in the wrong order.

course it is possible for the same spectator to read the scene in more than one way at the same time. Take another scene from *Howards End*, the scene when Henry Wilcox is showing Margaret Schlegel round his London house, and proposes to her on the stairs. It is a wonderful scene, perfectly capturing the emotional turmoil of the characters, their propriety and their repressiveness. It also has some magnificent decor, furnishings, and interior designs on display. The space and the props are clearly used expressively, with the emotional distance between the characters conveyed by the distance between them on the stairs, and the staircase itself, the props, and the cavernous dimensions of the building literally overwhelming them. But there can be no denying that the scene also makes the most of the opportunity to display some fine authentic period artefacts and interiors, which are of course the property of a very privileged class. It is interesting to compare the scene in the film to the equivalent passage in the novel, where Margaret's ironic view of the *mise-en-scène* suggests a much sharper criticism of the overdecoration and the masculinity of the space, and its source in colonial exploitation: 'Such a room admitted loot', writes Forster.[86]

These features—the way in which the story is told, the studied attention to both surface realism and psychological realism, the pictorialist camera style—owe as much to art-cinema style as they do to the mainstream film. This self-consciously different and distinctive film style operates as a sort of authorial signature—and it is the exercising of this signature which, as it were, 'explains' the developments in the film that seem to lack a clear narrative motivation. That signature was also central to the promotion of the film. The words 'Merchant Ivory Productions Presents' may not have been in quite as large a typeface as the names of the stars, but they still appeared prominently on every poster, advertisement, and video sleeve. Thus while there is no doubting that *Howards End* works in part as a woman's picture, with its attention to heterosexual romance, domestic and familial concerns, and the role of women, it is clear from the way the film is organized that it also works as a heritage film and draws on the conventions of art cinema.

CRITICAL RECEPTION: 'SHEER CLASS TRIUMPHS . . .'[87]

How did reviewers respond to the film? How were the film's diverse attractions handled in the critical discourse about the film? What sorts of signals did reviewers give their readers about whether they might enjoy the film, and for what reasons? Let's look first of all at the responses of reviewers writing for the various trade papers produced by and for those working in the film industry. It is perhaps surprising that a business as hard-nosed as the film industry should applaud the qualities of a low-budget, specialist film like *Howards End*, but there is no

---

[86] E. M. Forster, *Howards End* (London: Penguin, 1989), 166–7.

[87] Derek Malcolm, *Guardian*, quoted in advertisement for video rental release, *Video Home Entertainment*, 2/9 (1993), inner front page frontsheet.

question that they did. Trade reviewers thus heralded 'a sumptuous visual delight
. . . 140 minutes of cinematic bliss . . . [with] breathtaking cinematography . . .
[and] splendid actors', from film-makers whose names are 'synonymous with
quality'.[88] It was 'polished in all departments' and boasted 'impressive performances' and 'top-notch' production values; accordingly, it 'will find no critics'
among their 'stable of admirers'.[89] It almost seemed there was no faulting 'this film
jewel',[90] this 'lushly detailed period drama', this 'complex, dense and literate' film.[91]
'How do you find anything better than "Howards End"?' asked one reporter, after
a special screening of the film in Los Angeles. His report, drawing on interviews
with the many guests from the film business, is littered with superlatives: 'magnificent, a theatrically elegant work of art', 'a masterpiece', 'sheer genius', 'flawless
performances', 'eye-feasting period detail', and so on.[92]

Less surprisingly, most of the reviewers for British broadsheet newspapers and
middle-brow publications also registered strong approval for 'this perfectly
delightful film', this 'beautiful', 'resplendent' and 'near-perfect' film.[93] It was 'a
genuine triumph . . . their most fully achieved screen version of [Forster's] work',
'a colossal achievement', 'a gorgeous film . . . distinguished and enjoyable . . . If
you like illustrated classics of quality, waste no time in connecting with it.'[94] The
particular qualities of the film were repeatedly stressed. Thus it was 'literate,
vibrant, intellectually urgent', where most contemporary cinema was 'flashy, fashionable and evasive'.[95] This was no mere genre piece or studio crowd-pleaser; on
the contrary, it was 'a very handsome, intelligent, witty piece of work', 'a masterful film . . . with style, atmosphere and . . . sensitivity . . . a wholly absorbing and
enjoyable experience', 'a triumph of wit and delicacy, of non-obsequious faithfulness to Forster and of mind over narrative maze'.[96]

Reviewers for the equivalent publications in the USA saw no reason to disagree
with their British counterparts. Indeed, many of them surpassed the Brits in their
praise for a film that was 'so good I wouldn't have believed it if I hadn't seen it
with my own eyes'.[97]

Surrender to 'Howards End'. Give yourself willingly to this most assured motion picture,
to its remarkable acting and storytelling and the plush richness of its setting. For everyone
who's yearned for the dimly remembered satisfactions of traditional filmmaking, for

---

[88] Menell, 'Howards End', 9, 34.   [89] Dobson, 'Howards End', 23.

[90] Cohn, 'Howards End', 247.   [91] Thompson, 'A Classics Tale', cutting.

[92] George Christy, 'The Great Life', *Hollywood Reporter* (12 Mar. 1992), cutting.

[93] Errigo, 'Howards End', 24; Philip French, 'Be-all and End-all for Triumph', *Observer* (3 May 1992),
52; Geoff Brown, 'Passion Amid Period Props', *The Times* (30 April 1992), cutting; French, 'Be-all and
End-all for Triumph', again.

[94] Hugo Davenport, 'A Triumph of Period Passion', *Daily Telegraph* (30 Apr. 1992), 14; McGillivray,
'Homes and Gardens', 61; Usher, 'Fine Probe into Past Prejudices', 34.

[95] French, 'Be-all and End-all for Triumph', 52.

[96] Errigo, 'Howards End', 24; Iain Johnstone, 'All the Best Connections', *Sunday Times*, section 6 (3
May 1992), 10; Nigel Andrew, 'Prose and Passion Personified', *Financial Times* (30 Apr. 1992), 19.

[97] Stuart Klawans (cutting—title missing), *The Nation* (27 Apr. 1992), 570.

movies of passion, taste and sensitivity that honestly touch every emotion, this is the one you've been waiting for.[98]

Certain adjectives recur over and again in reviews: 'elegant', wrote Vincent Canby, 'elegant and powerful', wrote Richard Corliss, an 'elegant, complex and satisfying film', wrote Richard A. Blake.[99] No question then that this was a film of 'taste and elegance'.[100] It was also 'brilliant',[101] 'exquisite',[102] 'refined',[103] 'resplendent',[104] 'sumptuous',[105] 'stunning',[106] and 'sublime'.[107] These are not the sorts of adjectives used to describe most Hollywood studio films, and they show the same good taste and refined vocabulary as the film itself. Intelligent cinema deserves intelligent and articulate criticism, and there is no denying that this is an 'impeccably intelligent' film, 'a handsome and intelligent piece of work: a faithful, well-paced, and carefully crafted dramatization of a very good story', which 'meets the challenge of Forster's intellectual rigor'.[108]

A consensus was reached by many British and American reviewers about certain characteristics of the film. Thus the 'impeccable' quality of the acting was frequently commented on; this is 'acting of the most subtle, delicate sort', performed with 'nuance, taste and restraint', 'acted to perfection', by 'a dream cast'.[109] 'Although some of them could be considered Edwardian costume-drama regulars, even Merchant Ivory regulars, there is no trace of the generic in their performances'[110] The 'intensely visual' look of the film drew extensive praise too.[111] 'The first thing that anyone notices about a Merchant Ivory film is its sheer beauty—the backgrounds ... and the absolute "rightness" in the detail of the interiors.'[112] This 'classic costume drama' was no exception, precisely because it was exceptional in

[98] Kenneth Turan, ' "Howards End": Splendor in the Grass', *Los Angeles Times* (15 Apr. 1992), F1.

[99] Vincent Canby, 'A Drawing-Room War with Edwardian Grace', *New York Times* (13 Mar. 1992), C1; Richard Corliss, 'Doing it Right the Hard Way', *Time* (16 Mar. 1992), 72; Richard A. Blake, 'A Tired Season', *America* (11 Apr. 1992), 299.

[100] Stanley Kauffmann, 'Forster—Again and Better', *New Republic* (23 Mar. 1992), 27.

[101] Julie Salamon, 'Film: Merchant Ivory's "Howards End" ', *Wall St Journal* (12 Mar. 1992), cutting; see also Blake, 'A Tired Season', 299.

[102] Molly Haskell, 'Simply Sublime', *Harper's Bazaar* (Mar. 1992), 144; Rita Kempley, ' "Howards End": Resplendent Return to Forster's England', *Washington Post* (24 Apr. 1992), D8.

[103] Haskell, 'Simply Sublime', 144.

[104] Kempley, ' "Howards End" ', D1.

[105] Pristin, 'Old Novels, New Screenplays', 4; Kempley, ' "Howards End" ', D1.

[106] Anon., 'A Cinematic Journey to E. M. Forster's Howards End', *Victoria* (Apr. 1992), 62.

[107] Haskell, 'Simply Sublime', 144; Peter Travers, 'Howards End', *Rolling Stone* (2 Apr. 1992), 41; Kempley, ' "Howards End" ', D1.

[108] Tom Crow, 'Regarding *Howards End*', *Village View* (17–23 Apr. 1992), cutting; Terence Rafferty, 'The Current Cinema: Yes, But', *New Yorker* (4 May 1992), 74; David Denby, 'Class Action', *New York* (9 Mar. 1992), 73.

[109] Turan, ' "Howards End" ', F1, F7; Crow, 'Regarding *Howards End*', cutting; Travers, 'Howards End', 41; David Ansen, 'Forster Revisited', *Newsweek* (16 Mar. 1992), 66; for British variants, see e.g. Errigo, 'Howards End', 24; French, 'Be-all and End-all for Triumph', 52; Johnstone, 'All the Best Connections', 10.

[110] Joan Juliet Buck, 'Movies', *Vogue* (Mar. 1992), 192.

[111] French, 'Be-all and End-all for Triumph', 52.

[112] David Holloway (title missing on fiche), *Daily Telegraph* (5 May 1992), 12.

its achievement, 'characteristically honey-toned and handsomely dressed'.[113] It is 'a film of dazzling visual splendor' and 'exquisite design', 'elegantly photographed', 'almost perfectly realized . . . visually stunning', and marked by 'leisurely grace' and 'painstaking authenticity'.[114]

It was widely recognized that 'the frugal budget ha[d] been used to fund an imperial vision'.[115] Thus it had the look of 'a truly lavish production', with its 'mouth-watering choice of classic English locations' and 'the magnificence of its teeming set pieces'.[116] Some critics were so impressed with the period detail and the acting that they no longer felt they were dealing with the illusory world of fiction: 'The cast is so immaculately turned out and behaves so perfectly in such glorious English Heritage locations that . . . it seems that we are actually watching a dramatised documentary made in 1910', and that the actors are 'spied on in life rather than delivering lines'.[117]

For others, the fictionality of the film was vital, given the fact that it was an adaptation of a canonical novel by E. M. Forster, an 'unabashedly bookish movie'.[118] It was 'a superb adaptation', 'one of their finest and most elegant', displaying 'fidelity to the art of the novel, truthfulness to the film's craft'.[119] Several of the broadsheet and upmarket magazine reviews have as much to say about Forster and the novel as they do about the film, bolstering their views with references to eminent literary critics.[120] There were also a number of companion think pieces and interviews, which used the concurrent release of *Howards End* and *Where Angels Fear to Tread* as the excuse for a more general discussion of Forster, the film/literature relationship, and the process of literary adaptation.[121] There is a strong literary bias to this sort of reviewing, which almost treats the film as if it were literature. The adaptation is thus applauded because it is 'literate', because it has 'achieved just the right balance between the literate and the cinematic'.[122]

One reviewer favourably compared Merchant Ivory's Forster adaptations with what he saw as the dire Hollywood versions of English literature classics in the

---

[113] Shaun Usher, 'The Secret Passions that Smoulder behind the Windows of Howards End', *Daily Mail* (27 Mar. 1992), 32–3; Mat Snow, 'The Films of Merchant Ivory', *Premiere* (UK, Dec. 1993), 62–3.

[114] Ansen, 'Forster Revisited', 66; Tookey, 'Christopher Tookey on "Howards End" ', cutting; Bruce Williamson, 'Movies', *Playboy* (Apr. 1992), cutting; Crow, 'Regarding *Howards End*', cutting.

[115] Alexander Walker, 'Edwardian Emma Tops the Class', *Evening Standard* (30 Apr. 1992), 30.

[116] Jeff Sawtell, 'An Edwardian Tale of Middle-Class Morality', *Morning Star* (2 May 1992), 7; Davenport, 'A Triumph of Period Passion', 14; Hutchinson, 'Period Piece Making its own History', 39.

[117] McGillivray, 'Homes and Gardens', 61; Usher, 'Fine Probe into Past Prejudices', 34.

[118] Williamson, 'Movies', cutting.

[119] Barry Norman, 'Why Television is a Power Player in the British Film Industry', *Radio Times* (7–13 Oct. 1995), 56; Tookey, 'Christopher Tookey on "Howards End" ', cutting; Walker, 'Edwardian Emma Tops the Class', 30.

[120] See e.g. Holloway, *Daily Telegraph* (5 May 1992), 12; see also interviews that focused on the process of adaptation, e.g. Helen Dudar, 'In the Beginning the Word: At the End, the Movie', *New York Times* (8 Mar. 1992), 15, 20–1.

[121] See e.g. Dudar, 'In the Beginning the Word', 15, 20–1; Caryn James, 'Why Forster's Novels have Star Quality', *New York Times* (22 Mar. 1992), 11, 18; Blake Morrison, 'Only Connect! England Saved by an Ideal Home', *Independent on Sunday* (3 May 1992), 21.

[122] Salamon, 'Film', cutting; Crow, 'Regarding *Howards End*', cutting.

1930s, as well as the populist British adaptations produced in the immediate post-war period.[123] *Newsweek* was even more sweeping: 'Everyone says great books don't make great movies. Howards End is one grand exception'.[124] The reviewer for the American edition of *Vogue* was equally complimentary: 'This is literature on-screen at its best; it sent me scurrying to the book, which only confirmed the achievement of Mr. Ivory and Mrs. Prawer Jhabvala'.[125] This reviewer was evidently not the only one to move in that direction. While the film was still showing in only one cinema in New York, the novel appeared in the *Newsday* paperback best-seller list.[126] There were however a few dissenting voices. Thus there was nothing unique about the fact that Terence Rafferty wrote at length in the *New Yorker* about Forster. What was unusual was that, while he thought Howards End 'handsome and intelligent', in his view it still came nowhere near the novel, lacking as it did the distinctiveness of the author's voice.[127]

Others though identified a very distinctive authorial voice in the film, the voice of Merchant Ivory. An intelligent, artistic film by definition needed an auteur with a fine pedigree and a recognizable signature. What was unusual about the identi-fication of the auteur in this case was that it was not an individual, not the direc-tor of the film, but the composite 'Merchant Ivory', which meant in fact the triumvirate of Ivory, Merchant, and Prawer Jhabvala, the director, the producer, and the scriptwriter. Dozens of reviews identified Howards End not just as a Merchant Ivory film, but as their 'finest' film,[128] 'the crowning achievement of their careers'.[129] The Merchant Ivory team itself was 'civilized', 'culturally refined', 'the quality lit team of contemporary cinema', dedicated to producing 'intelligent', 'relatively highbrow films'.[130] Their trademark—the term is used in several reviews[131]—was literary adaptations, one reviewer joking that 'It's time for legis-lation decreeing that no one be allowed to make a screen adaptation of a novel of any quality whatsoever if Ismail Merchant, James Ivory and Ruth Prawer Jhabvala are available'.[132]

The idea of the trademark is worth considering further. It is not after all quite the same as an author's signature, being more associated with trade, commerce,

[123] Holloway, *Daily Telegraph* (5 May 1992), 12.

[124] Ansen, 'Forster Revisited', 66.   [125] Buck, 'Movies', 192.

[126] Pristin, 'Old Novels, New Screenplays', 4.

[127] Rafferty, 'The Current Cinema', 74; compare Vanessa Letts, 'Cosily Connected', *The Spectator* (9 May 1992), 37.

[128] See e.g. Mather, 'Another Round of Forster's', 47; Walker, 'Edwardian Emma Tops the Class', 30; Davenport, 'A Triumph of Period Passion', 14; Corliss, 'Doing it Right the Hard Way', 72; Derek Malcolm (cutting—title missing), *Guardian* (30 Apr. 1992), 26; Snow, 'The Films of Merchant Ivory', 62–3; Travers, 'Howards End', 41.

[129] Ansen, 'Forster Revisited', 66.

[130] Ibid.; *USA Today* (author and title of article missing from cutting) (22 Apr. 1992), D6; Dudar, 'In the Beginning the Word', 15; Morais, 'A Reverence for the Theater', 42.

[131] See e.g. Turan, ' "Howards End" ', F1; James, 'Why Forster's Novels have Star Quality', 18; Davenport, 'A Triumph of Period Passion', 14; Dobson, 'Howards End', 23; Gilbert Adair, 'The Last Detail: Film's Latest Fashion Victims?', *Independent* (3 July 1992), 16; also Johnstone, who uses an alternative term, benchmark: 'All the Best Connections', 10.

[132] Canby, 'A Drawing-Room War with Edwardian Grace', C1.

and craftsmanship than with the output of an individual artist. It thus draws attention to the teamwork common to all feature films, and to the fact that cinema is a business, an industry. Of course it also draws attention to the distinctiveness of Merchant Ivory's output. At the same time it suggests that James Ivory is not perceived as a true artist, but as a film-maker who has, for better or worse, allied himself to the demands of the marketplace. This is perhaps one of the reasons why the Merchant Ivory team have become such a middle-brow success, for they have neither cut themselves off from the market, nor lost sight of the principles of Art, Culture, and Quality. Indeed, they have successfully married the two, found a safe middle ground. And by establishing a recognizable trademark, a brand name that guarantees those very qualities, they have been able to establish for themselves a firm place in the crossover market, a niche where they can sell their goods and exploit that trademark.

LAURA ASHLEY, MASTERPIECE THEATRE, AND THE POLITICS OF THE MIDDLE-BROW

The trademark is a way of both guaranteeing certain qualities and warning off those who don't appreciate such qualities. Thus, as several reviewers intimated regarding *Howards End*, 'fans of Merchant-Ivory will be delighted'.[133] The implication was that many cinemagoers were not fans of Merchant Ivory, and they would not be delighted. One might expect the more downmarket tabloid newspapers, more aligned with popular culture than with either Forsterian modernism or middle-brow quality, to be less delighted than the broadsheets, so it is no surprise to find the following, from *Today*: 'It was with heavy heart and stiffening sinews that I braced myself for another $2\frac{1}{2}$ hours of corset-creaking E. M. Forster.' Even if this reviewer could think *Howards End* 'by far the best film the team have produced', she still complained that it was 'Crammed with corsets, bustles and stiff collars' and 'grown[ed] under the weight of starry thesps'.[134] More surprising, perhaps, is the fact that, when the film first showed on British television, *The Sun* awarded it a five-star rating in its TV listings, while the *Mirror*, which described the cast as 'exceptional', and the *People*, which described the film as 'virtually flawless', both awarded it a maximum four stars.[135]

Mainstream fan magazines like *Empire* and *Premiere* might also be thought of as publications whose core readership would not be in sympathy with tasteful period drama—and again the reception was ambivalent:

What drearier prospect than a gaggle of London's most renowned thespians—Royal Academy types with caramel stuck in their back teeth and umbrellas rammed you-know-

---

[133] Mark Sanderson, 'Howard's [sic] End', *Time Out* (29 Apr. 1992), 62.
[134] Sue Heal, 'Ivory Coasts through Feast of Forster', *Today* (1 May 1992), 24.
[135] *Sun* (7 Oct. 1995), 12; *Daily Mirror* (7 Oct. 1995), 13; *People* (8 Oct. 1995), 3.

where—smothered in period costumes by 'Masterpiece Theatre'-meisters Merchant and Ivory, comporting themselves languorously through stately British homes with the intention of embalming some Allan Bloom-inspired Great Book. What greater surprise, therefore, when the army of talent so assembled—Emma Thompson et al.—give E. M. Forster's masterpiece a whole new life. Even for those who prefer Harvey Keitel to Laurence Olivier, it's a lesson in cultural humility.[136]

We will need to return to the 'Masterpiece Theatre' jibe in due course. Let us stay for the moment with Emma Thompson and all that she might be thought to offer a female audience. For it is widely assumed, by the industry, by critics, and by the academy, that costume dramas appeal above all to the female audiences. How then did women's magazines respond to the film? Surprisingly, neither *Vogue* nor *Elle* were initially very enthusiastic about the film. As far as *Vogue*'s Joan Juliet Buck was concerned, however, 'The slight lassitude with which one might greet yet another adaptation of a piece of Edwardian literature costumed in beige linen and dotted with carriages dissipates with the opening shot'.[137] The reviewer for *Elle* was less easily persuaded. Yes, it was 'glamorously nostalgic', yes, Emma Thompson gave a fine performance, but otherwise this was 'basically . . . an agreeable period soap opera'—on the one hand, implying that period soap provided agreeable pleasures; on the other hand, suggesting that the quality tag was not really justified.[138]

Clearly, no single film is going to be to everyone's taste. As we've seen, one of the purposes of the marketing campaign for *Howards End* was to broaden the appeal of the film so that it didn't just reach confirmed Merchant Ivory fans. But at the level of critical reception, there was also a struggle over taste, a debate on the one hand about whether the film really was in good taste, and on the other about whether the 'good taste' it embodied was to be applauded or derided. On the whole, middle-brow reviewers loved the film, but some of their colleagues despised it because of its very middle-brow qualities, which meant for them that it could not be perceived as a 'genuine work of art'.[139] Some recognized it as middle-brow, and argued that as such it could engage in valid social criticism. Others argued that these same middle-brow qualities prevented it from having any contemporary political relevance whatsoever. Two cultural reference points are central to this debate. For the Brits, the key cultural reference was Laura Ashley; for the Americans it was Masterpiece Theatre.

For some, to invoke Masterpiece Theatre was simply to indicate the positive qualities of the film. As one reviewer put it, the work of Merchant Ivory 'has become synonymous with *Masterpiece Theatre* aesthetics, stateliness, sumptuous interiors and lavish detail. Never have the team's gifts been put to higher service than in this elegant adaptation of E. M. Forster's novel . . . a feast for the eyes as well as the soul.'[140] Others recognized that the Masterpiece Theatre reference could

[136] Anon., 'Premiere Recommends' (video review), *Premiere* (US June 1993), 102.
[137] Buck, 'Movies', 189.
[138] Ben Brantley, 'Howards End', *Elle* (Apr. 1992), cutting—no page given.
[139] James Bowman, 'Fashion Plays', *American Spectator* (July 1992), 53.
[140] Joanne Kaufman, 'Picks and Pans', *People Weekly* (13 Apr. 1992), 19.

be double-edged: 'Merchant Ivory films have often been admired, and reviled, for their dogged gentility, the *Masterpiece* theatricality of their style'.[141] Several other-wise complimentary reviews adopted this strategy of acknowledging that others disliked such films for their 'enervated "Masterpiece Theatre" gentility', yet claimed the taunt was inappropriate for *Howards End*.[142] The *New York Times* was particularly ambivalent:

Though intensely serious in its concerns, it is as escapist as a month in an English coun-tryside so idyllic that it probably doesn't exist. . . . It's easy for us to shake our heads with Forster over the inequities built into England's class system, although that same system pro-vides the stability of the structure in which such drawing-room wars can be fought. Forster was a social critic capable of savagery, but for today's film audiences, 'Howards End' is so much fun that it becomes a guilty pleasure. Thank heaven for inequities.[143]

Serious social criticism or escapist fun? The question reverberates through the critical debate about *Howards End*. Thanks to a cartoon by the film-maker Alan Parker, the key reference point for the debate in the UK was the Laura Ashley fashion and fabrics chain (see Fig. 11). In the cartoon, a couple are seen leaving a cinema showing a Merchant Ivory film, one of them commenting, 'God, how I hate the Laura Ashley school of film making'.[144] The criticism took root, and numerous reviewers found themselves alluding to the criticism while at the same time trying to distance themselves—and the film—from it.

It has become fashionable in certain leftish circles to sneer at the 'Laura-Ashley' school of costume drama, and it's true that the success of Room with a View spawned a flood of dull, inferior imitations . . . But Howards End is not a celebratory, nostalgic film: . . . it's a complex, unsentimental, intellectually meaty piece. And while its debates are of their period . . . you're constantly reminded of how topical and contested they continue to be.[145]

In review after review, the same sentiments are rehearsed, almost in the same terms: 'It's rather trendy nowadays to sneer at Merchant-Ivory films as being merely beautiful costume dramas that bury their heads in the sands of nostalgia and have nothing to say about modern times.'[146] Or, as a variant, try: 'Recently there has been grumbling about Britain's so-called "white flannel" school of film-making. The complaint is that we are making too many films in which well-bred young things pose languidly in the grounds of country houses in an England long gone.'[147] To be fair, the conclusions are not always the same. For some reviewers, the apparent lack of social relevance is an irrelevance: 'this is to criticise them for not being what they never set out to be in the first place. . . . they . . . follow a dif-ferent agenda—to please the eye and the ear and, yes, the mind too with well-told,

---

[141] Corliss, 'Doing it Right the Hard Way', 73   [142] Ansen, 'Forster Revisited', 66.
[143] Canby, 'A Drawing-Room War with Edwardian Grace', C1–15.
[144] *Making Movies: Cartoons by Alan Parker* (London: British Film Institute, 1998), 43; see p. 68 above.
[145] Sheila Johnston, 'Character Building', *Independent*, arts section (1 May 1992), 18.
[146] Norman, 'Why Television is a Power Player', 56.
[147] McGillivray, 'Homes and Gardens', 61.

well-mounted stories of human love and conflict'.[148] Art, it seems, is sometimes more important than politics: 'Yes, we've seen quite enough of this sort of thing, you may think. But then along comes a classic example of the genre. *Howards End* . . . is so captivatingly exquisite in every detail that all criticism is disarmed. In fact, it may even induce you to wonder why we don't make more films like this nowadays.'[149]

If quite a number of reviewers felt they had to defend the film from others that dismissed it as too similar to Laura Ashley and Masterpiece Theatre, who exactly were the real culprits? They were in effect the aesthetes (or to put it more bluntly, the snobs), and they had two overriding concerns. First, they saw it as their duty to defend literature from Merchant Ivory's dangerous talent for 'razing master-pieces'—'the book is nothing like the tasteful, lugubrious costume piece'. Secondly, they also felt they had to defend cinema from becoming too dependent on liter-ary culture, proclaiming that 'the qualities of such illustrated English Lit are not cinematic'.[150] Thus they were concerned at the way 'this overlong exercise in schmaltz', this 'inert', 'respectfully dull' film, paid 'stuffy tribute' to Forster's novel.[151] By paying tribute in the wrong way, it seemed that Merchant Ivory destroyed everything that was good about Forster's novel. 'Modernist texts like *Howards End* were once thought challenging and dangerous. Now they are the safe screenplays of the art-film circuit.'[152] All that was left after the process of adapta-tion had been completed was a 'Mills and Boon period melodrama for the literary set.'[153]

It was not just the film-makers that were at fault, apparently, but the audiences too: 'It's essentially for those PBS-weathered audiences used to sitting things out—just for the Britishness of it all.'[154] Worthiness, stultifying good taste—and of course the pretty pictures and nice frocks: 'Now, I'm all for pretty pictures and nice frocks, but there's a limit. The limit is reached when these things start being hailed as a great movie.'[155] Here we see the critical discourse about the film most overtly taking on the form of a struggle over taste. For their detractors, the real problem was that Merchant Ivory had made a career 'out of peddling plastic as cinematic art, as . . . *Howards End* triumphantly confirms'.[156]

What is so awful about the film, then, from this point of view? A review in *Cineaste* sums it up in one telling comment: 'Admittedly [Ivory's] approach to lit-

---

[148] Norman, 'Why Television is a Power Player', 56.

[149] McGillivray, 'Homes and Gardens', 61.

[150] John Simon, 'Demolition Jobs', *National Review* (13 Apr. 1992), 57; Georgia Brown, 'Homes of the Brave', *Voice* (17 Mar. 1992), 56; Anne Billson, 'Our Kind of People', *New Statesman and Society* (29 May 1992), 33.

[151] Desson Howe, 'Never-Ending: Forster on Film', *Washington Post* (24 Apr. 1992), WW39; Compton Miller, 'Classic Meets with a Sorry End', *Daily Express* (1 May 1992), 40.

[152] Morrison, 'Only Connect!', 21.

[153] *Gay Times* (author and title missing from cutting) (May 1992), 68.

[154] Howe, 'Never-Ending', 39.   [155] Billson, 'Our Kind of People', 32.

[156] Simon, 'Demolition Jobs', 56.

erary adaptation is middlebrow.'[157] This is clearly meant as a damning indictment. An article by James Bowman in *The American Spectator* explains the problems in more detail, this time using the term 'designer movie' to establish the middle-brow quality of the film, its difference from real art. Designer movies are:

typically 'Masterpiece Theatre' style costume dramas. Designer movies are like fine art reproductions in that the point of them is not to convey a genuinely artistic experience but to make a statement about the taste of those who make them and those who consume them. Their appeal is to a limited—indeed, a select—audience on the strength of their associations with approved cultural artifacts, especially classic novels. Each of them offers a whole set of challenges to the filmmaker: not to entertain or thrill or move us but to get right the costumes and the customs, the period detail of dress, décor, manners, and language. . . . You could say that these films are really educational . . . For a post-literate culture they are the equivalent of the ornamentation on medieval cathedrals: the only way for ordinary folk to know anything about history. Such sermons on celluloid cannot be judged as artistic experiences but only as one would judge a *National Geographic* documentary.[158]

The designer movie, then, 'is a way of conveying a simulacrum of artistic experience to those who are not interested in the real thing but only in having their good taste ratified'. With the 'genuine work of art', on the other hand, 'the point of the costumes and the scenery, the music and the manners, is not to register a designer trademark but to serve a dramatic purpose'. The presence of the canonical book, its themes and characters, is necessary so that 'we know that it *is* classic art. Once we know that, we are then free to enjoy the film for the pretty pictures of exotic places, the costumes, the music, and the sweetly melancholy ambiance of a past that is safely dead.'[159]

For those who did enjoy *Howards End*, this was of course no mere simulacrum, but an impressively humanist work of art, 'timelessly relevant'.[160] Some of its admirers also found a much sharper political sensibility in play, enabling the film to engage in 'scathing social criticism' of 'a social system built on exploitation'.[161] Even if it 'displays the trademark Merchant-Ivory prettiness, it has more than surface beauty', such critics argued.[162] It was felt inappropriate 'to deal out "lace-hankie" insults' because the film's vision of the past had been 'coloured, ironised and toughened by a modern sensibility'.[163] 'For all the gracious, spacious setting of the country house of its title, this is no white-linen-suits-and-cucumber-sandwiches period piece, but a clash of attitudes, classes, sexes, soaring ambitions and deep-running passions springing from "who shall inherit England?" concerns at the turn of the century.'[164] Some reviewers argued that those concerns remained relevant in the 1990s, and that the film should not therefore be dismissed as

[157] Peter Bates, 'Howards End', *Cineaste*, 19/2–3 (1992), 69.
[158] Bowman, 'Fashion Plays', 52.   [159] Ibid. 53.
[160] Usher, 'Fine Probe into Past Prejudices', 34.   [161] Blake, 'A Tired Season', 298.
[162] James, 'Why Forster's Novels have Star Quality', 18.
[163] Andrew, 'Prose and Passion Personified', 19.   [164] Usher, 'The Secret Passions', 32–3.

escapist.[165] Some even argued that *Howards End* had more contemporary relevance than much more self-conscious state-of-the-nation dramas made and set in the present day—that, 'with much greater subtlety than most "Thatcher's Britain" movies', it 'establishes an agenda . . . for the Nineties'.[166] But there always seemed to be a lingering doubt about how far such a line could be pushed; always, it seemed, the alternative view had to be acknowledged:

There is a prevailing view that the British film industry . . . no longer requires films like *Howards End*. They are despised as the Laura Ashley school of film-making; an Edwardian nirvana where Helena Bonham Carter is always tripping through the grass in a long frock. Where is the contemporary relevance? The answer is that *Howards End* is more subtly relevant than any anarchic offering from, say, Derek Jarman or Hanif Kureishi.[167]

The implication very often seems to be that the film must work on two levels, the subtle politics residing beneath the surface prettiness, as in both of the following reviews:

The film remains, of course, a period piece, and it would be stretching a point to find too much contemporary resonance in the fate of Leonard Bast. But the darker tone underlying the film's immaculately polished surface takes it far beyond the dubious attractions of a gratuitous wallow in nostalgia, and should banish once and for all the charge that Merchant Ivory's prime contribution to our culture is no more than a branch of the heritage industry.[168]

Howards End, the cottage in the country, with its sunburst of flowers and refined conversation at tea, presents a surface of elegant gentility, all that we outsiders are tempted to admire in the English of the era, but Forster and Ivory remind us from the outset that it is a property gained by corruption and maintained by deceit.[169]

What is emerging in this critical discourse is the same tension I outlined at the start of this chapter. On the one hand, there is this potentially conservative 'surface of elegant gentility'. On the other hand, if we probe beneath this surface, we find a much darker narrative exploring the social inequities of the period in a way that makes the film relevant to the 1990s. The problem was that the prettiness of the surface was often so intense it was distracting: 'As usual with a Merchant-Ivory production, the film is art-directed to within an inch of its life. You'd think the picture would choke on all those gewgaws and draperies and decorative mouldings.'[170] It certainly seemed that 'in some scenes, actors can barely move for potted palms, ornate stairways, cushions and umbrellas'.[171] And if it wasn't the interiors, then it was the 'ravishing' countryside, the 'romantic celebration of the English landscape—Englishness for export, as their detractors are fond of saying'.[172]

[165] See e.g. Corliss, 'Doing it Right the Hard Way', 72; Graham Fuller, 'Movie Column', *Interview* (March 1992), cutting; Travers, 'Howards End', 41; Kempley, ' "Howards End" ', D8; Walker, 'Edwardian Emma Tops the Class', 30.

[166] French, 'Be-all and End-all for Triumph', 52.   [167] Mather, 'Another Round of Forster's', 47.

[168] Davenport, 'A Triumph of Period Passion', 14.   [169] Blake, 'A Tired Season', 299.

[170] Klawans, *The Nation* (27 Apr. 1992), 570.

[171] Brown, 'Passion Amid Period Props', cutting.   [172] Johnston, 'Character Building', 18.

THE DISCOURSE OF HERITAGE: TOURISM AND THE HERITAGE
INDUSTRY

One of the central criticisms of the film's detractors was that they saw in *Howards End* not a great work of art or a trenchant piece of social criticism, but an 'Edwardian theme park'.[173] The reviewer for the left-leaning *New Statesman and Society*, for instance, felt she 'was trapped in a sub-standard slice of British heritage', while the communist *Morning Star* complained that, 'As usual with Merchant Ivory productions, this is a heritage industry film' (which meant, by definition, that it failed to explore the situation of the working classes).[174] Its attractions were thus as blatantly commodified as in any Hollywood genre film—where films like *Basic Instinct* were accused of having 'gratuitous car chases and explicit sexuality', *Howards End* had 'equally gratuitous scenes of Heritage England'.[175] Surprisingly, such views could be heard on both the right and the left. Thus the right-wing *Sunday Express* also accused Merchant Ivory of being 'high class purveyors of high-gloss nostalgia to the British cinema', creators of 'museum pieces'—or worse, 'a theme-park Howards End . . . all period and no passion'.[176] The achievements of the film-makers were ruthlessly satirized: 'Director James Ivory—the Laura Ashley of the lens—ensures that throughout the seasons Howards End is an extremely desirable residence',[177] so that 'there are times when it feels as though the major literary influence at work is not E. M. Forster, but *House and Garden* magazine'.[178] This 'grating, oppressive movie', this 'nostalgic . . . catalogue of collectibles, . . . stuffed full of objects most of us would love to possess', should be 'the envy of . . . our new Heritage Minister'.[179] Indeed, it should be 'bought up by the National Trust, though it doesn't need to be preserved. It has already been pickled in the formaldehyde of nostalgia.'[180]

There was worse to come, since the heritage pleasures of the Edwardian theme park were seen by the more politically concerned critics as bolstering an unacceptably exploitative social system. The more sympathetic might note simply that the film 'studiously attacks the greed and heartlessness of the rich while quite happily revelling in their splendid lifestyle'.[181] Others pushed the point further, arguing that the film 'extols the virtues of the snooty English class system, posh property rights and stultifyingly good behaviour'.[182] The problem in a nutshell was that 'If *Howards End* is supposed to be an indictment of snobbery and greed, it

[173] Billson, 'Our Kind of People', 33.
[174] Ibid. 32–3; Sawtell, 'An Edwardian Tale of Middle-Class Morality', 7.
[175] Mary Evans, 'Woolf in Lamb's Clothing', *The Times Higher* (11 Sept. 1992), 16.
[176] Sheridan Morley, 'Class Acts', *Sunday Express* (3 May 1992), 63.
[177] Sanderson, 'Howard's End', 62.
[178] James Pallot (ed.), *4th Virgin Film Guide* (London: Virgin, 1995).
[179] Brown, 'Homes of the Brave', 56; Adair, 'The Last Detail', 16; Morley, 'Class Acts', 63.
[180] Billson, 'Our Kind of People', 33.
[181] *Video Home Entertainment*, 2/10 (1993), 20.
[182] Michael Kilian, *Chicago Tribune*, quoted in Ben Macintyre, 'America Plays Down British Oscar Hopes', *The Times* (29 March 1993), 3.

fails, because it revels in the snobbish and greedy way of life: the idyllic country cottages, the grand mansions, the perfect lawns.'[183] *Howards End* was thus one of those films

that make white middle-class audiences feel safe, happy, content and unchallenged. They're non-threatening 'quality' films, set in the past, exquisitely photographed, meticulously designed, beautifully acted but they bear absolutely no resemblance whatsoever to the Britain we live in today. They inform us about our past, not the grim reality of our present. There is no sign of contemporary urban decay, or people sleeping in cardboard boxes and begging in the streets. They bear no relevance to Britain in 1992 and, though it would be wrong to say that these films should not be made, it is worrying that they should be chosen for much sought after film budgets when the social realities of living in 1990s Britain are so harsh and ignored in the cinema. They're self-indulgent, nostalgic coffee-table fantasies for the middle-classes.[184]

In a rather less dismissive discussion piece in a Sunday broadsheet newspaper, Blake Morrison pondered the ways in which *Howards End* and Forster's other novels and their film adaptations could both invoke nostalgia for an idealized England and articulate other themes relevant to the 1980s and 1990s. At stake once again is the tension between tradition and modernity, and between surface prettiness and social criticism. On the one hand, there was a vogue for Forster adaptations in the period of Tory rule in the 1980s and 1990s, 'because the national mood is so nostalgic'. On the other hand, Forster, as a modernist writer,

would have hated to be used as a piece of heritage industry. . . . It isn't all Laura Ashleyism and white linen suits. Forster's subjects are class, money, property, culture, sexuality, race. They are the subjects of our time even more than they were of his. . . . Mr Wilcox is a Thatcherite before his time . . . His antagonists are the Schlegel sisters . . . if this were 1992 they might appear . . . in Labour Party election broadcasts . . .[185]

Again, ambivalence: Forster would have hated being part of the heritage industry, but that has been his destiny—even if, at the same time, his novels and his themes connect with contemporary Britain (and indeed the USA) in other ways as well. Ambivalence notwithstanding, there is no disputing that one of the key ways in which *Howards End* was taken up in critical debate was in terms of notions of heritage, authenticity, and conservation—and often quite explicit links could be made between the film and other aspects of the heritage industry.

It does not seem unfair to summarize many of the press responses to *Howards End*, whether positive or negative, as articulating a sense of anxiety about the way it seemed to draw on the terms and conditions of the heritage industry. Many of the British and American reviewers, as we've seen, allude to the way in which the film can be seen as part of the heritage industry. Some dismissed it for the way it seemed to commodify a conservative, elite national identity that belonged in the past, but was embodied in the period details of the film's *mise-en-scène* and its

---

[183] Billson, 'Our Kind of People', 33.   [184] *Gay Times* (May 1992), 68.
[185] Morrison, 'Only Connect!', 21.

consumerist aesthetic. In contrast, some more right-leaning reviews celebrated the film for its nostalgia and for promoting *This England* patriotism, now the preferred version of the national past. The bid for historical authenticity and the spectacular display of pastness, from this perspective, was seen as admirable—and also allowed the film to be exploited in terms of the discourses and practices of cultural tourism. Some commentators, as we've seen, tried to have it both ways, praising the film, while at the same ironically acknowledging the heritage problem as perceived by others. A particularly clear example of this strategy can be seen in the *Mail on Sunday*'s review. It seems both to acknowledge the difficulties of the heritage project, and to celebrate the film for its 'quintessential Englishness'. It seems to be both ironic and patriotic, enabling the film to come across as on the one hand carefully historical, speaking poignantly to present-day audiences, and on the other as superficially nostalgic. Like the film itself, the review offers itself up for a variety of competing readings:

This is an instant national treasure. . . . [This] is because historic insights into British character—social snobberies, self-sacrifice—still ring as true as village church bells. The past speaks to the present as The Laura Ashley School of Nostalgic Film-making finally gets a masterpiece with an E. M. Forster story about Edwardian morality. . . . The film . . . is one to lift the spirits with the magnificence of its teeming set pieces and the eloquence of its intimate moments. In retreating into the past, the Ivory–Merchant–Jhabvala team has finally returned with something relevant and contemporary—the timelessness of a great movie. That it should be a country-house classic makes it the ultimate confirmation of their style. But that it should be an epic about class makes it an immediate part of the British heritage.[186]

Many of the discourses circulating around *Howards End* expressed fascination with the concern for period authenticity in the production of the film's *mise-en-scène*: 'Authenticity is important to our movies', Ismail Merchant is quoted as saying in one such article. 'In 30 years we have never shot in a studio.'[187] This concern mirrored the contemporary vogue for period style, antiques, and the renovation of period properties. Articles thus appeared celebrating the authenticity of the film's interior designs, especially the wall-coverings. A long article in *The Times*, for instance, was devoted to a discussion of the 'painstaking' archival research that went into planning the 'authentic Edwardian interiors' of the film, the techniques the set designer had used for ageing and distressing fabrics and materials, and the exhibition of designs for the film that was held at Sanderson's in London, source of most of the wallpaper designs.[188] This wasn't the only occasion on which the film appeared in the lifestyle sections of the quality press. A similar piece of writing appeared in the Home section of *The New York Times*, for instance, proclaiming that the film

---

[186] Hutchinson, 'Period Piece Making its own History', 39.

[187] Jane Warren, 'On Location for Romance', *Daily Express* (4 May 1992), 13.

[188] Swengley, 'And Now, an Oscar for the Wallpaper', 5; 'Designs on Film', an exhibition at Sanderson's, London, 4 Apr. to 9 May 1992.

spectacularly emphasizes the Merchant–Ivory team's attention to domestic detail. In addition to that ubiquitous silver, the film also makes abundant use of antique china and crystal, potted palms, leather-bound volumes, lace anti-macassars and elaborate period costumes for its interior shots, not to mention the vintage cars and trains, striking architecture, wicker furniture and luxuriant flower gardens that add color to its outdoor scenes.

The article also quotes James Ivory: 'Sometimes you have to be careful that the surroundings don't distract from what's going on . . . Other times you can lay it on with a trowel, and you should . . . That's part of the production value of a movie.'[189]

The costumes too were a selling point, an attraction that could be exploited by the fashion industry. Thus Betty Goodwin, in a regular column on 'Screen Style' in the *Los Angeles Times*, noted that the 'free-spirited' Schlegel sisters 'wear some men's clothing, such as fitted cotton shirts sometimes with neckties. If you like the look, consider that Ralph Lauren's fall collection pairs the very same shirts and ties.'[190] (In another film/fashion tie-in, *Harper's Bazaar* featured full-page colour photos of three of the film's female stars, Jemma Redgrave (who plays Henry Wilcox's daughter), Helena Bonham Carter, and Emma Thompson, dressed in Nicole Farhi clothes and Herbert Johnson hats.[191])

Attention was drawn elsewhere to the picturesque settings in which the film was shot. As an article in the *Daily Express* proclaimed, 'the true star of the film is the English countryside—the unspoilt village with its picturesque houses'. An article in *Vogue* in the USA was illustrated with a beautiful half-page colour photograph of the bluebell woods in the film, proclaiming that 'Tony Pierce-Roberts's camera is in love with England'.[192] Another American magazine, the Anglophile *Victoria*, featured a two-page spread illustrated with six large colour photographs from the film, showing off costumes and props. It treated the film as delightfully nostalgic,

a cinematic journey . . . back to an age when motor cars were stirring up dust, when women debated suffrage over tea, and a quaint country house named Howards End inextricably bound two very different families. Those who couldn't get enough of 'A Room with a View' will applaud 'Howards End' . . . all the trappings [are] glorious—from wicker baby carriages and beautiful London apartments to the dresses worn [by the female stars].[193]

The same magazine much later ran another slightly eccentric single-page spread that tied the film into a celebration of an upper-class, olde-worlde, 'English' summer, celebrating the house in a colour photo—and plugging the book *Merchant Ivory's English Landscape*.[194] This love affair with the English landscape had clearly been envisioned from the outset. Thus, in an interview during the shooting of the film, Ivory claimed that: 'There's hardly a scene without trees in

[189] Maslin, 'Finding Realities to Fit a Film's Illusions', C1 and C6.
[190] Betty Goodwin, 'Phooey on Froufrou', *LA Times* (24 Apr. 1992), cutting.
[191] Haskell, 'Simply Sublime', 144–5.
[192] Buck, 'Movies', 189–92.   [193] Anon., 'A Cinematic Journey', 62.
[194] Anon., 'Houses for Happiness', *Victoria* (July 1995), 44.

full leaf and beautiful flowers. We could have filmed in winter, but it seemed more important to show England at its best whenever we could'.[195]

The *Daily Express* article quoted above used the then recently released *Howards End* as the lead in to a discussion of how to enjoy 'the Great British outdoors' by searching out 'some wildly romantic film location . . . the beautiful countryside and forgotten villages which give British films their unique atmospheric appeal'. It goes on to list ten such spots, and where they can be found, including *Howards End*'s bluebell woods.[196] The film's locations have since been celebrated in a series of travel guides and coffee-table books. *On Location: The Film Fan's Guide to Britain and Ireland*, for instance, suggests that 'Fans can follow in Anthony Hopkins's and Emma Thompson's footsteps by eating at Simpson's-in-the-Strand, shopping at Fortnum and Mason's in London's Piccadilly and visiting numerous other public locations that represent England at its most elegant and charming.'[197] Each of these locations carries with it its own proud heritage:

For Howards End [the house], Merchant Ivory used Peppard Cottage, overlooking Peppard Common, near Henley-on-Thames, Oxfordshire. The name suggests a fairly small house, but the seventeenth-century, ivory and wisteria-covered building has four public rooms, six bedrooms and a self-contained flat. Forster was a friend of Lady Ottoline Morrell, who owned the house in the early part of this century, prompting speculation that it was the model for Howards End in his novel, which was published in 1910.[198] (Fig. 23)

The Schlegel home 'was another private residence, among the white townhouses of London's Victoria Square, not far from Buckingham Palace'.[199] Fortnum and Mason's is described as 'grocers and provision merchants by royal appointment' who 'began trading on the same Piccadilly site way back in 1707'.[200] Even the Bast's flat, included as an impoverished contrast with everything else in the film, 'was located in Park Street, Southwark, London—venue for the Borough Market, a very old wholesale fruit and vegetable market held every morning except Sundays'.[201]

Other coffee-table travel guides give the locations similar treatment. *The Movie Traveller*, another *Film Fan's Travel Guide to the UK and Ireland*, lists all the same locations, even helpfully pointing out that Peppard Cottage is a privately owned house, 'not open to the public, but it can be seen from Peppard Common which is crossed by the B481'.[202] At the time of the release of the film, an article in the *New York Times* had also played on the appeal of Peppard Cottage—'the epitome of the picturesque cozy cottage', according to Ivory—noting its Bloomsbury heritage and reproducing a scene from the film.[203] Elsewhere, an article in the

---

[195] Quoted in Sheila Johnston, 'Another Round of Forsters', *Independent* (5 July 1991), art section, 17.

[196] Warren, 'On Location for Romance', 13.

[197] Brian Pendreigh, *On Location: The Film Fan's Guide to Britain and Ireland* (Edinburgh and London: Mainstream, 1995), 30.

[198] Ibid.   [199] Ibid. 31.   [200] Ibid. 32.   [201] Ibid. 31.

[202] Allan Foster, *The Movie Traveller: A Film Fan's Travel Guide to the UK and Ireland* (Edinburgh: Polygon, 2000), 118.

[203] Eve Kahn, 'On the Home Front', *New York Times*, section 2 (8 March 1992), 15; see also James Delingpole, 'A Home Movie Starring Anthony Hopkins', *Daily Telegraph* (4 Apr. 1992), 9.

23. Peppard Cottage as Howards End

Independent mused over the life and times of another house on which Forster sup-posedly modelled Howards End, and the Poston family who occupied it for some years. The article opens: 'Thanks to Merchant-Ivory's justly acclaimed film adap-tation of *Howards End*, Rooks Nest House near Stevenage can expect a busy summer'.[204] A couple of years after the release of the film, the *Daily Telegraph* and *The Times* even ran articles about the sale of Peppard Cottage, again giving details of its heritage.[205]

A much more lavish coffee-table publication than the two film fan's guides to locations is John Pym's *Merchant Ivory's English Landscape*.[206] In part, this is a crit-ical examination of Merchant Ivory's English films, but in part it too is a heritage travel guide. At the front of the book is an olde-worlde map of southern England, showing selected locations from the films. A beautifully illustrated chapter is devoted to each of the films, at the end of which actually appears a gazetteer, which tells readers how to find each of the locations, and comes complete with details of local tourist offices. *Howards End* also featured on the 'Movie Map' produced in 1998 by the British Tourist Authority (see Fig. 8). The entry for *Howards End* informs us that 'Peppard Cottage, overlooking Peppard Common near Henley-

[204] Andrew Green, 'A Womb with a View', *Independent* (30 May 1992), 38.

[205] Michael Smith, 'Howards End Home Goes on the Market', *Daily Telegraph* (26 May 1994), 10; Rachel Kelly, 'Just as Pretty as a Picture', *The Times* (25 May 1994), 33; see also Anthea Massey, 'The Homes that Make it in the Movies', *Mail on Sunday* (20 June 1993), 82.

[206] Pym, *Merchant Ivory's English Landscape*.

on-Thames, Oxfordshire, was used to play the house, while for the local village, the filmmakers shot at Dorchester-on-Thames in Oxfordshire. London locations were used, including the department store Fortnum and Mason's, St James's Court Hotel, Victoria Square, Admiralty Arch and St Pancras Station.'[207]

There is little in this discourse of cultural tourism to suggest a vision of an unstable, fluid, changing Englishness, and much to suggest the reproduction of a fixed idea of a traditional national identity. As I suggested earlier, visually the film often seems to promote an image of an unchanged, pastoral England, while in other scenes splendid heritage buildings, furniture, ornaments, costumes, and vehicles seem as much on display as the characters and their relationships. For some critics, the apparently quite liberal explorations of class and gender relations and ideas of national identity that I identified above are overwhelmed by what they see as the seamless allure of the visually splendid *mise-en-scène*. Social subtleties in this sense are obscured by the exhibition of heritage properties and their commodification as image. The pictorial aesthetic adopted by the film-makers, the aesthetics of display, as I suggested above, is ideal for the display of heritage properties. Landscapes, grand or picturesque buildings, antique furnishings, elegant costumes, and so on, are allowed to linger on the screen, whether foregrounded in their own right or displayed as either backdrop to or adornment of characters framed in long shot and medium shot. This aesthetic thus feeds into those discourses of heritage and cultural tourism that circulate around the film. There are some nice ironies in this aesthetic of display too. Thus at one point, Mrs Wilcox says of her son Charles: 'he truly *loves* England—not of course London . . . it's so—it makes one feel so unstable, impermanent, with houses being pulled down on all sides.' The irony of this is that the new blocks of flats so despised by the characters is displayed visually as a splendid heritage property by the film. Once more, the ambivalence of the film seems to suggest that identities are fluid, they change, they are historically specific—not stable, or timeless.

CONCLUSIONS

What can we learn from this detailed examination of the marketing and the critical reception of *Howards End*? There are a number of conclusions that we can draw. Foremost among these is surely that *Howards End* is a multivalent text, which has been appropriated by different agencies at different times for different reasons. The sense those agencies make of the film depends on what they bring to the film, which aspects of the film they focus on, and to what uses they put it. Distributors use the film as a commodity they can sell in the marketplace as a means of making a profit. Reviewers use films as a way of appealing to their readers and reinforcing certain values and tastes. Audiences use films as a way of generating different sorts of pleasures. And so on. Films have a particular shape

---

[207] 'Movie Map', London: British Tourist Authority, 1999.

and style, a particular set of attractions, but meaning is not inherent in the text itself. Rather, it is produced in the negotiation between different readers, the texts with which they are confronted, and the circumstances under which that confrontation takes place.

At the outset of this chapter, I advanced two competing readings of *Howards End*. One concentrated above all on the visual qualities of the film, its iconography, and its surface prettiness, and resulted in a conservative interpretation. The other concentrated much more on the narrative of the film, and its exploration of social relations, resulting in a much more liberal interpretation. There is plenty of evidence that other spectators besides me—in this case, professional film reviewers—read the film in these ways too, underlining the extent to which the film was multivalent, and capable of being read in different ways. It is neither 'better' nor more 'correct' to read the film as an expression of a hybrid and shifting Englishness than to read it as a conservative celebration of a traditional core Englishness. From the point of view of reception studies, both readings are equally valid, representing as they do different positions taken by audiences in relation to these films.

How much was that a result of the marketing campaign for the film? While there is little evidence that this campaign was designed to promote political readings of the film, it is certainly the case that the distributors wanted a debate to emerge around the film. This would be a sign that the film was intelligent and worth debating—and would create the sort of word-of-mouth that they knew would sell the film. There is much more evidence that the film was carefully marketed as a quality product, a tasteful period drama, that would appeal to 'sophisticated' audiences, educated middle-class audiences, older audiences. These were identified as making up the core audience, which was understood by the distributors as a niche consumer group by comparison with what they perceived as the mainstream audience. The particular form and style of the film suggested arthouse pretensions, which again appealed to that core audience. But it was also important that the film could be sold as a middle-brow, crossover product—not too low-brow, yet with enough of the right ingredients to ensure that it would have some appeal within the so-called mass market; nor too high-brow, yet with enough to appeal to the more rarefied patrons of the art-house circuit. The film was thus also marketed as a romantic woman's film, and one which might appeal especially to a younger audience.

Different things to different people: this was one of the key reasons why the film was able to become such a success. By aiming for the middle ground, of course, there was always the risk that certain audiences would be offended, seeing the film as neither one thing nor the other. Hence the derision reserved in certain quarters for its middle-brow qualities—its failure to present itself as either 'genuine art' or as genuinely popular (oddly, from both perspectives, the film could seem 'stuffy'). It was here too that political readings of the film emerged, with the film being presented variously as politically suspect, as delightfully nostalgic, or as capable of liberal social criticism.

The film-makers clearly went out of their way to create a product that could showcase heritage properties—the source novel, the costumes, the buildings and their interiors, the landscapes. This 'surface prettiness', these heritage attractions, were undoubtedly a selling point. They worried some people too, of course, but for others, they were one of the delights of the film—and could be extended beyond the viewing experience itself. Inevitably, in confronting such attractions, audiences might—and some reviewers certainly did—engage in a debate about national identity, and thereby exhibit the sense of struggle that takes place over the meaning of Englishness. This complex ambivalence—the fact that the film could appeal to a range of connoisseurships, taste groups, and interests—is not of course unique to *Howards End*. On the contrary it is typical of texts in general and of heritage films in particular.

6
Case Study II: *Elizabeth*

Elizabeth (1998), a film set in the mid-sixteenth century, dealing with one of England's great historical personages, Queen Elizabeth I, represented a new stage in the development of the quality 'British' costume drama of the 1980s and 1990s. This is a film that delights in the unrestrained passions of the early modern period rather than the genteel reserve of Austen's drawing-rooms or the bourgeois respectability of Forster's. Where *Howards End* (1992) had emerged at the tail-end of the Thatcher period, *Elizabeth* was a product of Tony Blair's 'Cool Britannia'. Even so, the film is not unique; rather, its difference from earlier heritage films is one of tone, and a tone that became increasingly familiar as the 1990s wore on. There were in fact three Elizabeths in English heritage films made in that decade: Quentin Crisp's cross-dressed queen in *Orlando* (1992), Cate Blanchett's interpretation in *Elizabeth*, and Judi Dench's Oscar-winning outing in *Shakespeare in Love* (1999). Each represents a far more irreverent take on the national past than, say, Merchant Ivory's earlier offerings in the heritage cycle. Think too of other historical films made in Britain in the 1990s that reach back beyond the drawing-room—*Restoration* (1996), and *The Madness of King George* (1997), for instance, the various Shakespeare adaptations, but also more populist fare such as *Braveheart* and *Rob Roy* (both 1995). *Elizabeth* also shares much with other late 1990s 'British' costume dramas such as *The Wings of the Dove* (1997), *Plunkett and Macleane* (1999), and *Shakespeare in Love* in their efforts to reach wider audiences than earlier quality 'British' costume dramas—partly by blending in attractions usually reserved for other genres.

Elizabeth was released in the UK and the USA in the autumn of 1998. Nominally a British film, it was directed by Shekhar Kapur, an Indian, and featured an Australian actress, Cate Blanchett, in the lead role. The official website for the film described it thus:

Based on the remarkable story of the rise of the young Elizabeth Tudor to Queen of England, *Elizabeth* depicts the early life of a woman of independent spirit who ascended to the throne in 1558 to a reign of intrigue and betrayal. The conflict of her private passions and personal friendships with her duty, as monarch, to achieve national unity, form the basis of a story that is both heartbreaking and inspiring. . . .

To survive, Elizabeth must suss out hidden agendas in her court, on the battlefield, in the church, and in those closest to her. The male-dominated ruling class would appear to have the advantage, but Elizabeth will deploy whatever means necessary to keep, or take, what is rightfully hers. This young woman of intelligence and vitality will toughen herself into the imposing icon of legend ... Elizabeth I.[1]

The language of 'sussing out hidden agendas' and 'male-dominated ruling classes' should immediately signal to us that among the audiences the film-makers hoped to attract were a street-wise youthful audience and a politically aware feminist audience—neither of which are conventionally thought of as the core audience for romantic costume dramas or historical period pieces. Is this then really the sort of film I should be addressing at length in this book? One review of the film implies not, suggesting that it was 'a far cry from the sterility of British heritage movies'.[2] But how could a film about one of the most familiar English monarchs, an intelligent drama about a key moment in the national past, a film which so blatantly explores questions of national identity, a period film with fine costumes, authentic locations, and prestigious performers—how could such a film *not* be a heritage film? This sense of ambivalence—the different interpretations that could be made of the film—will become one of the central concerns of this chapter.

The bid by the makers of *Elizabeth* to reach new audiences was clearly partially successful. While *Elizabeth* was no blockbuster in the *Titanic* mould, it did make a mark with audiences, it did become a cultural presence for a short period at the end of 1998 and the beginning of 1999, when it was one of the top ten films at the British box office—and even, for a while, at the American box office. Box-office success on this scale is not insignificant when we are talking about a modestly budgeted costume drama. *Elizabeth* was also a prize-winner—including five BAFTAs, a Golden Globe, and an Oscar (it had actually been nominated for seven Oscars, including Best Picture)—and a great critical success. It was 'a stunning film', 'dazzling, vertiginous', 'one of the top movies of the autumn ... one of the must-sees of the month'.[3] It was selected as one of the films of the week or the month in numerous periodicals—for several issues running in some cases.[4] Even a senior Los Angeles trade journalist had it earmarked for his 1998 Top Ten list.[5]

Arguably, *Elizabeth* could not have been made without four crucial developments having taken place. The first was the relative success of the various English costume drama/heritage film cycles of the 1980s and 1990s, but also related films such as *Braveheart* and *La Reine Margot* (1994). The second was the relative success of the new British cinema of the mid-1990s, and especially films like *Trainspotting* (1996). The producers of *Elizabeth* in effect attempted to combine the attractions of these two film cycles and address their relatively distinct audiences. The third

[1] Official website, at www.elizabeth.themovie.com.
[2] Stella Bruzzi, 'Elizabeth' (review), *Sight and Sound*, 8/11 (1998), 48.
[3] Alison Boshoff, untitled cutting, *Daily Telegraph* (5 Sept. 1998), 18; Beverley D'Silva, 'Easy Sits the Crown', *Sunday Times*, section 2 (20 Sept. 1998), 4; Lisa Richards, 'Long Live the Queen', *Boyz* (3 Oct. 1998), 12.
[4] See e.g. the women's magazines *She* and *Marie Claire*, the gay men's magazine *Boyz*, the weekly Guide in the national newspaper the *Guardian*, and the London listings magazine *Time Out*, for Oct. and early Nov. 1998.
[5] Martin A. Grove, 'Web Site and Tarot Cards Augur Well for *Elizabeth*', *Hollywood Reporter* (28 Oct. 1998), 8.

crucial development was the strength and ambitions of PolyGram. The fourth was the increasing interest of the Hollywood majors in well-made and marketable independent films with the capacity to cross over from the specialized circuits to the multiplexes. The part each of these developments played in the genesis of *Elizabeth*, and the influence they had on the look and feel of the film, will emerge as the chapter unfolds.

As in the analysis of *Howards End*, another of my tasks in this chapter is to look at the ways in which the initial idea for an historical drama was opened up and turned into a successful cultural commodity for a range of consumers. In compiling evidence of the extent to which the film opened up interpretations rather than closed them down, I will look at the range of discourses which circulated around the film, the range of ways in which the film was taken up in the culture at large, the debates that have unfolded about the cultural status and significance of the film. This will involve looking at the extent to which the film engaged with heritage discourses, but it will also involve acknowledging the range of other discourses with which it engaged. In order to understand how the film was able to generate such a range of interpretations and debates, I shall explore the contexts of production, promotion, and presentation. Much of the chapter will be about reception, however, although I will be focusing on commentary that is publicly available, on the internet or in print, rather than on empirical audience research. Much of this publicly available material can be seen as promotional material. Promotion—the business of drawing a film to the attention of potential audiences— is a vital ingredient in the cultural presence and success of any film. What we will see in this case is the way in which particular aspects of the film were prepared for and promoted to particular segments of the audience, the way in which specific interest groups and taste communities were encouraged to engage with the film in specific ways. The distributors of *Elizabeth*, for instance, made a special effort to reach what they called 'upscale, educated female viewers'.[6]

Of course audiences didn't necessarily take up the film in the expected ways and some alternative, perhaps even resistant, interpretations and evaluations of the film emerge in press and internet commentary, especially in relation to the question of historical authenticity. Films also get caught up in other cultural discourses circulating at the time of release, discourses that may be regarded as incidental to the promotional thrust behind the film but which may have a profound effect on the film's reception and its cultural presence—in the case of *Elizabeth*, for instance, the post-feminist discourse of 'girl power' played an interesting role in the take-up for the film. The film's promoters may not necessarily have foreseen that audiences would engage with the film through such discourses. Other discourses they may have deliberately avoided: for instance, the production team went out of its way to distance *Elizabeth* from the Merchant Ivory version of heritage cinema. Thus producer Tim Bevan stated on more than one occasion,

---

[6] Telephone interview by the author with PolyGram Filmed Entertainment (PFE) theatrical distribution staff, 23 Nov. 1998.

that 'We were keen to do a period movie, but one that wasn't in the recent tradition of what I call "frock flicks." We wanted to avoid, as it were, the Merchant Ivory approach'. The quotation is taken from the Press Booklet issued to the British press. The booklet issued to the American press was identical, except for one tiny, almost imperceptible change: given the box-office appeal of Merchant Ivory in the USA, the reference to them was dropped, so that Bevan was now reported as saying 'We wanted to avoid *the classical approach*'.[7] Good marketing will always involve attending to such details. Bevan went on to explain what their goals were with the film:

we thought it would be great to do a picture set in Tudor times, as that was the most exciting of historical periods. We settled on Elizabeth I and her early life, a period that hasn't been particularly well documented on the screen, and one which would give us more dramatic life. We also wanted to stamp a contemporary feel onto our story, and with the early part of her reign being filled with such uncertainty, we decided to structure it as a conspiracy thriller.

Co-producer Alison Owen added, 'We were a lot more influenced by films like *The Godfather* than by previous historical dramas.'[8] This of course is good promotional material, with the *Godfather* (1972) reference designed to attract an audience that would not normally attend a costume film: this is a film, after all, that not only has an immense reputation as an intelligent and artful thriller but was also a major box-office hit. The reference is also of course nicely controversial, the idea that one might depict a national hero in terms of a Mafia film. Similarly controversial, and still with an eye on the market, was the decision to allow the Virgin Queen of national history to enjoy copious sex before becoming the virgin of legend. This irreverence was tempered by an attention to historical detail and an engagement with the discourse of authenticity—to lose that altogether would have meant losing a whole audience stratum who enjoy and appreciate such detail; to insist on the irreverent approach on the other hand was an attempt to encourage a less familiar audience to catch the film.

There is nothing new about this irreverence, of course. It was, for instance, a vital ingredient in Alexander Korda's 1933 British film, *The Private Life of Henry 8th*, an important reference point for understanding *Elizabeth* historically. We also know that some interpretations of even the Merchant Ivory films see them as irreverent and culturally radical. We can certainly situate *Elizabeth* in the cycle of what Claire Monk has called post-heritage films, films like *Orlando, Carrington* (1995), *Wilde* (1997), and *Wings of the Dove*, all of which share with *Elizabeth* a concern with the depiction of transgressive sexuality and/or sexual activity,

---

[7] Tim Bevan quoted in British and American versions of the Press Booklet, and on the official website; my italics. See also Candice Hughes, 'Bombay Director Tackles Tudor England', Fox News on the net, http://foxnews.com/js_index.sml?content=/news/international/0909/i_ap_0909_90.sml, 9 Sept. 1998.
[8] Tim Bevan and Alison Owen, quoted in the Press Booklet and on the official website.

though always against a backdrop of luxurious aristocratic or Bohemian lifestyles and living spaces.[9]

This mix of genres, sensibilities, and, in the end, audiences involved in the *Elizabeth* experience is in many ways typical of the media product aimed at a relatively 'mass' audience. The production and promotion of relatively populist texts must almost by default encourage a range of readings, and perhaps even encourage antagonistic readings: it is a vital means of maximizing audiences. The core heritage audience, in so far as one exists, was just one of the social groups at whom the producers and distributors aimed this particular film, though it is also clear that the whole question of historical interpretation and representation was at the heart of many responses to the film.

'THE REVENGE OF THE COLONIALS': QUESTIONS OF NATIONALITY[10]

Elizabeth is described on the official website as 'a film about a very English subject'. Stella Bruzzi, writing in *Sight and Sound*, suggests however that it would be inappropriate to see *Elizabeth* as 'a celebration of Englishness'. She is not alone in arguing that the film is, instead, 'marked by its distance from rather than veneration for its subject'.[11] If the film is not a *celebration* of Englishness, it can certainly be read as an *exploration* of Englishness, a historical meditation on the making of modern England and the construction of a central icon of the national heritage, the image of the Virgin Queen. No surprise, perhaps, that such a film should have emerged in a period when New Labour were seeking to rebrand Britain, to give it a more modern face while not ignoring established traditions. Nor indeed that such a film should prove successful so shortly after the death of that modern 'Virgin Queen', Princess Diana.

But if the film seemed radical in some respects, a break with tradition, some commentators thought it was still only going to work for 'serious Anglophiles'.[12] More than that, for one American reviewer, 'England has never seemed more English than in the exterior scenes of rude merrymaking.'[13] We can also find uncompromisingly patriotic views closer to home, in the pages of the *Daily Mail*, for instance: 'England furnishes a wealth of wonderful too-long neglected loca-

---

[9] Claire Monk, 'Sexuality and the Heritage', *Sight and Sound*, 5/10 (1995), 32–4.

[10] Shekhar Kapur, quoted in Gary Susman, 'Not Like a Virgin', *Boston Phoenix*, 19–26 Nov. 1998, from website (www.bostonphoenix.com).

[11] Bruzzi, 'Elizabeth', 48; see also Julianne Pidduck, '*Elizabeth* and *Shakespeare in Love*: Screening the Elizabethans', in Ginette Vincendeau (ed.), *Film/Literature/Heritage: A Sight and Sound Reader* (London: British Film Institute, 2001), 130–5; and Pamela Church Gibson, 'From Dancing Queen to Plaster Virgin: *Elizabeth* and the End of English Heritage?', *Journal of Popular British Cinema*, 5 (2002), 133–41.

[12] Rob Blackwelder, 'Elizabeth' (review), *PopcornQ*, www.planetout.com/popcornq.

[13] J. Hoberman, 'Drama Queens', *Village Voice*, Arts section (3–9 Nov. 1998), from www.villagevoice.com.

tions and they offer a marvellous setting for the big set-pieces', while the cinematographer 'revels in the Englishness of the settings'. In an interesting interpretation of how the film might be best understood by his readers, the *Mail's* reviewer went on to suggest that 'The film's other lesson . . . is that it's admirable to serve one's country. Kapur sees that Elizabeth flourished by putting the national interest first. He portrays this as a fine thing, even over-embellishing the patriotic finale by bringing in some anachronistic Elgar music.'[14]

This interpretation is surely a little perverse in its almost wilful refusal to acknowledge the post-colonial make-up of the film's most important creative workers, or to see the question marks that the film puts around the question of national identity and tradition. It also of course underlines the extent to which texts are open to interpretation, including to interpretations that may be quite at odds with the intentions of the film-makers. Perhaps the *Daily Mail* reviewer was being deliberately perverse in an effort to rescue *Elizabeth* for a conventional and conservative reading of national history, but that in itself simply underlines the fact that readings of films (or any other texts) will often be purposive rather than innocent, designed to serve the interests of the reader, consciously or otherwise.

As far as the film-makers were concerned, *Elizabeth* was clearly not intended to come across as a conventional presentation of a slice of the national past. On the contrary, in Kapur's words, it was conceived in part as 'the revenge of the colonials . . . I am the last person, in the world who should be directing *Elizabeth* . . . To ask an Indian who knows nothing about British history to make a film about a British icon. It was such a mad thing, I just had to do it.'[15] Alongside Kapur were the Australian actors Cate Blanchett and Geoffrey Rush, the French actors Fanny Ardant, Eric Cantona, and Vincent Cassel, and two more Australians, the editor, Jill Bilcock, and the composer, David Hirschfelder. As the reviewer for the British publication *Asian Age* points out, 'few doublet-and-hose movies feature such an international spread. . . . A multi-national cast working for a multi-ethnic creative team is, of course, laudable, and just one of the ways in which the modernity of *Elizabeth* cannot be impugned.'[16]

What we are confronted with from this point of view is an 'outsider's view of British history', a position which Kapur relished: 'I was excited by what they were expecting from me . . . something very dangerous', 'something raw and informal, a bit melodramatic and chaotic'.[17] This perspective clearly appealed to others involved with the film (which makes it even more surprising that the *Daily Mail* chose to see none of this danger). Geoffrey Rush, for instance, said in an interview that 'Shekhar has no cultural reverence for English history, and I enjoy that'.[18] Cate Blanchett recalled that 'Shekhar kept saying "This is my Elizabeth"; he was

[14] Christopher Tookey, 'Tonic for Heroine Addicts', *Daily Mail* (2 Oct. 1998), 44.
[15] Kapur quoted in Susman, 'Not Like a Virgin', from website.
[16] Matt Wolf, 'Make Way for the Tudor Twins', *Asian Age* (17 Nov. 1998), 14.
[17] Hoberman, 'Drama Queens', from website; Shekhar Kapur, quoted in Gerard Raymond, 'Ardor in the Court', *Village Voice* (3–9 Nov. 1998), from www.villagevoice.com; Tom Charity, 'Virgin Records', *Time Out*, 1466 (23 Sept. 1998), 16.   [18] Charity, 'Virgin Records', 17.

liberated by the fact that he's Indian. Being both from the colonies, we have quite a skewed perception.'[19] Michael Hirst, the scriptwriter, was of a similar view:

The idea of an Indian directing a quintessentially English subject must have surprised some—but it delighted me. Shekhar had made a remarkable film called *Bandit Queen* . . . which was raw with emotion . . . not a quality easily associated with British films, at least 'historical' ones. He brought with him no preconceptions about Elizabeth. Without perhaps even being conscious of it, many English people are protective about the image—and virginity—of Elizabeth I; after all, she remains one of the greatest icons in our history. But the last thing the film needed was a reverential camera.[20]

From this point of view, the view of the outsider, *Elizabeth* is not so much English as an irreverently post-colonial take on a core moment in English history. This sense of irreverence, this sense of a 'skewed perception' towards 'a quintessentially English subject', emerges time and again in the discourses which emerged around the film. It suggests that at the centre of the narrative is a theme typical of the heritage film: not the celebration of a fixed and pure national identity, but the hesitant exploration of the crisis of inheritance, the struggle over the meaning of Englishness, and the question of national ownership. *Elizabeth*, from this perspective, confronts us with the 'Howards End' questions. To whom does England belong? To whom *should* it belong? And how will this struggle be resolved? (Catholic or Protestant? Insular or allied with the Vatican, the French, the Spanish, or the Scots? And so on.) The 'skewed perception' also produces what can be seen as a very hybrid, exotic, cosmopolitan, and fluid English court in the Elizabethan period, a reflection on the strangeness of the English inheritance and the impurity of nationhood. Or at least, this is one way of looking at the film.

If this way of seeing, this sense of irreverence, can in part be attributed to Kapur's outsider status, then it is worth remembering just how many English costume dramas have been made by non-English film-makers. It is worth noting too just how much else is conventional about *Elizabeth*, with its emphasis on an iconic English monarch; its showcasing of no less than twelve period properties; its overall sumptuousness and visual splendour; its fine period costumes, decor, and architecture; its seductive performances; and its narrative exploring English history and a crisis of national inheritance.

PRODUCTION, DISTRIBUTION, AND EXHIBITION

Despite the multinational make-up of the filmmaking team, *Elizabeth* was officially classified as a British film, and proudly described by one of its producers as 'a real British film, financed, produced, written and shot in Britain'.[21] It was made

---

[19] Sheila Johnston, 'G'day to You Queen Bess', *Sunday Telegraph Review* (20 Sept. 1998), 9.

[20] Michael Hirst, 'Introduction', in Michael Hirst, *The Script of Elizabeth* (London: Boxtree, 1998), 10.

[21] Eric Fellner, quoted in Michael Ellison, 'Bard Battles for Oscars against Private Ryan', *Guardian* (10 Feb. 1999), 5.

by one of the leading British film and television production companies of the period, Working Title. The budget was around £13 million, with some of the funding coming from Channel 4, some from the European Union's MEDIA Programme, but most from PolyGram Filmed Entertainment.[22] When production began in September 1997, PolyGram was a European entertainments conglomerate owned by a Dutch parent company, Philips. During 1998, as I noted in an earlier chapter, Philips sold PolyGram to Seagram's, the Canadian leisure conglomerate and owner of one of the Hollywood majors, Universal. The American links were already well established, however, since PolyGram had, with Universal, set up their own American distributor, Gramercy, in 1992 (when Universal was still owned by the giant Japanese company, Matsushita). Thus if *Elizabeth* was nominally a British film, it was in other respects a typical product of the now global entertainments industry, in which almost all products have some sort of multinational status. Typical in some ways, but in others, unique. According to PolyGram executive Stuart Till, '*Elizabeth* would never have been greenlit in Hollywood . . . but it has the ability to work on a world-wide basis.' (Box-office figures subsequently confirmed the substance of this claim.) If it was not the sort of film that Hollywood would make, Till was keen to promote it as an ideal European film, screening it for the EU's audio-visual commissioner Marcelino Oreja 'to show what the European film industry should be about'.[23]

The size of the budget for *Elizabeth* is worth pondering. By Hollywood standards, £13 million was a small budget; by British standards, it was a fairly big budget. It was certainly a big budget for a British costume drama: few of the heritage films made earlier in the 1980s or 1990s could command that sort of budget, but the relative box-office success of many of those earlier films undoubtedly paved the way for *Elizabeth*. At the same time, there was clearly a gamble attached to this film—as there is for any film. That gamble is routinely played off in the industry by setting the familiar and predictable against the new and unpredictable. In the case of *Elizabeth*, on the one hand, it was a standardized product, working in what one trade journalist called 'a safe genre'; on the other hand, it was innovative and risky, given its relatively high budget and the lack of a high-profile cast or director.[24] Kapur in particular 'represent[ed] a £15 million gamble. After all, he [had] never made a film outside India before.'[25]

The gamble was typical of the way in which PolyGram and Working Title were operating in the mid-1990s. Working Title's link with PolyGram meant it had access to far greater funds than it would have had as a fully independent company. It also had access to a well-established and successful British, American, and international distribution system. PolyGram, on the other hand, could leave the creative risks of the production process to a relatively small company with a strong track record. The American market, and the involvement of both PolyGram and

---

[22] Eddie Dyja (ed.), *BFI Film and Television Handbook 1999* (London: British Film Institute, 1998), 18.
[23] Stuart Till, quoted in Adam Minns, 'What Dreams may Still Come?', *Screen International* (23 Oct. 1998), 34.
[24] Ibid. 32.   [25] Charity, 'Virgin Records', 16.

Universal in Gramercy, who distributed *Elizabeth* in the USA, was vital to the strategies of both PolyGram and Working Title: a budget the size of *Elizabeth*'s would be inconceivable without buoyant box-office takings in the USA. Indeed, a film on the scale of *Elizabeth* would never have been made were it not for the proven interest of the Hollywood majors in well-made and marketable independent films, and the success of such films in the crossover market. The bottom line for PolyGram, Universal, and the other major corporations is of course to make a profit by exploiting a particular commodity in as many markets as possible. It is this bottom line which paradoxically created the space for an irreverent, genre-busting, European production like *Elizabeth*. The apparently monolithic Hollywood machine thus allows for—indeed, enables—the production of difference.

In order to cross over from specialist to more mainstream markets, and to appeal to American distributors, films like *Elizabeth* have to embody a range of appeals. In the case of *Elizabeth*, the producers and distributors invested in a 'safe genre', a known product-type, and sought to attract the core audience for that genre, a slightly more upmarket, older, and more female audience than the Hollywood mainstream. At the same time, they developed a strategy for opening up the costume drama market and attracting new, younger, and more male audiences alongside that core customer base. The plan was to build on the success of the costume drama/heritage film production cycle, lift it out of the specialized art-house circuit, insert it into the multiplexes, and attract more mainstream cinemagoers and more male cinemagoers than would normally patronize a costume film. This meant maintaining some allegiance to Merchant Ivory and the 'frock flick', but it also meant engaging with the *Trainspotting*–cult film–MTV generation. The strategy had an impact on the way the film was handled from the initial idea through production, promotion, and distribution. It was this strategy which allowed the producers to take a gamble on an 'outsider' like Kapur, to create a space for his radical ideas and eclectic, postmodern style, which was much more in tune with contemporary youth culture than, say, James Ivory.

The distributors developed a marketing strategy which involved defining a primary and a secondary target audience. The primary target audience was, in effect, the core patrons of the costume drama, and was defined in the marketing plan as an 'older audience, 25–44 age group, upscale educated, with a female bias'.[26] In other words, it was older, more middle class, and more predominantly female than the mainstream cinemagoing population. Market research by PolyGram had confirmed for them that this was the traditional audience for costume drama: 'Dramas tend to play older . . . and costume dramas *always* play older'.[27] Publicity was designed in particular to attract this core audience, deemed more likely

[26] Telephone interview with PFE staff, 23 Nov. 1998. Unless otherwise indicated, information below comes from the same source.
[27] Julia Short of PolyGram, quoted in Nick Roddick, 'Shotguns and Weddings', *Mediawatch '99*, a supplement to *Sight and Sound*, 9/3 (1999), 13.

to read film reviews; there was, for instance, a careful push to get the film noticed in women's magazines.

The secondary target audience was less rigorously defined, but was understood as 18–35 with a similar class and gender skew. As trade journalists selling the film to distributors and exhibitors noted, while 'the *Armageddon* crowd will not go to see this', 'this richly entertaining saga is accessible enough to go beyond upscale crowds and possibly find wider appeal'.[28] The distributors designed a careful release plan for the film in the British and American markets, a platform release that would enable the film to move out relatively slowly from exclusive, specialized cinemas to the multiplexes, and in so doing attract as many different audience groups as possible. The film was also released in the UK in October, a slot 'traditionally popular for independent movies', since it comes between the summer blockbusters and Christmas releases, thus both ensuring less severe competition, and maximizing its appeal to those audiences who do not appreciate the full Hollywood marketing onslaught.[29]

In the UK, *Elizabeth* opened on fourteen West End screens the first weekend and was deliberately restricted to these screens for three weeks. On the one hand, this was very different from the nationwide openings of the Hollywood blockbuster; on the other hand, it was also different from *Howards End*'s opening in just one cinema. The distributors managed to get what they regarded as 'the best sites in the whole of London', including the Odeon West End and the Leicester Square showcase cinema, 'arguably the most prestigious screen in the UK'.[30] This first platform for the film enjoyed a full advertising push and generated excellent reviews, word-of-mouth, and box office, which were crucial to the success of the platform release. In its fourth week, the film moved up a platform, showing nationally on 160 screens; in its sixth week, it climbed to its third and highest platform of 197 screens.

The London release is vital for any films distributed in the UK. Between 1993 and 1997, for instance, London admissions were, on average, 27 per cent of the total admissions for the whole of the UK.[31] Further, with the national media based in London, screenings there will inevitably generate more copy than those elsewhere. Thus 'London cinemas provide a springboard for releases into the regions'.[32] This of course is particularly important for a film given a platform release, which is precisely designed to exploit this springboard effect. Chris Bailey, then head of theatrical distribution at PolyGram, explained the rationale: 'With these more specialist titles, a platform release can raise the awareness of a film outside London. It builds up heat and is a hotter film when you open it regionally.'[33] With the London opening, and therefore the national newspaper reviews

[28] Lee Marshall, 'Elizabeth' (review), *Screen International* (18 Sept. 1998), 28; David Rooney, 'Elizabeth' (review), *Variety* (14 Sept. 1998), 33.

[29] Mary Scott, 'Box-office Roundup', *Screen International* (9 Oct. 1998), 31.

[30] Telephone interview with PFE staff, 23 Nov. 1998; anon., 'Platform Shoo-ins', *Screen International* (23 Oct. 1998), 54.

[31] Anon., 'Platform Shoo-ins'.   [32] Ibid.   [33] Chris Bailey, quoted ibid.

and all the attendant publicity and word-of-mouth, coming some weeks before a platformed film moves into the regions, it is given a head start when it does eventually go nationwide over other films released in the regions at the same time: 'A platform release . . . has the benefit of leap-frogging stiff competition going wide on the same date.'[34]

A platform release is seen by the industry as the ideal way of doing things for the more upmarket, artistic end of the mainstream, for the sort of film that is going to be enjoyed by people who read reviews and depend on word-of-mouth, as opposed to those who are more influenced by the hard-sell of television advertising. The success of the strategy depends heavily on the quality of the reviews generated: 'You have to try to ascertain what reviews you are likely to get. If you have bad reviews, it will not be a success'.[35] The platform release was seen as ideal for *Elizabeth*, which the distributors saw as a typical 'upscale, literate dinner-party crowd, prestige movie'.[36] This was a film they were confident was going to review well and get good word-of-mouth, and they wanted to be in a position to exploit that publicity.

The platform release is a relatively sophisticated form of distribution which requires careful and regular attention to how the film is faring, and allows for minor adjustments to the advertising campaign week by week: 'In using a platform opening we can shape and evaluate the wide release. We can put new quotes [from reviews] into our roll-out campaign to sustain advertising.' Because the distributors were also wanting to attract a more mainstream audience, they 'grasped the nettle and ploughed in money for TV ads'.[37] The use of television—there was also a short programme about the making of the film—once again signals the difference of this film from earlier quality costume dramas like *Howards End*, and the attempts being made to consolidate the mainstream end of the crossover market. The television advertisements for *Elizabeth* focused heavily on chivalry and on the powerful soundtrack, which were seen as among the key selling points for more regular cinemagoers.

If *Elizabeth* had been released straight onto 200 screens, the distributors believed it would probably have had a reasonably good opening but then have sunk very quickly, which would have been a very inefficient way of milking the market. A more likely release for a modestly budgeted costume drama like *Elizabeth* would have been to rely heavily on a run of art-house screenings, and then possibly build up to the metropolitan independents and more upmarket multiplexes. In fact, this was never the intention with *Elizabeth*, as can be ascertained from the size of the production budget, far in excess of what could have been recouped from such a modest release. The plan was always to start in upmarket multiplexes and selected independents before going to the art-houses and Regional Film Theatres.

---

[34] Chris Bailey, quoted Anon., 'Platform Shoo-ins'.   [35] Ibid.
[36] Telephone interview with PFE staff, 23 Nov. 1998.
[37] Chris Bailey, quoted in Mary Scott, 'Box-Office Roundup', *Screen International* (16 Oct. 1998), 27.

The business of promotion followed a similar series of stages. Initially, magazines, and especially women's magazines, were targeted, 'followed by the "quality" dailies. When the film went wide, the press campaign was extended to mid-market papers like the *Daily Mail*, and TV spots also kicked in.' Teaser trailers were shown in participating cinemas prior to the arrival of the film, while a limited poster campaign with a very striking design was run in metropolitan centres, especially London. At each stage, advertisements quoting carefully selected reviews were placed in the 'quality' newspapers and in listings magazines such as *Time Out*. According to Julia Short of PolyGram, 'we did a great deal of research into previous costume dramas, and we took *The Madness of King George* as our ruler. When we saw that we were doing better than *Madness*, we did more TV.' The television advertising campaign was very selective, with advertisements appearing mainly on Channel 4, 'grouped around "upscale" programmes like *Friends* and *Frasier*'.[38]

The promotional strategy was thus twofold. On the one hand, it was designed to maximize the appeal of the film to its core target audience. On the other hand, it was intended to extend that appeal to a wider audience, both younger and more male, but without ignoring or alienating the primary target audience.[39] The attempt to reach a wider audience was readily apparent in the design of the poster and advertising copy used in the UK, with its stark close-ups of the four main characters, described in bold lettering as, respectively, heretic, lover, traitor, and assassin (Fig. 24): hardly the keywords of Merchant Ivory-style costume drama. The use of expressionist lighting and colour and the framing of the close-ups emphasized the harsh, piercing looks of the gangster rather than the soft glances or warm embraces of the romantic lover. And where other heritage films have used flowing, organic text-dividers depicting natural forms such as flowers or leaves, *Elizabeth*'s publicity preferred a bolder, more threatening crossed swords design.

The UK release strategy and promotional campaign proved highly successful, with an excellent opening weekend and very strong average takings per screen. It was the second highest grossing film of the week in London, and even though it was only showing on fourteen screens, all in London, it still managed to secure eighth place nationwide because of the exceptionally strong showings at each of the cinemas in which it was playing (in week six of its release, it was showing at less screens than all but one of the rest of the national top ten—it was number eight that week—but it had a higher average box-office take per screen than all but the top three). By its fourth week of release, when it had opened outside London, it had overtaken *Lock, Stock and Two Smoking Barrels* (1998) in terms of box-office takings that week to become the leading British film currently on release. By this stage, it was riding a wave of strong publicity and reviews, which served to attract the 'upscale audience', while the television adverts were evidently working on the more mainstream audience. The film eventually stayed among the top ten films at the British box office for ten weeks, and although its release was

[38] Roddick, 'Shotguns and Weddings', 13.   [39] Ibid.

24. Costume drama as conspiracy thriller: the poster used in the UK for *Elizabeth*

not yet complete by the end of the year, it was still the third most successful British film of 1998, behind *Sliding Doors* (1998) and *Lock, Stock*. By the end of its run, it had sold 1.24 million tickets and taken £5.5 million.[40]

The film also did well in other European markets, opening in over eighteen countries over a nine-month period. It was in the box-office top ten for five weeks in the Netherlands and Denmark, for four weeks in Italy and Sweden, for two weeks in Germany, and for one week in Spain. More than 100,000 tickets were sold in each of France, Greece, and Portugal, nearly a quarter of a million in Spain, and nearly half a million in Germany and Italy.[41] It was equally successful in other territories. In Japan, for instance, it was the eighteenth highest grossing film for 1999, staying in the box-office top ten for ten weeks; in Australia and Brazil, it was

---

[40] *Screen International* (9 Oct. 1998), 30; *Screen International* (13 Nov. 1998), 22; Derek Malcolm, 'One Smoking Barrel', *Guardian*, G2 (29 Dec. 1998), 11; Eddie Dyja (ed.), *BFI Film and Television Handbook 2000* (London: British Film Institute, 1999), 32, 34; Lumiere database at http://lumiere.obs.coe.int; A. C. Nielsen EDI Ltd., cumulative box-office statistics.

[41] Data from *Elizabeth* page on ShowBIZ Data online at http://www.showbizdata.com; weekly international box-office charts in *Screen International* for 1998 and 1999; Lumiere database; Danish Film Institute.

in the top ten for seven weeks and six weeks respectively.[42] It was also a major box-office winner in the USA, where it was one of the top-ranked independent productions released in 1998, with 6.18 million tickets sold, compared to 3.07 million for the whole of Europe.[43] While it took at least $40 million in all other territories, it took $30 million in the USA.[44] We should put these statistics in perspective, however, for if this was an impressive performance for a modestly budgeted British film, it hardly compared with the takings of unreservedly mainstream productions. Thus *Saving Private Ryan*, released in 1998, took $216 million at the US box office, while *The Phantom Menace*, released the following year, took $431 million.[45]

These box-office statistics underline a bald fact about contemporary media activity: that it is increasingly difficult to ascribe national identity to media products. For if *Elizabeth* is variously an English film, a British film, a European film, and a post-colonial film, it is also, as I noted above a product of the now global entertainments industry, a transnational commodity.

With a November release in the USA, *Elizabeth* was up against much stronger competition than in the UK, with several major films released for the holiday season. But this was also the beginning of the period for art-house distributors to release films which it was hoped would attract the attention of those making the Academy Award nominations:[46]

The initial signs of holiday event titles pushing out niche fare was evident as the month's top 10 grossing titles cornered 75% of all ticket sales. . . . Still, a couple of titles have managed to hold against the big guns—notably Gramercy's *Elizabeth* and Miramax's *Life Is Beautiful*, which have done slow rollouts and will add more playdates later in December.[47]

As in the UK, *Elizabeth* was given a platform release in the USA. Initially, it opened at nine specialized cinemas in Chicago, Los Angeles, and New York, moving up a platform to 144 screens in its third week, when it went 'into exclusives in almost every market'. The following week, it moved up to yet another platform, showing on 516 screens (which was of course still some way short of the number of screens on which mainstream Hollywood films played). As in the UK, however, the film had two lives running in parallel. While its carefully orchestrated national release saw it go to more and more screens and do well as a crossover film in the multiplexes, it was also doing the rounds in the art cinemas, and the trade press

[42] *Screen International* (9 Oct. 1998), 30, (16 Oct. 1998), 27, (6 Nov. 1998), 30–1, (13 Nov. 1998), 22–3; Don Groves, 'Rookies Fall Flat', *Variety Extra online* (10 Oct. 1998), at Variety.com; Don Groves, ' "Truman" Awakens O'seas B.O.', *Variety Extra online* (17 Nov. 1998), at Variety.com.

[43] *Variety* (21 Dec. 1999), 20; Lumiere database.

[44] Bhavan Lall, '*Elizabeth* Reigns on', *Screen International* (1 Oct. 1999), 35; Nielsen EDI.

[45] American box-office statistics from the Internet Movie Database, at IMDb.com.

[46] Andrew Hindes, ' "Elizabeth" Rules', *Variety Extra online* (9 Nov. 1998), at Variety.com.

[47] Leonard Klady, '*Waterboy* Buoys Nov. B.O.', *Variety Extra online* (2 Dec. 1998), at Variety.com.

continued to discuss it as an 'exclusive' film, presented by 'arthouse distributors' on 'the specialised circuit', and addressed to 'niche' audiences.[48]

For a relatively small British period drama, *Elizabeth* thus proved an enormous success, with weekly average box-office takings per screen described as 'resounding' and 'stunning'.[49] Even on its first weekend, when it was showing on only nine screens, it managed to take enough money on those screens to reach number 27 in the box-office charts; indeed its average takings per screen were higher than any other film in the top 30. By the third week of its release, *Elizabeth* had become the most successful British film currently on release in the USA. By week four, when it was showing at more than 500 cinemas, the film broke into the American box-office top ten.[50] As one British newspaper commented, this was 'most surprising . . . This, remember, is a bit of black-teeth-and-boils English history not zapped up or modernised [*sic*], with an Indian director and an Australian lead. And we don't think Eric Cantona or Kathy Burke are pulling them in either.'[51] *Elizabeth* eventually remained in the box-office top thirty in the USA for twenty-two weeks. In early February, it was still on more than 400 screens. When the Oscar nominations were announced in mid-February (*Elizabeth* received seven), it was on 624 screens, but thereafter gradually tailed off. The overall box-office takings were of course minuscule compared to the two major studio films released around the same time, *The Waterboy* (1998) and *RugRats* (1999) (by week three, *Elizabeth* had taken nearly $7 million, but *Rugrats* by that stage had taken $53 million and *Waterboy* $119 million; even after twenty-two weeks in the top thirty, the box-office gross for *Elizabeth* was still only $29.1 million).

Although Russell Schwartz, president of Gramercy, the film's American distributors, claimed that 'this is better than we'd hoped for', it is clear that in fact a carefully finessed marketing plan was coming to fruition: 'We have a populist period movie here. . . . We're selling it as a historical thriller . . . with the emphasis on thriller.'[52] In order to exploit the film to its maximum, Gramercy 'mounted a costly campaign for *Elizabeth*, including TV spots and two-page ads, . . . betting it [would] surpass the typically limited grosses that period pieces usually achieve'.[53] Another strand to the promotional campaign was a brilliantly designed website for the film, which included an elaborate game, 'Traitor in Our Midst', 'where you can try to find the traitor in Elizabeth's court. You gain points, you get clues— otherwise, you get beheaded'. According to Schwartz, the website was created

in our ongoing hope to get men interested in the picture, which is obviously one of the marketing challenges. . . . [T]he obvious sell is to women. But because the movie is so much

[48] Monica Roman, ' "Elizabeth" Reigns in Niche B.O.', *Variety Extra online*, 1 Dec. 1998, at Variety.com; Andrew Hindes, ' "Elizabeth" Rules'; *Screen International* (13 Nov. 1998), 21; Andrew Hindes, ' "Waterboy" Douses Field', *Variety Extra online* (16 Nov. 1998), at Variety.com; *Variety* (16–22 Nov. 1998), 11.
[49] *Variety* (16–22 Nov. 1998), 11; *Screen International* (13 Nov. 1998), 21.
[50] Box-office statistics here and below from *Elizabeth* page on ShowBIZ online at http://www.showbizdata.com, and from weekly box-office charts in *Variety* and *Screen International*.
[51] 'Film charts', *Guardian*, Friday review (4 Dec. 1998), 29.
[52] Russell Schwartz, quoted in Hindes, ' "Elizabeth" Rules'.   [53] Ibid.

a thriller and actually has a lot of action in it, a lot of murders, a number of beheadings and burnings at the stake—it's got a lot of *Braveheart*-type spectacle to it—we wanted to make sure we were able to expose the film to men as well. . . . [T]hings like the web are 70% male (in their demographics) and there's no reason why we shouldn't try to get to [a male audience] and, at least, let them (see) what the movie's about rather than just saying, 'No, because it's a period picture I'm not interested.'[54]

Positioning the film as both a traditional costume drama and a thriller that could appeal to a wider audience was the central strategy of the marketing campaign:

It's making sure that the early word-of-mouth audiences know what to expect. The television campaign, the trailer and things like the Web site are trying to not only paint a full picture of what it is, but also show it's not all about costumes—there's a really fascinating story of backstabbing and adventure. There's a lot in this movie.[55]

The success of the marketing campaign can be gauged by the comments of the manager of a film website on the internet:

In the last two weeks . . . my preview page for this movie has been visited enough to rocket *Elizabeth* up to the top ten of my most visited previews, an honor not often granted by my visitors to period piece dramas. I think what may be drawing some of the attention, and may be the key to this movie's success, are the surprisingly riveting commercials that have been showing in some theaters and on cable TV. Rather than a limp British drama, *Elizabeth* is being marketed as a dark Machiavellian historical thriller about a young woman who steered her country down her own path, in the face of much opposition. Another thing that jumps out in the commercials is the cinematography and lighting of the film, which is very rich and enticing . . .[56]

The main promotional image used in the USA was different to the poster and advertisement design adopted in the UK (although the same key image was used for British book and CD tie-ins, see Fig. 28). The image foregrounds Cate Blanchett in a glorious golden dress, blending in with her auburn-coloured hair. Although she is looking straight to camera in a potentially challenging way, Schwartz saw it as an image of 'a very vulnerable woman. I haven't met one man who hasn't liked that shot. . . . Both sexes have quite taken to this movie.'[57] He also saw it as 'a very contemporary shot of her. I don't think people think of Elizabeth the Queen as a 25-year-old. They think of her giving a speech (in 1588 when England repelled) the Spanish Armada or (in the classic shot) in all the white pancake makeup.'[58]

Other promotional materials indicated a much stronger appeal to the traditional costume drama audience: older, more educated and upmarket, and female. A packet of seeds, emblazoned with a mock-authentic *E1R* logo topped off with a crown, allowed the owner to 'plant your own Royal wildflowers'. A bookmark

[54] Grove, 'Web Site and Tarot Cards', 8.   [55] Ibid.

[56] Greg Dean Schmitz, 'Elizabeth', *Upcomingmovies.com*, at http://www.upcomingmovies.com/elizabethi.html.

[57] Russell Schwartz, quoted in Grove, 'Web Site and Tarot Cards', 8.

[58] Russell Schwartz, quoted in Martin A. Grove, '*Elizabeth*: Crowning Gramercy Achievement', *Hollywood Reporter* (23–25 Oct. 1998), 8.

25. Girl power: Cate Blanchett in *Elizabeth*

with the same logo gave a thumbnail biographical sketch of Elizabeth's life, concluding with the quotation, 'I may be a woman, Sir William—but if I choose, I have the heart of a man.' A package of elegant postcard-sized 'tarot cards' (Fig. 26) came in a mock-parchment case tied with a blue ribbon, the cards themselves illustrated with painted versions of promotional stills of the main characters, with historical details on the reverse.[59]

As we look more closely at the reception of the film in subsequent sections of this chapter, the success or otherwise of a production and marketing strategy designed to interest different audiences and maximize the takings for a relatively unconventional film will become clear.

WHAT SORT OF A FILM IS IT? GENRES AND LABELS

What is the most appropriate generic label to apply to *Elizabeth*? Is it a 'lavish costume drama' or a 'a mesmerising rollercoaster of a thriller'? 'An astounding historical spectacle, a costume romp' or 'the darkest costume picture ever to emerge from a British studio'? 'A sexually-charged romantic drama' or an 'artfully deco-

---

[59] My thanks to Anne-Marie Cook for showing this material to me.

26. Mock tarot cards used to publicize *Elizabeth* in the USA

rated history lesson'? 'A cracking political thriller' or a 'superior historical soap opera that shrewdly sidesteps all the clichés of British costume drama with its bold, often modern approach'? A 'bodice ripper' or 'an intelligent think piece about women and politics that transcends its time and place'?[60]

Clearly, at one level, it is all these things. Some reviewers consequently thought the film-makers were unable to make up their minds about what they were producing: 'Kapur can't decide if he's making an art movie or a melodrama, an opera or a soap opera.'[61] Others recognized that this might have been a deliberate strategy to maximize audience reach: 'in a valiant effort to snare moviegoers who wouldn't go to a period picture if it came with a free diamond tiara', the distributors are 'pleased [to] call [*Elizabeth*] a "historical thriller"'.[62] It was in this sense a strategy designed to provide something for all tastes:

[60] Jami Bernard, 'Elizabeth, Queen of Hearts', *New York Now* (6 Nov. 1998), from website (www.nydailynews.com); Pauline McLeod, 'Best Movie', *Woman's Own* (5 Oct. 1998), 9; Andrew Wilson, 'All the Queen's Castles', *Daily Mail* (Magazine) (10 Oct. 1998), 20; Philip French, 'Life beyond the Ocean Wave', *Observer*, Review (27 Dec. 1998), 5; extract from review by Bruce Kirkland, originally from *Toronto Sun*, reproduced on Toronto Film Festival website, at http://www.canoe.ca/FilmFestToronto98/jul22_fest.html; *Guardian*, Guide (3 Oct. 1998), 20; Barry Norman, 'New Releases', *Radio Times* (3 Nov. 1998), 70; Rooney, 'Elizabeth', 33; Victoria Newton, 'Bess Actress', *Sun* (10 Feb. 1999), 9; Ella Taylor, 'Lese-Majeste', *LA Weekly* (6–12 Nov. 1998), 65.

[61] Jeff Giles, 'Review', *Newsweek* (23 Nov. 1998), no page given.

[62] Taylor, 'Lese-Majeste', 65.

Conspiracy buffs will love [the plotting] ... Feminists will delight in seeing a romantic, frightened woman take charge of her own (and her nation's) destiny. Historians will happily debate the sexy melodramatics with which the Protestant–Catholic conflict over the throne is stated. In short, this darkly sumptuous, hypnotically complex movie ought to have many constituencies ... The largest of them may turn out to be moviegoers hungry for rich, old-fashioned historical spectacle ...[63]

As far as the American distributors were concerned, because it was 'much more of a historical thriller than a standard period film ... [*Elizabeth*] creates somewhat of a new genre'.[64] There was indeed widespread recognition that this was not a pure genre film, but a hybrid, a 'political thriller cum romance' that was yet 'replete with smashing finery and looks as sharp as daggers', a film that could be described in the same publication as both a 'ravishing costumer' and a 'blazing historical thriller'.[65]

At the same time, the film belongs to a generic tradition that can be traced back to the beginnings of the quality European heritage movie in the silent period, from *films d'art* to Lubitsch's *Anna Boleyn* (1920) and Gance's *Napoleon* (1927). In the 1930s, following the international success of *The Private Life of Henry 8th*, a whole series of films was made in both Hollywood and Europe that explored, often in quite irreverent terms, the private lives of prominent figures from European history. (Indeed, Elizabeth appeared in two of them, *Fires over England* (1937) and *Elizabeth and Essex* (1939)). *Henry 8th* in particular makes an interesting comparison with *Elizabeth*: although it was nominally a British film, it too was made by a multinational production team, led by the Hungarian director, Alexander Korda. Several commentators also linked *Elizabeth* to both Eisenstein's *Ivan the Terrible* (1942), and *La Reine Margot* (1994) and other recent French costume dramas of that ilk.[66] To situate *Elizabeth* in such a context is to begin to suggest that it might be genuinely European in sensibility. Even if the focus of the film is English, it deals with a key moment in Western European history, tentatively exploring the prevailing relationships between England, France, Spain, Scotland, and the Vatican: when Elizabeth is crowned queen of England, Ireland and France, a very unfamiliar political geography is writ large.

The one trait of *Elizabeth* that is not thoroughly signalled in this list of generic forebears is the thriller element. Yet there is no denying that, if this is a costume drama that tries to authenticate its fiction in various ways (but also to fictionalize its history), it is also a thriller full of intrigue, violence, and the expression of brute power. The thriller element is tempered or counteracted by the elements of the woman's film, historical romance fiction, and the costume drama. The focus

[63] Richard Schickel, 'Review', *Time* (16 Nov. 1998), cutting.

[64] Schwartz, quoted in Grove, '*Elizabeth*: Crowning Gramercy Achievement', 8.

[65] Sandra Contraras, 'Girl, Interrupted', *TV Guide Entertainment Network* (18 Nov. 1998), posted on Internet Movie Database, at IMDb.com; *Time Out*, Critics' Choice (30 Sept. 1998), 88; *Time Out*, Critic's Choice (28 Oct. 1998), 88.

[66] See e.g. Philip French, 'Another Fine Bess', *Observer*, Review (4 Oct. 1998), 6; Ryan Gilbey, 'The Big Picture', *Independent*, Review (1 Oct. 1998), 13; Rooney, 'Elizabeth', 33–4.

on Elizabeth, on her desires and sexuality, and especially her love affair with Robert Dudley, Earl of Leicester, is important here. So too is the sense of female community established in the entourage of young women (the ladies-in-waiting) that surround Elizabeth. Then there is the attention to lavish dress, the use of romantic music, and the overt discussion of a woman's role and the tension between duty and love.

If for some viewers, then, *Elizabeth* was a fairly conventional costume drama with the right ingredients of romance, spectacle, and period detail, for others, this was 'no ordinary period film', since they did not usually offer their audiences such a 'rollicking good time'.[67] For the boys who did not care for the pleasures and concerns of costume drama, it was especially important to be able to sell the film as 'a rousing adventure . . . a fine historical melodrama, with enough adventure, intrigue, and romance to keep the proceedings from dragging', a film that might be compared with the likes of *Braveheart* and *Rob Roy*.[68] The thriller elements—the tortuous plotting, the conspiratorial, noirish sensibility, the often gruesome action sequences—were thus never allowed to disappear. The description of the film as a thriller was carefully foregrounded in the Press Booklet, on the official website, and in other publicity. In fact, for some viewers, the romantic costume drama element was lost altogether, and the film became solely a historical thriller:

Elizabeth has just the right running time for a film of this genre. When compared to *Nixon*, *JFK* and other reasonably historically based conspiracy films, Elizabeth emerges as easily the most watchable, in one sitting. Clever use of editing during the scene in which Elizabeth is working out how to address parliament, alludes to a *Taxi Driver*-style insight into another's mind. The whole story draws interesting parallels with *The Godfather, Part II*, as a ruler wanting to emulate his/her father's successes, [who] slowly destroys all those around him/her. The films conclude by showing how lonely such an achievement can be in reality, leaving Elizabeth as the 'Virgin Queen' and Don Michael Corleone isolated from the remainder of his family, sitting on his throne, by Lake Tahoe.[69]

More typical, however, was a recognition that the film brought together the thriller template and the costume drama template, 'the costume drama escap[ing] its mothballs in Kapur's vertiginous, labyrinthine conspiracy movie'.[70] The hybridity of the film is visible from the start, rendering it very difficult to reduce the film entirely to one or other generic tradition. The opening sequence, for instance, is both highly stylized at the level of sound and image and, in the use of titles giving historical information, a fragment from a worthy educational drama. As such, it offers a heady mix of aesthetic pleasure and historical authenticity. These tensions,

[67] Charity, 'Virgin Records', 16; Taylor, Lese-Majeste', 65.
[68] James Berardinelli, 'Elizabeth, A Film Review', at http://www.bomis.com/cgi-bin/ring.cgi?page=3&ring=elizabeth; compare the comments of one of the producers, Tim Bevan: 'I thought that *Braveheart* had done a good job in broadening the range of historical film dramas and I hope this will be similar', quoted in Alison Boshoff, 'Hunt for Star to Play Virgin Queen', *Daily Telegraph* (13 May 1997), 5.
[69] Patrick James, 'Elizabeth' (user comments), posted on IMDb, 3 Nov. 1998.
[70] Tom Charity, 'Elizabeth' (review), *Time Out* (30 Sept. 1998), 79.

between stylistic innovation and the conventional period drama, and between romantic costume drama and the modern political thriller, frequently emerge in responses to the film, some calling for a purer generic experience, others delighting in the hybrid formation of the film, its exotic qualities, its inclusion of non-indigenous elements.

This struggle between the pure and the impure was figured thematically in the film too. At one level, the state of the nation in the Elizabethan period, the position of its boundaries, the nature of its allegiances, was at issue. This was yet another British costume drama in which inheritance was in crisis, except that on this occasion, the nation was to be inherited literally, not simply metaphorically. After escaping the terrors of her sister Mary, Elizabeth is crowned queen of England, Ireland, and France, but spends most of the film resisting further alliances with either France or Spain. Violently removing those who plot against her throne, she claims to 'have rid England of her enemies'. In her final act of the film, reinventing herself as the Virgin Queen ('I have become a virgin'), sexual purity has become consonant with the safety and sovereignty of the nation. Earlier, sexual activity has been more transgressive than pure, with the implication that both Walsingham and Anjou are gay, or at least bisexual, and the onscreen evidence of Elizabeth's secret pre-marital sex, Anjou's cross-dressing, and the orgy. Of course, Elizabeth's ultimate virginal purity has dual implications: both the refusal of men ('observe, Lord Burghley, I am married to England') and the adoption of a masculine persona ('I may be a woman, but if I choose, I have the heart of a man'), both the Virgin Mary and the patriarchal ruler. As one reviewer commented, 'Kapur cunningly confuses gender roles', enabling us to read this film, like other heritage films, as a liberal treatise on gender and sexuality.[71]

For some, though, *Elizabeth* was not to be taken too seriously—it was 'rip-roaring historical soap', after all, and as such 'destined to be a crowd-pleaser'.[72] For others, the same ingredients meant that it was a gratifyingly conventional costume film and historical bio-pic—indeed, 'costume dramas just don't come any more powerful and satisfying'.[73] As a fairly conventional costume drama, it could engage with a variety of audiences. Thus it could please reviewers in women's magazines—'this scary, stark but sexy historical drama . . . [which] captures the creepy, cold feel of an era and the magical, Madonna-like transformation of the virgin queen'—and in gay men's magazines—'We're closet crinoline fans here at Boyz Towers, and despite the gaping historical errors in this period dramarama, we loved this epic of a movie . . . with the most luscious costumes, sweeping breathtaking shots, a cheeky underlying humour and a loud, in-yer-face soundtrack.'[74] For a discerning, upmarket British broadsheet newspaper, it could, by 'deploying

[71] Tom Charity, 'Elizabeth' (review), *Time Out* (30 Sept. 1998), 79.

[72] David Rooney, 'In Venice, U.S. Gives "Lola" a Long Look', *Variety Extra online* (8 Sept. 1998), at Variety.com.

[73] Jay Carr, 'Blanchett Portrays "Elizabeth" for the Ages', *Boston Globe* (20 Nov. 1998) from website (boston.com).

[74] Anon., 'Film of the Month', *She* (Oct. 1998), 71; Richards, 'Long Live the Queen', 12.

the richness of a pageant and the sweep of a thriller', become 'the very model of a successful historical drama—imposingly beautiful, persuasively resonant, unfailingly entertaining. It's tempting to suggest that if Shakespeare had come back four centuries later to make a movie about his Queen, this is how it might have turned out.'[75] At a pinch, it might even appeal to some of the working-class readers, or at least the female readers, of the more downmarket tabloids— although evidently the lingering taste of history is a bit too much for those with least attachment to the joys of a middle-class education; historical drama is still a class-bound pleasure, an exclusive taste, not for the real mainstream, or at least this is how I think we must interpret the *Sun*'s distaste for the film:

> I think it's time [the European Parliament] started to pay film producers not to make certain types of films. Top of my list would be costume period dramas. There is a world glut of them. But if you really feel the need to see one, you could do worse than *Elizabeth*. . . . It looks great and the acting is top drawer, although that doesn't mean it's much fun to watch. But if you need to see a frock pic before they bring in the much-needed European costume drama ban, this isn't a bad choice.[76]

Some of course appreciated the film precisely because it was like 'an enjoyable history lesson'.[77] Even if, for others, it may have been no more than 'quasi-historical' or 'pseudo-biographical', it still helped some commentators 'open . . . a window into the culture that gave birth to Christopher Marlowe, Edmund Spenser, Francis Bacon, and William Shakespeare': for all its failings, in other words, it did have some historical clout.[78]

Knowing that the fans of costume drama are sensitive souls, some commentators were gratified that the necessary danger signs had been posted around this rather impure version of the generic type. 'Both pageantry and cruelty are on display and the opening execution scene serves notice that this is no delicate costume drama—though the frocks are magnificent'.[79] Others felt they should erect their own signs: 'Be warned . . . this is not a Jane Austen period drama; this is very gory stuff.'[80] Nor, with its stench of conspiracy, its gruesome murders, its severed heads, its scenes of torture and people burning at the stake, and its between-the-sheets frankness, was this a tasteful Merchant Ivory adaptation of a Forster novel. Tastes were being both protected and extended by the film, and by the danger signs proliferating around it: 'Anyone expecting a typically stately, in manner and in pace, British historical drama will be jolted by Shekhar Kapur's stylish and fast-paced "historical thriller"'.[81]

[75] Richard Williams, 'Liz the Lionheart', *Guardian*, section 2 (2 Oct. 1998), 6.

[76] Nick Fisher, 'Elizabeth', *Sun* (3 Oct. 1998), 21.

[77] Nick Cannon, 'Cinema', *Woman* (5 Oct. 1998), 50.

[78] Anon., 'Elizabeth', *Premiere* (US, Nov. 1998), 28–9; Berardinelli, 'Elizabeth, A Film Review', from website.

[79] Mark Wyman, 'Elizabeth' (review), *Film Review* (Nov. 1998), 20.

[80] Nikki Lesley, 'Elizabeth (1998)' (review), posted to the rec.arts.movies.reviews newsgroup.

[81] Michael Dequina, 'Elizabeth (1998)' (review), posted to the rec.arts.movies.reviews newsgroup.

Elsewhere, a different sort of danger sign was raised, one that was designed to seduce viewers *to* the film, rather than steer them gently *away*: 'If period pieces send you running in the opposite direction, be warned: Elizabeth is not your average frock fest . . . [T]his historical epic . . . moves with the crackling urgency of a contemporary political thriller.'[82] If the traditional audience for the quality costume drama is older, female-skewed, and safely middle-brow, then *Elizabeth* was determined to attract and, with the help of the critical and promotional machine, prepare new, more youthful, and more modern audiences for its version of the period film. Although it was 'a rich historical biography', as one reviewer explained, '*Elizabeth* isn't your grandma's English historical epic' and moviegoers should therefore 'forget all that "virgin queen" stuff and Bette Davis' 1939 and 1955 movies about the 16th Century monarch.'[83] Instead, audiences were urged to prepare for 'barbarism in silks and velvets and brocades', for 'a dazzling entertainment that never attempts to hide its frankly contemporary slant.'[84]

This 'dark historical thriller', in which 'sixteenth century England is a sordid, deadly place' was thus 'far removed from the colourful pageant of most British historical movies'; this 'vibrant, red-blooded biofilm' was 'a far cry from the sterility of British heritage movies.'[85] But let's not forget that, for some commentators, the heritage film was far from sterile. The implication is obvious: that, where *Elizabeth* is passionate and libidinal, Merchant Ivory films, or Jane Austen adaptations, for instance, lack any such characteristics. Yet, as we saw earlier, for some audiences the Merchant Ivory film is the film of preference precisely because of its passionate sensibility, its engagement with emotionality and desire—even if it is very often the *repression* of desire that is explored.

Still, there is no denying that, for many commentators, there was a clear distinction between the usual 'bland British bore' and the 'uninhibited' *Elizabeth*, between 'the traditionally stuffy and aloof British costume drama' and the more 'accessible . . . entertaining and exciting' *Elizabeth*.[86] With Kapur 'throwing decorum aside', *Elizabeth* could be presented as a more democratic text, by comparison with the inaccessible elitism of the more conventional costume drama; this was 'a far cry from traditional British masterpiece theater filmmaking', and as such could be offered as a film to be enjoyed by a wider audience 'who like their period costume dramas defrocked of aristocratic poise.'[87] This defrocking brought with it what some saw as a more enlightened view of history, the warning signs making it 'safe to assume . . . that this won't be your average swishily attired, pro-monarchy Crimplene and corsets costume drama'. On the contrary, 'this subver-

---

[82] Kevin Maynard, 'Mr Showbiz Movie Guide', online at http://www.bomis.com/cgi-bin/ring.cgi?page=4&ring=elizabeth.

[83] Blackwelder, 'Elizabeth', from website.

[84] Carr, 'Blanchett Portrays "Elizabeth" for the Ages', from website.

[85] Angie Errigo, 'Elizabeth' (review), *Empire*, 113 (1998), 42; French, 'Another Fine Bess', 6; Carr, 'Blanchett Portrays "Elizabeth" for the Ages', from website; Bruzzi, 'Elizabeth', 48.

[86] Anon., 'Elizabeth', *Premiere* (US), 28–9; Dequina, 'Elizabeth (1998)'.

[87] Charity, 'Elizabeth', 79; Grove, '*Elizabeth*: Crowning Gramercy Achievement', 8; James Cary Parkes, 'Elizabeth', *Gay Times* (Oct. 1998), 92.

sive rollercoaster of a royalty flick shows up, say, *The Madness of King George* for the lily-livered reactionary tosh it was'.[88]

The distinction between *Elizabeth* and 'your typical Tudor pageant' was in part explained in terms of the mixing of templates and Kapur's 'aversion towards the staid and the settled'.[89] This was a history film, yes, but it was '*revisionist* history' which allowed 'the lush *Elizabeth* to bust free of period torpor. Stuffy it's not.'[90] This was 'an English period piece', yes, but it had come 'by way of Bombay', producing 'a cross-cultural revelation' that was 'full of sensual, tactile detail and blistering dramatic heat'.[91] This was a costume drama, yes, but it was also a historical thriller. *Elizabeth* was promoted as a 'historical thriller' because this was seen as a more populist touch, a bigger audience draw than a more conventional costume drama. Yet for those in the cinema trade, it was still very much an 'exclusive' film.[92] At its North American premiere at the Toronto Film Festival, it was offered as 'a very intelligent film about power and power politics', a film with 'a recognizable theme ... a moral quandary', while a mainstream British fan magazine discerned 'a decidedly arty bent'.[93] This was still, in other words, a relatively upmarket film, for a discerning, educated audience.

GIRL POWER

Costume drama is traditionally seen as a genre with a strong appeal for female spectators. While the producers and distributors of *Elizabeth* were at pains to reach a wider audience, particularly by building in the thriller element, they also attempted to maximize the female appeal of the film. In the UK, they carefully targeted women's magazines,[94] and were rewarded with *Elizabeth* being selected as 'film of the week' or 'film of the month' in several titles, including *She* and a cluster of IPC magazines, including *Woman, Woman's Own, Woman's Journal*, and *Marie Claire*.[95] Gossip about the film's stars also appeared in magazines aimed at a younger readership, including *19* and *Frank*.[96] Interest in these outlets focused on romance and sex, though not to the exclusion of the thriller element ('a glorious study of the early reign of Elizabeth Tudor ... the "Virgin Queen", who had

[88] Kevin Harley, 'The Violence of Elizabeth I', *Pink Paper* (2 Oct. 1998), 14.

[89] Errigo, 'Elizabeth'; Charity, 'Elizabeth', 79.

[90] Peter Travers, 'Elizabeth', *Rolling Stone* (26 Nov. 1998), cutting.

[91] Gemma Files, 'Elizabeth' (review), *eye Weekly*, at http://www.eye.net/eye/issue/issue_09.10.98/film/filmfest.html.

[92] See e.g. Monica Roman, '*Elizabeth* Crowned Queen of Exclusives', *Variety Extra online* (10 Nov. 1998), at Variety.com.

[93] Festival director Piers Handling, quoted in Tamsen Tillson, '*Elizabeth* Bows in Toronto', *Variety Extra online* (22 July 1998), at Variety.com; Errigo, 'Elizabeth', 42.

[94] Telephone interview with PFE staff, 23 Nov. 1998.

[95] Anon., 'Film of the Month'; Cannon, 'Cinema', 50; McLeod, 'Best Movie', 9; Liz Hoggard, 'Elizabeth' (review), *Woman's Journal* (Oct. 1998), 18; Demetrios Matheou, 'Elizabeth' (review), *Marie Claire*, 123 (1998), 143.

[96] Anon., 'Joe's *So* Fienne!', *19* (Nov. 1998), 10; Anon., 'Talent Who', *Frank* (Nov. 1998), 35.

her heart broken by Robert Dudley, Earl of Leicester . . . and who survived the murderous duplicity of her courtiers. A mesmerising rollercoaster of a thriller'[97]). Interest also focused on the fact that this was a film with a strong female central protagonist and a theme of female empowerment. 'The main interest of the film is in its reading of Elizabeth's iconic status as the "Virgin Queen". As played by Cate Blanchett, she is a beautiful, independent force of nature'.[98] This was a film with 'some unsettling modern parallels. Can female icons (from Madonna to Margaret Thatcher) ever have a private life?'[99] For younger audiences, the parallels were pursued in terms of the then current Spice Girls-inspired discourse of girl power. *19*, for instance, charted some of the problems 'Liz' faced, concluding that 'Worst of all, her childhood sweetheart Robert Dudley (the not altogether unattractive Joseph Fiennes) has been lying to her . . . Despite it all, Elizabeth's courage and tenacity help her emerge a winner—now *that's* Girl Power.'[100]

The appeal, power, and modernity of the central character were in fact widely commented on, not just in women's magazines. This was a film about 'a very modern women . . . [with] an independent spirit and an iron will . . . [who] ruled in a male dominated age', 'a smart, strong woman stretched to survive and command in a man's world, while her sense of duty conflicts with her romantic inclinations', 'a female figurehead struggling to gain purchase in a patriarchal society'.[101] It was also a film about 'a sexy queen', a 'hell-cat Virgin Queen', 'the ultimate bitchy queen', 'a guffawing good-time girl toughened up in the courtly school of hard knocks', 'the first Iron Lady', 'the world's greatest career woman', 'a feisty modern woman who wants it all but is unlucky enough to be trapped in a time-warp', 'a stressed out modern woman who must cope with a super-intense case of having it all', 'a woman torn between her bodily fluids . . . and her duty to secure the monarchy in a time of raging conflict'.[102]

These different interpretations together suggested the film might be seen as 'proto-feminist', an attempt 'to synthesize Shakespeare, Harlequin and a Perspectives in Feminist History course', or 'an intelligent think piece about women and politics that transcends its time and place'.[103] This was certainly one of the ways in which the film was promoted, with the official website and the Press Booklet both quoting producer Alison Owen saying,

[97] McLeod, 'Best Movie', 9.   [98] Matheou, 'Elizabeth', 143.
[99] Hoggard, 'Elizabeth', 18.   [100] Anon., 'Elizabeth' (review), *19* (Nov. 1998), 18.
[101] *Odeon Preview*, leaflet distributed at Odeon (UK) cinemas, Oct./Nov. 1998; Errigo, 'Elizabeth', 42; Gilbey, 'The Big Picture', 13.
[102] Peter Rainer, 'Reviews', *New York* (16 Nov. 1998), cutting; Travers, 'Elizabeth'; Harley, 'The Violence of Elizabeth I', 14; Matthew Sweet, untitled cutting (review), *Independent on Sunday*, Culture section (4 Oct. 1998), 5; Shlomo Schwartzberg (Review of *Elizabeth*), Boxoffice online reviews, at http://www.bomis.com/cgi-bin/ring.cgi?page=3&ring=elizabeth; Kapur, quoted in Raymond, 'Ardor in the Court', from website; Janet Maslin, 'Amour and High Dudgeon in a Castle of One's Own', *New York Times* (6 Nov. 1998), E16; Harley, 'The Violence of Elizabeth I', 14.
[103] Bernard, 'Elizabeth, Queen of Hearts', from website; Katherine Duncan-Jones, 'Why Then, O Brawling Love!', *TLS* (5 Feb. 1999), 18; Jeff Millar, 'Elizabeth is Fun, But Hard to Take Seriously', *Houston Chronicle* (20 Nov. 1998), from website, HoustonChronicle.com; Taylor, 'Lese-Majeste', 65.

For me, it was very appealing that the central character is a woman. Her story seemed to have lots of parallels with modern twentieth-century women who are often faced with that choice between career and personal life. It is a dilemma many contemporary women are trying to resolve in their own lives that Elizabeth had to face. She had to give up the chance of marriage and children in order to achieve stability in the country. I thought that was very interesting.[104]

For the more misogynistic commentators, of course, the feminist label was intended as a criticism, expressing concern at the way in which 'Elizabeth shed her girl-next-door image to become a thundering feminist', or simply 'another female autocrat who brought her government to its knees'.[105] For the more committed feminist writers, Elizabeth's feminism was merely 'half-baked'.[106] Most commentators fell somewhere in between, seeing this film about 'a woman in a man's world, who battles between love and duty, and defiantly carves out her own path', as *post*-feminist rather than *proto*-feminist, as 'HERstory with big gowns': ' "I am not your Elizabeth," she cries, "I am no man's Elizabeth." Talk about Girl Power.'[107] Many did indeed talk about girl power, for this was seen very much as a bio-pic for the late 1990s: 'Kapur keeps this tale from turning into a dusty old history lesson by taking a cue from England's current rulers—the Spice Girls. The film wields a feisty, wholly anachronistic girl-power edge.'[108] Anachronism, though, was helpful in marketing *Elizabeth* to a modern, youthful audience with its own fashionable reference points: 'the appeal of the Tudor boss-lady is undiminished as Girl Power takes hold'.[109]

Elsewhere, other contemporary parallels were drawn: 'In fact, this Elizabeth is just your average working gal, Ally McBeal in brocade instead of Banana Republic'.[110] Kapur himself saw Elizabeth as Indira Gandhi; others saw 'a Tudor Princess Diana'; 'a 16th-century Margaret Thatcher; a secular Virgin Mary'.[111] The range of references suggests some of the problems with seeing Elizabeth in this film as *feminist*. 'Cate Blanchett, as everyone has noted, is magnificent in the role of Elizabeth. She's fun, she's haughty, she's naive, she's strong at all the right times, making an Elizabeth who's believable and sympathetic while at the same time being something of a hero.'[112] But what sort of a hero was she? She may have been

[104] Alison Owen, quoted on official website.
[105] Harvey S. Karten, 'Elizabeth (1998)' (review), posted to rec.arts.movies.reviews newsgroup; Alexander Walker, 'Ruff Justice', *Evening Standard* (1 Oct. 1998), 27.
[106] Duncan-Jones, 'Why Then, O Brawling Love!', 18.
[107] Geoff Brown, untitled cutting (review), *The Times* (1 Oct. 1998), 37; tagline in the 'Go See' section of *Boyz* (24 Oct. 1998), 12; Brown, untitled cutting (review), 37.
[108] Alicia Potter, 'Queen Size', *Boston Phoenix* (19–26 Nov. 1998), from website.
[109] Online film review for *This is London* (Nov. 1998), posted at http://www.thisislondon.com/dynamic/hottx/film.html Hot Tickets—Films.
[110] Potter, 'Queen Size', from website.
[111] Kapur quoted in Raymond, 'Ardor in the Court', from website; Michael Fitzgerald, 'Twentieth-Century Tudor', *Time* (2 Nov. 1998), 44, from website, Time.com; Tookey, 'Tonic for Heroine Addicts', 44–5.
[112] Lesley, 'Elizabeth (1998)' (online review).

'an independent woman of forthright but naively utopian ideals', but she 'became the very core of the monarchy she had fought to change'; as such, 'Elizabeth breathlessly exemplifies the double-edged sword that is true girl power.'[113] Again, this may be a prime selling-point: double-edged swords are good marketing tools, since they appeal simultaneously to two different interpretations, two different audience experiences. For others, of course, there was a more simple problem: the contemporaneity of Elizabeth's characterization got in the way of history: 'She is a bit too much a 1990s woman . . . She may be written a little too much like a modern woman.'[114]

One edge of girl power is that the girl is sexy, and this was certainly perceived to be the case with *Elizabeth*. 'Kapur infuses the young monarch with some distinctly contemporary female sensibilities. For one thing, she's no virgin. . . . *Elizabeth* is the story of a woman with a healthy sexual appetite'; it is the story of 'the sexually charged early life of the Tudor queen.'[115] Consequently, this was not only 'the sexiest bit of power-play I've seen at the cinema this year', but also, of all things, 'an enjoyable history lesson.'[116] Several commentators indeed moaned wistfully, 'If only history had been like this at school—riveting, thrilling and sexy', 'full of sex, violence, intrigue, and fabulous wardrobes'.[117] Sex, and the eventual renunciation of sex, of course plays a central role in *Elizabeth*'s exemplary 'tale of female empowerment', depicting 'the journey from canoodling girlhood to the threshold of an imperial monarchy', the journey 'from a girl into an iron-willed monarch who put aside her personal desires to transform herself into an icon: The Virgin Queen'.[118] The telling of this tale, the depiction of this journey, may have been influenced by 'gals' guides to empowerment', but it also raised 'some interesting questions about women holding power in male-dominated societies and the sacrifices of personality and sexuality, involved in retaining that power'.[119]

STYLIZATION AND SUPERFICIALITY

One thing that most commentators agreed upon was that *Elizabeth* was 'a stylised film of broad, dramatic gestures',[120] perhaps even 'excessively stylised, particularly

---

[113] Maynard, Mr Showbiz Movie Guide (online).

[114] Mark R. Leeper, 'Elizabeth' (review), posted to rec.arts.movies.reviews newsgroup.

[115] Jack Mathews, 'A Prideful Queen Cuts to the Chaste', *Newsday online*, at Newsday.com; Cannon, 'Cinema', 50.

[116] Tom Shone, *The Sunday Times*, quoted in advert, *Time Out* (28 Oct. 1998), 79; Cannon, 'Cinema', 50.

[117] McLeod, 'Best Movie', 9; Mary Ann Johanson, 'What's Love got to do with it?', The Flick Filosopher, online at http://www.bomis.com/cgi-bin/ring.cgi?page=3&ring=elizabeth.

[118] Bernard, 'Elizabeth, Queen of Hearts', from website; Williams, 'Liz the Lionheart', 6; Hughes, 'Bombay Director Tackles Tudor England', from website.

[119] *Entertainment Weekly*, 461 (4 Dec. 1998), 68; Anon., 'Elizabeth (1998)' (user comments), Internet Movie Database, at IMDb.com.

[120] French, 'Another Fine Bess', 6.

in its camerawork'.[121] Promotional material proclaimed that 'the film . . . spared no expense in the production values department';[122] the more positive reviewers thought this expense had paid off: it was 'wonderful to look at, highly atmospheric and splendidly acted . . . Credit must go to [the] producers . . . for ensuring that so much ended up adorning the screen'.[123] For those who enjoyed the film, 'the visual potency of *Elizabeth* is never less than compelling, thanks to Kapur's swash-buckling camera, John Myhre's meticulous production design and [the] eye-popping splendor of Alexandra Byrne's costumes'.[124] As a result, 'this handsomely mounted and vigorous bio-pic' was 'the richest looking and most colourful [film] produced in this country for ages', its 'luscious, monumentalist pictures', its 'gor-geous' costumes, and its 'sumptuous freneticism' providing 'a visual magnificence rarely seen in British cinema'.[125]

From the outset, *Elizabeth* signals that it is to be visually a very exciting film. Even the opening credits sequence is visually and aurally impressive, with its montage of colours, faces, images, and symbolism, overlaid with stylized titles pro-viding historical background information, and choral music on the soundtrack. We are invited to enjoy the sequence as a self-conscious sign of both great cinema and educative historical drama, both aesthetic pleasure and authenticity. As we settle into the first diegetic scene, of a group of Protestants being prepared for and burnt at the stake, we are confronted with a relentlessly moving camera, big close-ups, overhead shots, and a veritable chaos of voices, music, sounds, and images. There is no letting up either: the final scene of the film, as Elizabeth becomes the Virgin Queen, is equally stunning as a virtuoso piece of cinema, poignant, passionate, and stylized.

How should we respond to such scenes? It is the task of the film's promoters and reviewers to guide us in this respect (although we may of course choose to reject their guidance). Thus, 'while the opening sequences are perhaps over-directed—full of whirling cameras and lofty overhead shots—the film settles in to establish a painterly but unmannered visual style full of bold strokes'.[126] The latter part of this quotation is typical of the many positive comments about the film in its identification of a self-consciously artistic, in this case painterly, feel to the film. In order to situate the film stylistically, or to help identify its ideal audi-ence (and warn off others), as we've seen, commentators cited numerous influ-ences and reference points, from *The Godfather* to Bollywood, from B movies to *La Reine Margot*, from *Dynasty* to MTV, and from Eisenstein and Welles to Greenaway and Jarman. The *Godfather* reference was pervasive, as we know. In an

---

[121] Bruzzi, 'Elizabeth', 48.

[122] Anon., 'New British Expo', *Screen International* supplement (Sept. 1998), 11.

[123] Tookey, 'Tonic for Heroine Addicts', 44–5.

[124] Rod Dreher, 'A Liz Tailored to MTV', *New York Post* (6 Nov. 1998), 55.

[125] Anthony Quinn, 'The Lust Years of the Virgin Queen', *Mail on Sunday*, Night and Day (4 Oct. 1998), 42; Alexander Walker, 'Queen of the Screen', *Evening Standard* (25 Aug. 1998), 19; Sweet, *Independent on Sunday* (4 Oct. 1998), 5; Tookey, 'Tonic for Heroine Addicts', 44–5; Bruzzi, 'Elizabeth', 48; Sweet, *Independent on Sunday* (4 Oct. 1998: again), 5.

[126] Rooney, 'Elizabeth', 33.

interview with the director, another influence unexpected in the context of the period drama comes through equally strongly:

Kapur's copy of Michael Hirst's screenplay begins with a mission statement citing the intrigue of *The Godfather* and the shooting style of *Trainspotting*. The latter influence is chiefly a question of attitude. 'I thought that film was brilliant—it frightened me, it was so good. It's the new cinema: it gave me the confidence to do this,' Kapur says. He adopts a rich, florid, fluid syntax of jump-cuts, high camera angles and fast tracking shots. *The Godfather* is immediately felt in the finished film's murky sense of paranoia and veiled conspiracy.[127]

The idea that *Elizabeth*, via *The Godfather*, was 'a conspiracy thriller in Tudor dress' struck more than one reviewer.[128] For others, the definitive reference point was further afield: 'the style is Bollywood: rhythmic, spectacular and lit and lensed . . . like a giant fresco in motion'.[129] Again, such references are to be expected, given that Kapur's career to date had been in that context, including his previous film, *Bandit Queen* (1994), which had made such a mark in Western circles. Thus 'the film's operatic visual style owes much to Kapur's training in Bollywood'.[130] In this context, Bollywood clearly signifies both a genuine influence and a particularly stylized cinema. For reviewers in some of the more upmarket publications, however, Bollywood does not have quite the required cultural cachet and another, more prestigious reference point is required:

Elizabeth may not have too much to do with real history, but it has much to do with real cinema. Swirling overhead crane-shots, chiaroscuro by the gallon, inventive cutting, a showmanship that is never merely show-off. Never mind Bollywood. Welles and Eisenstein come to mind at the movie's high points and you cannot get higher than that.[131]

Other reviewers suggested the design of the film was 'an intelligent mainstream assimilation of the visual vernacular created by Peter Greenaway and Derek Jarman—a stylised and ornate idiom'.[132]

There were some dissenters, though, who thought the film failed to live up to these art-house qualities, finding instead a 'lurid sensationalism. This is Masterpiece Theater for the MTV generation, a Virgin Queen for people raised on Like a Virgin.'[133] Another reviewer found 'the bouncy, kinetic flow of images and the shafts of light that too artfully pierce through the shrouded chambers of various castles' resembled nothing more than 'a pop video'.[134] A third thought the film 'vulgar and vacuous'; in the scene where Elizabeth dances in a meadow with her girlfriends, for instance, 'we almost expect a voice-over advertising hair condi-

---

[127] Charity, 'Virgin Records', 17–18.
[128] Brown, *The Times* (1 Oct. 1998), 37.
[129] Nigel Andrew, 'The Queen of All Pictures', *Financial Times* (7 Oct. 1998), 20.
[130] Raymond, 'Ardor in the Court', from website.
[131] Andrew, 'The Queen of All Pictures', 20; see also J. Hoberman, 'Drama Queens', from website.
[132] Williams, 'Liz the Lionheart', 6.
[133] Dreher, 'A Liz Tailored to MTV', from website.
[134] Sweet, *Independent on Sunday* (4 Oct. 1998), 5.

tioner'.[135] A fourth was worried by what he saw as 'the director's fashionable film-making' and especially the way in which background information was presented in 'the opening credits' Gothic, Pop-Up Video-style paragraphs'.[136] Quality drama has been tainted, it would seem, by the empty populism, the 'overall flashiness' of contemporary youth culture ('Generation X in Elizabethan England').[137] Superficiality, the bane of postmodern culture ('looks great but lacks focus and depth'), and the low-brow, sensationalist pleasures of melodrama, for long the whipping-boy of aesthetes and intellectuals, were not infrequent criticisms:

> *Elizabeth* has flash, dash and panache on the surface, but little more. While no one wants a corseted, airless recitation of historical occurrences, turning the passions of dynastic politics into a got-up *Dynasty* is tremendously off-putting. . . . whereas Coppola ennobled pulp melodrama with his artistry, Kapur vulgarizes dramatic history with his garish sensibilities.[138]

For another reviewer,

> The gore and brutality of the early scenes suggest that Kapur is still locked into the sleazy, B-movie mode which was so inappropriate to the complexity of *Bandit Queen*, but which could conceivably prove fitting now that any royal thriller has to live up, or rather down, to *La Reine Margot*. . . . he communicates ideas in the most rudimentary cinematic language. . . . the icy lighting and frozen compositions . . . strongly suggest[ing] the genre of Gothic horror . . .[139]

If for some, the 'dark, Gothic look . . . befits the lush dramatics of the piece', for others it is typical of Kapur, whose 'touch isn't exactly gentle. He cudgels home the impact of Catholic zealotry with plenty of God-is-watching aerial shots'; other passages are 'overwrought' and there is 'a predilection for artful grotesqueries . . . Such slickness elevates style over sentiment'.[140] But if there was a problem with 'a hardcore English historical drama . . . directed by a muckraker who betrays influence from *The Godfather* films [with] moments of dramatic import coincid[ing] with thunderstorms', it perhaps did not matter too much because the film was 'too anachronistic and punched-up to be taken seriously'; and if it was, at times, watchable, it was only 'embarrassingly, soapily watchable'.[141]

We will need to return to the dissenters below, but for the time being, we should simply record the differences of opinion between those who saw the film as a worthy cinematic—for which read artistic—achievement, and those who saw it as vulgarly downmarket. (We should perhaps also record that many of both the

[135] Duncan-Jones, 'Why Then, O Brawling Love!', 18.
[136] Blackwelder, 'Elizabeth', from website.
[137] Sweet, *Independent on Sunday* (4 Oct. 1998), 5; jg-8, 'Elizabeth' (user comments), posted on Internet Movie database, at IMDb.com.
[138] Schwartzberg (Review of *Elizabeth*), from website; Sweet, *Independent on Sunday* (4 Oct. 1998), 5.
[139] Gilbey, 'The Big Picture', 13.
[140] Rooney, 'Elizabeth', 34; Potter, 'Queen Size', from website.
[141] Millar, 'Elizabeth is Fun', from website.

celebrants and the dissenters work for the same sorts of relatively upmarket publications, British broadsheet newspapers and the like: there is, in other words, no obvious class divide here.)

STORY-TELLING AND SYMBOLISM

Let's look a little more closely at some more specific aspects of the film's style, beginning with the mode of narration adopted and the way in which the story has been organized. *Elizabeth* is presented as a fairly complex, multi-layered narrative, embracing as it does both a love story and a story of political intrigue and infighting, while at the same time trying to be reasonably faithful to history. Michael Hirst, the scriptwriter, stated in his introduction to the published script that he 'wanted the film to be thick with plots', since this indicated something of the 'complex, labyrinthine and bizarre' politics of the Renaissance period and of Elizabeth's circumstances: 'By allowing into the script a number of plots, rather than teasing out the thread of one, I knew I risked leaving the door of confusion, if not open, then at least ajar. But the risk seemed worthwhile', since it allowed the sensibility of the period to come through.[142] Narrative complexity was thus intended not as a self-conscious stylistic flourish (it is after all very often a mark of art-house cinema), but as a symbolic representation of contemporary politics. Unfortunately at least one otherwise sympathetic reviewer found intention did not have the required effect, in that the film seemed to avoid 'the didactic and the over-explanatory to the point of being occasionally obscure'.[143]

The action within each scene of the film is often frenetic, but the plotting is highly episodic and the overall pacing artfully slow. This pacing again left commentators divided. For the celebrants, while 'This may be considered a slow ride for some, . . . so are novels and they usually read better than movies. Like a novel, this story comes across more finely paced than most of the rushed 2 hour jobs out there today.'[144] For some of the dissenters, on the other hand, this was indeed, 'despite all the gore and periodic melodrama, . . . a very slow paced film with a rather confusing plot—unfortunately often consequences of attempts to keep, however vaguely, to historical facts. Often, it ended up as just a series of tableaux of beautifully shot scenes in large churches.'[145] At the other extreme, for another type of dissenter, the adrenaline rush of MTV was too evident in the 'feverish pacing', the 'giddy plotting': 'Michael Hirst's scattershot, often disorienting script, coupled with the breakneck pace of Kapur's narrative, drives you crazy. You wish

---

[142] Hirst, 'Introduction', 9–10.

[143] French, 'Another Fine Bess', 6.

[144] Timothy Voon, '*Elizabeth*' (user comment), posted to rec.arts.movies.reviews newsgroup.

[145] Anon., '*Elizabeth*' (user review), 16 Oct. 1998, posted on Internet Movie Database, at IMDb.com; see also Parkes, '*Elizabeth*', 92 ('a slow-paced, muddled melodrama'), and Schwartzberg (review of *Elizabeth*), from website ('Royal intrigue is inherently dramatic but "Elizabeth" is pretty sedate stuff, despite multiple murders and sexual shenanigans.').

the movie would stop long enough to catch its breath and give us at least a far-thing's worth of historical context.'[146] For Hirst, though, historical context might actually be symbolically represented through what others might see as the disorienting narrational device of montage (we should not however assume that intention is the same as effect). Violent juxtapositions within the film

like the burning of the martyrs and the dancing of the women . . . could as a matter of fact bring us much closer to some kind of historical 'truth' than any amount of dead facts and inert details . . . whether of costume, language or furniture. The film itself, the way it was made, as much as its content, was the message.[147]

Narrative always effects a dual pull, both the attraction of each individual moment, and the forward drive of the unfolding drama. I argued earlier that this tension is intensified in the costume film because of the attention paid to the allure of the *mise-en-scène*. As a decidedly episodic narrative, *Elizabeth* certainly affords room to explore the discrete pleasures of each scene; as a conspiracy thriller, or indeed as a romance whose outcome is unclear, the film also possesses a relatively strong hermeneutic energy. This dual function was again intended by the scriptwriter:

I wanted the film to be intimate and personal . . . to vibrate with the nervous system of a young woman . . . but also to have a sense of scale, of grandeur, for the young woman was also a Queen. For me, the midsummer pageant on the Thames performed both these functions, and was always a pivotal and seminal scene.

Hirst goes on to explain that he saw the pageant as an intensely romantic moment for Elizabeth and Dudley ('one of the great romantic images in European culture'); but he also wanted to interrupt the scene with political intrigue in the shape of the assassination attempt.

Such scenes have a resonance for me over and above their narrative importance . . . but since this is a film, they must also carry the narrative forward, serve a function. Hence at this point we decided to interrupt the idyll, to reintroduce political reality, in the shape of the assassination attempt. But to hold these two things in tension—the independent and free content of the scene, and then its narrative function—is, I think, one of the principal jobs of the screenwriter.[148]

Kapur in fact felt 'the plot should be simpler . . . but Michael Hirst said, "Plot is like a serpent, slithering around you all the time", and so the camera . . . became the serpent and a co-conspirator, representing all the myriad conspiracies that I personally didn't understand.' Kapur thus sought 'to tell the plot with the way the camera moved.'[149] If for some of the dissenters the film consequently seemed overly episodic, this was in part blamed on Kapur, whose 'panache [was] not quite

---

[146] Maynard, Mr Showbiz Movie Guide (online); Taylor, 'Lese-Majeste', 65; Dreher, 'A Liz Tailored to MTV', from website.
[147] Hirst, 'Introduction', 9–10.   [148] Ibid. 8.
[149] Raymond, 'Ardor in the Court', from website; Charity, 'Virgin Records', 17.

enough to hold the episodic script smoothly together' and who, at his best, was only just able to 'keep a story juddering along'.[150]

MISE-EN-SCÈNE AND THE CAMERA EYE

It is not just the narrative organization of the film that is distinctive, since the visual style—the *mise-en-scène*, the camerawork, and the editing—is equally eye-catching. In part what is at stake here is the aesthetics of spectacle. Earlier 'British' period films and costume dramas of the 1980s and 1990s—especially the Merchant Ivory films—developed an aesthetic that was ideal for the spectacular display of heritage properties. As we've seen, this meant slow-paced narratives, a slow cutting rate, and a preponderance of long shots and medium shots rather than close-ups, which allowed heritage iconography to linger on the screen. The difference of some of the shots—the length of time they are on the screen, the spectacular vantage point from which many of them are framed, their detachment from the classical conventions for marking establishing shots and point of view shots—invites a reading of them as exceeding narrative requirement. This gap between narrative requirement and the attraction of the *mise-en-scène* thus allows the image to come to the fore precisely as image, as spectacle, as the unfettered display of heritage properties.

Elizabeth adopts a very different aesthetic. It has a much faster moving narrative, given its thriller elements. There is much more editing, and there are far more close-ups than in most of the earlier 'British' costume dramas of the 1980s and 1990s. In other words, there is less scope for *Elizabeth*'s camera to linger over or display heritage iconography. Where the average shot length of *Howards End* was 8.92 seconds, the average shot length of *Elizabeth* is little more than half that, at 4.67 seconds (with one montage sequence cutting together nineteen shots in sixteen seconds). *Elizabeth* is thus up there with the fastest cut American films ('when it came to making zippy movies, the Americans were always in front'[151]). There is consequently much less time for the spectator to gaze uninterruptedly at spectacular architecture, landscapes, interiors, and costumes by comparison with *Howards End*, but this doesn't stop the film appearing decidedly spectacular. What we are faced with, however, is a very different regime of spectacle. Where the Merchant Ivory films are contemplative, *Elizabeth* is frenetic. The speed of developments and the constant bustle of activity leave no room for the camera to caress period details. It would however be misleading to reduce the spectacle of *Elizabeth* to a dynamic cutting rate or to narrative energy. Spectacle is more properly about what we see and how we see it—how the images are organized, how audiences are invited to look at or participate in the image. At the same time,

---

[150] Walker, 'Ruff Justice', 27; Gilbey, 'The Big Picture', 13.

[151] Barry Salt, *Film Style and Technology: History and Analysis* (London: Starword, 1983), 213.

clearly the very *rush* of images in *Elizabeth*—the speed of the editing, the speed at which the images pass before us—contributes to its spectacular visceral feel.

Elizabeth's spectacular attractions are drawn from the eclectic range of genres mixed together in the film. Thus the film draws on Kapur's background in Bollywood, with its intense colour scheme, its dramatic camera movements, and its sense of theatricality. It draws on the conventions of the historical epic, with its crowd scenes and cavernous sets, its set-piece sequences of pageantry and courtly ritual, its shots of horsemen thundering across open landscapes, and its panoramic view of the battlefield strewn with dead and dying bodies after the English army has been destroyed by Mary of Guise's troops in Scotland. It draws on the rich *mise-en-scène* of the quality film, from Sternberg and Eisenstein to *La Reine Margot*, but also the choreographed violence and expressionism of *The Godfather* and the post-MTV aesthetics of *Trainspotting*. In each case, the sense of spectacle is greatly enhanced by the sheer scale, magnitude, or intensity of the strategy—the size of the crowds or the breathtaking expanse of the battlefield, with the castle looming behind, for instance. In part, what is at stake in this visual extravagance is the size of the budget and the consequently relatively high production values, certainly for a European film. But the sense of visual extravagance is also partly the result of the excessively and self-consciously stylized way in which the film-makers put the film together.

Despite this eclectic range of stylistic influences, *Elizabeth* still shares some formal and iconographic characteristics with earlier heritage films. There are for instance still plenty of heritage costumes, properties, and landscapes on display in the film, even if there is much less sense of the camera lingering on those properties, mainly because of the relative brevity of the shots. And if some of the shots are brief, some are also very flamboyant—and once again frequently divorced from the conventional means of establishing space or character point of view. The most marked shots in this respect are the frequent towering vertical shots, some of them bird's eye shots, others taken from an extreme low angle looking vertically up. The film also uses a constantly moving camera, which often seems to be looking through or around something at the proceedings (shooting through gauze and other materials, or round bars, stone carvings, or vast pillars, or through architectural frames within the camera frame). Such shots can again be understood as artistically rather than narratively motivated, although they clearly also have an expressive function (Kapur talks about them as expressing the voice of destiny, of something greater than the mere individual[152]). Thus they accentuate the aesthetic difference of the film while at the same time creating a spectacular feel that is closely related to the use of heritage properties.

The *mise-en-scène* throughout the film is rich and artful. Many of the interiors are set in castles, and while there are obviously some cavernous spaces, the film-makers have also created some frighteningly dark and claustrophobic areas,

---

[152] In the voice-over commentary he provides to the film on the American version of the DVD.

27. Architectural lighting in *Elizabeth*

especially in the opening scenes during Mary's reign of terror. When Elizabeth succeeds her sister on the throne, more light is thrown on the proceedings. The banquet scenes especially are riots of colour, sound, and music, while there are some gloriously busy crowd scenes at court. As I've already noted, *mise-en-scène* in the period drama must perform several functions. It must provide a diegetically plausible narrative setting, but it must also provide a relatively historically accurate setting; most film-makers will also ensure that the *mise-en-scène* is both aesthetically pleasing and capable of carrying symbolic narrative weight. These functions will not always or necessarily operate in unison. *Elizabeth*, not unexpectedly, demonstrates the difficulty of achieving a meaningful blend of functions.

At one level there was the problem of how to achieve an authentic period look, with landscapes for instance untainted by modern developments. In this context, the fact that the film-makers had shot the film in heritage properties underlined 'the authoritative tread of the production'. In period drama, though, the authentic must very often be newly manufactured: 'Sixteenth century England does not exist,' as Kapur noted, 'so we had to create it.'[153] That process of recreating the past is of course very often as much about blending in with well-established convention as it is about 'historical accuracy'. In attempting to create an authentic look

---

[153] Wilson, 'All the Queen's Castles', 20.

in *Elizabeth*, the film-makers actually attempted to break with convention to achieve a renewed realist effect—to achieve what has been called *transgressive realism*.[154] Northumberland, for instance, was chosen as one of the key locations for the film because of its 'bleakness': 'We wanted to get away from the "chocolate box" feel so many period movies have', explained producer Alison Owen. 'Northumberland is beautiful, but in a very stark way.'[155]

Starkness, bleakness, a bid for transgressive realism: this may have been one motivation for selecting Northumberland, but the acknowledgement that Northumberland is also beautiful should remind us of another function of *mise-en-scène* as spectacle. As one reviewer put it, 'the real scene-stealers are the locations'.[156] Promotional material was not slow to alert people to the claim that *Elizabeth* was filmed 'amid some of the most spectacular historical locations in the UK' (nor was it slow to suggest to other film-makers around the world that they might consider using some of these same locations).[157] For some reviewers, as I noted earlier, these locations were not simply spectacular but had a patriotic function too: 'The film delivers splendidly in the way it looks. England furnishes a wealth of wonderful, too-long neglected locations and they offer a marvellous setting for the big set-pieces . . . [The] cinematographer . . . revels in the English-ness of the settings'.[158] For other reviewers, while the spectacle of the locations was not in doubt, there was a definite sense that the *mise-en-scène* was conventional, familiar: 'lots of the pageantry that goes traditionally with the territory of historical chronicle . . . [much of it] set among stunning shots of Merchant Ivory-type heritage locations such as Haddon Hall and Durham Cathedral'.[159] For still others, it was the mixture of the unexpected—'filmed in the vibrant colours and rich textures of Indian cinema'—and the more predictable—'stunning locations from Haddon Hall in Derbyshire to Durham Cathedral'—that made 'the entire movie . . . a sensual adventure'.[160]

Another of the undoubted pleasures of *Elizabeth* was the 'ornate costumes', remarkable for both their number and their splendour: 'Blanchett had a total of 27 different costumes for her role, ranging from relatively simple smocks to fantastic, bejewelled gowns.'[161] Indeed, 'this film is all about costumes. . . . It becomes just a succession of costumes and images, like a music video.'[162] As a result, as one

[154] See Roman Jakobson, 'On Realism in Art', in Ladeslav Matejka and Krystyna Pomorska (eds.), *Readings in Russian Poetics* (Ann Arbor, Mich.: University of Michigan Press, 1978), 38–46; Paul Willemen, 'On Realism in the Cinema', in John Ellis (ed.), *Screen Reader I* (London: SEFT, 1977), 47–54.
[155] Wilson, 'All the Queen's Castles', 20.
[156] Ibid.
[157] Anon., 'Elizabeth I', *British Film and TV Facilities Journal* (Spring 1998), 43; see also the Press Booklet.
[158] Tookey, 'Tonic for Heroine Addicts', 44–5.
[159] Gerald Kaufman, 'Royal Flush', *New Statesman* (2 Oct. 1998), 36–7.
[160] Danae Brook, 'Elizabeth I is Known as the Virgin Queen. So Why does a New Film Show Her Having Sex with a Courtier?', *Mail on Sunday* (13 Sept. 1998), 52–3.
[161] Hoggard, 'Elizabeth', 18; Wilson, 'All the Queen's Castles', 20.
[162] iago-6, 'Elizabeth' (user comments), posted on Internet Movie Database, at IMDb.com.

reviewer put it, 'the film looks fabulous, and in the costume dramas ... that's often enough.'[163] For others, though, part of the success of the film was not simply that it looked good, that some splendid costumes and locations were on display, but that they were 'skilfully used', they had a narrative function.[164] Thus the castle locations may have added to 'the authoritative tread of the production' but they did so 'not just as backdrops': 'The large hewn stones are a visual analogue of Elizabeth's hard stony era. The walls, rooms, and spaces speak of people playing for high stakes—and for keeps.'[165] Similarly, while 'the photography and design' and 'the regulation silks, cloisters and candelabras' are 'sumptuous', they 'also help to carry part of the burden of explanation, as this is a world in which objects and architecture speak as loudly as words and glances'.[166]

In this instance, intention and effect are in unison. According to the official website for the film, Kapur and his production designer, John Myhre, were influenced by a Russian film version of *Macbeth*:[167] 'When I watched *Macbeth*,' Myhre is reported as saying, 'I knew exactly why Shekhar wanted me to see it: the use of stone. The film literally starts on the stone of the castle, which looks like it has been carved out of a cliff. Shekhar loved that look: to him, the stone represented England and destiny. We used this look for the Whitehall Palace scenes in particular.' Myhre found other narratively useful details in the architecture of Durham Cathedral, one of the main settings for the film's interiors: 'doorways that felt like they had teeth, and windows that looked like eyes peeping in ... We were trying to get this feeling that Elizabeth is never alone—even when she is alone—and to capture this whole feeling of conspiracy and intrigue that is prevalent throughout the Palace.' Clearly, then, settings were chosen for reasons of both historical authenticity and narrative meaning. Myhre underlines the narrativity of *mise-en-scène* still further when discussing the influence of another film, Josef von Sternberg's *The Scarlet Empress* (1934):

In *The Scarlet Empress*, the Princess leaves her beautiful home to live in this wonderful castle, only to find that the castle is a frightening place to be, full of unsettling imagery. In a way, this is what goes on with Elizabeth. She leaves the security of Hatfield House for the isolation of Whitehall Palace. Shekhar also latched on to the way that Josef von Sternberg liked to photograph scenes through veils. I thought this would be a very interesting look to heighten the intrigue of the romantic scenes between Elizabeth and Dudley.[168]

What emerges from this quotation is that the narrative functionality of props and settings is in part a question of their presentation in filmic terms. The reverential and tasteful tableau shot may be typical of heritage cinema, but *Elizabeth* is certainly not a film in which the camera stands back and simply observes the

---

[163] Mathews, 'A Prideful Queen Cuts to the Chaste', from website.

[164] French, 'Another Fine Bess', 6.

[165] Carr, 'Blanchett Portrays "Elizabeth" for the Ages', from website.

[166] Marshall, 'Elizabeth', 28.

[167] I've been unable to identify which film this is.

[168] John Myhre, quoted on the official website for *Elizabeth*, in the section on John Myhre and production design.

settings, interior designs, costumes, and performances. On the contrary, as one reviewer put it, 'instead of squatting for minutes on end observing some inspiring tableau, the camera soars overhead, glides or jabs, eager to follow the action'.[169] Indeed, the camera is constantly moving, and is in fact quite often *unmotivated* by action or narrative. As I noted above, the film-makers also favour the eccentric or unexpected angle, with the camera not infrequently looking vertically up from the ground, or down from lofty ceilings. But if some of the camera positions do tend towards the distanced, observational and spectacular tableau, the film-makers are certainly not afraid to use the close-up. Nor are they afraid to use non-naturalistic effects, such as slow motion, fades to white, heavily out of focus backgrounds, jump-cuts, and flashbacks.

TASTE WARS

The film's style split reviewers. The danger with such a rich, stylized film is that it will come over as no more than 'a variety show, full of stunt effects', but in fact the film's celebrants found it 'an organic and intelligent whole', its style integral to the meaning of the film.[170] This was because for some the style functioned symbolically. Thus one reviewer argued that 'its dramatic overheads, deep-focus compositions, and baroque bustling through cold castles . . . emphasize the heroine's search for a center in this unbalanced world'. Another saw 'the dramatic contrasts of chiaroscuro, and the sinister lighting of flesh against funereal gloom [intensifying] the ominous patterns of plotting and counterplotting'. A third enjoyed the way Kapur interpreted the 'themes of illusion, imprisonment, and subterfuge in rich, rhapsodic imagery. Curtains—yards and yards of 'em—emerge as the dominant leitmotif'.[171] For others, the style was indicative of an intelligent reworking of the generic conventions of the period drama. The way it pushed at so many of those conventions enabled it to work as a successful piece of contemporary film-making, 'made with as much concern for modern sensibilities as for its selected facts of history'.[172] Thus while the film has 'the requisite scenes of court ceremony and spectacle', the stylistic innovations of the film mean that they are presented without any of the 'conventional stuffiness' and thus have 'an anarchy and spirit about them that seem entirely fresh'.[173] As a result, not only is *Elizabeth* 'far removed from the colourful pageant of most British historical movies', but also 'no recent cinema trip into the past has been so enjoyable'.[174]

But the film also had its detractors, for whom its style was indulgent, 'obtru-

[169] Brown, *The Times* (1 Oct. 1998), 37.
[170] Ibid.
[171] Hoberman, 'Drama Queens', from website; Quinn, 'The Lust Years of the Virgin Queen', 42; Potter, 'Queen Size', from website.
[172] Brown, *The Times* (1 Oct. 1998), 37.
[173] Rooney, 'Elizabeth', 33–4.
[174] French, 'Another Fine Bess', 6; Brown, *The Times* (1 Oct. 1998), 37.

sive', a confused, sensationalist variety show, desperately in need of 'a firmer production hand' to bring its disparate strands together:

> Kapur's direction . . . is a curious mixture of the conventional and the outré. He provides lots of the pageantry that goes traditionally with the territory of historical chronicle . . . And then, disconcertingly scattered throughout the movie, are those Berkeleyesque overhead shots, interspersed with slow-motion sequences and moments in which camera exposures are bleached with light. This melange sometimes works well and sometimes seems rum . . .[175]

This is not outright dismissal, but an anxiety about what is a typically postmodern mixing of genres and styles, the imposition of 'an ultra-modern approach' to the representation of the past, but also to a genre with well-defined conventions.[176] Under the pressure of this

> of-the-moment style . . . the picture begins to unravel. Entire scenes seem out of character for the mood of the film—like shots of a Vatican spy skulking through castle shadows in action movie-style slow-motion . . . and Kapur's use of upside-down camera angles, meant to portray disorientation . . . instead are so out of place they jar the audience out of the story.[177]

Where the celebrants had seen *Elizabeth* as a successful intervention in the genre, several of the dissenters thus experienced its style as jarring. And if it wasn't jarring, then it was superficial, style for style's sake. Thus for one reviewer, it seemed 'annoyingly enamored with its own campy, post-feminist cleverness'. For another, it was

> too self-conscious in its desire to leave most English costume dramas, well, in the closet. . . . The problem is that it [boasts] a showy, highly resistible artiness that may put off as many moviegoers as it attracts. One minute the screen blurs and bleeds to white, the next Kapur indulges in a horror movie technique or two that suggest a corseted equivalent of *Halloween*. . . . Like its star, *Elizabeth* is smart and savvy and more than a shade too knowing. If it weren't so determined to be cool, it might even generate some heat.[178]

This sense that style had erased all feeling was not atypical. For one reviewer, 'A stark montage of corpses on a battlefield feels too art-directed really to shock.' For another, 'despite the sumptuous regalia, exterminating priests, misty castle ramparts, feverish couplings and occasional violence, the conspicuous lack of emotional resonance makes this film *Queen Margot*'s poor cold English cousin'. A third was also

> left cold. I hadn't been able to invest emotionally in the protagonist because I didn't understand her motives . . . I didn't know where she was coming from, or what she was after.

[175] Blackwelder, 'Elizabeth', from website; Walker, 'Ruff Justice', 27; Kaufman, 'Royal Flush', 36–7.
[176] Blackwelder, 'Elizabeth', from website.
[177] Ibid.
[178] Travers, 'Elizabeth'; Blackwelder, 'Elizabeth', from website; Wolf, 'Make Way for the Tudor Twins', 14.

That's strange, since Elizabeth is largely a character study, and if I didn't get a good insight into the main character, it could have only been moderately successful.[179]

As one generally sympathetic reviewer puts it, Kapur's risk-taking intervention in the stylistics of the costume drama at its best 'captures the danger of the times, a confusion and vulnerability that extends to gender and sexuality . . . what Kapur calls the chaos of the moment.' But risk-taking is a risky business: 'Chaos cuts both ways, and the movie is sometimes clumsy and crude.'[180]

What can we learn from this dissent amongst commentators on *Elizabeth*? At the very least, we should note that form does not determine meaning, that interpretation and pleasure are not bound by the structure and style of a film, that intention cannot necessarily dictate effect, that one's man's meat is another man's poison. But does this mean simply that there's no accounting for taste, or can we explain the grounds on which the dissent takes place? In very broad terms, we might suggest that those who favour the film's stylistic innovations do so in what is now, at least in the West, more or less an art-house or cult-film context (Eisenstein, Welles, Jarman, Greenaway, foreign-language film-making). Many (though admittedly not all) who *dislike* the film, however, seem worried precisely that what *ought* to be an art-house film, or at least a safe, upmarket quality film, has broken out of the confines of the specialist circuit and into the multiplexes, addressing the MTV generation in what seems a pretentious, flashy, attention-grabbing manner too much a part of contemporary consumer culture. There is undeniably a struggle over taste taking place here.

There was also perhaps a struggle over what sort of film we are watching, a struggle which is surely symptomatic of a period film which tries to be different, to work like *Trainspotting*, but which, at the same time, does not want to be too irreverent, does not want to break entirely with the conventions of historical authenticity or with the taste of the Merchant Ivory audience. Taste wars are in some ways inevitable when the film in question tries to be both a modern conspiracy thriller in Tudor dress and a romantic period costume drama. The different responses of dissenters and celebrants are in this sense the product of a film addressed to markedly different audiences at the same time.

CAMEOS, CASTING, AND STAR APPEAL

The attempt to maximize audience reach is evident too in the casting of the film—and again the strategy came in for some criticism. In some ways, the problem is a familiar one of the tension between the discrete attraction and the overarching narrative: to what extent are the attractions of stars, locations, production design, costumes, music, romantic plot, and so on, integrated into an organic, cohesive

[179] Sweet, *Independent on Sunday*, 5; Contraras, 'Girl, Interrupted', from website; Luke Buckmaster, 'Elizabeth' (user review), posted to rec.arts.movies.reviews newsgroup.
[180] Charity, 'Virgin Records', 17–18.

whole?[181] The problem is not of course unique to this film, or even this type of film, but is typical of any cultural practice which engages thoroughly with the demands of consumerism, with the exigencies of promotion and the marketplace. In attempting to resolve the problem, we are inevitably faced with the question about how best to analyse mainstream cinema. Should we follow David Bordwell, for instance, who sees classical cinema primarily as an aesthetic project, a cinema of narrative integration, in which story is paramount, the organizing feature for the film as a whole? Or should we go with Richard Maltby, for whom mainstream cinema is primarily a consumerist project, a cinema of attractions, in which films appear as a conglomerate of marketable ingredients?[182]

The critical response to the casting of *Elizabeth* falls roughly into these same two camps. There are those who want the film to function as an organic whole and who therefore want the cast to be inconspicuous, the performers at one with their roles and with their generic and narrative context. There are others who recognize that cinema must also reach an audience large enough to justify the cost of the film, and who recognize therefore that casting may at times be conspicuous in its effort to reach out to particular taste groups and spectators. The question of genre is crucial here: the attempt to produce a hybrid film which breaks out of the confines of the traditional costume drama or historical film brings with it the possibility of casting against the familiar conventions of the genre. But possibilities are also risks.

The casting of *Elizabeth* was certainly eclectic. Thus we have cameos from footballer Eric Cantona, comic television performer Angus Deayton, and theatrical legend John Gielgud, alongside old film hands like Richard Attenborough, up-and-coming stars like Cate Blanchett, Christopher Eccleston, and Kathy Burke, equally at home in cinema and television, and relatively new faces like Joseph Fiennes. For producer Tim Bevan, 'This is not stunt casting . . . It is going back to our original concept of not wanting to see actors popping up who had been seen in other "frock flicks." It was a deliberate strategy, and one that helps give the film its freshness.'[183]

For the dissenters, however, this fresh look was on the contrary simply 'odd', with its 'absurdly-cast cameos', which 'encumber the narrative with a distracting, celebrity-turn gaudiness'.[184] Angus Deayton provided the most problems, giving 'one early scene the feeling of a sitcom', his cameo courtier 'smack[ing] more of

---

[181] Claire Wills, 'Elizabeth', *Flicks Trailers* (Nov. 1998), 13 (*Flicks* is a promotional freebie circulated in British cinemas).

[182] See David Bordwell, Janet Staiger, and Kristin Thompson, *Classical Hollywood Cinema* (London: RKP, 1985); David Bordwell, *Narration in the Fiction Film* (London: Methuen, 1985); and Richard Maltby, *Hollywood Cinema: An Introduction* (Oxford: Blackwell, 1995).

[183] Brown, *The Times* (1 Oct. 1998), 37; *The Genesis of Elizabeth*, from the official movie website. It's ironic then that Joseph Fiennes and Geoffrey Rush went straight from *Elizabeth* to another Elizabethan costume drama, *Shakespeare in Love*.

[184] French, 'Another Fine Bess', 6; Parkes, 'Elizabeth', 92; Quinn, 'The Lust Years of the Virgin Queen', 42.

the *Black Adder* version'.[185] The cameo performers are names, they are precisely *attractions*, and the dissenters worry that they are not sufficiently integrated and absorbed into the narrative: 'The celebrity casting is all of a piece with the movie's overall flashiness'.[186] Others are more sympathetic to what they see as a knowingly camp aesthetic, 'the potential silliness of a film which puts a legion of British character actors into tights'; one reviewer suggested that Kapur had drawn on Ken Russell's *The Devils* (1970) and *Carry on Henry* (1971): 'he can skip comfortably from horrific scenes of heretic-burning to jokey sequences staffed by almost-actors like Angus Deayton and Eric Cantona'.[187]

For the producers, however, the casting is much more closely related to the marketability of the film. Cantona, for instance, has a huge following outside cinema: 'Cantona's presence has created huge advance awareness. . . . It will have been calculated that curiosity to see him act will bring in the armchair fans of Manchester United who might otherwise have given the film a wide berth.'[188] For others, there was love interest in the two youthful leads, Cate Blanchett as Elizabeth and 'the not altogether unattractive Joseph Fiennes' as Robert Dudley, Earl of Leicester, 'her childhood sweetheart'.[189] Both Blanchett and Fiennes made good gossip copy in teenage girls' and women's magazines: 'Joe's *so* Fienne! If you fancy Ralph Fiennes, get a load of little bro' Joseph. . . . Check out his new flick, *Elizabeth*, where he plays Elizabeth I's lurve interest (lucky her!).'[190] Another audience segment to whom the film is addressed is that for which the 'serious' (for which usually read 'theatre-based') actor is a draw: 'Buttressed by the likes of . . . Gielgud, . . . Attenborough, . . . Ardant . . . Rush and . . . Eccleston . . . Blanchett's unsurpassed turn as Elizabeth might be enough to float the film for serious Anglophiles.'[191]

EXTRA-FILMIC ATTRACTIONS: TIE-INS AND TOURISM

While the film itself was designed to appeal to a range of audiences, with its eclectic casting, and its mix of different styles and genres, the marketing strategy for *Elizabeth* embraced much more than simply a film. While there were none of the plastic toys, lunchboxes, or computer games that the successful blockbuster generates, there were still a variety of tie-ins, notably a soundtrack CD, a book version of the screenplay (Fig. 28), and a novelization. There was careful marketing across the various products in the UK, each of them using the same stunning image on the front cover, of Cate Blanchett as Elizabeth, in a beautiful gold dress, staring

[185] Tookey, 'Tonic for Heroine Addicts', 44; Wyman, 'Elizabeth', 20.
[186] Quentin Curtis, 'Good Queen Bess as a Born-Again Virgin', *Daily Telegraph* (2 Oct. 1998), 23.
[187] Sweet, *Independent on Sunday* (4 Oct. 1998), 5.
[188] Jasper Rees, 'From Goals to Roles', *Independent*, Review (20 Aug. 1998), 12.
[189] Anon., 'Elizabeth' (review), *19*, 18.
[190] Anon., 'Joe's *So* Fienne!', 10; see also Anon., 'Talent Who', 35.
[191] Blackwelder, 'Elizabeth', from website.

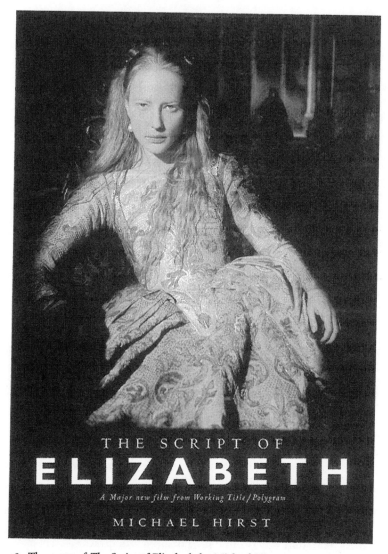

THE SCRIPT OF

ELIZABETH

A Major new film from Working Title / Polygram

MICHAEL HIRST

28. The cover of *The Script of Elizabeth*, by Michael Hirst

haughtily into the camera, with the shadowy figure of a would-be assassin behind her. Although this is similar to the image used in American publicity, it is different to the main publicity image used in the UK.

The CD provides a typical example of the way in which the modern media work, since it was published by the Decca label, which was owned by PolyGram, who also funded the film. Film and CD thus fed off each other to the mutual benefit of PolyGram. While the CD was available in the usual outlets and bought by fans of the film, it also had a more specific, upmarket appeal given its classical music connotations, with performances by the New London Consort, directed by Philip Pickett, and several pieces of 'authentic' period music, ranging from Tallis and Byrd to Mozart and Elgar. A sticker on the front of the CD suggested another selling angle: 'From the composer of *Shine*' (David Hirschfelder). The CD was in fact heavily promoted in classical music outlets, which both ensured that the CD sold well (indeed, it sold out of its first UK imprint), and publicized the film to the sort of upmarket consumers seen as the core audience for the film.

Another way of reaching that audience was through literary tie-ins. Unlike many of the English heritage films of the 1980s and 1990s, *Elizabeth* was not directly based on a literary source, but the marketing for the film still managed to establish literary connections for the film. First, there was the published screenplay, a large format, beautifully designed book, with dozens of wonderful production stills and portrait photographs in colour, and a 'serious' introduction by Hirst. In other words, it was a relatively upmarket publication. In his introduction to the screenplay, Hirst further invokes a literary heritage, noting that the image of Elizabeth and Dudley (Leicester) at the midsummer water pageant drew on a passage in T. S. Eliot's *The Waste Land*, while his attempts to juxtapose the beautiful and the violent in the film were inspired by Elizabethan poetry, and particularly the work of Sir Thomas Wyatt.[192]

Secondly, and at the other end of the literary scale, there was a novelization of the film, a much more downmarket publication, which made no attempt to aspire to the literary high-brow, and was quite clearly addressed to a female readership. The novelization is of course a despised, non-canonical literary format, and this one is written according to the conventions of popular historical romance fiction, an equally despised genre. Fact and fiction are quite openly woven together in the novelization, but if the historical background, the political intrigue, and the violence of the film are consistently maintained in the novelization, it is also much more blatantly focused on affairs of the heart, on desire, romance, and sex. The back cover blurb stresses the romantic elements too, whereas the blurb for the screenplay makes more of *Elizabeth*'s filmic connections. It is in such promotional details, in the differences between the back-cover blurbs for screenplay and novelization, that the marketing strategy for *Elizabeth* is laid bare, its address to different audiences and tastes displayed for all to see.

Another important way in which the appeal of *Elizabeth* spills over the edges of the film itself is through its insertion into the culture of heritage tourism. As we've already noted, heritage iconography is still very much present in *Elizabeth*, and it is still very beautiful, even if it is displayed much less languorously than in a film like *Howards End*. Majestic castles and pastoral landscapes act as the fleeting backdrop to narrative episodes or scenes of pageantry and ritual; ancient interiors provide the magnificent settings for numerous scenes both intimate and epic; the camera will often foreground architectural details; and the costumes are

---

[192] Hirst, 'Introduction', 8–9.

stunning. This iconography was then carefully exploited in a way that tied the film into the wider field of heritage, travel, and the tourist gaze. Thus, however much the film-makers may have wanted to distance themselves from the Merchant Ivory tradition, this aspect of the film's reception was shared with earlier costume dramas.

It is not simply that the film was 'a sumptuous historical drama', but also that it 'tours some of 16th century England's most desirable residences'; it is not simply that the film was 'an astounding historical spectacle, a costume romp', but that it took 'us on a breathtaking tour of some of the most stunning buildings in Britain, many of which are open to the public'.[193] For all its difference, there was still a concerted exploitation of heritage spectacle in discourses surrounding the film; this was still one way of opening the film up, engaging with different audience interests, encouraging different ways of consuming heritage spectacle, spectacle that may be detached from narrative requirement. It is also at this point that *Elizabeth* becomes more than a film, more than something to be appreciated in the confines of the cinema auditorium. Through its textual formation—its aesthetic of display—and through the discourses that circulate around it, that vaunt and valorize it, *Elizabeth* becomes a tourist brochure, an intervention in the wider heritage culture. The Press Booklet, the official website, and various other promotional organs, listed all twelve 'period' locations, including Haddon Hall, Alnwick Castle, Bamburgh Castle, Warkworth Castle, Raby Castle, Chillingham Castle, Durham Cathedral, and York Minster, giving details of their history, their architecture, and how they were used in the film.[194] Perhaps this does suggest a gradual change in the secondary discourses that circulate around heritage films, a shift from seeing costume dramas, historical films, and quality literary adaptations in terms of a culturally refined, object-venerating museum aesthetic to seeing them in more populist terms through the discourses and practices of heritage travel and cultural tourism. ('Seen the film?' asks the *Daily Mail*. 'Now visit the location . . . [and] relive the movie'.[195]) At the same time, there is still a clear sense in which heritage materials become the focus of secondary discourses in the promotion and reception of the film. And as we've seen this discourse was already being mobilized around the much more culturally refined *Howards End*.

The discourse of heritage tourism, the presentation of *Elizabeth* as heritage showcase, is foregrounded in two full-page articles in British newspapers, both of which were organized around *Elizabeth*'s spectacular historical attractions. The *Daily Mail* devoted a page to situating the *Elizabeth* experience historically (Fig. 29). Alongside a long article on the making of the film, the *Mail* presented readers with a tour guide to the twelve 'period' locations. Under the headline, 'Reel history. How you can visit the historic locations used in *Elizabeth*', the article identified

---

[193] Rees, 'From Goals to Roles', 12; Wilson, 'All the Queen's Castles', 20.
[194] See e.g. the Press Booklet, 31–4, and Anon., 'Elizabeth I', 43.
[195] Uncredited clipping on the 'Elizabeth' fiche at the British Film Institute National Library, *Daily Mail* (3 Apr. 1999), 55.

the scenes shot in each place and gave details of how the locations could be visited, complete with phone numbers. The article was illustrated with an 'olde worlde' map showing the locations, and glossy postcard images of Bamburgh Castle and Durham Cathedral.[196]

Another full page in the *Travel* section of the *Independent on Sunday* was given over to a piece on Northumberland's castles, using *Elizabeth*'s locations as the entry-point—or perhaps more precisely, the selling-point: '*Elizabeth* is just the latest of many films to be made in Northumbria. The dramatic castles and coastline are hard to beat: centuries of keeping marauding Scots at bay has left a rich heritage for the film industry.' The article was illustrated with a huge half-page colour photograph of Warkworth Castle seen across a lake and greenery (courtesy of the British Tourist Authority). It transpires that the locations have a heritage even as locations: 'Shakespeare, as well as Shekhar Kapur, knew Warkworth, and chose it as one of the settings in *Henry IV, Part 1*, describing it as "this worm-eaten hold of ragged stone".'

But it is Bamburgh which gets into all the films. The splendid sweep of sands with the complete castle on the cliff is irresistible to location managers, and has starred in *Ivanhoe, Kidnapped, The Secret Life of Ian Fleming*. Derek Jarman made his acclaimed film *The Tempest* here. Even *El Cid*, starring Charlton Heston, has a shot of Bamburgh Castle. Inside the entrance hall is a plaque recounting the films: *Hunting Tower* 1927, *Becket* 1964, *The Devils* 1969, *Mary Queen of Scots* 1972. Naturally, it had a bit part in *Elizabeth* as well. . . . Such star quality is always recognised.

This particular newspaper article functions very much as a tourist guide, with a 'Factfile' giving details of how to get there, where to stay, what to visit (with contact details), the address of the Northumbria Tourist Board, and a map showing key locations. The article also tells you which approach to take to some of the castles, to ensure the least twentieth-century view.[197] *Elizabeth* also featured on the 'Movie Map' issued by the British Tourist Authority in the summer of 1999, another invitation to visit heritage locations that have appeared in films.

Moya Luckett argues that there is something different about the heritage spectacle in *Elizabeth*, in that it reveals not just a romanticized touristic vision of historical Englishness but also its other side, the cruelties that took place inside the majestic castles.[198] It is certainly the case that, by moving back to the sixteenth century, the film-makers have created a sort of pre-modern space in which to play out dangerously primitive and irrational passions. While not strictly medieval, it draws on the connotations of medievalism with its scenes of murderous priests, grotesque torture and gory violence. But is this really a new departure in the way in which heritage space is used in English costume dramas and historical films? I

---

[196] Wilson, 'All the Queen's Castles', 20.

[197] Hilary Macaskill, 'A Castle Fit for a Celluloid Queen', *Independent on Sunday*, Travel section (25 Oct. 1998), 7.

[198] Moya Luckett, 'Image and Nation in 1990s British Cinema', in Robert Murphy (ed.), *British Cinema of the 1990s* (London: British Film Institute, 2000), 90–1.

29. 'You've seen the film, now visit the castle': a full page 'heritage tourism' spread from the *Daily Mail*

argued earlier that even the far more polite adaptations of the work of Jane Austen, E. M. Forster, Oscar Wilde, Henry James, and Evelyn Waugh used heritage space ambivalently. In films from *Chariots of Fire* to *Howards End* to *The Wings of the Dove*, matters of class, gender, and ethnic oppression were explored and illicit sexual liaisons took place in heritage settings. At the level of the narrative, the national past was almost always depicted as troubled, with inheritance and identity in crisis. In *Howards End*, Leonard Bast even dies a sort of medieval death after being attacked with a sword by Charles Wilcox!

Such examples notwithstanding, there is no denying that the move further back into the past in *Elizabeth*—but also in another Working Title film, *Plunkett and Macleane*—takes us from genteel drawing-rooms to vast stone castles where less decorous and much more overtly threatening passions can be played out. In effect, the studiedly picturesque landscapes and buildings of so many other English costume dramas have been reworked according to the aesthetics of the sublime. In part, it is a shift in scale, from the relative intimacy of the drawing-room to the awesome magnitude of the castle. In part, it is a question of sensibility, the re-assuring surface decorum of the earlier films replaced by the terror and aston-ishment of *Elizabeth*'s sublime imagery. As the English costume drama meets the thriller genre on the one hand and retreats towards medievalism on the other, her-itage England becomes a far more dangerous space to inhabit. But that has by no means been a hindrance to the tourist industry; for all its differences from earlier heritage films, *Elizabeth* was still taken up within the same discourse of heritage and tourism.

'IT'S 1554—SO NO MACDONALD'S, THEN': MODERNITY, IRREVERENCE, AND THE INTERPRETATION OF HISTORY[199]

The heritage industry repackages the past for modern-day consumers and par-ticipants. The same impulse—to re-present or modernize history—lay behind the production of what one of the producers called 'a "modern" film about a histor-ical character'. Their view was that 'Elizabeth I . . . had so much potential for a modern audience'.[200] (Apparently the screenplay was originally titled 'Elizabeth I', but the American distributors 'felt that made the film seem more dated'.[201]) This bid for modernity meant that the film-makers were not overly concerned to estab-lish historical accuracy during the unfolding of the narrative. There is no inser-tion of dates as new developments take place, for instance, and in any case chronological time is quite radically conflated in the film. Although the events depicted probably cover about twenty years of official history, there is little sense of time passing in this manner; Elizabeth herself hardly seems to age, for instance. The film thus often glosses over the facts as they are accepted by most historians, and the producers and distributors of the film made little effort to suggest other-wise. Their approach is neatly summarized in one of the taglines used in public-ity for the film:

Forget About Pulp Fiction
Anyone For A Slice Of Pulp Fact

[199] Anon., 'Elizabeth' (review), *19* (Nov. 1998), 18.
[200] Quoted on the official website.
[201] Schwartz, quoted in Grove, '*Elizabeth*: Crowning Gramercy Achievement', 8.

This is a clever promotional gambit, given its reference to one of the most talked-about and influential cult films of the 1990s, its frank acknowledgement of the populist sensibility, and its play on the relation between fact and fiction (indeed the published screenplay was presented as 'a masterly weaving of fact and fiction'[202]).

Yet at the same time this *is* a historical film and it is presented as such in various ways, even if historical accuracy is not allowed to become a fetish. The titles at the beginning and end of the film do establish dates and facts, most of the characters are based on actual historical personages, chronology may be condensed but it is still in broad terms maintained, and costume and production design do not fly entirely in the face of authenticity. The historical discourse is further invoked on the official website for the film, which offers several pages of 'proper history' as background to the film, covering the period from the reign of Henry VIII to that of James I. A similar parade of historical detail could be found on the reverse of the 'tarot cards' distributed by the American distributors ('It's all about giving background').[203] This ambivalence of the film with regard to history generated considerable debate; it will, I hope, prove instructive to examine the terms of this debate.

In his introduction to the screenplay, Michael Hirst wrote:

The first thing to say about *Elizabeth* is that it is a film, not a documentary. Many of the scenes are based on historical fact (or what passes for historical fact), but others are not. Of course, before I even began to write I had done a huge amount of historical research; but the reason behind the research was to discover a way into the material, a lever to shift it with, what film people call 'an angle'. Unlike life, films have to have a dramatic shape.[204]

What this suggests is that history is *Elizabeth*'s backstory; it is the setting for other dramatic narratives, but is not the narrative itself. For a journalist writing for one of the industry's trade papers, and thus attuned to the requirements of entertaining film-making, this relegation of history to backstory does not constitute a problem: 'The life of Elizabeth I is not an easy subject for a film . . . —there is a risk of all that history congesting the drama. Here, except briefly in the first part, it doesn't.'[205] Drama is the important thing for the mainstream audience, not historical accuracy, which can get in the way of a good story. Thus, if *Elizabeth* 'plays fast and loose with history', it does so in order to be able to present 'a vivid, sweeping portrait of her early life and times'.[206] If 'historians will no doubt have a ball quibbling over the telescoping of events into a movie-friendly time-frame', this does not mean the rest of us have to: 'Kapur . . . doesn't really give a damn that some of the film's finer historical points wander away from the truth. And nor do we'.[207]

[202] Back-cover blurb, Hirst, *The Script of Elizabeth*.
[203] Schwartz, quoted in Grove, 'Web Site and Tarot Cards', 8.
[204] Hirst, 'Introduction', 7.   [205] Marshall, 'Elizabeth', 28.
[206] Charity, 'Elizabeth', 79.
[207] Unattributed comment from *Sunday Telegraph*, quoted in Teri Grenert, 'Show People', *Guardian*, Guide (24 Oct. 1998), 20; Richards, 'Long Live the Queen', 12.

The most controversial aspect of the film was that it was 'decidedly erotic' for a biography of Elizabeth I, daring to suggest that she had a healthy sex-life before she became the Virgin Queen of history.[208] Hirst justified this sexual experience as a necessary plot development, a logical narrative motivation, something that needed to take place in order for the film to proceed:

For putting Elizabeth into bed with Dudley, I have already been branded a heretic. Now neither you nor I, nor any of the rent-a-quote historians know with any certainty whether they were actually lovers. Nobody disputes that they behaved like lovers, but her virginity is still highly prized, and an essential part of her status as an icon. . . . [By] showing them as lovers, I have not changed the course of English history . . . The characters in the film sleep with one another, because that is the logical expression of their desire, their passion, their love . . .[209]

It was here that the tension between official history and filmic narrative came into sharpest focus. The film-makers were trying to tell a love story that was also a story of political intrigue and infighting, but they were also trying to be reasonably faithful to history. For them, certain plot developments had to be there; the problem for historians was that certain agreed historical facts were eased out of the picture while others were reworked for the purposes of the story. If the film is regarded as simply another product of the entertainment industry, then this is hardly a problem:

Much of what happens in Elizabeth did not happen that way . . . There are also several outright distortions of the historical record. . . . Ultimately, however, all of this is, if not irrelevant, then inconsequential. Those who want a factual account of Elizabeth's reign can read a history book; *Elizabeth* does what it sets out to do: provide a solidly entertaining two hours. . . . [Its] factual inaccuracies . . . really don't represent a flaw, especially to viewers who are only passingly conversant with English history.[210]

Of course, others will see this as the dumbing down of culture, the reduction of history to entertainment, a denial of the responsibility to ensure that viewers are more than passingly conversant with English history. The danger is that the naïve and ignorant viewer will think that what they are watching is history, wish that 'history had been like this at school', or suggest that '*Elizabeth* is historical moviemaking the way it should be: swift, smart and sexy—anything but dry'.[211] If, from this point of view, *Elizabeth* may suggest that 'education in action never looked so pretty, or packed such a punch', the worry is that anyone should think that education should be either pretty or punchy.[212] To put it mildly, the film 'is perhaps a little too insistent in the modern parallels it draws'.[213]

Education was clearly not a primary concern of film-makers attempting to make a product that would sell. The educational value of a film may be one

[208] Potter, 'Queen Size', from website.   [209] Introduction to screenplay, 11.
[210] Berardinelli, 'Elizabeth, A Film Review', from website.
[211] McLeod, 'Best Movie', 9; Files, 'Elizabeth', from website.
[212] Files, 'Elizabeth', from website.   [213] French, 'Another Fine Bess', 6.

marketing angle, but it must coexist with others. The discourse of authenticity was thus not discarded altogether; but if it was not discarded, nor was it promoted above all other considerations. In particular, it had to compete with the discourse of irreverence and rule-breaking which was so carefully promoted by those marketing the film. If Kapur thought Working Title had asked him to direct this film 'because they knew I wasn't going to be all reverent',[214] then in interview after interview, other members of the cast and crew confirmed without any embarrassment or hesitation that they were not interested in 'historical accuracy'.[215]

According to the official website and the Press Booklet, Kapur was chosen to direct the film because his 'lack of western baggage, and his fresh perspective, meant that he would bring a new approach to a period drama', and 'would really interpret [the script and] . . . not get bogged down with the sort of tradition that we have of our own history'. Kapur himself noted that his previous film, *Bandit Queen*, had 'none of the formality of an English period drama'; he also claimed that 'I never wanted to do a traditional English period film . . . I've turned the period film on its head. I've made a contemporary film out of a 16th-century life'.[216] Elsewhere, he argued that 'the cinema has too many rules . . . the challenge is to break the rules'. If that meant breaking the 'rules' of history, then so be it: 'History is interpretation. And this is ours.'[217]

A central part of that interpretation, for scriptwriter, director, and producers, was the effort to get to grips with the inner life of the characters, according to the conventions of twentieth-century psychological drama: 'Most historical characters are approached from the outside: we take what we know about how they dressed, spoke, behaved, and try to recreate them from these externals. Shekhar [Kapur] needed to know the characters from the inside.'[218] If this meant loosening the attachment to 'historical veracity', the film-makers still claimed the film was 'very true in spirit to the Tudor times'.[219] This is clearly a different conception of historical truth to that conventionally employed by the academic historian. Hirst felt he 'had to make a choice . . . whether I wanted the details of history or the emotions and essence of history to prevail'.[220] He suggested that the purpose of the film was to explore how the familiar 'white-faced, pearl-encrusted icon of [Elizabeth's] later years and of historical memory' was created. He wanted to get behind that historical mask, to recreate a living human being, to invest the icon with psychological depth, with desires and anxieties, to speculate about 'the motivations, political and personal, behind the myth of the Virgin Queen'. In a wonderful formulation, he explained that what had interested him as the scriptwriter

---

[214] Shekhar Kapur, quoted on official website and in Press Booklet.
[215] See e.g. D'Silva, 'Easy Sits the Crown', 4; Susman, 'Not Like a Virgin', from website; Sarah Gristwood, 'The New Nicole Kidmans', *Evening Standard* (30 Sept. 1998), 30; Johnston, 'G'day to You Queen Bess', 9. Imogen Edwards-Jones, 'Cooler Shekhar', *Times Metro* (25 Nov. 1997), 24.
[216] Susman, 'Not Like a Virgin', from website; all other quotations from official website.
[217] Hughes, 'Bombay Director Tackles Tudor England', from website.
[218] Hirst, 'Introduction', 10.   [219] Owen, quoted on official website.
[220] Shekhar Kapur, quoted in Williams, 'Liz the Lionheart', 6.

had been the idea that the film should end with 'the moment at which Elizabeth became "historical", an icon, a public image'.[221] Prior to that point where the myth was originated, the film should be free to speculate on a less familiar set of affairs. The promotional line was thus that the film was 'about a human being rather than a monarch'.[222] For the less hidebound reviewers, this effort to create a psychological history could be regarded as a success, the film 'breath[ing] life into the revered historical figure, transforming her from an old picture on an encyclopedia page to a flesh-and-blood individual whom an audience can root for and care about'.[223]

Psychologizing a familiar image from the national heritage, transforming it into a living character with desires and anxieties, inserting that character into an engrossing narrative: this was part and parcel of the effort to offer a modern film about a historical character. For celebrants of the film, this modernity was to be embraced and praised:

The time and place, we are reliably informed at the start, is England, 1554—a time associated in cinemagoers' minds with dusty history lessons at school, or some vintage piece of Hollywood swash and buckle. Nothing relevant; nothing for today. But *Elizabeth* is no dead slab of cinema. The film offers a new brand of history, styled to catch the attention of restless modern youth.[224]

Of course this is not the only film 'to give history a kick in the pants' but what is remarkable about it is that it is 'a British film . . . and it is hard to stop us getting soggily reverential about our past'.[225] In other words, what is admired about the film is its modernist irreverence. America's *Time* magazine admired the film for the same reasons, delighting in the way 'a postcolonial cast and crew free England's Virgin Queen from the prison of historical reverence':

The weight of history can stultify the most well-intentioned of film biographies. Rather than releasing life, worthiness sometimes embalms famous figures in a formaldehyde of historical accuracy. Tudor England's Virgin Queen is no exception. Despite the merits of the 1971 BBC-TV series *Elizabeth R*, her image remains fixed in the pancake makeup, frilly fright wig and imperious tones of Glenda Jackson's icy old-maid matriarch. It is one of the pleasures of *Elizabeth* to watch Indian director Shekhar Kapur remove that mask. . . . He lets down her hair, loosens her bodice and frees her from constraints.[226]

Other commentators suggested that the achievement of *Elizabeth* was less about removing a mask and finding the real person, and more about reconstructing the person and creating a new mask in the light of contemporary mores and concerns. 'Period movies inevitably reflect more on the period in which they're made

---

[221] Hirst, 'Introduction', 7.

[222] Schwartz, quoted in Grove, '*Elizabeth*: Crowning Gramercy Achievement', 8.

[223] Berardinelli, '*Elizabeth*, A Film Review', from website (see also Williams, 'Liz the Lionheart', 6: 'For once the commitment to emotional truth appears to have incurred no penalty in terms of historical integrity').

[224] Brown, *The Times* (1 Oct. 1998), 37.   [225] Ibid.

[226] Michael Fitzgerald, 'Twentieth-Century Tudor', *Time* (2 Nov. 1998), from website Time.com.

than on the period of their subject, and rarely has that fact been more evident, or more distracting, than it is with . . . *Elizabeth*.'[227] Because Elizabeth is such a central figure in the national mythology, she is constantly reworked for each new generation, presented to that generation in ways that are meaningful to it. This process can be traced through the various cinematic impersonations of the queen, from Flora Robson and Bette Davis in the 1930s, via Glenda Jackson in the 1970s, to Cate Blanchett in the 1990s. 'Each age, and each great actress, has been able to reinvent her anew, always with something apposite to say to her own time.' From this point of view, *Elizabeth* could be seen by a sympathetic historian as 'contriv[ing] to be both true and timely'.[228] The timeliness was twofold: on the one hand, the film chimed with the then-current post-feminist discourse of girl power; on the other hand, several commentators saw echoes of another unfolding narrative about the private life of a powerful public figure, since *Elizabeth* was released as revelations about President Clinton's sexual transgressions seemed about to bring him down.

Virginity, illegitimacy, politics, conspiracy . . . How could those elements go through the mental filters of a storyteller working at the end of the millennium and not emerge as an allegorical blend of sex, dysfunction, feminism and melodrama? Stubborn historians may insist that Elizabeth went to her grave a virgin, or that she at least deserves the benefit of the doubt. But this is not the Golden Age, or even a period of polite discretion. If we can unzip a sitting president, we can deflower a dead queen.[229]

AUTHENTICATING THE FICTION

How does the film's modernity accord with the discourse of authenticity? On the one hand, an authentic representation of the national past is surely at odds with a modernized pastiche. On the other hand, an authentic representation is still precisely that: nothing more than a representation. What passes as verisimilitudinous in such representations is often the conventional; that is to say, it is often designed to reproduce a familiar version of the past, to match audience expectations rather than scholarly rigour, to adhere to a pre-constructed vision. The codes of authenticity, the conventions for establishing a realistic representation of the past, are not fixed in stone but are subject to change. In this sense, a period film will tell us something about both the period represented and the period in which the film is made. In this sense, too, it is possible for *Elizabeth* to seem both 'true' and 'timely', both authentic and modern.[230] A more common view is that period authenticity and modernity are at odds with each other.

---

[227] Mathews, 'A Prideful Queen Cuts to the Chaste', from website.

[228] David Starkey, 'The Drama Queen', *Sunday Times*, section 2 (20 Sept. 1998), 5.

[229] Mathews, 'A Prideful Queen Cuts to the Chaste', from website.

[230] Starkey, 'The Drama Queen', 5.

This tension is clearly there in the film itself and in the discourse about the film. If the film-makers were proud to proclaim the distinctive irreverence of their modern interpretation of history and to deny any interest in historical accuracy, they were at the same time striving for a certain authenticity. The film's ambivalence towards history was clearly a part of the production process, with different members of the cast and crew pulling in different directions. According to several interviews and publicity put out by the distributors, Blanchett immersed herself in the Queen's letters, writings, portraits, and biographies ('the in-depth research [Blanchett] did for *Elizabeth* could have garnered her a ... degree in Elizabethan social politics'[231]). But if his leading lady 'was addicted to playing Elizabeth' then Kapur 'was addicted to telling my [his] story ... she wanted to bring everything about Elizabeth into the role. I actually felt relieved that someone else was carrying that burden. I pulled her into my view of the story, and she clung to detail. So we're both in there.'[232]

Several commentators remarked on Blanchett's 'eerie resemblance to the portraiture images of Elizabeth'; 'Physically, she's so similar to the actual Elizabeth that it's like watching a ghost caught on film'.[233] In fact, of course, what is being remarked on is less physicality and more the efforts of the make-up and wardrobe departments to create an authentic look, one which is familiar from paintings of the period. Kapur may suggest that Blanchett has 'a translucent quality that is ageless—not in terms of age, but in terms of century ... There is something about her face that has the quality of being very modern yet very period'.[234] We may respond by saying that period quality is a matter of convention, and that Blanchett's Elizabeth is clearly cloaked in the discourse of authenticity, while being given a modern twist at the same time: 'We were consistent with the look of the period. We went to the National Portrait gallery to find authentic pictures of Elizabeth. But we also had to make Elizabeth a "today" girl for earlier scenes.'[235]

We may also recall that, for many commentators 'the well-chosen castle locations' contributed 'to the authoritative tread of the production'.[236] But we also noted that these locations very often had to be worked on in order to produce the desired authentic period look. Each location had to be prepared so that signs of modernity were erased by 'the foam matting that looked like slabs of stone, the polystyrene rocks to supplement the real ones, the care—and the brown paper—that went into covering up the signs'.[237] Period films are about dressing up,

[231] Quotation from Baz Bamigboye, 'Cate's Coronation', *Daily Mail* (11 Sept. 1998), 42; see also the official website and Press Booklet; D'Silva, 'Easy Sits the Crown', 4; Johnston, 'G'day to You Queen Bess', 9; Hughes, 'Bombay Director Tackles Tudor England', from website.

[232] Shekhar Kapur, quoted in Charity, 'Virgin Records', 16–18.

[233] Mathews, 'A Prideful Queen Cuts to the Chaste', from website.

[234] Kapur quoted on the official website.

[235] Jenny Shircore, make-up artist, quoted in Benedict Carver, 'Benigni: Hold the Pope; Dench Stole Scenes', *Variety Extra online*, at Variety.com (22 Mar. 1999).

[236] Carr, 'Blanchett Portrays "Elizabeth" for the Ages', from website.

[237] Macaskill, 'A Castle Fit for a Celluloid Queen', 7.

pretending to be someone else, and even the castles had to enter into the spirit of the game, with 'Alnwick Castle masquerading as Mary of Guise's Scottish strong-hold', for instance.[238] There was also the problem of matching twelve different locations with scenes to be shot at Shepperton Studios. 'On the screen, it needed to be one cohesive whole. To achieve this, Myhre and his art department team created sculptural elements and large carved wall pieces, which were integrated into both location and studio settings.' Historical accuracy was an important goal: 'We started out doing the period research to find out exactly what was correct for the period, deciding on the areas that we were going to keep absolutely authen-tic'. But it was not the only goal: they also wanted to use the locations themati-cally, 'to create a more interesting atmosphere'. For the purposes of the drama, the Tower of London, for instance, needed to 'look darker, danker, and more claus-trophobic than it really was'.[239]

Other special effects were used to enhance the production design of the film, further underlining the extent to which the past was recreated in *Elizabeth*, but also the extent to which historical authenticity was achieved through illusion. Certain Hollywood blockbusters are sold on the visibility of their special effects—this is one of their main attractions. For a period film like *Elizabeth*, it was *invis-ible* special effects which were required, since they 'allow filmmakers to achieve higher production values for less money', while at the same time not drawing attention to the means by which the effects are achieved: '*Elizabeth* is a good example of the use of invisible effects to enhance the narrative and the [period] setting rather than as a basis for the movie itself.'[240]

A special effects company, Men in White Coats, used techniques such as crowd replication and two-dimensional composites to create vast crowd scenes by shoot-ing much smaller crowds in different positions and putting them together at the post-production stage: 'For the coronation sequence in *Elizabeth*, Men in White Coats put 20 layers over original footage, adding stained glass, additional sunlight, raised seating tiers and removing a non-period organ', turning 'a sparsely popu-lated York Cathedral into a full-to-bursting Westminster Abbey'.[241] One of the ways in which they created these effects was through Domino, a Quantel com-puter software package providing creative compositing for films. A full-page advertisement in a British trade publication celebrated the way in which Domino had been used 'to recreate this bygone age . . . The result is a movie of immense style and dramatic impact, bringing to life the queen's coronation, set-piece battles, and royal pageants—all with stunning authenticity. And throughout, Domino is transparent, enhancing production values and building an epic story.'[242]

[238] Macaskill, 'A Castle Fit for a Celluloid Queen', 7.
[239] Extracts from the section on John Myhre, on the official website and in the Press Booklet.
[240] Anon., 'Staying Alive', *Screen International* (23 Oct. 1998), 28; Anon., 'Men in White Coats Apply Invisible Effects to *Elizabeth*', *Broadcast* (9 Oct. 1998), B+ supplement, S18.
[241] Anon., 'Staying Alive', 28; Anon., 'Men in White Coats', S18.
[242] *Screen International* (23 Oct. 1998), 55.

30. Costumes on display: Elizabeth with her ladies-in-waiting

Authenticity and illusionism, historical artefact and modern technology: the past was thus recreated, to produce both a functional space in which the narrative might unfold, and something that matched the film-makers' ideas of how the past would have looked, both a narrative space and a historical space. This same blend of narrative requirement and period look can be seen in the design of the costumes for the film, but that blend also created a tension around the discourse of authenticity (Fig. 30). On the one hand, costume designer Alexandra Byrne wanted to research the period thoroughly; on the other hand, 'every time I was reading a reference book . . . Shekhar would tell me to close it and throw it away, because he didn't want us to be tied to the fact and reality of it'. Byrne felt the research was important, however: 'I felt that I needed to initially make the audience feel safe in a world they would be expecting from a period film.' Period authenticity in this sense is thus precisely about recreating the familiar, working conventionally, trying to meet audience expectations. For the purposes of dramatic cinema, those conventions and expectations had to allow space for narrative requirements to be fulfilled. Thus 'with Cate [Blanchett] as Elizabeth, we had certain clear codes to what we were doing', Byrne explained. 'For example, the neckline starts low and gradually closes up and up, working towards that final icon look.'[243]

[243] Alexandra Byrne, quoted on official website and in Press Booklet.

If Byrne's work was in some ways conventional, and deliberately so, in another way it was unconventional: 'a film of this particular period had not been done for so long. . . . *Elizabeth* was a chance to re-examine the period, interpret it, and not get caught up in a set way of doing it.'[244] As with the choice of locations, so with the costumes: there was a partial bid for a transgressive realism, in which some familiar conventions might be adhered to, while others might be broken to create a sense of freshness in the representation. Byrne's working method is explained on the official website and in the Press Booklet:

The only reference is the portraiture, and, being rich people, they would have had new clothes made purely for the portraits. So, that reference has nothing to do with real life and the practicality of the clothes. . . . I usually work by doing a lot of reading and looking at paintings, trying to understand the period enough so that I can then almost stop looking at it. I tried to find out what was the 'T-shirt and jeans' of Elizabethan times—what they would have worn when they weren't formally dressed but were formal enough to meet and greet people. It's that kind of thing I really enjoy in making the clothes. There is no refer- ence for it. No one is going to say, 'That's wrong.' Providing you can create a world that is believable, you can be much more theatrical within that world, and make a statement about the character without being distracting.

The bid for authenticity comes through very strongly, but so does the desire to make the costumes narratively and thematically functional. Unfortunately for Byrne, there were some prepared to say 'That's wrong'. Costume expert Betty Goodwin, for instance, complained about the lack of historical accuracy in an article on costumes in the *LA Times*, arguing that only the gold brocade dress from the coronation scene approaches authenticity, that no white gown was ever worn by Elizabeth, regardless of what the final scene shows, and that the curved corsets worn by women in the film did not become standard until three centuries later— true Elizabethan corsets were ruler straight.[245] The question is, did such details detract from the believability of the world created by the film? For Goodwin, clearly they did. For most audiences, that is unlikely to be the case: there is enough in the costumes that meets the expectations of most audiences about the details of period dress. Still, the tension between historical accuracy and a modern approach was clearly felt in the production of the film and, for all her own back- ground research, Byrne could still remark that 'all the actors were very hooked into the research they were doing on their characters. They would come in with all this academic research, which I had to gradually unbutton, as it were.'[246]

It was important not to undo too many buttons, since the film-makers had decided to use certain standard historical references: 'we knew there were moments of portraiture that we were going to achieve, like the Coronation and the icon, so those were landmarks.'[247] The use of paintings as historical reference

---

[244] Byrne, quoted on official website.
[245] Betty Goodwin, 'Costume', *LA Times* (13 Nov. 1998), cutting.
[246] Byrne, quoted on official website and in Press Booklet.   [247] Ibid.

points lends the film a strong sense of art-historical realism.[248] The invocation of this principle underlines the extent to which we know history through previous representations. One of the pitfalls of such an approach is that the reference points are not pure versions of history—they are precisely representations, and in the case of the portrait, as Byrne has already explained, this was a special event, not a depiction of everyday dress. Further, one set of representations may be laid over another—the representations congeal, become conventional. Thus for many audiences, the historical reference points, the means by which we know the past, are less the paintings of the period, more previous films (or even the waxwork museum, another populist version of history[249]). While numerous commentators enjoyed the way in which the bulk of the film broke with convention by depicting Elizabeth *before* she became the familiar icon, they also saw the finale of the film through filmic eyes: 'only at the end does she reinvent herself as the immaculate, forbidding figurehead . . . we're familiar with from Glenda Jackson, Flora Robson or Bette Davis'. 'The Elizabeth I we usually see in engravings and movies is the later Elizabeth, the one who had locked herself into a certain image and never let the facade chip. (Think Bette Davis in *The Private Lives of Elizabeth and Essex*.)'[250] The use of such familiar historical reference points is a way of situating the film's audiences, though some found this superficial and preferred the irreverent side of *Elizabeth*: 'Occasionally Kapur seems to fall back on research in order to reassert the historical basis of the story, simplistically using famous portraits and miniatures as the basis for costumes and compositions. . . . But much of the time he approaches his subject with fresh eyes, and gives the film a dynamism rooted in difference.'[251]

The mix of the familiar and the different caused more upset with the music, with several commentators bemoaning the mix of authentic sixteenth-century music (Thomas Tallis, William Byrd, Tielman Susato) with music from later periods: the use of 'some misplaced Mozart (wrong century, I think)' was 'very unfortunate'; and while some found the use of Elgar 'inspired', others thought it 'rum' at best, 'hopelessly inappropriate' at worst.[252] Few however commented on the music specially written for the film by David Hirschfelder, though one musical connoisseur thought it 'a pastiche of a pastiche, with all the lumbering dullness of so many bad period costume dramas of the past'.[253] The eclectic mix of musics

---

[248] For further discussion of this issue, see Luckett, 'Image and Nation', 88–99; and Kara McKechnie, 'Taking Liberties with the Monarch: The Royal Bio-pic in the 1990s', in Claire Monk and Amy Sargeant (eds.), *British Historical Cinema* (London: Routledge, 2002), 215–36.

[249] See e.g. Walker, 'Ruff Justice', 27.

[250] Charity, 'Virgin Records', 18; Bernard, 'Elizabeth, Queen of Hearts', from website.

[251] Bruzzi, 'Elizabeth', 48.

[252] Wills, 'Elizabeth', 12; Anon., 'Elizabeth' (user review), posted on Internet Movie Database, at IMDb.com, 7 Nov. 1998; Williams, 'Liz the Lionheart', 7; Kaufman, 'Royal Flush', 36–7; Agm, 'Elizabeth' (user comment), posted on IMDb.com, 26 Oct. 1998; see also Ross W. Duffin, 'Early Music Gets Short Shrift in *Elizabeth*', *LA Times*, 21 Dec. 1998 (cutting).

[253] Agm, 'Elizabeth', from website.

is a symptom of both the period film as a genre and the ambivalence of this par-·
ticular film towards historical accuracy. The period film will routinely employ specially written mood music to enhance narrative effect and emotional tone, but it
will also frequently nod towards historical authenticity, either in the form of pastiche or by including extracts from appropriately period music. The irreverence
of *Elizabeth* meant that it could find space for both sixteenth-century music and
period music from other centuries: if Mozart and Elgar seemed appropriate, then
they could be included. Such music may thus signify the archaic, the classical, and
the tasteful, in a general sense; it may also signify both the regal (Mozart) and the
English (Elgar).

THE DANGERS OF POP HISTORY:
CREATING A MORAL PANIC

If *Elizabeth*'s irreverent 'reinvention of history', meant 'an Oliver Stone-like stance
towards the facts', and 'gaping historical errors' then it was, at the very least,
'unlikely to please historians or historical purists'. This was 'historical drama for
anyone whose idea of history is back issues of *Vogue*'. But even non-historians
were advised to 'close your eyes when the last scene fades; to know what Lizzie
did next, find a decent textbook'.[254] The right-wing press were not slow to respond,
not simply to the question of historical inaccuracies, but also to what they saw as
distinctly unpatriotic behaviour, especially the depiction of Elizabeth I, national
icon, Virgin Queen, engaging in a passionate sexual relationship. Both the *Daily
Telegraph* and the *Mail on Sunday* went out of their way to brand the film controversial, to generate a moral panic. In a piece on the news pages rather than the
arts pages of the *Daily Telegraph*, and some months before the film was released,
a headline blazed 'Film changes sexual history of Elizabeth I, the Virgin Queen'.
The reporter explained that 'the reputation of Elizabeth I as the Virgin Queen is
called into question by a new . . . film depicting her life, to the chagrin of many
historians of the period. . . . That [Kapur] has now seen fit to tamper with English
history is going down badly with some eminent British historians.' Dr Simon
Adams, 'a senior lecturer at Strathclyde University and an expert on the Tudor
period', was quoted as saying that the 'treatment of Elizabeth I's sexual antics [was]
"fiction" . . . There is no doubt among serious historians that Elizabeth I died
virgo intacta'. The problem was that 'many popular films gave the impression of
being historically accurate. "That is why they are so dangerous"'.[255]
　　The struggle was continued by the paper in an editorial comment on the same
day:

[254] D'Silva, 'Easy Sits the Crown', 4; Susman, 'Not Like a Virgin', from website; Richards, 'Long Live
the Queen', 12; French, 'Another Fine Bess', 6; Maslin, 'Amour and High Dudgeon in a Castle of One's
Own', E16; Wyman, 'Elizabeth', 20.
[255] Amit Roy, 'Film Changes Sexual History of Elizabeth I, the Virgin Queen', *Daily Telegraph* (9
Mar. 1998), 3.

A new film denying Elizabeth I's chastity says rather more about our morals than hers. The obsession with sullying the reputations of dead heroes and heroines is one of the ugliest features of our age. This is bad enough when there is actual proof of their transgressions, but all the evidence suggests that Elizabeth went intact to her grave. . . . The patriotism of Elizabethan Englishmen was imbued with a sense of gallantry towards their Queen. Elizabeth used her virginity as an instrument of statecraft, flirting with continental noblemen as the national interest dictated. . . . To question Elizabeth's virtue 400 years after her death is not just a blackguardly slur upon a good, Christian woman, but an insult to our fathers who fought for her. It should rouse England to chivalrous anger.[256]

It certainly roused the *Mail on Sunday*'s version of middle England into action:

The two bodies are naked, intertwined. Young lovers in the heat of passion, cocooned in the intimacy of a double bed from which the curtains cascade. It's the sort of scene that is only too familiar in Hollywood and at first glance it would be no more shocking than most. But what is truly startling is that the woman on the screen is Elizabeth I, the 'Virgin Queen'. The sex scenes form a key part of a controversial film . . . Such graphic scenes may stick in the throat of historians and anyone who remembers their history lessons. . . . For all the undoubted glamour and vivid drama of the film, . . . there will be many who resent the explicit reinterpretation of the life of one of England's most cherished monarchs.[257]

Education, in the form of history lessons, is good; popular culture, in the form of Hollywood sex scenes, is bad, however glamorous and dramatic it is made out to be. In fact, the reporter in this case seems to quite like the film, though this did not hold her back from suggesting that 'the interpretation will stun audiences', from reporting that the film 'has already attracted criticism from historians', or from finding her own friendly expert to quote: 'Historian Alison Weir, who has just published a book about Elizabeth and her courtiers, thinks Kapur has taken "a lot of liberties with the truth" and dismisses some of his claims as "nonsense". . . . [She] maintains there is no evidence to support the film's reinterpretation of history.'[258]

Somewhat surprisingly, this struggle over the meaning of the film and the interpretation of history took a slightly different form in the *Daily Mail*, a newspaper that could usually be relied upon to take a similar critical line. Rather than chastizing the film for its irreverent deviation from what is conventionally regarded as the historical facts, the *Mail* claimed the film for a conservative vision of nationhood and national identity. It commended the film-makers for dealing with a great British hero, and for the way they 'neatly avoid an anachronistically feminist reading of history, for they make it clear that in order to become "a strong woman" and a sixteenth century equivalent to *The Godfather*, Elizabeth had to sacrifice important, feminine areas of her personality'. As noted earlier, the *Mail* also celebrated the Englishness of the film's landscapes and architecture.[259]

Where other conservative commentators expressed concern over the moder-

---

[256] Anon., 'Elizabeth *Intacta*', *Daily Telegraph* (9 Mar. 1998), 21.
[257] Brook, 'Elizabeth I is Known as the Virgin Queen', 52–3.   [258] Ibid.
[259] Tookey, 'Tonic for Heroine Addicts', 44–5.

nity of the film, the *Mail* found a different, more positive interpretation of the film, one more in keeping with the presumed interests of its readers.

The film avoids becoming a history lesson; yet its messages for the present are instructive. One is that the neat division of a ruler's life between public and private is an impractical one. The public always takes precedence, whether one likes it or not. This is a lesson younger members of our Royal Family, and those who feel called to high government, may do well to ponder. It has clearly come too late for President Clinton.

Here, apparently, was a film that could speak to the great and the good, and to all right-thinking people. This seems a risky line for the *Daily Mail* to have taken, given the danger signs so many others had felt it necessary to erect in order to warn audiences of what was in store for them. In fact, there were some danger signs: the film 'will irritate some historians'; it was 'certainly no masterpiece and not to be taken altogether seriously as history'; it was marked by 'occasional errors of taste and imprecision in story-telling'; and it 'play[ed] fast and loose with chronology, compressing events that took years to unfold'. The overall tone, however, was that *Elizabeth* was to be welcomed, that it remained 'commendably true to the spirit of its heroine', and indeed that it could be used as an object-lesson for the British film industry as a whole:

it is high time that our film industry made more movies about Britain's heroes. It is ridiculous that only in wartime do the British produce films about their great commanders, such as Nelson, when the French and Americans make film after film about their national heroes. Why are there no halfway decent pictures about such fascinating figures as Wellington or Sir Francis Drake? Feminism, pacifism, Marxism and just plain cynicism have all contributed to British filmmakers' habit of heckling our heroes, or simply ignoring them . . .

The title of this article—'Tonic for heroine addicts'—suggests it should be seen in part as a riposte to the success of *Trainspotting*. On the one hand, *Elizabeth* is a film which will appeal to those who want to see their national heroines depicted on the screen. On the other hand, it is the perfect antidote for a country that first produces a film about heroin addiction (*Trainspotting*), then allows it to become one of its biggest ever box-office successes. It seems almost perverse that the *Daily Mail* should both advance such an interpretation of *Elizabeth*, and use that interpretation for such old-fashioned, patriotic ends. For cultural historians of a different persuasion, it was the film's old-fashioned qualities, and its attachment to well-trodden myth which were its downfall. For such commentators, the film did not do enough by way of developing a revisionist historical perspective. 'This film's queen is predictably and uninterestingly "normal"', suggested one critic:

if the writers had stuck to it, and been willing to sift the sources creatively, they might have come out with a genuinely modern psychodrama . . . An emotionally damaged young queen, daughter of a psychopath, who had suffered sexual abuse and was herself strongly suspected of complicity in murder, would have made a far more interesting heroine for today . . . [260]

[260] Duncan-Jones, 'Why Then, O Brawling Love!', 18.

SOME CONCLUSIONS

It should by now be clear that, if some found *Elizabeth* dangerously irreverential, others found it delightfully so. That a progressive cultural historian might find aspects of the film 'uninterestingly normal' adds to the complexity of the debate, as does the *Daily Mail* finding a way of interpreting the film as a celebration of an uncomplicated Englishness. All this is surely testament to the ambivalence of the film and to the way in which meanings and interpretations are negotiated between reader and text. What this study of the critical reception of a film thus reveals is the extent to which any film is open to alternative readings, the extent to which a text is a contested terrain.

The discourses circulating around the film provide a series of takes on the film, a series of routes into, through, and away from the film itself. Heritage tourist brochure; upmarket historical drama with an artistic bent;[261] controversial talk-piece; conspiracy thriller for the boys; costume romance for the girls: each of these 'versions' of *Elizabeth* constitutes at the same time an interpretation of the text and a selling-point, an audience engaged with the film and a means of generating revenue. To some extent the film has to be open to alternative readings, to be able to appease different audience interests, to be accessible in different markets. The details of the production and marketing of the film confirm the extent to which these different versions of the film were explicitly encouraged by those responsible for the success of the film, in their efforts to create a mid-budget crossover film. Their goal was to produce a film that could appeal to the core heritage cinema audience while at the same time attracting new audiences.

So is it still appropriate to label *Elizabeth* a heritage film? Labelling is a key means of containing the polysemy of a text—though it can also be used to open the text up to other interpretations. In this case, to label *Elizabeth* a heritage film is both to limit our understanding of the way the film operates, and to offer an explanation about how the film works, as a text, but also as a commodity. The label limits our understanding of *Elizabeth* since there are other ways in which the film can be taken up which do not situate it as a part of the heritage industry or link it to heritage discourses. The reading of the film in terms of girl power is perhaps the most obvious example. That is not to deny that the Merchant Ivory adaptations of E. M. Forster or film versions of Jane Austen also have strong female protagonists, or work on a romantic level, or appeal to female audiences. It is to acknowledge simply that the heritage label foregrounds an aspect of the film but does not exhaust the meaningfulness of the film. To discuss *Elizabeth* in the context of a debate about heritage does however help us to understand another aspect of the appeal of the film. It draws attention to the film's relationship to the tourist industry, to the ongoing fascination with the past, to the concern for period authenticity, and to discourses of national identity and nationhood.

Elizabeth's eclecticism, its hybridizing of elements from different filmic

---

[261] Handling, quoted in Tillson, '*Elizabeth* Bows in Toronto'.

traditions, is not simply a matter of critical debate, however. It was also an important part of the process of producing a widely marketable commodity. What the phenomenon of *Elizabeth* demonstrates is that to define popularity in terms of the capacity of a cultural product to reach a mass audience is misleading. The mass is always a collection of niches. *Elizabeth* was a specialized product designed to exploit that fact by bringing together attractions that appealed to different audience groups and interests. The relatively large budget enabled the producers to develop the film on a scale that was extravagant by the standards of much European film-making. That extravagance is itself an acknowledgement of the increasing interdependency of the major Hollywood studios and the tradition of the specialized European film.

Conclusion

At the time of writing, a new English heritage film is doing excellent business at the box office in both the USA and the UK. The film is *Gosford Park* (2001), about an elaborate weekend party at a grand country house in the early 1930s, but also about the last of aristocratic England. We see as much of the enormous army of servants as we see of the hosts and guests, allowing the film to focus on relations between the different classes. If we are looking for an engrossing story, then we should surely concentrate on the narrative that emerges around Sir William McCordle, owner of the country estate and host of the house party. It turns out that he had several affairs with working-class girls who worked in his factories, two of whom are now on the staff at his estate. One of these affairs produced a son, who turns up at the house party as valet to one of the guests. The son apparently murders the father, although in fact his mother, now Sir William's housekeeper, has already poisoned him.

But there are many other little narratives circling around this one, and one of the great attractions of the film is its huge number of protagonists, its enormous ensemble cast of mainly British thespians, including such heritage film stalwarts as Kristin Scott Thomas, James Wilby, Maggie Smith, and Jeremy Northam. There are many other familiar ingredients of the heritage film too: the narrative revelations about the seedy underside to the aristocratic veneer; the sense of class exploitation; the transgressive, cross-class sexual relationships; the ennui and eccentricity of the financially troubled upper classes; aristocratic concerns about society interlopers—Americans, media types, 'new money'; and so on. Narratively, England is in flux. Visually, though, it looks splendid, even if the country house is only ever seen in bad weather. The heritage iconography is all in place, the dressing of the sets and the costumes of the characters is thoroughly picturesque. And the shooting style is languid, affording plenty of opportunities to display the cast, their costumes, and the production design.

It should come as no surprise to learn that the film won BAFTA Awards for Best British Film and Best Costume Design. Indeed, the film has been positively garlanded with prestigious nominations and prizes and celebrated by critics on both sides of the Atlantic. There is nothing new here, either—nor is there anything new in the fact that the film was directed by veteran *American* film-maker Robert Altman, whose preferred shooting style perfectly matches the standard aesthetics of the heritage film. Once again, an outsider's view seems both to capture an authentic version of the English national character and to dissect it ruthlessly.

There is much that is familiar about the funding and marketing of the film too. The film was in part financed by lottery money, in the form of the Film Council's Premiere Fund, set up to support popular, commercially viable, mainstream films.

But it was also an Anglo-American co-production, with additional money from an Italian company. With a reported budget of $19.8 million,[1] it was towards the top end of the range of heritage film productions, and clearly intended for the crossover market, for this was not the sort of budget that could be covered in the specialized market alone. The film opened first in the USA, where it was given a platformed release, rolling out much more slowly than a typical mainstream film with its saturation opening weekend, but much more quickly than the year-long rollout of earlier films like *Howards End*. It opened initially on nine screens in December 2001, with such impressive takings on each screen that it already appeared at number twenty-two in the box-office charts. By week two, it was in the top twenty, and by week three, in the top ten. By the end of its second month on release, it was on more than 800 screens—although the top nine films in the box-office chart were all on more than 2,000 screens. Throughout its run, the film was in fact listed in both the mainstream and the independent charts, a clear indication that the trade perceived it as a specialized film that had crossed over into the multiplexes as well.[2]

In the UK, the film was given a wider release from the outset, opening on 156 screens and taking enough on those screens to reach number four in the box-office charts. By comparison, seven of the top ten films were on more than 200 screens, *Harry Potter and the Philosopher's Stone* (2001) was on 363, and *The Lord of the Rings: The Fellowship of the Ring* (2002) on 480 screens. By the end of April 2002, the film had taken over £12 million in the UK and over $40 million in the USA.[3] Observing audiences at my local multiplex, it was clear that the film was attracting both the core under-35 multiplex audience, and the core over-35 heritage film audience—and it was not unusual to hear members of the latter niche commenting in middle-class accents as they left the cinema how much they enjoyed a good British film.

This was the sort of box-office success the makers of *Mansfield Park* (1999) and *The Golden Bowl* (2000) must surely have been hoping for, and with two other specialized films with period settings also being exploited in the crossover market at the same time—*Iris* (2001) and *Charlotte Gray* (2002)—perhaps the quality costume drama cycle hasn't wound down after all. In the case of *Gosford Park*, the marketing of the film was crucial to its success, with advertisements making the most of the ensemble cast and the awards and accolades it received—initially in upscale newspapers, but eventually taking in television advertising as well, a strategy usually reserved for solid multiplex fare. The film was sold both as a country-house drama, a frock flick, and as a murder mystery, like *Elizabeth* (1998) deliberately tapping into two relatively distinct markets, the tagline used in publicity perfectly capturing this sense of generic hybridity: 'Tea at Four. Dinner at Eight. Murder at Midnight'.

---

[1] Adam Dawtrey, ' "Park" Bench', *Variety* (18–24 Feb. 2002), 9.
[2] See the weekly box-office charts in *Variety* for Jan. and Feb. 2002.
[3] See the weekly box-office charts in *Screen International* for Feb., Mar., and Apr. 2002.

Although the focus of this book has been the 1980s and 1990s, such neat peri-odization rarely works in practice. I've identified two convenient cut-off points—at one end, the rash of 'British' costume dramas that appeared in the early 1980s, and in particular the success of *Chariots of Fire* (1981); at the other end, the rela-tive failure of some fairly prestigious and expensive period films. But as the success of *Gosford Park* indicates, the production trend didn't die off in the year 2000 as Tony Blair's rebranded Britain looked forward to the millennium, rather than back to the national past. Equally, as others have noted, there was plenty of period work in British film and television in the years before *Chariots of Fire*, work that often shares much with the films of the post-*Chariots* production trend.[4]

Even within the 1980s and 1990s, I've identified a much wider range of films than is normally taken into account when discussing heritage cinema. Do these films constitute a genre? Well, genres are critical categories, and there is no denying that the heritage film is a critical construct, and that there is by now a fairly exten-sive body of academic work that more or less treats the heritage film debate as if it were about a genre. Equally, there's no denying that the period film or costume drama has been a key production trend in British film-making in the 1980s and 1990s, with distinctive but gradually changing commercial characteristics. I would suggest that the question of whether these films constitute a genre or not is much less important than attending to the critical debate about those films, to the details of the films themselves, and to the market conditions under which those films cir-culated. It's certainly been important to the way this book has developed to have been able to relate the films to the contexts of production, distribution, and exhibition, to funding opportunities, markets, and audiences.

But to establish these relations is also to reveal a paradox at the heart of the heritage film economy. On the one hand, these are films that stand in for British national cinema, and that are different from mainstream (Hollywood) films, a feature that is central to the perception of them both at home and abroad. To this extent, their very presence as films is indicative of a certain cultural diversity, a certain attention to the local within our increasingly globalized film culture. On the other hand, this attention to the local and the national is only possible because of transnational funding, and especially American funding. Equally, these 'national' films are intended for and enjoyed by international audiences, and they have transnational appeal. Paradoxically, it is the support of the Hollywood majors as much as anything else that has enabled such films to be made. Hollywood's interest in specialist film thus suggests that the monolithic machine that some see in Hollywood actually allows for—indeed, encourages—the production of

---

[4] See e.g. D. L. LeMahieu, 'Imagined Contemporaries: Cinematic and Televised Dramas about the Edwardians in Great Britain and the United States, 1967–1985', *Historical Journal of Film, Radio and Television*, 10/3 (1990), 243–56; Tana Wollen, 'Over our Shoulders: Nostalgic Screen Fictions for the Eighties', in John Corner and Sylvia Harvey (eds.), *Enterprise and Heritage: Crosscurrents of National Culture* (London: Routledge, 1991), 178–93; and Claire Monk, 'The British Heritage-Film Debate Revis-ited', in Claire Monk and Amy Sargeant (eds.), *British Historical Cinema* (London: Routledge, 2002), 176–98.

difference. It ensures that a certain market segment is served, a segment that does not normally feel well served by the film industry.

One reason for this interest may of course be that Hollywood perceives in the niche market and the specialized film a great deal of potential: in a sense, the low-budget, specialized film provides a research and development site for mainstream cinema. It is certainly possible to read the heritage film economy in this way. Think for instance of the shift from the minuscule budget but major box-office success of *A Room with a View* (1986), to the much better funded *Howards End* (1991), the success of which paved the way for later and even more expensive costume films, such as *Sense and Sensibility* (1996) and *Mansfield Park*. Think too of the way *Elizabeth* borrowed from both the frock flick tradition and from more mainstream films like *Braveheart* (1995), while *Shakespeare in Love* (1998) mixed the worthiness of the Shakespeare film with the romantic period comedy of *A Room with a View* and some of the Austen adaptations. Important here is the shift that many have perceived in the 1990s, from reverential authenticity to irreverence and playfulness, but it is equally important to acknowledge how much remains familiar in the heritage films of the late 1990s and early 2000s.

There are other ways in which we might see the heritage film as one of Hollywood's research and development operations. Think for instance of the way director Mike Newell moved from small-scale, low-budget period pieces like *Dance with a Stranger* (1985) and *Enchanted April* (1991), to the enormously successful *Four Weddings and a Funeral* (1994), and then on to a Hollywood career. *Four Weddings* itself spawned further global successes in the form of *Notting Hill* (1999), and even *Bridget Jones's Diary* (2001). Those three films, along with mainstream blockbusters such as *Titanic* (1997), *Lara Croft—Tomb Raider* (2001), and *Harry Potter and the Philosopher's Stone*, all managed to incorporate English heritage iconography or literary references. *Harry Potter* could also be seen as a quality British literary adaptation, and was hooked into the discourses of heritage tourism.[5] What such developments suggest is that the niche English costume drama has crossed over so far that it has now become a thoroughly mainstream film.

Others will no doubt disagree with my reading of such films—but then the ambivalence of film texts and the richness of the reception process have been central features of my argument about how heritage films work with their audiences. The different readings of the films I've discussed in previous chapters indicate above all the extent to which texts are precisely open to interpretation, including interpretations that may be quite at odds with the intentions of the filmmakers. As such, this book has been as much about the process of reception as about the films themselves, although I have of course focused on critical reception, rather than undertaken empirical studies of filmgoers in their natural habitat. The range of meanings generated by a particular film—or rather by the

---

[5] Gareth McLean, 'Hogwarts and All: Harry Potter's Britain', *Guardian*, Friday Review (19 Oct. 2001), 1–4.

interaction of that film with its audiences—should make us wary of 'reading' films, or at least of granting too much status to our readings.

Indeed, I trust I haven't given the impression that films have inherent or fixed meanings. Of course, films have a particular form and content, a particular set of attractions, but this need not imply that meaning is inherent in the text itself. I've certainly resisted indulging at length in modes of analysis that suggest as much, since I'm increasingly dissatisfied with the implications of such analysis. It seems to me more interesting to acknowledge the range of readings a film has generated or enabled, the impact of marketing on the reception process, and the critical debate that has raged around heritage films more generally. As we've seen in the case of *Howards End* and *Elizabeth*, promotional material invites different audiences and taste groups to engage with a film in particular ways. In part, this is an acknowledgement on the part of the industry that to open up a film to a range of readings is more profitable than closing it down to one particular reading.

There's certainly a great openness about the films I've discussed in this book, and there's no denying that they are a relatively eclectic group, drawing on several different generic categories and incorporating a range of attractions. The attractions of heritage by no means exhaust the appeal of films such as *Howards End* and *Elizabeth*. In the case of *Elizabeth*, for instance, for some audiences and reviewers, the feminist potential of the eponymous character was more important. For others, the narrative energy and complexity of the conspiracy thriller appealed. For yet others, it was the eclectic visual style that held the attention. What, perhaps a little too obstinately, I've called the heritage film, others have seen as romantic comedies, woman's pictures, queer dramas, middle-brow classics. My previous work on the heritage film foregrounded what I've here called the leftist cultural critique, and insisted on reading the films politically, relating them to the social conditions of the period, arguing that they produced a very limited and limiting vision of Englishness for global consumption. In fact, the films themselves are rarely about politics in any conventional sense, and are much more frequently about romance and desire, narrative and spectacle, history and tourism. But there's still a debate to be had here—and if there's one thing that my discussion has, I hope, demonstrated, it is that films don't close down meanings, but rather generate debate. And I've no doubt that that claim itself will provoke debate.

Select Filmography: 'British' Costume Dramas of the 1980s and 1990s

The filmography lists costume dramas made or first released in the 1980s and 1990s, with some British connection, and at least partly set before the Second World War (with one or two exceptions!). The British connection might be that the film is set all or partly in Britain, or deals with the English abroad; or it might be that the film is an adaptation of a work by a canonical British author; and most but not all of the films have some British production involvement. It is important to note that these categories are not hard and fast, and some decisions that will no doubt seem arbitrary have had to be taken.

The first set of details given indicate title, director, country of production, and date of production. This is followed by the source of the screenplay (where it is based on historical figures, it is identified as a bio-pic; where it is an adaptation, the title of the source is only given where it differs from the title of the film). Next comes the date in which the film is set (and the place where it is set if this is mainly other than England). Where the film uses a modern-day framing device from where the past is remembered this is represented as, for instance, 1930s/1980s (meaning that the film cuts between the 1930s and the 1980s). Where a film was an Academy Award (Oscar) winner, this is indicated by AA, followed by the category and year of the award. Finally, the date of the full credits and review in *Monthly Film Bulletin* (*MFB*) or *Sight and Sound* (*S&S*, from May 1991) is given.

Adam Bede (Giles Foster, UK, 1991; from novel by George Eliot; turn of 18th/19th cent.; *S&S*, Apr. 1992)

Amy Foster (Beeban Kidron, UK/USA/France, 1997; from novel by Joseph Conrad; late 19th cent.; *S&S*, May 1998)

Angels and Insects (Philip Haas, UK/USA, 1995; from novella, *Morpho Eugenia*, by A. S. Byatt; mid-19th cent.; *S&S*, Dec. 1995)

Another Country (Marek Kanievska, UK, 1984; from play by Julian Mitchell; 1930s/1980s; *MFB*, June 1984)

August (Anthony Hopkins, UK, 1995; from Anton Chekhov's play *Uncle Vanya*; 1890s [Wales]; *S&S*, Aug. 1996)

Black Beauty (Caroline Thompson, UK/USA, 1994; from novel by Anna Sewell; late 19th cent.; *S&S*, Feb. 1995)

Bram Stoker's Dracula (Francis Ford Coppola, USA, 1992; from novel by Bram Stoker; 1890s [partly set in Transylvania]; *S&S*, Feb. 1993)

Braveheart (Mel Gibson, USA, 1995; bio-pic, original screenplay; late 13th cent. [Scotland]; AA, 1995, Make-up; *S&S*, Sept. 1995)

Bridge, The (Sydney MacCartney, UK, 1990; bio-pic in part, from novel by Maggie Hemingway; 1890s; *S&S*, Jan. 1992)

Carrington (Christopher Hampton, UK/France, 1995; bio-pic, based on biography by Michael Holroyd, *Lytton Strachey*; 1910s–1930s; *S&S*, Sept. 1995)

Century (Stephen Poliakoff, UK, 1993; original screenplay; 1899–1900; *S&S*, Jan. 1994)

Chaplin (Richard Attenborough, UK, 1992; bio-pic, original screenplay; 1890s–1970s [partly set in the USA and Switzerland]; *S&S*, Jan. 1993)

Chariots of Fire (Hugh Hudson, UK, 1981; bio-pic, original screenplay; 1920s/1980s [partly set in Scotland]; AA, 1981, Best Picture, Original Screenplay; *MFB*, May 1981)

Chasing the Deer (Graham Holloway, UK, 1994; original screenplay; early 18th cent. [Scotland]; S&S, Jan. 1995)

Claim, The (Michael Winterbottom, UK/Canada/France, 2000; inspired by Thomas Hardy's novel, *The Mayor of Casterbridge*; mid-19th cent. [USA]; *S&S*, Mar. 2001)

Clandestine Marriage, The (Christopher Miles, UK, 1999; from play by George Coleman and David Garrick; late 18th cent.; *S&S*, Dec. 1999)

Cold Comfort Farm (John Schlesinger, UK, 1995; from novel by Stella Gibbons; 1920s; *S&S*, May 1997)

Comrades (Bill Douglas, UK, 1986; bio-pic, original screenplay; 1830s [partly set in Australia]; *MFB*, Sept. 1987)

Dawning, The (Robert Knights, UK, 1988; from Jennifer Johnston's novel, *The Old Jest*; 1920s [Ireland]; *MFB*, Nov. 1988)

Deceivers, The (Nicholas Meyer, UK, 1988; from novel by John Masters; 1820s [India]; *MFB*, Sept. 1988)

December Bride (Thaddeus O'Sullivan, UK/Ireland, 1990; from novel by Sam Hanna Bell; 1900s, 1910s [Ireland]; *MFB*, Feb. 1991)

Draughtsman's Contract, The (Peter Greenaway, UK, 1982; original screenplay; 1690s; *MFB*, Nov. 1982)

Edward II (Derek Jarman, UK, 1991; from play by Christopher Marlowe; early 14th cent.; *S&S*, Nov. 1991)

1871 (Ken McMullen, UK, 1989; bio-pic of sorts, original screenplay; 1870s [mostly set in France]; *S&S*, Aug. 1991)

Elephant Man, The (David Lynch, USA, 1980; bio-pic, from various memoirs; 1880s; *MFB*, Oct. 1980)

Elizabeth (Shekhar Kapur, UK, 1998; bio-pic, original screenplay; mid-16th cent.; AA, 1998, Make-up; *S&S*, Nov. 1998)

Emma (Douglas McGrath, UK/USA, 1996; from novel by Jane Austen; early 19th cent.; AA, 1996, Score; *S&S*, Sept. 1996)

Enchanted April (Mike Newell, UK, 1991; from novel by Elizabeth von Arnim; 1920s [partly set in Italy]; *S&S*, Feb. 1992)

English Patient, The (Anthony Minghella, USA, 1996; from novel by Michael Ondaatje; 1930s, 1940s [Egypt, Italy]; AA, 1996, Best Director, Art Direction; *S&S*, Mar. 1997)

Englishman Who Went Up a Hill and Came Down a Mountain, The (Chris Monger, UK, 1994; loosely autobiographical; 1910s [Wales]; *S&S*, Aug. 1995)

Excalibur (John Boorman, USA, 1981; based on *Le Morte d'Arthur* by Thomas Malory; 5th–6th cent.?; *MFB*, June 1981)

Fairytale A True Story (Charles Sturridge, USA, 1997; bio-pic, original screenplay; 1910s; *S&S*, Mar. 1998)

Firelight (William Nicholson, USA/UK, 1997; original screenplay; 1830s; *S&S*, Aug. 1998)

Fool, The (Christine Edzard, UK, 1990; bio-pic, partly based on Henry Mayhew's *London Labour and the London Poor*; mid-19th cent.; *MFB*, Dec. 1990)

Fools of Fortune (Pat O'Connor, UK, 1990; from novel by William Trevor; 1920s [mostly set in Ireland]; *MFB*, July 1990)

French Lieutenant's Woman, The (Karel Reisz, UK, 1981; from novel by John Fowles; 1860s/present day; *MFB*, Oct. 1981)

Gandhi (Richard Attenborough, UK/India, 1982; bio-pic, original screenplay; various episodes, 1900s to 1940s [South Africa, India]; AA, 1982, Best Picture, Best Director, Original Screenplay, Best Actor, Art Direction, Costume, Cinematography; *MFB*, Dec. 1982)

Golden Bowl, The (James Ivory, UK/France/USA, 2000; from novel by Henry James; 1900s [partly set in Italy]; *S&S*, Nov. 2000)

Gothic (Ken Russell, UK, 1986; bio-pic, original screenplay; 1810s; *MFB*, Feb. 1987)

Governess, The (Sandra Goldbacher, UK/France, 1997; original screenplay; mid-19th cent.; *S&S*, Nov. 1998)

Greystoke: The Legend of Tarzan, Lord of the Apes (Hugh Hudson, UK, 1984; from Edgar Rice Burroughs's novel *Tarzan of the Apes*; 1880s-1900s [partly set in Africa]; *MFB*, May 1984)

Hamlet (Kenneth Branagh, UK/USA, 1996; from play by William Shakespeare; 19th cent. [Denmark]; *S&S*, Feb. 1997)

Handful of Dust, A (Charles Sturridge, 1987; from novel by Evelyn Waugh; 1930s; *MFB*, June 1988)

Heat and Dust (James Ivory, UK, 1982; from novel by Ruth Prawer Jhabvala; 1920s/present [India]; *MFB*, Jan. 1983)

Hedd Wyn (Paul Turner, UK, 1992; bio-pic, original screenplay; 1910s [Wales]; *S&S*, July 1994)

Henry V (Kenneth Branagh, UK, 1989; bio-pic, from play by William Shakespeare; 15th cent. [partly set in France]; AA, 1989, Costume; *MFB*, Oct. 1989)

House of Mirth, The (Terence Davies, UK/USA, 2000; from novel by Edith Wharton; 1890s/1900s [New York]; *S&S*, Nov. 2000)

Howards End (James Ivory, UK, 1992; from novel by E. M. Forster; 1900s; AA, 1992, Best Actress, Art Direction; S&S, May 1992)

Ideal Husband, An (Oliver Parker, UK/USA, 1999; from play by Oscar Wilde; 1890s; *S&S*, May 1999)

Innocent, The (John MacKenzie, UK, 1984; based on Tom Hart's novel *The Aura and the Kingfisher*; 1930s; *MFB*, June 1985)

Jane Eyre (Franco Zeffirelli, UK/Italy/France, 1995; from novel by Charlotte Brontë; 1820s; *S&S*, Oct. 1996)

Jude (Michael Winterbottom, UK, 1996; from Thomas Hardy's novel *Jude the Obscure*; mid-19th cent.; *S&S*, Oct. 1996)

Keep the Aspidistra Flying [in USA, *A Merry War*] (Robert Bierman, UK, 1997; from novel by George Orwell; 1930s; *S&S*, Nov. 1997)

Lady and the Highwayman, The (John Hough, UK, 1988; from Barbara Cartland's novel, *Cupid Rides Pillion*; mid-17th cent.; no review)

Lady Jane (Trevor Nunn, UK, 1985; bio-pic, original screenplay; mid-16th cent.; *MFB*, June 1986)

Last September, The (Deborah Warner, UK/Ireland/France; 1999; from novel by Elizabeth Bowen; 1920s [Ireland]; *S&S*, June 2000)

Little Dorrit (Christine Edzard, UK, 1987; from novel by Charles Dickens; mid-19th cent.; *MFB*, Dec. 1987)

Little Lord Fauntleroy (Jack Gold, UK, 1980; from novel by Frances Hodgson Burnett; late 19th cent.; *MFB*, Feb. 1981)

Love's Labour's Lost (Kenneth Branagh, UK/France/USA, 2000; from play by William Shakespeare; late 1930s; *S&S*, Apr. 2000)

Macbeth (Jeremy Freeston, Scotland, 1997; from play by William Shakespeare; 11th cent. [Scotland]; *S&S*, June 1997)

Madness of King George, The (Nicholas Hytner, UK, 1995; bio-pic, from Alan Bennett's play *The Madness of George III*; 1780s; AA, 1994, Art Direction; *S&S*, Apr. 1995)

Mansfield Park (Patricia Rozema, USA/UK, 1999; from novel by Jane Austen; early 19th cent.; *S&S*, Apr. 2000)

Mary Reilly (Stephen Frears, USA, 1996; from novel by Valerie Martin; 19th cent.; *S&S*, May 1996)

Maurice (James Ivory, UK, 1987; from novel by E. M. Forster; 1900s; *MFB*, Nov. 1987)

Midsummer Night's Dream, A (Adrian Noble, UK, 1996; from play by William Shakespeare [and RSC stage production]; ancient Athens; *S&S*, Jan. 1997)

Missionary, The (Richard Loncraine, UK, 1981; original screenplay; 1900s; *MFB*, Feb. 1983)

Moll Flanders (Pen Densham, USA, 1995, from novel by Daniel Defoe; 18th cent.; *S&S*, June 1997)

Month by the Lake, A (John Irvin, USA/UK, 1994; from novella by H. E. Bates; 1930s [Italy]; *S&S*, Aug. 1996)

Month in the Country, A (Pat O'Connor, UK, 1987; from novel by J. L. Carr; 1920s; *MFB*, Dec. 1987)

Mrs Brown [in USA, *Her Majesty, Mrs Brown*] (John Madden, UK/USA/Ireland, 1997; bio-pic, original screenplay; 1860s, 1880s; *S&S*, Sept. 1997)

Mrs Dalloway (Marleen Gorris, USA/UK/Netherlands, 1997; from novel by Virginia Woolf; 1920s/1890s; *S&S*, Mar. 1998)

Much Ado About Nothing (Kenneth Branagh, UK/USA, 1993; from play by William Shakespeare; 16th cent. [Sicily]; *S&S*, Sept. 1993)

My Life So Far (Hugh Hudson, USA/UK, 1998; from Sir Denis Forman's book *Son of Adam*; 1920s [Scotland]; *S&S*, June 2000)

Mystery of Edwin Drood, The (Timothy Forder, UK, 1993; from unfinished novel by Charles Dickens; 19th cent.; *S&S*, May 1993)

On the Black Hill (Andrew Grieve, UK, 1987; from novel by Bruce Chatwin; various episodes from 1890s to present; *MFB*, May 1988)

Orlando (Sally Potter, UK/Russia/France/Italy/Netherlands, 1992; from novel by Virginia Woolf; various episodes from 16th cent. to present [partly set in Central Asia]; *S&S*, Mar. 1993)

Oscar and Lucinda (Gillian Armstrong, USA/Australia, 1997; from novel by Peter Carey; 19th cent. [partly set in Australia]; *S&S*, Apr. 1998)

Othello (Oliver Parker, UK, 1995; from play by William Shakespeare; 1570s [Venice]; *S&S*, Feb. 1996)

Pascali's Island (James Dearden, UK, 1988; from novel by Barry Unsworth; 1900s [Aegean island]; *MFB*, Jan. 1989)

Passage to India, A (David Lean, UK, 1984; from novel by E. M. Forster; 1920s [India]; AA, 1984, Supporting Actress; *MFB*, Apr. 1985)

Persuasion (Roger Michell, UK, 1996; from novel by Jane Austen; early 19th cent.; no review)

Photographing Fairies (Nick Willing, UK, 1997; bio-pic, from book by Steve Szilagyi; 1910s; *S&S*, Sept. 1997)

Plunkett and Macleane (Jake Scott, UK, 1999; bio-pic, original screenplay; mid-18th cent.; *S&S*, Apr. 1999)

Portrait of a Lady, The (Jane Campion, UK/USA, 1996; from novel by Henry James; 1870s; *S&S*, Mar. 1997)

Prospero's Books (Peter Greenaway, Netherlands/France/Italy, 1991; based on *The Tempest*, by William Shakespeare; early 17th cent. [imaginary setting]; *S&S*, Sept. 1991)

Quartet (James Ivory, UK/France, 1981; from novel by Jean Rhys; 1920s [France]; *MFB*, July 1981)

Rainbow, The (Ken Russell, UK, 1988; from novel by D. H. Lawrence; various episodes, late 19th and early 20th cent.; *MFB*, Jan. 1990)

Regeneration (Gillies MacKinnon, UK/Canada, 1997; from novel by Pat Barker; 1910s; *S&S*, Dec. 1997)

Remains of the Day, The (James Ivory, UK/USA, 1993; from novel by Kazuo Ishiguro; 1930s/1950s; *S&S*, Dec. 1993)

Restoration (Michael Hoffman, UK/USA, 1996; from novel by Rose Tremain; mid-17th cent.; AA, 1996, Costume; *S&S*, Apr. 1996)

Return of the Soldier, The (Alan Bridges, UK, 1982; from novel by Rebecca West; 1910s; *MFB*, Jan. 1983)

Richard III (Richard Loncraine, UK, 1995; from play by William Shakespeare [and stage production by Richard Eyre]; 1930s; *S&S*, May 1996)

Rob Roy (Michael Caton-Jones, USA, 1995; from novel by Walter Scott; early 18th cent.; *S&S*, June 1995)

Robin Hood (John Irvin, UK, 1990; bio-pic, original screenplay; 12th cent.; *S&S*, June 1991)

Robin Hood: Prince of Thieves (Kevin Reynolds, USA, 1991; bio-pic, original screenplay; 12th cent. [partly set in the Holy Land]; *S&S*, Aug. 1991)

Robin Hood: Men in Tights (Mel Brooks, USA, 1993; bio-pic, original screenplay; 12th cent. [partly set in the Holy Land]; *S&S*, Jan. 1994)

Room with a View, A (James Ivory, UK, 1986; from novel by E. M. Forster; 1900s [partly set in Italy]; AA, 1986, Art Direction, Costume; *MFB*, Apr. 1986)

Rudyard Kipling's Jungle Book (Stephen Sommers, USA, 1994; from novel by Rudyard Kipling; 19th cent. [India]; *S&S*, Mar. 1995)

Scarlet Tunic, The (Stuart St Paul, UK, 1997; from Thomas Hardy's short story, *The Melancholy Hussar*; 1800s; *S&S*, July 1998)

Secret Agent, The (Christopher Hampton, USA/UK, 1996; from novel by Joseph Conrad; 1880s; *S&S*, Apr. 1998)

Secret Garden, The (Agnieszka Holland, USA, 1993; from novel by Frances Hodgson Burnett; 1900s [partly set in India]; *S&S*, Nov. 1993)

Sense and Sensibility (Ang Lee, UK/USA, 1996; from novel by Jane Austen; late 18th cent.; AA, 1995, Adapted Screenplay; *S&S*, Mar. 1996)

Shadowlands (Richard Attenborough, UK/USA, 1993; bio-pic, based on play by William Nicholson; 1950s; *S&S*, Mar. 1994)

Shakespeare in Love (John Madden, USA/UK, 1998; bio-pic, original screenplay; late 16th cent.; AA, 1998, Best Film, Supporting Actress, Original Screenplay, Art Direction, Costume Design, Score; *S&S*, Feb. 1999)

Shooting Party, The (Alan Bridges, UK, 1984; from novel by Isabel Colegate; 1910s; *MFB*, Feb. 1985)

Sirens (John Duigan, Australia/UK, 1994; original screenplay; 1920s [Australia]; *S&S*, Aug. 1994)

Solomon and Gaenor (Paul Morrison, UK, 1998; original screenplay; 1910s [Wales]; *S&S*, May 1999)

Stiff Upper Lips (Gary Sinyor, UK, 1997; parody of other period dramas, original screenplay; 1900s; *S&S*, July 1998)

Summer Story, A (Piers Haggard, UK, 1987; from short story by John Galsworthy; 1920s; *MFB*, Nov. 1988)

Tea with Mussolini [*Te con Il Duce*] (Franco Zeffirelli, Italy/UK, 1998; loosely autobiographical, original screenplay; 1930s, 1940s [Italy]; *S&S*, Apr. 1999)

Tempest, The (Derek Jarman, UK, 1980; from play by William Shakespeare; imaginary setting; MFB, Apr. 1980)

Tess (Roman Polanski, France/UK, 1979; from novel by Thomas Hardy; mid-19th cent.; AA, 1980, Costume, Art Direction, Cinematography; *MFB*, May 1981)

Tichborne Claimant, The (David Yates, UK, 1998; bio-pic, original screenplay; 1870s [partly set in Australia]; *S&S*, Dec. 1999)

Tom and Viv (Brian Gilbert, UK, 1994; bio-pic, from play by Michael Hastings; 1910s–1940s; *S&S*, May 1994)

Topsy-Turvy (Mike Leigh, UK/USA, 1999; bio-pic, original screenplay; 1880s; AA, 1999, Costume Design, Make-up; *S&S*, Mar. 2000)

Twelfth Night (Trevor Nunn, UK/USA, 1996; from play by William Shakespeare; imaginary setting; *S&S*, Nov. 1996)

Victory (Mark Peploe, UK/France/Germany, 1995; from novel by Joseph Conrad; 1910s [Dutch East Indies]; *S&S*, Dec. 1998)

War Requiem (Derek Jarman, UK, 1989; from oratorio by Benjamin Britten; 1910s; *MFB*, Feb. 1989)

Where Angels Fear to Tread (Charles Sturridge, 1991; from novel by E. M. Forster; 1900s [partly set in Italy]; *S&S*, July 1991)

White Mischief (Michael Radford, UK, 1987; from novel by James Fox; 1940s [East Africa]; *MFB*, Feb. 1988)

Wicked Lady, The (Michael Winner, UK, 1983; based on Magdalen King-Hall's novel, *The Life and Death of the Wicked Lady*, and 1945 film version; mid-17th cent.; *MFB*, May 1983)

Wilde (Brian Gilbert, UK/USA/Japan/Germany, 1997; bio-pic; 1880s, 1890s; *S&S*, Oct. 1997)

Wings of the Dove, The (Iain Softley, USA/UK, 1997; from novel by Henry James; 1900s [partly set in Italy]; *S&S*, Jan. 1998)

Winslow Boy, The (David Mamet, USA, 1998; from play by Terence Rattigan; 1910s; *S&S*, Nov. 1999)

Woodlanders, The (Phil Agland, UK, 1997; from novel by Thomas Hardy; 1870s; *S&S*, Feb. 1998)

Wuthering Heights (Peter Kosminsky, USA/UK, 1992; from novel by Emily Brontë; late 18th–19th cent.; *S&S*, Oct. 1992)

Table *The Contribution of Women to the Writing, Producing, or Directing of 'British' Costume Dramas of the 1980s and 1990s*

Title	Director	Author of Source Novel	Screenwriter	Producer/ Executive Producer
Adam Bede		George Eliot	Maggie Wadey	
Amy Foster	Beeban Kidron			
Angels and Insects		A. S. Byatt		Belinda Haas, Joyce Herlihy
August				June Wyndham-Davies, Pippa Cross
Black Beauty	Caroline Thompson	Anna Sewell		
The Bridge		Maggie Hemingway		
Cold Comfort Farm		Stella Gibbons		Alison Gibley
The Dawning		Jennifer Johnston	Moira Williams	Sarah Lawson
Edward II				Sarah Radclyffe
Elizabeth				Alison Owen
Emma		Jane Austen		
Enchanted April		Elizabeth von Arnim		Ann Scott
Fairytale A True Story				Wendy Finnerman
The Fool	Christine Edzard			
Fools of Fortune				Sarah Radclyffe
The Golden Bowl			Ruth Prawer Jhabvala	
The Governess	Sandra Goldbacher		Sandra Goldbacher	Sarah Curtis
Heat and Dust		Ruth Prawer Jhabvala	Ruth Prawer Jhabvala	
The House of Mirth		Edith Wharton		Olivia Stewart, Pippa Cross

Table 269

Table (*cont.*):

Title	Director	Author of Source Novel	Screenwriter	Producer/ Executive Producer
Howards End			Ruth Prawer Jhabvala	
The Innocent				Jackie Stoller
Jane Eyre		Charlotte Brontë		
The Last September	Deborah Warner			Yvonne Thunder
Little Dorrit	Christine Edzard			
Little Lord Fauntleroy		Frances Hodgson Burnett	Blanche Hanalis	
Mansfield Park	Patricia Rozema	Jane Austen	Patricia Rozema	Sarah Curtis
Mary Reilly		Valerie Martin		
Mrs Brown				Sarah Curtis
Mrs Dalloway	Marleen Gorris	Virginia Woolf	Eileen Atkins	Lisa Katselas Paré
The Mystery of Edwin Drood				Mary Swinedale
On the Black Hill				Jennifer Howarth
Orlando	Sally Potter	Virginia Woolf		
Oscar and Lucinda	Gillian Armstrong		Laura Jones	
Persuasion		Jane Austen		
Photographing Fairies (1997)				Fiona Finlay Michele Camarda
The Portrait of a Lady	Jane Campion		Laura Jones	
Quartet		Jean Rhys	Ruth Prawer Jhabvala	
Regeneration		Pat Barker		Saskia Sutton
The Remains of the Day			Ruth Prawer Jhabvala	

Table (*cont.*):

Title	Director	Author of Source Novel	Screenwriter	Producer/ Executive Producer
Restoration		Rose Tremain		
The Return of the Soldier		Rebecca West		
Richard III				Lisa Katselas Paré
A Room with a View			Ruth Prawer Jhabvala	
The Secret Agent				Norma Heyman
The Secret Garden	Agnieszka Holland	Frances Hodgson Burnett	Caroline Thompson	
Sense and Sensibility		Jane Austen	Emma Thompson	Lyndsey Doran
The Shooting Party		Isabel Colegate		
Sirens				Sarah Radclyffe
A Summer Story			Penelope Mortimer	
The Wicked Lady		Magdalen King-Hall		
The Winslow Boy				Sarah Green
Wuthering Heights		Emily Brontë		Mary Selway

Select Bibliography

Ashby, Justine, and Andrew Higson (eds.), *British Cinema, Past and Present* (London: Routledge, 2000).

Austin, Guy, *Contemporary French Cinema: An Introduction* (Manchester: Manchester University Press, 1996).

Auty, Martin, 'But is it Cinema?', in Martin Auty and Nick Roddick (eds.), *British Cinema Now* (London: British Film Institute, 1985), 57–70.

——and Nick Roddick (eds.), *British Cinema Now* (London: British Film Institute, 1985).

Balio, Tino (ed.), *Hollywood in the Age of Television* (Boston and London: Unwin Hyman, 1990).

Balio, Tino, *The History of the American Cinema,* v. *Grand Design: Hollywood as a Modern Business Enterprise, 1930–1939* (New York: Charles Scribner's Sons, 1993).

——'Adjusting to the New Global Economy: Hollywood in the 1990s', in Albert Moran (ed.), *Film Policy: International, National and Regional Perspectives* (London: Routledge, 1996), 23–38.

——' "A Major Presence in All the World's Important Markets": The Globalization of Hollywood in the 1990s', in Steve Neale and Murray Smith (eds.), *Contemporary Hollywood Cinema* (London: Routledge, 1998), 58–73.

——'The Art Film Market in the New Hollywood', in Geoffrey Nowell-Smith and Steven Ricci (eds.), *Hollywood and Europe: Economics, Culture, National Identity 1945–95* (London: British Film Institute, 1998), 63–73.

Ballaster, Ros, 'Adapting Jane Austen', *English Review* (Sept. 1996), 10–13.

Bennett, Susan, *Performing Nostalgia: Shifting Shakespeare and the Contemporary Past* (London: Routledge, 1996).

Bordwell, David, *Narration in the Fiction Film* (London: Methuen, 1985).

——*On the History of Film Style* (Cambridge, Mass.: Harvard University Press, 1997).

——Janet Staiger, and Kristin Thompson, *Classical Hollywood Cinema* (London: RKP, 1985).

Bradbury, Malcolm (ed.), *Forster: A Collection of* Essays (Englewood Cliffs, NJ: Prentice-Hall, 1966).

Bruzzi, Stella, *Undressing Cinema: Clothing and Identity in the Movies* (London: Routledge, 1997).

Cannadine, David, 'Beyond the Country House', in *Aspects of Aristocracy* (New Haven, Conn.: Yale University Press, 1994), 242–5.

Cartmell, Deborah, I. Q. Hunter, Heidi Kaye, and Imelda Whelehan (eds.), *Pulping Fictions: Consuming Culture across the Literature/Media Divide* (London: Pluto Press, 1995).

Chase, Malcolm, 'This is No Claptrap: This is our Heritage', in Colin Shaw and Malcolm Chase (eds.), *The Imagined Past: History and Nostalgia* (Manchester: Manchester University Press, 1989), 128–46.

Church Gibson, Pamela, 'Fewer Weddings and More Funerals: Changes in the Heritage Film', in Robert Murphy (ed.), *British Cinema of the 90s* (London: British Film Institute, 2000), 115–24.

Church Gibson, Pamela, 'From Dancing Queen to Plaster Virgin: *Elizabeth* and the End of English Heritage?', *Journal of Popular Birtish Cinema*, 5(2002), 133–41.

Colls, Robert, and Philip Dodd, *Englishness: Culture and Politics, 1880–1920* (London: Croom Helm, 1986).

Cook, Pam, *Fashioning the Nation: Costume and Identity in British Cinema* (London: British Film Institute, 1996).

—— 'Neither Here Nor There: National Identity in Gainsborough Costume Drama', in Andrew Higson (ed.), *Dissolving Views: Key Writings on British Cinema* (London: Cassell, 1996), 51–65.

Corner, John, and Sylvia Harvey, 'Mediating Tradition and Modernity: The Heritage/ Enterprise Couplet', in John Corner and Sylvia Harvey (eds.), *Enterprise and Heritage: Crosscurrents of National Culture* (London: Routledge, 1991), 45–75.

Craig, Cairns, 'Rooms without a View', *Sight and Sound*, 1/2 (1991), 10–13.

Dale, Martin, *The Movie Game: The Film Industry in Britain, Europe and America* (London: Cassell, 1997).

Daniels, Stephen, *Fields of Vision: Landscape Imagery and National Identity in England and the United States* (Cambridge: Polity Press, 1983).

Dave, Paul, 'The Bourgeois Paradigm and Heritage Cinema', *New Left Review*, 224 (1997), 111–26.

Deutchman, Ira, 'Independent Distribution and Marketing', in Jason E. Squire (ed.), *The Movie Business Book* (New York: Fireside, 1992), 321–7.

Docherty, David, David Morrison, and Michael Tracey, *The Last Picture Show? Britain's Changing Film Audiences* (London: British Film Institute, 1987).

Dyer, Richard, 'Feeling English', *Sight and Sound*, 4/3 (1994), 17–19.

—— 'Heritage Cinema in Europe', in Ginette Vincendeau (ed.), *The Encyclopaedia of European Cinema* (London: British Film Institute and Cassell, 1995), 204–5.

—— 'Nice Young Men Who Sell Antiques: Gay Men in Heritage Cinema', in Ginette Vincendeau (ed.), *Film/Literature/Heritage: A Sight and Sound Reader* (London: British Film Institute, 2001), 43–8.

—— and Ginette Vincendeau (eds.), *Popular European Cinema* (London: Routledge, 1992).

Eberts, Jake, and Terry Ilott, *My Indecision is Final: The Rise and Fall of Goldcrest Films* (London: Faber & Faber, 1990).

Edson, Barry, 'Film Distribution and Exhibition in the UK', in Mundy Ellis (ed.), *British Film Institute Film and TV Yearbook 1983* (London: British Film Institute, 1983), 140–6.

Elsaesser, Thomas, *New German Cinema: A History* (London: Macmillan, 1989).

Forster, E. M., *Maurice* (London: Penguin, 1972; 1st publ. 1908).

—— *Howards End* (London: Penguin, 1989).

Foster, Allan. *The Movie Traveller: A Film Fan's Travel Guide to the UK and Ireland* (Edinburgh: Polygon, 2000).

Friedman, Lester (ed.), *Fires were Started: British Cinema and Thatcherism* (Minneapolis and London: University of Minnesota Press and UCL Press, 1993).

Gomery, Douglas, *Shared Pleasures: A History of Movie Presentation in the United States* (London: British Film Institute, 1992).

Gunning, Tom, 'The Cinema of Attractions: Early Film, its Spectator and the Avant-Garde', in Thomas Elsaesser and Adam Barker (eds.), *Early Cinema: Space–Frame–Narrative* (London: British Film Institute, 1990), 56–62.

Hall, Sheldon, 'Hard Ticket Giants: Hollywood Blockbusters in the Widescreen Era', unpublished Ph.D. thesis, University of East Anglia, Norwich, 1999.

—— 'The Wrong Sort of Cinema: Re-fashioning the Heritage Film Debate', in Robert Murphy (ed.), *The British Cinema Book* (London: British Film Institute, 2nd edn., 2001), 191–9.

Herbert, James D., *Fauve Painting: The Making of Cultural Politics* (New Haven, Conn., and London: Yale University Press, 1992).

Hewison, Robert, *The Heritage Industry: Britain in a Climate of Decline* (London: Methuen, 1987).

Higson, Andrew, 'Re-presenting the National Past: Nostalgia and Pastiche in the Heritage Film', in Lester Friedman (ed.), *Fires were Started: British Cinema and Thatcherism* (Minneapolis and London: University of Minnesota Press and UCL Press, 1993), 109–29.

—— 'The Victorious Re-cycling of National History: *Nelson*', in Karel Dibbets and Bert Hogenkamp (eds.), *Film and the First World War* (Amsterdam: Amsterdam University Press, 1995), 108–15.

—— *Waving the Flag: Constructing a National Cinema in Britain* (Oxford: Oxford University Press, 1995).

—— (ed.), *Dissolving Views: Key Writings on British Cinema* (London: Cassell, 1996).

—— 'The Heritage Film and British Cinema', in Andrew Higson (ed.), *Dissolving Views: Key Writings on British Cinema* (London: Cassell, 1996), 232–48.

—— 'Heritage Discourses and British Cinema before 1920', in John Fullerton (ed.), *Celebrating 1895: Proceedings of the International Conference on Film before 1920* (Sydney: John Libbey, 1998), 182–9.

—— 'The Instability of the National', in Justine Ashby and Andrew Higson (eds.), *British Cinema, Past and Present* (London: Routledge, 2000), 35–47.

—— 'Heritage Cinema and Television', in Dave Morley and Kevin Robins (eds.), *British Cultural Studies: Geography, Nationality and Identity* (Oxford: Oxford University Press, 2001), 249–60.

Hill, John. 'Government Policy and the British Film Industry 1979–90', *European Journal of Communication*, 8 (1993), 203–44.

—— *British Cinema in the 1980s: Issues and Themes* (Oxford: Clarendon Press, 1999).

Hipsky, Martin A., 'Anglophil(m)ia: Why does America Watch Merchant-Ivory Movies', *Journal of Popular Film and Television*, 22/3 (1994), 98–107.

Hirst, Michael, *The Script of Elizabeth* (London: Boxtree, 1998).

Hoskins, Colin, Stuart McFadyen, and Adam Finn, *Global Television and Film: An Introduction to the Economics of the Business* (Oxford: Oxford University Press, 1997).

Ilott, Terry, *Budgets and Markets: A Study of the Budgeting and Marketing of European Films* (London: Routledge, 1996).

Jakobson, Roman, 'On Realism in Art', in Ladeslav Matejka and Krystyna Pomorska (eds.), *Readings in Russian Poetics* (Ann Arbor, Mich.: University of Michigan Press, 1978), 38–46.

Johnston, Sheila, 'Charioteers and Ploughmen', in Martin Auty and Nick Roddick (eds.), *British Cinema Now* (London: British Film Institute, 1985), 99–110.

Krämer, Peter, 'Would You Take your Child to See This Film? The Cultural and Social Work of the Family-Adventure Movie', in Steve Neale and Murray Smith (eds.), *Contemporary Hollywood Cinema* (London: Routledge, 1998), 294–311.

Laemmle, Robert, 'The Independent Exhibitor', in Jason E. Squire (ed.), *The Movie Business Book* (New York: Fireside, 1992), 360–4.

Landy, Marcia, 'Looking Backward: History and Thatcherism in the Recent British Cinema', *Film Criticism*, 15/1 (1990), 17–38.

LeMahieu, D. L., 'Imagined Contemporaries: Cinematic and Televised Dramas about the Edwardians in Great Britain and the United States, 1967–1985', *Historical Journal of Film, Radio and Television*, 10/3 (1990), 243–56.

Long, Robert Emmet, *The Films of Merchant Ivory* (London: Viking, 1992).

Lowenthal, David, *The Past is a Foreign Country* (Cambridge: Cambridge University Press, 1985).

—— *The Heritage Crusade and the Spoils of History* (London: Viking, 1997).

Luckett, Moya, 'Image and Nation in 1990s British Cinema', in Robert Murphy (ed.), *British Cinema of the 90s* (London: British Film Institute, 2000), 88–99.

Lukk, Tiiu, *Movie Marketing: Opening the Picture and Giving it Legs* (Los Angeles: Silman-James Press, 1997).

McKechnie, Kara, 'Taking Liberties with the Monarch: The Royal Bio-pic in the 1990s', in Claire Monk and Amy Sargeant (eds.), *British Historical Cinema* (London: Routledge, 2002).

Macnab, Geoffrey, *J. Arthur Rank and the British Film Industry* (London: Routledge, 1993).

Maltby, Richard, *Hollywood Cinema: An Introduction* (Oxford: Blackwell, 1995).

Medhurst, Andy, 'Inside the British Wardrobe', *Sight and Sound*, 5/3 (1995), 16–17.

—— 'Dressing the Part', *Sight and Sound*, 6/6 (1996), 28–30.

—— 'Licensed to Cheek', *Sight and Sound*, 7/10 (1997), 32–5.

—— 'The Mike-Ado', *Sight and Sound*, 10/3 (2000), 36–7.

Monk, Claire, 'Sex, Politics and the Past: Merchant–Ivory, the Heritage Film and its Critics in 1980s and 1990s Britain', unpublished MA dissertation, British Film Institute and Birkbeck College, 1994.

—— 'The British "Heritage Film" and its Critics', *Critical Survey*, 7/2 (1995), 116–24.

—— 'Sexuality and the Heritage', *Sight and Sound*, 5/10 (1995), 32–4.

—— 'Heritage Films and the British Cinema Audience in the 1990s', *Journal of Popular British Cinema*, 2 (1999), 22–38.

—— 'The British Heritage-Film Debate Revisited', in Claire Monk and Amy Sargeant (eds.), *British Historical Cinema* (London: Routledge, 2002), 176–98.

—— and Amy Sargeant (eds.), *British Historical Cinema* (London: Routledge, 2002).

Muraleedharan, T., 'Imperial Migrations: Reading the Raj Cinema of the 1980s', in Claire Monk and Amy Sargeant (eds.), *British Historical Cinema* (London: Routledge, 2002), 144–62.

Murphy, Robert, 'Three Companies: Boyd's Co., HandMade and Goldcrest', in Martin Auty and Nick Roddick (eds.), *British Cinema Now* (London: British Film Institute, 1985), 43–56.

—— (ed.) *The British Cinema Book* (London: British Film Institute, 1997).

—— (ed.), *British Cinema of the 90s* (London: British Film Institute, 2000).

Neale, Steve, *Genre and Hollywood* (London: Routledge, 2000).

Ogan, Christine, 'The Audience for Foreign Film in the United States', *Journal of Communication*, 40/4 (1990), 58–77.

Parker, Alan, *Making Movies: Cartoons by Alan Parker* (London: British Film Institute, 1998).

Pendreigh, Brian, *On Location: The Film Fan's Guide to Britain and Ireland* (Edinburgh and London: Mainstream, 1995).

Petley, Julian, 'Reaching for the Stars', in Martin Auty and Nick Roddick (eds.), *British Cinema Now* (London: British Film Institute, 1985), 111–22.

Pidduck, Julianne, 'Of Windows and Country Walks: Frames of Space and Movement in 1990s Austen Adaptations', *Screen*, 39/4 (1998), 381–400.

—— '*Elizabeth* and *Shakespeare in Love*: Screening the Elizabethans', in Ginette Vincendeau (ed.), *Film/Literature/Heritage: A Sight and Sound Reader* (London: British Film Institute, 2001), 130–5.

Powrie, Phil, 'On the Threshold between Past and Present: "Alternative Heritage" ', in Justine Ashby and Andrew Higson (eds.), *British Cinema, Past and Present* (London: Routledge, 2000), 316–26.

Pratten, Stephen, and Simon Deakin, 'Competitiveness Policy and Economic Organization: The Case of the British Film Industry', *Screen*, 41/2 (2000), 217–37.

Pym, John, *Merchant Ivory's English Landscape: Rooms, Views and Anglo-Saxon Attitudes* (London: Pavilion, 1995).

Rice, Jenny, and Carol Saunders, 'Consuming *Middlemarch*: The Construction and Consumption of Nostalgia in Stamford', in Deborah Cartmell, I. Q. Hunter, Heidi Kaye, and Imelda Whelehan (eds.), *Pulping Fictions: Consuming Culture across the Literature/Media Divide* (London: Pluto Press, 1996), 85–98.

Richards, Jeffrey, *Films and British National Identity: From Dickens to Dad's Army* (Manchester: Manchester University Press, 1997).

Roddick, Nick, 'If the United States Spoke Spanish, We would have an Industry . . . ', in Martin Auty and Nick Roddick (eds.), *British Cinema Now* (London: British Film Institute, 1985), 3–18.

—— 'Shotguns and Weddings', *Mediawatch '99*, special supplement to *Sight and Sound* (Mar. 1999), 10–13.

Rushdie, Salman, 'Outside the Whale', *Granta*, 11 (1984), 125–38.

Sales, Roger, *Jane Austen and Representations of Regency England* (London and New York: Routledge, revised edn., 1996).

—— 'In Face of All the Servants: Spectators and Spies in Austen', in Deidre Lynch (ed.), *Janeites: Austen's Disciples and Devotees* (Princeton: Princeton University Press, 2000), 188–205.

Salt, Barry, *Film Style and Technology: History and Analysis* (London: Starword, 1983; also 2nd edn., 1992).

Samuel, Raphael (ed.), *Patriotism: The Making and Unmaking of British National Identity*, i. *History and Politics* (London: Routledge, 1989).

—— *Theatres of Memory* (London and New York: Verso, 1994).

Sargeant, Amy, 'The Darcy Effect: Regional Tourism and Costume Drama', *International Journal of Heritage Studies*, 4/3–4 (1998), 177–86.

—— 'Making and Selling Heritage Culture: Style and Authenticity in Historical Fictions on Film and Television', in Justine Ashby and Andrew Higson, *British Cinema, Past and Present* (London: Routledge, 2000), 301–15.

Schamus, James, 'To the Rear of the Back End: The Economics of Independent Cinema', in Steve Neale and Murray Smith (eds.), *Contemporary Hollywood Cinema* (London: Routledge, 1998), 91–105.

Shaughnessy, Nicola, 'Is S/he or isn't S/he?: Screening *Orlando*', in Deborah Cartmell *et al.* (eds.), *Pulping Fictions: Consuming Culture across the Literature/Media Divide* (London: Pluto Press, 1996), 43–56.

Silverstone, Matthew, 'Finding the Money', in Martin Auty and Nick Roddick, *British Cinema Now* (London: British Film Institute, 1985), 37–40.

Street, Sarah, *British National Cinema* (London: Routledge, 1997).

Street, Sarah, *Transatlantic Crossings: British Feature Films in the USA* (London: Continuum, 2002).

Swann, Paul, 'The British Culture Industries and the Mythology of the American Market: Cultural Policy and Cultural Exports in the 1940s and 1990s', *Cinema Journal*, 39/4 (2000), 27–42.

Tait, Archie, 'Distributing the Product', in Martin Auty and Nick Roddick (eds.) *British Cinema Now* (London: British Film Institute, 1985), 71–82.

Urry, John, *The Tourist Gaze* (London: Sage, 1990).

Vincendeau, Ginette (ed.), *Film/Literature/Heritage: A Sight and Sound Reader* (London: British Film Institute, 2001).

Wade, Graham, *Film, Video and Television: Market Forces, Fragmentation and Technological Advance* (London: Comedia, 1985).

Wayne, Mike, 'The Re-Invention of Tradition: British Cinema and International Image Markets in the 1990s', *EnterText*, 2/1 (2001/2), at http://www.brunel.ac.uk/faculty/arts/EnterText/issue_2_1.htm.

Widdowson, Peter, *E. M. Forster's 'Howards End': Fiction as History* (London: Sussex University Press and Chatto & Windus, 1977).

Willemen, Paul, 'On Realism in the Cinema', in John Ellis (ed.), *Screen Reader I* (London: SEFT, 1977), 47–54.

Williams, Raymond, *Keywords: A Vocabulary of Culture and Society* (Glasgow: Fontana, 1976).

Wollen, Tana, 'Over our Shoulders: Nostalgic Screen Fictions for the Eighties', in John Corner and Sylvia Harvey (eds.), *Enterprise and Heritage: Crosscurrents of National Culture* (London: Routledge, 1991), 178–93.

Wood, Robin, *The Wings of the Dove* (London: British Film Institute, 1999).

Wright, Patrick, *On Living in an Old Country* (London: Verso, 1985).

Wyatt, Justin, 'The Formation of the "Major Independents": Miramax, New Line and the New Hollywood', in Steve Neale and Murray Smith (eds.), *Contemporary Hollywood Cinema* (London: Routledge, 1998), 74–90.

Index

Compiled by Miranda Bayer